Objectivity in Law and Morals

Are there objectively right answers to legal questions? Can judicial decisions be objective when legal questions present moral issues? These and related questions about objectivity are at the center of current debate in legal theory. This volume is the first collection to bring the rich philosophical literature in metaethics that has developed since the 1970s into contact with fundamental problems in legal philosophy.

The seven original essays, written by some of the world's most distinguished moral and legal philosophers, bring a sophisticated philosophical perspective to bear on issues about the objectivity of legal interpretation and judicial decision making. They examine the intersection between objectivity in ethics and objectivity in law in the positivist and natural law traditions, and they develop a variety of approaches, constructive and critical, to the fundamental problems about the objectivity of morality. One of the key issues explored is that of the alleged "domain-specificity" of conceptions of objectivity, that is, whether there is a conception of objectivity appropriate for ethics that is different in kind from the conception of objectivity appropriate for the sciences and other domains.

As a whole, the volume presents a state-of-the-art survey of live issues in metaethics and examines their relevance to theorizing about law and adjudication.

Brian Leiter is Joe A. Worsham Centennial Professor in Law, Professor of Philosophy, and Director of the Law and Philosophy Program at The University of Texas at Austin.

Cambridge Studies in Philosophy and Law

Other books in the series:

Objectivity in Law and Morals

Edited by

Brian Leiter

University of Texas, Austin

CAMBRIDGE
UNIVERSITY PRESS

PUBLISHED BY THE PRESS SYNDICATE OF THE UNIVERSITY OF CAMBRIDGE
The Pitt Building, Trumpington Street, Cambridge, United Kingdom

CAMBRIDGE UNIVERSITY PRESS
The Edinburgh Building, Cambridge CB2 2RU, UK
40 West 20th Street, New York, NY 10011-4211, USA
10 Stamford Road, Oakleigh, VIC 3166, Australia
Ruiz de Alarcón 13, 28014 Madrid, Spain
Dock House, The Waterfront, Cape Town 8001, South Africa

http://www.cambridge.org

First published 2001

Printed in the United States of America

Typeface Times Roman 10/12 pt.   *System* MagnaType™ [AG]

A catalog record for this book is available from the British Library.

Library of Congress Cataloging in Publication Data
Objectivity in law and morals / edited by Brian Leiter

p. cm. – (Cambridge studies in philosophy and law)

Includes bibliographical references.

ISBN 0-521-55430-6 (hb)

1. Law and ethics. 2. Law – Philosophy. I. Leiter, Brian. II. Series.

K247.6.O25 2000
340'.112 – dc21   00-020002

ISBN 0 521 55430 6 hardback

Contents

Contributors

DAVID O. BRINK is Professor of Philosophy at the University of California at San Diego.

BRIAN LEITER is Joe A. Worsham Centennial Professor in Law, Professor of Philosophy, and Director of the Law and Philosophy Program at The University of Texas at Austin.

PHILIP PETTIT is Professor of Social and Political Theory in the Research School of Social Sciences at the Australian National University and Visiting Professor of Philosophy at Columbia University.

GERALD J. POSTEMA is Cary C. Boshamer Distinguished Professor of Philosophy at the University of North Carolina at Chapel Hill.

JOSEPH RAZ is Professor of the Philosophy of Law at Oxford University, Fellow of Balliol College, and Visiting Professor of Jurisprudence at Columbia Law School.

DAVID SOSA is Associate Professor of Philosophy at The University of Texas at Austin.

SIGRÚN SVAVARSDÓTTIR is Assistant Professor of Philosophy at Ohio State University.

Acknowledgments

I am grateful to Jules Coleman for commissioning this volume and for his helpful comments on a draft of the introduction. Michael Durham at Yale and Chad McCracken at Texas did excellent work on the bibliography. My colleagues Daniel Bonevac, Cory Juhl, and Robert C. Koons read through and discussed most of the contributions with me, and their comments and ideas were of great value to both me and many of the contributors. Finally, my sincere thanks to the contributors to this volume – for their excellent essays, their constructive response to criticism, and their patience.

B. L.
Austin, July 1999

Introduction

BRIAN LEITER

Ordinary language and thought are replete with claims to objectivity. "Abortion is objectively wrong, no matter what some people think." "Creationism is objectively false; evolution is just an objective fact." "Research on sex differences is rarely objective; it reflects the male-dominance of the field." "You're not being objective when you let your strong dislike of him affect your evaluation of his performance." "Calm down and try to be objective about the situation." "Supreme Court justices aren't any more objective than any other partisan political actors."

What is at stake in these claims about objectivity? This introduction sets out *one* conventional philosophical way of understanding these claims, in which we read them as raising issues in metaphysics and epistemology. So understood, we can distinguish two kinds of worries about objectivity implicit in ordinary language and thought. In some of the above examples, the demand to be objective is the demand to be free of *bias* or other factors that distort judgment, that prevent the things we are judging from presenting themselves clearly and accurately. This, then, is a demand for *epistemic* objectivity: that the cognitive processes and mechanisms by which we form beliefs about the world be constituted in such a way that they at least *tend* toward the production of accurate representations of how things are. Notice that epistemic objectivity does not require that cognitive processes always yield true representations: that would demand more than is attainable and more than what we have in mind when we worry about epistemic objectivity. We might think of *epistemic* objectivity as obtaining when either of the following is true: (1) the cognitive processes at issue *reliably* arrive at accurate representations, or (2) the cognitive processes are free of factors that we know to produce inaccurate representations.

Already, though, we have made reference here to another kind of objectivity. For the worry about the objectivity of our epistemic faculties has been explicated as a worry about their ability to deliver accurate representations of *the way things truly or objectively are.* This latter thought involves a demand for *metaphysical* objectivity: that things are what they are *independent* of how we take them to be.

This "independence requirement" is often thought to be central to metaphysical objectivity,[1] though its proper interpretation raises two important questions: independence *from what* and *how much* independence? The most plausible answer to the first question is that metaphysical objectivity demands *epistemic* independence: something is objective if its existence and character does not depend on what we *believe* or would be *justified* in believing about it. How much independence of this kind is demanded varies on different views. Traditional "metaphysical realists" demand absolute independence from epistemic constraints: even at the ideal end of inquiry, what we believe or are justified in believing could be false. Putnam's "internal realism" and related views demand less in the way of independence: only that the existence and character of a thing not depend on what we believe or would be justified in believing *except* under ideal epistemic conditions.

These tentative characterizations are, of course, not wholly uncontroversial, even among contributors to this volume. While some (including David Brink, myself, Philip Pettit, and Sigrún Svavarsdóttir) develop or defend this kind of approach to objectivity, broadly construed, others (especially Gerald J. Postema, but also, in some respects, Joseph Raz) resist this way of thinking about issues of objectivity. For these latter writers, as well as Ronald Dworkin, Thomas Nagel, "British" moral realists like John McDowell, and perhaps various Kantian constructivists, issues about objectivity arise "internal" to the practices of normative argument and do not lend themselves to translation into metaphysical and epistemological categories. Indeed, a recurring issue in this volume will concern the alleged "domain-specificity" of conceptions of objectivity, that is, whether there is a conception of objectivity appropriate for ethics that is different in kind from the conception of objectivity appropriate, say, for the sciences. For those committed to the domain-specificity of objectivity, the conceptualization offered in this introduction will be part of what is at issue in thinking about objectivity in ethics. Nonetheless, this conceptualization constitutes a natural starting point in the metaethical literature, one that even the defenders of domain-specificity recognize the need to argue against.

Two arenas of our practical life – law and ethics – present special, and important, cases for worries about objectivity. In ethics, these questions are familiar: when we ask about whether there are absolute moral standards, or whether morality is relative, we are asking about the objectivity of ethics. Those who deny that moral judgments have cognitive content (and thus deny that they can be evaluated as either true or false) are defending a view about the objectivity of ethics as well.

In law, too, issues about objectivity arise along a variety of dimensions. For example: (1) We expect the content of our laws to be objective in the sense of treating people the same unless they are "relevantly" different. (2) We expect judges to be objective in the sense of not being biased against one party or the other. (3) We expect legal decisions to be objective in the sense of reaching the result that the law *really* requires without letting bias or prejudice intervene. (4) In some areas of law, we expect the law to employ "objective" standards of conduct (like "reasonable person" standards) that do not permit actors to excuse their conduct based on their subjective perceptions at the time.

In this volume, we are interested in the objectivity of law primarily with respect to the issues posed in (3). Indeed, it is here, in particular, that questions about the objectivity of morality intersect with those about law. We may think of the central problematic in the following way.

Judges must decide cases. They must consult and interpret the relevant legal sources (statutes, precedent, custom, etc.) in order to determine the governing legal principles and rules, and then decide how these are to apply to the facts of the case. Let us call the "class of legal reasons" the class of reasons that judges may legitimately consider in deciding a legal question.[2] If the law is "rationally determinate" on some point that means the class of legal reasons justifies a unique answer on that point: there is, as is commonly said, a single right answer as a matter of law.

We may now speak of the law as *objective* along two possible dimensions:

1. The law is *metaphysically* objective insofar as there exist right answers as a matter of law.
2. The law is *epistemically* objective insofar as the mechanisms for discovering right answers (e.g., adjudication, legal reasoning) are free of distorting factors that would obscure right answers.

The scope of these claims about the objectivity of law may vary. We may think the law is metaphysically objective only with respect to a narrow range of cases (as the Legal Realists do), or with respect to nearly all cases (as Dworkin does). We may think the law is epistemically objective some of the time or almost none of the time. The claims to objectivity can diverge as well. The law may be metaphysically objective, but fail to be epistemically objective. On the other hand, the above characterization of epistemic objectivity presupposes for its intelligibility that the law be metaphysically objective: we can get no purchase on the notion of a "distorting factor" without reference to the "things" we are trying to know. Not all writers accept this link; in particular, Gerald Postema, in his contribution to this volume, questions whether an adequate account of the epistemic objectivity of law need make reference to an antecedent notion of the law as metaphysically objective.

How is the objectivity of ethics implicated in the objectivity of law? The metaphysical objectivity of law, as we have seen, is a matter of its rational determinacy, that is, it is a matter of the class of legal reasons justifying a unique outcome. If the class of legal reasons, however, includes *moral* reasons, then the law can be objective only if morality (and moral reasoning) is objective. The class of legal reasons can come to include moral reasons two ways.

First, and most obviously, the familiar sources of law – like statutes and constitutional provisions – may include moral concepts or considerations. The United States Constitution provides the most familiar examples, since it speaks of "equal protection," "liberty," and other inherently moral notions. For courts to apply these provisions is for them necessarily to apply the incorporated moral concepts. For the law to be metaphysically objective in these cases requires that these moral concepts have objective content. Of course, this objective content need not be fixed in virtue of morality being objective: an interpretive principle like "Interpret each provision as the framers of the provision would have intended" may suffice to make the application of the Equal Protection Clause of the Fourteenth Amendment determinate, without presupposing anything about the "objective" meaning of "equality." Yet in some cases, and under some theories of interpretation, what will be required is precisely to understand what equality *really* requires. Such an approach to legal interpretation is developed in David Brink's contribution to this volume.

Second, moral reasons might be part of the class of legal reasons because they are part of the very criteria of legal validity. Natural lawyers hold that for a norm to be a legal norm it must satisfy moral criteria:[3] thus, a judge wondering whether a particular norm (relevant to a particular case) is a valid legal norm must necessarily engage in moral reasoning. Some Legal Positivists ("soft" or "inclusive" positivists) accept a similar view: they hold that, as a contingent matter, morality can be a criterion of legal validity if it is the practice of legal officials in some society to employ moral considerations as criteria of legal validity. For these positivists – who include the century's leading defender of the doctrine, H. L. A. Hart[4] – legal reasoning in such societies will include moral reasoning.

Of course, even those positivists ("hard" or "exclusive" positivists) who deny that morality is ever a criterion of legality may still hold that it is a judge's duty in exercising discretion in hard cases to reach the morally correct result. Thus, while the objectivity of morality won't, for these positivists, affect the objectivity of law, it will still matter in thinking about what judges ought to do in hard cases.

In all these ways, then, the objectivity of morality may be implicated in how we think about the objectivity of law (or the objectivity of the adjudicative process).

The seven original essays that constitute this volume do not try to canvass all the different senses in which we make claims to objectivity. Their focus is more narrow: they consider objectivity in law, from both metaphysical and epistemological perspectives; they examine the intersection between objectivity in ethics and objectivity in law; and they develop a variety of approaches, constructive and critical, to the fundamental problem of objectivity in ethics.

The metaethics literature is, to date, far richer than anything that has been written about objectivity in law. Four of the contributors here – Sigrún Svavarsdóttir, Joseph Raz, Philip Pettit, and David Sosa – focus their attention on this rich literature, in some cases taking issue with positions developed by philosophers like John Mackie, Thomas Nagel, John McDowell, and David Wiggins, and in other cases trying to extend and develop existing lines of thought. Three of the essays (mine, David Brink's, and Gerald Postema's) explicitly examine the intersection of the objectivity of law and the objectivity of ethics, showing how positive or skeptical views about the latter have ramifications for the former. As a whole, the volume presents a state-of-the-art survey of live issues in metaethics and examines their relevance to theorizing about law.

David O. Brink's essay, which opens the volume, introduces a theme that, as noted, occupies many of the contributors: whether there are "domain-specific" conceptions of objectivity, or whether one conception of objectivity (typically, one drawn from the natural sciences) suffices for thinking about objectivity in all fields, including the practical domains of ethics and law. Brink's position is unchanged from his earlier work: objectivity is not a domain-specific concept. "[E]thics is or can be objective in much the same way" that the sciences are objective.[5] Insofar as certain legal questions depend on moral arguments and considerations, they too have objective answers. Brink's essay revisits and refines his earlier, well-known approach to the intersection of issues about objectivity in ethics and in law.[6] He begins with a critical discussion of the "verificationism" about law found in some of the American Legal Realists, the apparent view of writers like Holmes and most clearly John Chipman Gray that "law" is just what the court says it is.[7] He agrees with H. L. A. Hart that such skepticism is untenable (indeed, incoherent), but disagrees with Hart's modest concession to skepticism, namely, that there will be some cases in which the language of the applicable rule dictates no clear result, and so judges must exercise discretion. Hart, Brink believes, was driven to this conclusion by his tacit embrace of an outdated semantic theory. This outdated "descriptional view" of meaning (as Donnellan, Kripke, Putnam, and others have argued) fails to give an adequate account of the meaning of proper names and natural kind terms.[8] Brink argues in favor of the "new" or "causal" theory of reference, according to which reference fixes meaning, and in which reference is not mediated by the descriptions or beliefs a speaker associates with a term. Such a semantics, Brink argues, can be fruitfully applied not only to the interpretation of legal terms[9] but also to understanding the abstract intentions that underlie particular legal provisions (like an intent to prohibit "cruel and unusual" punishments), intentions that we must often consult given the limitations of textualism. This sets the stage for a wide-ranging defense of judicial review, in which the famous U.S. Supreme Court decisions in *Brown* and *Griswold* figure as central examples. In the process, Brink considers, refines, and in most cases criticizes the views of Bork, Dworkin, Sunstein, and various Critical Legal Studies writers about the objectivity of legal interpretation. He concludes by showing how the correct understanding of legal interpretation helps establish a middle ground between legal positivism and natural law theory regarding the relationship between law and morality.

My own contribution to this volume shares Brink's rejection of the domain-specificity of objectivity. I approach the topic by considering Ronald Dworkin's often perplexing writings on objectivity and right answers. According to Dworkin, the right answer to a legal dispute is the answer that follows from the principles that both *fit* the prior institutional history and provide the best *justification* of that history from the standpoint of morality. Dworkin's theory thus thrusts moral considerations into the center of law and makes the objectivity of morality a necessary condition for the objectivity of law. The kind of objectivity at stake, however, is domain-specific according to Dworkin, something that moral skeptics like John Mackie are said to misunderstand. While I argue that much that Dworkin says about this objectivity "internal" to morality is confused or mistaken, I do find a core animating idea from Dworkin worth salvaging, one that he shares with John McDowell: namely, the idea that it suffices for the objectivity of morality if moral views are (in McDowell's phrase) "susceptible to reasons." Dworkin and McDowell, in turn, reject a "naturalistic" conception of objectivity, which demands that moral facts be objective in precisely the same way the objects studied by the natural sciences are objective: namely, that they are both mind-independent and causally efficacious. I argue, against Dworkin and McDowell, that "susceptibility to reasons" is not adequate to account for objectivity and that, in any event, morality is only susceptible to reasons in the trivial sense that noncognitivists have long recognized, namely, that the factual and logical underpinnings of moral views are susceptible to reasons. This leaves Dworkin's theory of adjudication vulnerable, then, to the moral skeptic who denies the objectivity of law because he denies the objectivity of morality.

Gerald J. Postema's essay, "Objectivity Fit for Law," takes a different tack (as its title would suggest): he defends the domain-specificity of objectivity and develops an account of objectivity that makes sense for law and adjudication. In particular, Postema wants to vindicate the objectivity of law against some of the more radical and incautious claims made by law professors associated with Critical Legal Studies, Critical Race Theory, and feminist theory who believe, wrongly, that a role for political and moral values in adjudication is *incompatible* with the objectivity of law. Postema asks us to start with a "generic" concept of objectivity according to which a judgment is objective when the judger is "open" in the appropriate ways to the subject matter of that judgment. More precisely, the generic account requires, according to Postema, that the judgment be *independent* of the judging subject in the appropriate way; that the judgment be truth-evaluable, and that its truth-value be an objective matter; and that there be invariance of judgment across (competent) judging subjects. Postema develops these criteria in some detail, as well as exploring the motivations for expecting objectivity in practical arenas (like law and morality). This discussion sets the stage for Postema's own theory of "objectivity as publicity," which holds (very roughly) that a judgment is objectively correct if it can be vindicated by public practical reason,[10] that is, by sound reasoning in a public deliberative process. It is crucial on this view, then, to specify, as Postema does, the features of a public deliberative process whose issuances are eligible for objectivity. Law and adjudication, he then argues, are (or can be) such a process. Notice that Postema's account of the objectivity of law is *epistemic,* focusing on the *procedures* by which judgments are arrived at, rather than on the metaphysical status of some domain of legal facts to which such judgments answer. One of the especially interesting features of Postema's essay is his defense of the idea – against myself and others – that an account of epistemic objectivity does *not* presuppose an antecedent view about the metaphysical objectivity of the subject matter of our judgments.

Sigrún Svavarsdóttir's essay, "Objective Values: Does Metaethics Rest on a Mistake?," shifts the volume's focus from the objectivity of law and the intersection of law and ethics, to the objectivity of ethics itself. Yet central to her essay remains the question of the domain-specificity of conceptions of objectivity. Svavarsdóttir does not defend a particular account of objectivity, though like myself and Brink, she remains skeptical about the claim that there is a domain-specific notion of objectivity appropriate to ethics. Svavarsdóttir approaches the question through a sustained interpretation and critique of Thomas Nagel's views in metaethics. Nagel shares with Dworkin the thought that much skeptical writing about ethics (once again, Mackie is the prime target), as well as much moral realism, presupposes a mistaken picture of what the objectivity of ethics consists in – this is the alleged "mistake" of Svavarsdóttir's title. Like Dworkin, Nagel thinks this mistake consists, roughly, in treating moral realism as demanding that moral judgments correspond to some fact in an observer-independent external world. Rather, Nagel thinks, moral realism is vindicated from "within" value inquiry itself. To reach this understanding of Nagel, however, Svavarsdóttir first offers a careful discussion of the differing claims about objectivity at stake in Mackie's and Nagel's writings. Nagel's notion of objectivity, Svavarsdóttir shows, is primarily *epistemic* – and thus is silent on the metaphysical commitments of value realism – while Mackie is concerned with the *metaphysical* objectivity of moral facts, as well as their "normative objectivity," that is, the categoricity of moral demands that flows from their normative force being independent of agents' antecedent concerns and desires. Situating Nagel's views on normative realism with respect to those of Simon Blackburn and Peter Railton, Svavarsdóttir concludes that the real "mistake" in metaethics for Nagel is an allegiance to methodological naturalism,[11] to the idea that philosophical method is simply continuous with scientific method, and thus metaethical questions should be answered within the framework of a broadly scientific epistemology. To the contrary, Nagel argues, value realism must be sustained from within ethical inquiry itself, whose methods are not continuous with, but stand apart from, those of science. Svavarsdóttir concludes by arguing, contra Nagel, that giving up on methodological naturalism, in metaethics or elsewhere in philosophy, is deeply problematic.

Joseph Raz's essay offers both a substantive account of objectivity and a partial defense of the objectivity of practical thought itself. Raz begins by exploring an *epistemic* sense of objectivity (and cognate notions like *impartiality*) and what he calls "domain-objectivity" (not to be confused with what I have been calling "domain-specificity"). Domain-objectivity, according to Raz, is a property of thoughts, propositions, and statements that are properly objects of knowledge. If practical thought is to enjoy domain-objectivity it must satisfy various conditions, for example, that error in judgment about matters in the domain be possible, and that judgments concern an "independent" reality. These, and five other conditions, constitute what Raz calls "the long route" to understanding objectivity. After defending the "long route," Raz considers various doubts that might arise about the objectivity of practical thought. One set of doubts arises from the role of "parochial concepts" – concepts that cannot be mastered by all, often because they require parochial interests or imaginative capacities – in practical thought. Here Raz defends practical thought against objections from Nagel and Bernard Williams contesting the objectivity of any domain dependent on parochial concepts. Another set of doubts, again suggested by Williams (though elaborated in new directions by Raz), arises from the idea that knowledge of objective reality demands knowledge of "what is there anyway," independent of anyone's thought or experience. Since the truth-value of evaluative claims (Raz considers especially the case of thick concepts) depends on social facts, it is unclear how practical thought could meet this condition for objectivity. Raz argues that this worry about the objectivity of practical thought can be dispelled once we distinguish between different ways value judgments "depend" on shared (social) understandings. Rightly understood, Raz concludes, the dependence of practical thought on the social is no threat to its objectivity.

Philip Pettit's article picks up some related themes in the course of the volume's most systematic and sustained defense of the objectivity of ethics, along semantic, ontological (what we earlier called "metaphysical"), and justificatory dimensions. Indeed, those needing a thorough introduction to the basic issues in the metaethics literature of recent decades may find Pettit's essay an excellent place to start. Pettit's standpoint is resolutely naturalistic, and the ambition is to make sense of moral objectivity on a picture of the world as composed of microphysical elements governed by natural laws. The objectivity of values does not demand Platonism, that is, positing a nonnatural realm of transcendent values. (David Sosa, as we shall see, takes a different view about the necessity of Platonism.) We are to take our cue, as it were, from color properties, which have the trappings of objectivity, but which are neither transcendent nor even independent of human responses: something *is* red, we might say, just in case normal observers are disposed to judge it to be red under normal conditions; yet at the same time, it is natural to explain a correct judgment that "X is red" by appealing to the fact of its redness.[12] So, too, perhaps moral predicates like "good" or "right" just pick out the property that plays or realizes the dispositional role of making us judge something "good" or "right" in the appropriate circumstances. Thus, the extension of moral terms, like the extension of color terms, would be "response-dependent," but at the same time, objective because, in part, it remains independent of any particular agent's response. Pettit's proposal here, however, introduces one important modification to this basic idea.[13] Moral terms, Pettit argues, pick out natural properties that play not only a dispositional role (as above), but also a certain "functional" role, in the sense that the property realizes a functional role described by a network of shared working assumptions about the term. This "moral functionalism," as Pettit calls it, unlike functionalism in the philosophy of mind, is not limited to identifying only causal roles, but also includes inferential roles. Yet like its philosophy of mind cousin, moral functionalism maintains that we fix the content (in this case of moral terms) by understanding its place in an interconnected network of relations. Pettit devotes the remainder of his paper to a defense of moral functionalism, showing how it meets the demands for semantic, ontological, and justificatory objectivity with which he began.

David Sosa's paper, "Pathetic Ethics," which concludes the volume, is a sustained attack on the idea (found in related forms in Raz and Pettit) that making value dependent on human response or sensibility could really be adequate to capture the *objectivity* of value.[14] The famous "pathetic fallacy" refers to the projection of *our* feelings onto external objects. "Sensibility theories" of value are "pathetic" in this sense: they see the ethical qualities of things as dependent on our sensibilities, though they do not, of course, view this as involving any kind of "fallacy" or "error" – though Sosa does (hence his title). Rather, such theories are motivated by the idea that only when we demand of the objectivity of ethics that it be *independent* of human sensibility in a way it could not be are we driven to skepticism. Sosa wants to reject this idea (and thus reject the domain-specificity of objectivity), in favor of the idea that any genuinely objective property must be objective in the way "primary" qualities were thought to be objective: namely, as features of things that do not depend in any sense on how we take them to be (how we respond to them, what we judge about them, etc.). His route to this conclusion begins by a careful analysis of the dispute between Mackie and McDowell over the kind of objectivity ordinary ethical thought demands. Sosa finds McDowell's alternative account – the "no-priority view" – untenable. On this view, neither the features of things nor our sensibilities have priority one over the other. Funny jokes do have comic qualities that we respond to, but for a joke to be funny is just for it to have properties that dispose us to find it funny. The same is true for the ethical features of things, according to McDowell. This, Sosa shows, leads to vicious circularity, McDowell's protestations to the contrary notwithstanding. Moreover, there seems to be no noncircular way to fix the responses that would be properly constitutive of ethical value. Similar problems afflict David Wiggins's related account, which leads Sosa to consider variants of the theory developed more recently by Crispin Wright and Mark Johnston. These variants focus on the idea that the extension of certain concepts (like color concepts and perhaps also value concepts) could be given by biconditionals of the following form:

x is red $\leftrightarrow$ for any S: if S were perceptually normal and were to encounter x in perceptually normal conditions, S would experience x as red.

In the end, Sosa identifies a variety of ways in which these proposals fail to capture a suitably "full-blooded, hardcore" sense of objectivity – a sense captured best by traditional Platonism. He concludes by sketching how we might think of the objectivity of value precisely on the model of the objectivity of primary qualities.

Notes

1. For an overview of relevant issues, see Brian Leiter, "Objectivity and the Problems of Jurisprudence," *Texas Law Review* 72 (1993): 190–196. For related, and more detailed discussions, see Elliott Sober, "Realism and Independence," *Noûs* 16 (1982): 369–385, and Bruce W. Brower, "Dispositional Ethical Realism," *Ethics* 103 (1993): 238–246.
2. For this way of conceptualizing indeterminacy, see Brian Leiter, "Legal Indeterminacy," *Legal Theory* 1 (1995): 481–492.
3. Satisfying the moral criteria might simply be *necessary* for a norm to be a legal norm, or it might be both necessary and sufficient. The strongest forms of natural law theory hold the latter.
4. See the "Postscript" to the 2nd edition of P. Bulloch and J. Raz (eds.), *The Concept of Law* (Oxford: Clarendon Press, 1994).
5. David O. Brink, *Moral Realism and the Foundations of Ethics* (Cambridge: Cambridge University Press, 1989), p. 6.
6. David O. Brink, "Legal Theory, Legal Interpretation, and Judicial Review," *Philosophy & Public Affairs* 17 (1988): 105–148.
7. For doubts that this is really Holmes's view, see my "Legal Realism," in D. M. Patterson (ed.), *A Companion to Philosophy of Law and Legal Theory* (Oxford: Blackwell, 1996), p. 263.
8. Natural kind terms pick out natural properties that figure in the laws of the sciences.

9. Other writers have explored this approach as well. See, e.g., Michael S. Moore, "A Natural Law Theory of Interpretation," *Southern California Law Review* 58 (1985): 277–398; Nicos Stavropoulos, *Objectivity in Law* (Oxford: Clarendon Press, 1996).

10. See also Gerald J. Postema, "Public Practical Reasoning: An Archaeology," *Social Philosophy and Policy* 12 (1995): 43–86, and "Public Practical Reasoning: Political Practice," in I. Shapiro and J. DeCew (eds.), *NOMOS XXXVII: Theory and Practice* (New York: New York University Press, 1995).

11. See, e.g., Peter Railton, "Naturalism and Prescriptivity," in E. Paul et al. (eds.), *Foundations of Moral and Political Philosophy* (Oxford: Blackwell, 1990). For a general typology of *kinds* of naturalism, see Brian Leiter, "Naturalism and Naturalized Jurisprudence," in B. Bix (ed.), *Analyzing Law: New Essays in Legal Theory* (Oxford: Clarendon Press, 1998).

12. For Pettit's earlier and influential treatment of related themes, see his "Realism and Response-Dependence," *Mind* 100 (1991): 587–626. For other important literature on response-dependence and/or the analogy with colors, see, e.g., John McDowell, "Values and Secondary Qualities," reprinted in G. Sayre-McCord (ed.), *Essays on Moral Realism* (Ithaca: Cornell University Press, 1988); Crispin Wright, "Moral Values, Projection, and Secondary Qualities," *Proceedings of the Aristotelian Society* 62 (1988): 1–26; the papers by Mark Johnston, David Lewis, and Michael Smith on "Dispositional Theories of Value," *Proceedings of the Aristotelian Society* supp. vol. 63 (1989); and Mark Johnston, "Objectivity Refigured: Pragmatism Without Verificationism," in J. Haldane and C. Wright (eds.), *Reality, Representation, and Projection* (Oxford: Oxford University Press, 1993).

13. The idea was developed in conjunction with Frank Jackson in "Moral Functionalism and Moral Motivation," *Philosophical Quarterly* 45 (1995): 20–40.

14. Sosa does not specifically consider Pettit's version of the theory, but his objections to its antecedents in writers like McDowell and Wiggins bear on the viability of Pettit's version of the view as well.

1

Legal Interpretation, Objectivity, and Morality

DAVID O. BRINK

Much of traditional analytical jurisprudence concerns the nature of law and the relation between law and morality. One traditional debate about the nature of law concerns its objectivity or determinacy. A conception of law can be understood to be objective insofar as it represents the law in actual or hypothetical controversies as determining a uniquely correct outcome; it can be understood as skeptical insofar as it represents the law as indeterminate. Extreme skepticism would claim that the law is rarely, if ever, determinate, whereas complete objectivity would claim that the law is never indeterminate. By contrast, a more moderate skepticism maintains that the law is indeterminate when it is especially controversial what the law requires. Here, as elsewhere, extreme views may be difficult to accept. Few endorse complete objectivity; some strands in Legal Realism and in Critical Legal Studies appear to endorse extreme skepticism about the law; but moderate skepticism is probably the view more congenial to common sense.

Another traditional jurisprudential debate concerns the relation between law and morality. This debate is often cast between Legal Positivism and Natural Law. Whereas Natural Law theory asserts that there is some essential connection between law and morality, Legal Positivism denies this. In particular, Natural Law theory typically asserts that valid laws must have some significant moral content, without which they are not genuine legal norms. By contrast, Legal Positivism typically understands the law as a system of social norms or rules having an appropriate history or pedigree that distinguishes them from moral norms or rules; on this view, genuine laws might be significantly immoral.[1] Though Natural Law appears to be the more inspirational tradition, Legal Positivism may seem the more plausible.

I would like to thank David Lyons for several helpful conversations a few years ago about the issues discussed here, an audience at the University of Minnesota in April 1998 for discussion of an earlier version of this paper, and Brian Leiter for helpful written comments on the penultimate version of this paper.

Debates about the determinacy of the law and the relation between law and morality are, I believe, best seen and assessed in the context of debates about the nature of legal interpretation. For debates about the law's objectivity can be seen as debates about the extent to which legal interpretation is determinate. Debates between Legal Positivism and Natural Law can be seen as debates about the role of moral reasoning in legal interpretation. I begin with a critical discussion of some familiar forms of skepticism about the law and legal interpretation. In the wake of these criticisms of skepticism, I sketch a philosophical conception of legal interpretation, whose significance I then explore for familiar debates in constitutional jurisprudence about the nature of constitutional interpretation and judicial review. I conclude by examining the implications of this conception of interpretation for debates about the determinacy of the law and the relation between law and morality. This interpretive conception underwrites skepticism about the existence of significant indeterminacy in the law and finds an important element of truth in both legal positivism and natural law theory.[2]

I. The Model of Rules

A common view of the law and legal reasoning receives theoretical articulation in traditional positivist theories of law of the sort defended by John Austin and H. L. A. Hart.[3] On this view, the law is a system of social norms or rules having an appropriate pedigree that distinguishes them from various other norms or rules, including norms of etiquette and norms of morality. According to Austin, laws are commands of the sovereign. A command is a request backed by the threat of sanctions for noncompliance, and a sovereign is one (or more) who is habitually obeyed by the bulk of society but who is not in the habit of obedience to anyone else. According to Hart, a legal system is composed of primary rules and secondary rules of recognition, adjudication, and change. Primary rules regulate the conduct of citizens by way of requirements, permissions, and prohibitions. Secondary rules of recognition, adjudication, and change address concerns about a system of primary rules. A rule of recognition resolves uncertainty about which norms are part of the system of primary rules by specifying the criteria that mark a norm as part of the system of primary rules; rules of adjudication specify how disputes about the interpretation and application of the primary rules are to be resolved; and rules of change specify how the primary rules may be modified to accommodate changing circumstances, beliefs, preferences, and values. A rule of recognition is constituted by the norms that regulate, in the appropriate way, the behavior of the system's officials. Primary rules are valid laws by virtue of having the appropriate pedigree specified in the system's rule of recognition.

The model of rules claims that there are preexisting legal rules that judges can and, at least in decent legal systems, should apply. Presumably, these rules clearly require, forbid, and permit certain conduct. The rules clearly cover cases involving such conduct. These are *easy* cases in which the law is uncontroversial and determinate. But there are also *hard* cases involving conduct that the rules do not cover clearly, about whose resolution there is controversy. Hart's own view is that hard cases are legally indeterminate and that courts can resolve such cases only by exercising *discretion* – that is, a quasi-legislative capacity.[4] On this view, judges – at least in easy cases – can and do both *discover* and *apply* pre-existing law.

II. Legal Realism and Rule-Skepticism

However, this common view about the law and legal interpretation appears to be challenged by some strands in Legal Realism – especially the rule-skepticism found in the writings of Oliver Wendell Holmes and John Chipman Gray, among others.[5] Much of what Legal Realism was concerned with was psychological and sociological analysis of the judicial process – for instance, the way in which judicial decisions are correlated with the class background of the judiciary and the social and economic sources of litigation and consequences of judicial decisions. Insofar as this was the main concern of the realists, their claims may have little direct bearing on the traditional concerns of analytical jurisprudence. But many of the realists also made general, apparently philosophical claims about the nature of law and the responsibilities of judges, and they were critical of theories of law, like Hart's and Austin's, that treat the law as a body of rules. It is this aspect of Legal Realism on which I shall focus here.[6]

The realists criticized the sort of *mechanical jurisprudence* that they associated with thinking of law as a body of rules.[7] The mechanical jurist apparently thinks that all cases are easy cases and that legal reasoning takes a simple syllogistic form.

1. All Fs are forbidden (legal rule).
2. *A*'s action x is F (statement of fact).
3. Hence, x is forbidden (judicial decision).

Some Legal Realists are skeptical about whether there are exceptionless rules that can serve as the major premises in such syllogisms. They are *rule-skeptics*. Instead of identifying the law with legal rules, they think we should identify it in some way with the decisions of courts. Holmes suggests that we adopt the bad man's point of view on the law.

If you want to know the law and nothing else, you must look at it as a bad man, who cares only for the material consequences which such knowledge enables him to predict, not as a good one, who finds his reasons for conduct, whether inside the law or outside of it, in the vaguer sanctions of conscience.[8]

If we take the bad man's point of view, Holmes thinks, we will identify law with predictions of what courts will do.

Take the fundamental question, "What constitutes the law?". You will find some text writers telling you that it is something different from what is decided by the courts of Massachusetts or England, that it is a system of reason, that it is a deduction from principles of ethics or admitted axioms or what not, which may or may not coincide with the decisions. But if we take the view of our friend the bad man we shall find that he does not care two straws for the axioms or deductions, but that he does want to know what the Massachusetts or English courts are likely to do in fact. I am much of his mind. The prophecies of what the courts will do in fact, and nothing more pretentious, are what I mean by the law.[9]

But if we are really interested only in the "bottom line" from the bad man's point of view, then we should apparently identify law with what courts will in fact do, rather than with (fallible) predictions of what they will do. This is Gray's view. He distinguishes between law and sources for law. Whereas statutes, constitutional provisions, and precedents are sources of law, actual laws are just whatever the court in fact decides. In *The Nature and Sources of Law* he writes

[A]fter all, it is only words that the legislature utters; it is for the courts to say what those words mean; that is, it is for them to interpret legislative acts. . . . And this is the reason why legislative acts, statutes, are to be dealt with as sources of Law, and not as part of the Law itself. . . . It has sometimes been said that the Law is composed of two parts – legislative law and judge-made law – but, in truth, all the Law is judge-made law.[10]

Understood literally, this means that there is never any law prior to a court's decision and that, as a result, judges always *create,* rather than apply, the law. Though there are no legal constraints on how courts decide cases, cases can be decided in better and worse ways. One important strand in Legal Realism urges judges to base their decisions on a proper understanding of the social and economic consequences of their decisions.[11] Though courts can make no legal mistakes, they can make pragmatic and moral mistakes.

Ironically, rule-skepticism represents a kind of philosophical antirealism about the law.[12] Realism about a domain typically claims that there are facts or truths of a certain kind that are independent of our beliefs about them and our verification procedures. As such, realism implies *fallibility.* By contrast, anti-realist views deny or at least restrict fallibility. For example, verificationist views eliminate the possible gap between truth and our evidence by reducing the facts or truths in question to our evidence or verification procedures. One form of verificationism about the external world is phenomenalism, which holds that the truth of a claim that there is a table in the next room is nothing more than the truth of various claims about what one would experience were one to enter the room. Behaviorism is a verificationist view about mental states, according to which ascription of mental states is nothing more than the ascription of behavioral tendencies. And a standard verificationist position in philosophy of science is operationalism, which Percy Bridgman describes as the "attitude that the meanings of one's terms are to be found by an analysis of the operations which one performs in applying the term in concrete situations or in verifying the truth of statements or in finding answers to questions."[13] For instance, the temperature of an object, on this view, is just whatever reading would result if the object were connected to an appropriate thermometer (fact = verification procedure).

The model of rules is (in this sense) realistic; it treats judicial decisions (and the predictions of lawyers about the decisions of judges) as reliable, but not infallible guides to what the law is prior to and independently of those decisions. By contrast, the Legal Realists – or, at least, the rule-skeptics among them – were verificationists; this strand of Legal Realism removes the commonsense gap between the law and judicial reports about the law and so makes judicial decisions infallible.

Why should we embrace these counterintuitive claims? Gray and other Legal Realists defend verificationist claims about the law by appeal to the fact that in legal systems such as our own, it is the courts that have the authoritative say on what the laws mean.[14] There are two things worth distinguishing here. One issue concerns *finality*. Courts (ultimately the highest court) have (has) the final say in a particular case about what legal rights the parties to that case have. Another issue concerns *precedential value*. Other things being equal, a court's ruling in a relevantly similar case has the status of law; subsequent interpretations of the law must take that decision into account with other legal materials.

Gray certainly appeals to judicial finality as his principal argument for verificationism about the law. This is clear in the larger passage, which I have already quoted in part.

[A]fter all, it is only words that the legislature utters; it is for the courts to say what those words mean; that is, it is for them to interpret legislative acts; undoubtedly there are limits upon their powers of interpretation, but these limits are almost . . . undefined. . . . And this is the reason why legislative acts, statutes, are to be dealt with as sources of Law, and not as part of the Law itself. . . . It has sometimes been said that the Law is composed of two parts – legislative law and judge-made law – but, in truth, all the Law is judge-made law. The shape in which a statute is imposed on the community as a guide for conduct is that statute as interpreted by the courts. The courts put life into the dead words of the statute. To quote again from Bishop Hoadly . . . "Nay, whoever hath an *absolute authority* to *interpret* any written or spoken laws, it is *he* who is truly the *Lawgiver* to all intents and purposes, and not the person who first wrote or spoke them."[15]

It is important that there be some final arbiter for disputes at law, for parties to those disputes, and important that there be some consistency in the decisions governing similar cases, for those beyond the parties to a particular suit. But neither the finality nor precedential value of judicial decisions secures their infallibility, as the verificationist requires.

Even if there is no further appeal after the decision of a superior court, that doesn't mean that the court could not have made a legal mistake. Hart's analogy with the finality of umpires within the game of baseball is helpful here.[16] Because umpires have the final say on the interpretation and application of the rules of baseball, we might be tempted to say that the rules of baseball are what the umpire says they are. But to infer that there are no rules of baseball prior to and independently of the decisions of umpires – that the umpire is supposed to apply and against which his decision can be assessed – is to mistake the finality of an umpire's decisions for his infallibility. Indeed, it's hard to explain how the players regulate their behavior or the umpire is to make decisions if it is not normally as a good faith effort to follow or enforce the rules of the game.

There might seem to be some sense to the verificationist claim that final arbiters are infallible, where their decisions, however bad, have the force of precedent. For then there seems to be a clear sense in which even bad decisions are law. But this does not show that courts are infallible. Precedent implies that subsequent interpretations of the law must take that decision into account with other legal materials, including those rules that the earlier decision misinterpreted. We can agree that a bad decision can add to the law while insisting that that decision was not supported by the law that existed at the time of the decision. The forward-looking claim on behalf of bad interpretation and the backward-looking claim against it are fully compatible. So precedent does not imply infallibility. In fact, if the significance of precedent is that subsequent interpretations of the law must take that decision into account with other legal materials, then precedents are among the preexisting legal rules that any future decision must take into account.[17] But then precedent counts against legal verificationism, not in favor of it.

III. Indeterminacy in Hard Cases and Judicial Discretion

Legal Realism, understood as a verificationist view about the law, claims that there is no settled law on a matter prior to its judicial resolution. As such, it implies rampant indeterminacy in the law. As we have seen, such a view is wildly implausible. We have no reason to give up the commonsense view of law as a system of rules in favor of this sort of Legal Realism. However, even if there is no plausibility to the verificationist's claims about rampant indeterminacy, might a more restricted kind of indeterminacy be plausible? Verificationism is implausible as a general theory of law if only because there are legal rules that judges can apply in easy cases. These cases are legally determinate and the court's decision is legally correct just insofar as it corresponds to what the rules, properly interpreted, imply. But not all cases are easy cases. Some cases are hard cases in which, for a variety of reasons, it is controversial what the law requires or whether the law applies to the case at hand. It is significant that the realists were primarily appellate court judges and law professors who studied cases on appeal. As such, most of the cases that they were concerned with were hard cases, presenting controversial issues of law. Even if easy cases are legally determinate, it is not unreasonable to suppose that in hard cases there is no determinate answer about what the law is, with the result that if judges are to decide such cases they must do so on extralegal grounds. This suggests that we might best view Legal Realism's indeterminacy thesis not as a general claim about the law, but as a claim about hard cases.[18] So restricted, Legal Realism is much more plausible.

Indeed, Hart himself clearly accepts this more restricted realist claim. On this view, easy cases, to which the legal rules clearly apply, are legally determinate; insofar as it is the judge's duty to interpret and apply the law, it is her duty to decide the case as the law determines. But hard cases, in which it is controversial or unclear whether the rules apply, are, as a result, legally indeterminate. Hart thinks that such indeterminacy is an artifact of the "open texture" of language.

All rules involve recognizing or classifying particular cases as instances of general terms, and in the case of everything which we are prepared to call a rule it is possible to distinguish clear central cases, where it certainly applies and others where there are reasons both for asserting and denying that it applies. Nothing can eliminate this duality of a core of certainty and a penumbra of doubt when we are engaged in bringing particular situations under general rules. This imparts to all rules a fringe of vagueness or "open texture."[19]

Hard or controversial cases fall within the open texture of legal rules, precisely because they are cases in which reasons can be given on either side. But when a case falls within the open texture of language, Hart believes that it is legally indeterminate.[20] Judges cannot decide such cases by applying the law but only by exercising a quasi-legislative capacity – what Hart calls *judicial discretion.*[21]

Hart illustrates these claims about open texture, indeterminacy, and judicial discretion with an example involving a municipal ordinance that prohibits the introduction of vehicles into the park. He claims that the word "vehicle" has in this context a core of settled meaning that includes ordinary citizens' cars and motorcycles; as a result, the rule prohibits these vehicles from being in the park. But, Hart claims, bicycles and skateboards fall within the open texture of the term "vehicle" and so there is no fact of the matter as to whether the rule prohibits these vehicles. A judge deciding cases on the periphery must exercise discretion.

Hart makes clear that this sort of judicial legislation need not and should not be arbitrary; such judicial choice should reflect characteristic judicial virtues of impartiality, neutrality, and principled decision making.[22] Though there may in this way be better or worse resolutions of legally indeterminate cases, such resolution must ex hypothesi be based on extralegal considerations. We can reconstruct Hart's reasoning in something like the following way.

1. The law consists of legal rules formulated in general terms.
2. All general terms are "open textured": though they contain a core of settled meaning, they also have a periphery where their meaning is not determinate.
3. Controversial or hard cases, about which reasonable people with legal training disagree, fall within the open texture of legal terms within existing legal rules.
4. Hence, hard cases are legally indeterminate.
5. Hence, courts cannot decide hard cases on legal grounds; they could decide them only on extralegal (e.g., moral and political) grounds.
6. Hence, in hard cases courts must exercise judicial discretion and make, rather than apply, law.

On this view, judicial discretion does involve a quasi-legislative activity. By this sort of interstitial legislation, the courts gradually help fill in gaps in the law.[23]

We might raise various questions about this argument. For instance, we might worry about the move from indeterminacy to judicial discretion in the inference from (5) to (6). Of course, if courts are to decide legally indeterminate cases, they must exercise discretion. But should they decide such cases? A democratic worry is that judicial discretion involves judge-made law and, as such, violates the separation of powers doctrine that requires lawmakers to be politically accountable as, in principle, legislators are and many judges are not. Alternatively, we might worry that judicial discretion is unfair insofar as it would hold people legally liable for conduct whose legal status at the time was, by hypothesis, indeterminate.

Interesting and important as these worries are, I want to focus instead on the adequacy of Hart's argument for indeterminacy.[24] To assess Hart's argument for indeterminacy, it will be useful to examine briefly Dworkin's early criticism of the model of rules.

IV. Rules and Principles

In "The Model of Rules" Dworkin rejects Hart's argument about the need for judicial discretion in hard cases.[25] Whereas Hart defends moderate skepticism about the determinacy of the law, Dworkin defends its near complete objectivity. Dworkin argues that in virtually every case, including the hardest of hard cases, one litigant is entitled – as a matter of preexisting legal right – to a decision in his favor. This is a very strong claim about the determinacy of the law. Dworkin's disagreement with Hart rests on his rejection of the model of rules. According to Dworkin, the law is richer than a set of rules; in addition to explicitly enacted rules, the law also consists of principles that do not depend for their legal status upon any kind of prior official, social recognition or enactment. Dworkin uses two cases to illustrate this claim: *Riggs v. Palmer*[26] and *Henningsen v. Bloomfield Motors, Inc.*[27]

In *Riggs,* the court declared, contrary to the "plain meaning" of the relevant probate statutes, that an heir could not inherit under the provisions of an otherwise valid will if he or she murdered the testator. Though conceding that the statutes did not bar inheritance under such conditions, the court held that it is a fundamental principle of the common law that "no one shall be permitted to profit from his own fraud, or to take advantage of his own wrong, or to found any claim upon his own iniquity, or to acquire property by his own crime."[28]

In *Henningsen* there was a contract to buy an automobile, signed by both parties, that expressly limited the manufacturer's liability to "making good defective parts." The contract was properly executed, and there seemed no other established legal rule that could expand the manufacturer's liability. Henningsen's wife was injured as the result of defects in the manufacture of his car. Henningsen sued to collect compensatory damages, and the court found for Henningsen despite the express limitations in the contract. The court cited various general principles of law. Despite principles requiring the enforcement of freely made contracts, the court based its decision on the following principles: (1) manufacturers who produce potentially dangerous products such as automobiles are under special obligations that require courts to ensure that the terms of contracts involving such manufacturers are fair to both public and consumer interests; (2) courts will not be used as instruments of injustice; and (3) courts will not enforce contracts in which one party takes unfair advantage of the other's economic necessities.

It is an interesting question how exactly Dworkin's principles differ from Hart's rules.[29] But even if Dworkin can explain this satisfactorily, it remains unclear how supplementing the model of rules with principles can block Hart's argument for the indeterminacy of hard cases. If Hart's semantic claim in premise (2) of his argument is true, then we should expect to find legal indeterminacies even if the law consists of principles as well as rules. Legal principles, as well as legal rules, are expressed in language that contains general terms that have open texture. And it would be absurd to suppose that whenever the meaning of a legal rule is unclear, there is a legal principle whose meaning is clear. For instance, in *Henningsen* the court's decision that Henningsen's contract was too unjust to enforce could not, I think, be construed as settled by the core meaning of the term "injustice." But then we cannot resist something like Hart's indeterminacy thesis simply by supplementing the model of rules with principles.[30]

V. The Semantics of Indeterminacy

The claim that general terms are open textured in Hart's sense fits with a familiar view about meaning and reference that receives articulation in a semantic tradition that includes John Locke, Gottlob Frege, Bertrand Russell, C. I. Lewis, and Rudolph Carnap.[31] Simplifying somewhat, we might understand this tradition as making two claims about meaning and reference:

1. **A descriptional theory of meaning:** the meaning of a word or phrase is the set of (identifying) descriptions or properties that speakers associate with it.
2. **Meaning determines reference:** the extension of the word or phrase is all and only those things that satisfy the descriptions speakers associate with the term(s).

On this view, the meaning of a term is the set of criteria that speakers have in mind when they apply the word, and the extension of that term is the set of all and only those things that satisfy these criteria. So, for example, the meaning of the term "bachelor" is given by the description "man who has never been married" that people associate with the term, and the reference or extension of the term is all and only those things that satisfy this description, that is, all and only men who have never been married.

Hart appears to accept a version of the traditional semantic theory that identifies meanings of words with the properties or descriptions conventionally associated with them. The meaning of these legal terms is the set of criteria that are conventionally associated with them, and the law is a function of what satisfies those criteria. This explains his view that legal terms have determinate meaning just so long as speakers by and large agree in the properties or descriptions that they associate with particular legal terms. Though cases are either easy or hard, there are two kinds of easy case and so three kinds of case altogether. For a given word, there are

a. descriptions that almost everyone associates with the word,
b. descriptions that almost no one associates with the word, and
c. descriptions that some do associate with the word, and some don't.

Something that satisfies an (a)-description is part of the extension of the term; something that satisfies only (b)-descriptions is not part of the extension of the term; and about something that satisfies a (c)-description it is indeterminate whether it is part of the extension of the word. So a legal rule using this word determinately applies in the first case; it determinately does not apply in the second; and it is indeterminate whether it applies in the third. The first two kinds of case are easy cases, whereas the third is a hard case. In hard (and only hard) cases the law is indeterminate. So, on this view, judges in hard cases are not bound by determinate legal standards; if they are to decide such cases, they must do so on extralegal grounds.

However, a semantic theory that combines a descriptional view of meaning with the traditional view according to which meaning determines reference is problematic as an account of names and natural kind terms for a number of reasons. First, it does not allow us to use names and general terms to refer to individuals or properties about whom or which we are ignorant or have false beliefs. Intuitively, speakers can use names and general terms to refer to things about which they associate erroneous descriptions. We might wrongly associate the description "teacher of Plato" with the name "Aristotle." To explain how it is that we might say falsely of Aristotle that he was Plato's teacher, the name "Aristotle" must not refer via the satisfaction of an associated description (which might include "student of Plato"). The problem here for the descriptional theory is that it does not distinguish properly between what speakers' words refer to and what speakers believe.

This problem manifests itself in another way; the descriptional theory has difficulty representing disagreement. Genuine disagreement requires univocal meaning or reference but incompatible beliefs about the nature of the things one's words refer to. This is just to say that genuine disagreement requires the distinction between a difference in subject matter and a difference in belief. Because the traditional descriptional theory cannot make this distinction adequately, it cannot represent genuine disagreement. Consider synchronic disagreement. At any one stage in an intellectual inquiry there may well be a number of descriptions conventionally associated with the use of a general term. Suppose most speakers associate features XYZ with general term "G." Nonetheless it ought to be possible for a heretical inquirer to express disagreement with the prevailing view. A speaker ought to be able to say of the very thing that most speakers use "G" to refer to that it is not XYZ but rather ABC. But this must be ruled out by the traditional descriptional theory, for on this view the meaning and reference of "G" is given by the description – XYZ – that is conventionally associated with "G." If so, the heretic's claim is analytically false. But certainly not all heretical claims are false – much less analytically false – as the progressive nature of various inquiries shows us. This leads naturally to the case of diachronic disagreement. At any one stage in an intellectual inquiry there may well be a number of descriptions conventionally associated with the use of a general term. But as inquiry progresses, the descriptions associated with these terms are likely to change. In the normal case, we would like to say that there is diachronic disagreement and progress, but both judgments presuppose continuity of meaning and reference. But there will be no such continuity according to the traditional descriptional theory. The two linguistic communities associate different descriptions with their terms and, hence, mean and refer to different things by their terms. They no more disagree than do interlocutors one of whom says "The bank [= financial institution] is a good place for your money" and the other of whom says "The bank [= side of the river] is not a good place for my money." On this view, there can only be diachronic intellectual *change;* there can be no genuine intellectual disagreement, continuity, or progress.[32]

There are, of course, legal illustrations of these issues. People appear to disagree about the extension of legal phrases, such as "due care," "cruel and unusual punishment," and "equal protection of the laws." And, at least in some areas, we think legal interpretation has been progressive. For instance, most people think that the Court's decision in *Brown v. Board of Education*[33] declaring racially segregated public education unconstitutional is both inconsistent with and superior to the Court's earlier decision in *Plessy v. Ferguson*[34] upholding racially segregated public transportation under the separate-but-equal doctrine. But disagreement, continuity, and progress presuppose univocal meaning or reference, for instance, as regards the phrase "equal protection of the laws." This is what the traditional descriptional theory cannot deliver. It must represent heretical claims about the extension of legal terms as analytically false and must represent changed conceptions of equal protection as changes of subject matter.

These problems arise from the descriptional theory because it allows reference to be determined by senses. A natural alternative to this kind of mediated reference is a theory of *direct* reference that does not make reference depend upon speakers' associated descriptions or beliefs. One account of direct reference that grew out of suggestions made by Keith Donnellan and was developed by Saul Kripke and Hilary Putnam is the *causal* theory of reference.[35] According to the causal theory, names and natural kind terms refer to things in the world via complex causal histories. On this view, language users introduce terms (e.g., names and general terms) to pick out interesting features of their environment. In the idealized case, a group of speakers introduces a term in this way; what their term refers to is that bit of the environment (e.g., that object, property, or relation) that explains what they found interesting and intended to pick out. Subsequent speakers borrow this term with the intention of referring to the same thing; their use of the term inherits reference to the same features of the environment via a historical-causal chain extending from their use of the term, through the original "dubbing ceremony," to the relevant aspects of the environment. Thus, for example, the term "water" was introduced to pick out the colorless, odorless stuff found in lakes, rivers, etcetera that is suitable for drinking, bathing, supporting life, and so forth. This liquid is actually made of H_2O, and it is this chemical composition that allows it to serve these various functional roles. According to the causal theory, the reference of the term "water" is determined by this causal-historical chain; past, subsequent, and present use of "water" refers to H_2O, even as speakers' beliefs about water have been very different. Because people have not always realized that the chemical composition of water is H_2O or even that water has a chemical composition, the causal theory allows us to explain how speakers can use terms meaningfully while being quite ignorant, perhaps mistaken, about their extension and how speakers can speak about the same thing while disagreeing significantly in their beliefs about this subject matter. On this view, determining what the term "water" refers to involves reliance on scientific theorizing about the chemical structure that explains the liquid's properties. We appeal to, or defer to, experts – not because their beliefs determine what our terms refer to – but because they provide us with the best available evidence about the real nature of the referents of our terms.

The theory of direct reference is just one view about meaning and reference. But I think that any plausible view must observe two constraints that traditional semantic assumptions do not and that the theory of direct reference does.

1. It must distinguish between the meaning and/or reference of terms and the beliefs of speakers about the extension of their terms.
2. It must recognize that ascertaining the extension of general terms typically involves theoretical considerations of various kinds that may outstrip knowledge possessed by ordinary speakers.

Consider how these semantic claims would affect the interpretation of an environmental regulation imposing strict standards of due care in the handling of toxic substances enacted in, say, 1945. Relying perhaps on (then) current scientific evidence, the legislators in 1945 had beliefs about what substances are toxic, and this determined what substances the handling of which they expected the statute to regulate. We now have different and better theories about toxins. Should we place any weight on the descriptions that framers of the law associated with toxins or the scope they thought the statute has? Should we continue to impose strict liability only on the handling of those substances that the enacting legislators expected to be regulated? We might if we accepted traditional semantic assumptions. For then, failure to treat the enacting legislators' beliefs about toxins as authoritative for the meaning or reference of the word "toxin" in the regulation would apparently be a failure to interpret the statute in light of its original meaning. But appealing to original legislative beliefs in this way means failing to impose strict standards of due care on the handling of substances that are in fact toxic. Indeed, we might now have good reason to believe that substances that were not regarded as toxic in 1945 are actually *more* toxic than the substances that the legislators regarded as toxic. Only if we reject the traditional semantic assumptions and distinguish between the extension of a term and speakers' beliefs about the extension of that term can we get the right interpretative results here. The 1945 statute imposes new legal regulations on the handling of substances that are, in fact, toxic, and not on those substances that legislators then believed to be toxic. A given legal community can do no better than rely on the best available evidence in trying to determine the reference of "toxic substance." The conventional beliefs then or now about the extension of "toxin" and the scope of the statute are at most starting points in our own inquiry into the meaning of the statute, and where we have reason to believe that these beliefs are mistaken, they exercise no interpretive constraint at all.

Insofar as legal interpretation is concerned with the meaning and extension of the language in which legal provisions are expressed, it must make and defend substantive commitments about the nature and extension of the kinds and categories that legal terms refer to, and cannot simply appeal to conventional beliefs about the extension of those terms.[36]

VI. Interpretation and Intention

It is tempting to think that semantics exhausts interpretation. Isn't interpreting a phrase or text just the attempt to determine its meaning or reference? If so, then interpretation just is the determination of semantic content. This is the position of so-called textualists, such as Justice Scalia.[37] Scalia contends that the rule of law within a constitutional democracy requires that interpretation be constrained by the original meaning of legal texts, as applied to present circumstances, rather than by appeal to extratextual sources such as the intentions of the framers or past or present moral and political ideals. Only a textualist approach to interpretation, he thinks, will ensure the rule of law, rather than a rule by individuals.

But it is doubtful that semantics exhausts interpretation; a thoroughgoing textualism leads to absurd interpretive results. Consider Hart's municipal ordinance forbidding vehicles in the park. Does the ordinance, properly interpreted, forbid police cars from entering the park in pursuit of dangerous criminals? Presumably not. But on almost any semantic view "vehicles" clearly includes police cars within its extension. If semantics exhausted interpretation, the correct interpretation of this statute would clearly imply that police cars are forbidden in the park. Because this seems to be the wrong interpretive result (certainly, it is not clearly the right interpretive result), this casts doubt on a pure textualism.

Or consider the First Amendment's guarantee that "Congress shall make no law respecting an establishment of religion . . . or abridging the freedom of speech, or of the press, or the right of people to peaceably assemble." Here, too, at least part of the *meaning* of the amendment is clear; it applies to *all* speech, and it extends an *absolute* protection. But this has not been the traditional *interpretation* of the First Amendment; the Court distinguishes between protected and unprotected speech and subjects restrictions on different kinds of speech to different standards of review.[38]

If the semantic content of a legal provision does not exhaust its interpretation, what else does interpretation involve? The primary objects of legal interpretation – statutes, constitutional provisions, and precedents – like most objects of interpretation, are human artifacts, the products of purposeful activity. In interpreting the products of purposeful activity, it is common to think that we must appeal to the purposes that prompted and guided the activity whose product we are trying to understand. This suggests that legal interpretation should involve appeal to the reasons, purposes, and intentions of those who enacted the law.[39] So, for example, appeal to underlying purposes having to do with public safety might explain why various kinds of vehicles are excluded from the park and also why, at least under certain circumstances, law enforcement vehicles are not to be excluded. Similarly, if we could identify the purposes underlying the First Amendment, perhaps we could begin to distinguish, as the Court does, between central First Amendment liberties and "low value" speech.

The limits of textualism are nicely illustrated in a case that Scalia himself discusses. Scalia's brand of textualism insists that "a text . . . should be construed reasonably, to contain all that it fairly means."[40] He illustrates this brand of textualism by his dissent in *Smith v. United States*.[41]

The statute at issue provided for an increased jail term if, "during and in relation to . . . [a] drug trafficking crime," the defendant "uses . . . a firearm." The defendant in this case had sought to purchase a quantity of cocaine; and what he had offered to give in exchange for the cocaine was an unloaded firearm, which he showed to the drug-seller. The Court held, I regret to say, that the defendant was subject to the increased penalty, because he had "used a firearm during and in relation to a drug trafficking crime." I dissented.[42]

Scalia dissented on the ground that the proper interpretation of the statute would understand the reference to the use of firearms to be restricted to their use as weapons and not to include their use as barter. But this sensible interpretive claim cannot be defended by appeal to the meaning of the language of the enacted provision, independently of information about the general aims or goals the legislators were pursuing in enacting the provision. But this is just the sort of extratextual information that Scalia's textualism eschews.

A textualist literalism leads to interpretive absurdities. In rejecting textualism, we seek an account of interpretation that represents legal provisions in a favorable light. The way to do this is to understand interpretation as appealing not just to the meaning of the language of legal provisions but to reasonable conceptions of the principles and aims that underlie or rationalize those provisions.

VII. Abstract Intent

The relevance of the intentions of framers is a familiar view about both statutory and constitutional interpretation. But this claim establishes very little until we determine the *level of abstraction* at which we should characterize the purposes or intentions of the framers of a law. The purposes of the framers can be characterized in two quite different ways. The interpreter can look only to the specific activities that the framers sought to regulate – *specific intent* – or she can look to the abstract values and principles that the framers had in mind – *abstract intent* – and then rely on her own views about the extension of these values and principles. Indeed, one's specific intent is the product of one's abstract intent and collateral beliefs that determine one's beliefs about the extension of the values and principles that form one's abstract intent. So, for example, the framers of our 1945 environmental regulation had the abstract intent to regulate the manufacture and disposal of toxic substances and they had (or relied on) certain beliefs about which substances are toxic, which together led them to have specific intentions about which substances should be regulated. Or consider the intentions underlying the Eighth Amendment's prohibition of cruel and unusual punishment. The framers presumably had the abstract intent of prohibiting morally outrageous or disproportionate punishment, but their collateral moral beliefs about justifiable punishment and their previous experiences led them to expect the Eighth Amendment's prohibition on cruel and unusual punishment to prohibit some punishments and not others. For instance, they might have had the specific intent to prohibit the rack, the guillotine, and drawing-and-quartering; and it might not have been part of their specific intent to prohibit, as a matter of principle, capital punishment or hanging, in particular.

Typically both kinds of intentions or purposes exist. But then insofar as there is interpretive need to appeal to the intentions of framers, should we be constrained by their specific intentions or by their abstract intentions and our own collateral beliefs about the extension of these abstract values and principles? These two conceptions of the intentions of the framers assign quite different roles to judges and other legal interpreters. Ascertaining specific intent appears to be primarily a historical-cum-psychological task, whereas articulating abstract intent appears to be a more philosophical and value-laden task. Which intention should guide interpretation?

Meaning itself is often a good guide as to how abstract the intention is that we're looking for. If the environmental regulation demands the regulation of toxic substances, then this is evidence for the priority of abstract intent. Though evidence then available may have led its framers to expect the regulation to cover only certain substances, they chose the more general language. Because they could have chosen more specific language, regulating all and only those substances they then believed toxic, the fact that they didn't suggests that their dominant intent was to regulate those substances that are in fact toxic, and not just those they then believed to be toxic. Similarly, the abstract language of the Eighth Amendment seems to be evidence for the priority of abstract intent. Though the framers' moral beliefs about punishment may have led them to expect a prohibition on cruel and unusual punishment to prohibit only certain specific forms of torture and capital punishment, the fact that they chose the general language of "cruel and unusual punishment" is evidence that their dominant intention was to prohibit punishments that are in fact morally outrageous or disproportionate, not just these specific forms of torture and capital punishment. For it was certainly within their power to adopt a much more restricted amendment, explicitly prohibiting only these specific forms of torture and capital punishment. So when the language of the legal provision is abstract, this tends to show that the dominant intention was abstract.

But if we are to avoid the perils of pure textualism, language cannot be our only guide. One appropriate kind of evidence is counterfactual. Consider a different, but related, interpretive problem for a moment. Agents often possess many motives from which they might have acted or which their actions might be taken to express. In interpreting and assessing an agent's behavior in such circumstances, we often want to know what the agent's dominant motive was. The usual way we go about determining this is by trying to answer various counterfactual questions about what the agent would have done if certain of her beliefs or desires had been different in certain ways. If I want to know whether it was Bonny's conception of her own interest or her concern for Ben and Sam that made her keep her promise to them, I would try to decide, among other things, if she would have kept a similar promise to them had it required somewhat greater sacrifice on her part. It is not always easy to answer such counterfactual questions, but plausible answers to such questions seem to be a good guide to dominant motive.

We might rely on a similar sort of counterfactual test to determine which purpose or intention underlying a legal standard is dominant. Would the framers still have enacted the legal provision in question, in its current form, even if their beliefs about the extension of their abstract intent had been different?

Consider our environmental regulation. Suppose that we share an aim of subjecting the manufacture and disposal of toxic substances to stringent standards of care. We may disagree in our collateral beliefs about which substances are toxic; you may recognize both x and y as toxic substances, whereas I recognize only x as toxic. As a result, you may have the specific intention that the manufacture and disposal of both x and y be regulated, whereas my specific intention is that the manufacture and disposal of x but not y be regulated. If I were to come to believe that y as well as x is toxic, would I

a. come to believe that y, as well as x, ought to be handled with due care
or
b. cease to want to regulate the manufacture and disposal of toxic substances?

Here the answer seems clear: (a). My dominant aim is to regulate the manufacture and disposal of substances that are in fact toxic, not just those that I now believe to be toxic.

Or suppose that I have an abstract aim of prohibiting cruel and unusual punishment, that I do think drawing-and-quartering is cruel and unusual punishment, but that I do not think hanging is cruel and unusual punishment (for capital crimes). My specific intentions are to prohibit drawing-and-quartering but not to prohibit hanging. If I were to come to think that hanging is morally outrageous, would I

a. come to believe that the death penalty is cruel and unusual punishment and ought to be prohibited or
b. cease to want to prohibit cruel and unusual punishment?

It may be difficult for me to imagine some of my collateral beliefs mistaken in important ways. But if I really imagine what it would be like to change my collateral beliefs in this way, the answer, again, seems clear: (a). My dominant aim is to prohibit those forms of punishment that are in fact cruel and unusual, not just those that I now believe to be cruel and unusual.

Nor should this be surprising. Because specific conceptions result from a prior, though perhaps implicit, commitment to certain abstract values together with collateral beliefs about the extension of those values, the appropriate change in one's collateral beliefs would typically lead to a change in one's specific conceptions and intent.

These considerations tend to vindicate the interpretive priority of abstract intent. They also explain a similar point Dworkin makes. At one point, Dworkin draws a contrast between *concepts* and *conceptions,* which is related to our contrast between abstract and specific intent.[43] Dworkin distinguishes between fundamental moral or political concepts or values recognized in the Bill of Rights – such as freedom of association, due process, and equality – and conceptions of those concepts that articulate a theory about those values and that assign an extension to those values. On Dworkin's view, constitutional interpretation should seek to identify the best conception of the framers' concepts, rather than simply reproduce the framers' conceptions. The priority of abstract intent explains why.

Abstract intent also avoids or reduces certain familiar worries about the interpretive appeal to the intentions of the framers. What sort of historical evidence should be used to determine the specific intentions of framers who are no longer alive? How reliable is this information? Can framers be said to have intentions about situations that had not occurred to them or which they could not have envisaged? Whose intentions should we be concerned with: the leading intellectual proponents of the provision, all those who voted, only those who voted for it, or the citizens these people were supposed to represent? So, for example, in the case of constitutional provisions, we might wonder whether we are to appeal to the intentions of the leading Federalists (e.g., Madison, Hamilton, and Jay), all members of the Constitutional Convention, those of the participants in state ratification, or those of the people whom these participants were supposed to represent. Moreover, where there are competing or different intentions, how do we aggregate conflicting intentions?

These worries seem especially acute for specific intent, because specific intentions will vary among individuals to the extent that they differ in their collateral beliefs about the proper conception of the values expressed by a provision's abstract intent. However, insofar as parties to a disagreement differ only in their conceptions of shared abstract concepts, we should expect much less disagreement at the level of abstract intent. Moreover, the evidential problem will also be reduced when we shift attention from specific to abstract intent. For the language of these constitutional provisions and background knowledge about a society's general aims and principles will often be a fairly good guide as to the kind of principle or value underlying the provision.

VIII. Corporate Intentions

But if we continue to think of abstract intent as a part of an individual's psychology, some worries remain. For we may still wonder whose abstract intentions we should consider. Also, though there will be less disagreement in concept than in conception, it's not clear why there can't still be disagreement in concept, and then we need to know how to aggregate conflicting abstract intentions. Moreover, on this view, abstract intentions are still psychological states of individuals, and any claim that a particular principle was among the abstract intentions of the framers must be assessed as a historical-cum-psychological claim about various individuals. But when interpreters posit a principle or value as a purpose of the framers of a provision, they often make no attempt to document any such historical-psychological claim. Often they appeal to a principle that provides a plausible rationale for the provision and that may well have been held by the framers but need not have.[44]

We can accommodate this aspect of interpretive practice by recognizing that we are interpreting the acts of social and political bodies who are corporate agents. We are interpreting acts of legislatures at various levels, the Constitutional Convention, and various courts. Though they are composed of individuals, the acts are attributed to those individuals acting together. Insofar as we are interested in the intentions of the framers, we should be interested in the purposes or intentions of these corporate bodies – *corporate intentions* – rather than the individual persons who compose them. If so, we might understand appeal to underlying purpose as making no essential psychological or intentional claims – about individuals. Instead, we should understand interpretive ascriptions of underlying purpose as attempts to find *intellectual* or *explanatory structure* in the law. The purposes underlying a legal provision are the reasons that explain the adoption of the law. It should not be surprising if these reasons are often reflected in the language of the law or if individual framers of the law often possessed and understood these reasons, but neither of these things is necessary.

We might try to understand the explanation of corporate behavior on the model of the explanation of individual behavior. We explain an individual's intentional action by ascribing to her reasons for action. In so doing, we may be said to "rationalize" her behavior. These reasons consist of beliefs and aims whose existence and causal efficacy would explain why the person acted as she did.[45] Though a person's reports about her own motives and aims would be important evidence for us in deciding what purposes rationalize her behavior, they need not be authoritative. People often fail to understand fully their own aims, for instance, because they are moved by subconscious desires or because they are self-deceived about their true motives. In such cases, the reasons a person might adduce as underlying her behavior would not provide a good explanatory fit with her actions. If we consider any particular action, there are likely to be many eligible explanations. For instance, if a person keeps a promise that it was in her interest to keep, her reasons for action might be either prudential or moral. We decide between alternative explanations by seeing which better explains *patterns* in her behavior. We would like to know whether she would have kept her promise even if she had believed that it was disadvantageous to do so. If she would have, it seems her motive was moral; if not, it seems her motive was prudential. But often our best evidence for answering this counterfactual question is other behavior of hers. Has she kept other promises when she believed that it was imprudent or at least when the advantages of fidelity were uncertain? We might also look at associated forms of behavior. Is she generally faithful to her friends even when doing so is inconvenient or otherwise difficult? Does she generally maintain what she believes to be her obligations even when this is costly? A person's other behavior will be relevant to an intentional explanation of a particular action of hers to the extent that we think she has a fairly continuous, stable character. In a similar way, the reasons we ascribe to a particular person on a particular occasion will be constrained by our general knowledge of human nature and psychology. It is on this sort of holistic basis that we ascribe reasons and aims to a person. Sometimes, our background psychological knowledge and the person's behavioral history is insufficiently rich to allow us to decide between alternative explanations of her behavior. In some such cases, it seems reasonable to think that there is a fact of the matter about what her motive was and that the indeterminacy is just in our evidence. In other cases, however, it seems reasonable to think that her motives are more coarse-grained and do not distinguish between different features of her act, as the alternative motives we might ascribe to her do; here, there is a kind of psychological indeterminacy. If we were allocating praise and blame to her on the basis of our explanation of her behavior, it would be reasonable, in cases involving either sort of indeterminacy, to construe her motivation in the most favorable light available.

A structurally similar story about the explanation of corporate agents is plausible. We should look to the aims, values, and principles underlying particular legal provisions in interpreting those provisions in order to explain the adoption of those provisions. Of course, the semantic content of the provision is some evidence about what goals and values the framers collectively were trying to realize, and the provision may contain a preamble that explicitly sets out these goals and values. Moreover, we would do well to consider the beliefs, where they are available, of various individuals who were influential in the drafting and enactment of the provision about the aims of the provision. But none of this evidence need be decisive, for it may not succeed in rationalizing the adoption of the provision in light of what else we know about the corporate agent's behavior and the larger social and institutional background against which it acts. Often alternative rationales are eligible. If a particular regulation tends to promote two values F and G, it may be unclear whether the underlying purpose of the provision is to promote F, to promote G, to promote F and G, or to promote F or G. To decide among these alternative rationales, we would need to answer various counterfactual questions. For instance, it would help to know if the provision would have been adopted (in its actual form), all else being equal, had it promoted F but not G and had it promoted G but not F. If the provision would only have been adopted if both F and G were promoted, this is reason to think that the rationale of the provision is to promote both. If the provision would have been adopted if either F or G alone was promoted, this is reason to think that the rationale of the provision is to promote F or G. If the provision would not have been adopted had G alone been promoted, this is reason to think that the rationale of the provision is to promote F. And if the provision would not have been adopted had F alone been promoted, this is reason to think that the rationale of the provision is G. But often our best evidence for answering such counterfactual questions is other provisions that have been adopted. What effect do closely related provisions have on F and G? Are both promoted? If so, are they promoted individually or together? Is one not promoted? Do any provisions prevent or retard one of the values and, if so, which value? And we might ascribe rationales by finding wider patterns in the law, among provisions from different areas of the law (e.g., criminal and tort law). In a similar way, our ascription of rationale will also be constrained by our background knowledge about human psychology and social theory. The content and effect of other provisions and background social theory are relevant to the ascription of a rationale to a particular provision to the extent that we think our legal system operates in fairly continuous, principled ways. It is in this sort of holistic way that we ascribe values and principles to our legal system as the rationale for particular provisions. It is possible that in some cases these resources will be insufficiently rich to decide between alternative ascriptions of underlying purpose. Sometimes this will appear to be indeterminacy in our evidence; sometimes it will appear to be indeterminacy in the law. Because legal judgments determine people's entitlements and responsibilities, it would be reasonable, in cases involving either sort of indeterminacy, to construe the underlying purpose of a provision in the most favorable light available.

It is, I think, this sort of sympathetic or constructive interpretation of the explanatory structure of a legal system's provisions that best fits the interpretive practice surrounding the rhetoric of the intentions of the framers and allows us to recover a defensible interpretive constraint from that rhetoric.

IX. Principled Interpretation

On this view, the interpreter begins with the rules and principles expressed in various legal materials, including constitutional provisions, statutes, and judicial decisions. Interpreting these rules and principles requires ascertaining the meaning and extension of the words in which these rules and principles are expressed. This semantic constraint requires the interpreter to distinguish between the meaning of general terms in the law and conventional beliefs about their extension; she must make and defend commitments about the nature of the properties these terms pick out, commitments that may outstrip conventional wisdom about the extension of these terms. If the legal rules refer to scientific kinds (as our environmental regulation refers to toxins), then the semantic constraint requires the interpreter to make substantive judgments about the nature of the kinds (toxins); she should make use of the best available theories about the kinds in question (toxins), which may well outstrip conventional wisdom about the extension of the kinds (conventional wisdom about which substances are toxic). Similarly, when legal provisions are formulated using general terms that are normative, the semantic constraint requires interpreters to make and defend substantive normative judgments about the extension of the normative terms. Making normative commitments will be a feature of much legal interpretation, but especially of the interpretation of "open-ended" provisions in the Bill of Rights and the Fourteenth Amendment formulated in terms of "freedom of speech," "unreasonable search and seizure," "due process," "just compensation," "cruel and unusual punishment," and "equal protection of the laws." Here, the semantic constraint requires interpreters to make and defend substantive moral commitments about freedom of expression, the rights of the accused, fair procedures, compensatory justice, penal justice, and equal treatment.

To avoid the perils of textualist literalism, the semantic aspects of interpretation must be supplemented by construction of abstract corporate intentions of the provisions and decisions under interpretation. This requires identifying the values and principles that rationalize the actions of legal institutions and bodies in the sense of both fitting or explaining these legal events and in the sense of justifying them. One identifies principles by looking for patterns in existing provisions and decisions and tests them by seeing how well they account for existing provisions and decisions and how they would bear on the decision of related controversies. Principled interpretation will require recognizing legal mistakes. It is unlikely that all existing decisions track all the relevant similarities among cases; a principled conception of interpretation must treat those that do not fit the fundamental patterns as mistakes. But a principled interpreter might also decide a case according to principle A, rather than principle B, even though A requires recognizing more mistakes than B, if A projects much more plausibly to future controversies than B. This will be especially plausible where the mistakes that A recognizes are decisions themselves interpreting some prior provision or decision and A represents the meaning or purpose of the original provision or decision more faithfully. Mistakes should not be posited lightly, but this is the sort of reasoning responsible interpretation sometimes requires, as in the Court's decision in *Brown* to overturn *Plessy*'s separate-but-equal doctrine.

This conception of principled interpretation resembles Dworkin's account of "constructive" legal interpretation, which decides cases in terms of principles that represent existing legal materials in their best light.[46] It represents legal interpretation, especially the interpretation of legal provisions and decisions employing normative concepts, as a philosophical enterprise in which interpreters must identify substantive conceptions of these concepts that both explain the role of those concepts in the workings of the legal system and articulate those concepts in attractive ways.

X. Judicial Review and Constitutional Interpretation

We can see the importance of these interpretive claims by exploring their role in familiar and important debates in constitutional theory about the legitimacy of the Supreme Court's exercise of judicial review. The popular and political debate surfaces at just about every hearing over a Supreme Court nomination, though perhaps especially at more controversial (less centrist) nominations. It surfaced perhaps most clearly during the hearings over the nomination of (then) Judge Robert Bork. The popular and political debate is often framed as one between *judicial restraint* or *strict constructionism* and *judicial activism*. There has been a parallel debate in the scholarly literature about the nature of constitutional interpretation and the scope of legitimate judicial review. Judicial review is the judicial power to declare democratic legislation void for being unconstitutional. At one point not so long ago, this debate was framed as one between *interpretive* and *noninterpretive* review. We might say that the Court exercises interpretive review insofar as it invalidates legislation based on its interpretation of the Constitution and that it exercises noninterpretive review insofar as it invalidates legislation as embodying unsound policy or political morality.[47]

The debates about judicial activism and restraint and about interpretive and noninterpretive review typically concern a variety of landmark decisions over the last several decades – especially by the Warren and Burger Courts – concerning personal and civil rights. Much of the debate concerns various aspects of so-called substantive due process. Since the New Deal, the Court has rejected the doctrine of economic substantive due process, associated with *Lochner v. New York*,[48] that recognized the liberty of contract as a fundamental right deserving special protection. But whereas *Lochner* and economic substantive due process ended during the New Deal, substantive due process continued, insofar as the Court subsequently construed due process as protecting various fundamental personal and political liberties. Part of substantive due process concerns the "selective incorporation" of key provisions of the Bill of Rights (the first nine amendments) – such as the right to freedom of speech and religion, the right against unreasonable search and seizure, the right to counsel, the right against self-incrimination, the right to compensation for property appropriated by the state, and the right against cruel and unusual punishment – into the due process clause of the Fourteenth Amendment so as to make these provisions, applicable against the federal government, applicable against state and local governments as well.[49] Modern substantive due process also includes the recognition of nonenumerated substantive rights, such as the right to privacy.[50] Other controversial aspects of due process include the recognition of rights of the accused in criminal proceedings.[51] The debates also concern equal protection decisions that invalidated legislative districting plans that denied equal representation[52] and that mandated school desegregation.[53] Many claim that in these cases, among others, the Court has gone well beyond constitutional interpretation and has, instead, been legislating social policy and creating legal rights. In the popular debate, this part of the Court's record is represented as activist; in the scholarly debate, it is characterized as noninterpretive review. The critics reject activism and noninterpretive review, whereas many friends of the Court embrace activism and noninterpretive review.[54]

XI. Judicial Review in a Constitutional Democracy

Most parties to these debates assume that judicial review has an important role in a constitutional democracy; they are not skeptics about judicial review. Nonetheless, it is important to be clear about the rationale for judicial review. Within a constitutional democracy, such as our own, the constitution not only (a) creates a federal government, specifying its powers and dividing them among the branches of government, and (b) allocates power, at least by implication, between federal and local government, but also (c) recognizes certain rights of individuals against both local and federal government. Judicial review is the power of the judiciary to determine if governmental action conforms to these constitutional powers and constraints.

Though judicial review is not *explicitly* provided for in the Constitution, the structure of the Constitution appears to imply the legitimacy of judicial review. Article 3 of the Constitution defines the legitimate sphere of judicial power. Section 2 extends judicial power to cases "arising under this Constitution." That is, litigants claiming that a constitutional right has been violated present cases that fall within the scope of the federal judicial power. Article 6, section 2 says "This Constitution and the laws . . . which shall be made in pursuance thereof . . . shall be the supreme law of the land; and the judges in every state shall be bound thereby." This obligation to apply the law is presumably, by article 3, equally binding on federal courts.

The rationale at work here is an argument from *institutional role* that is also advanced by Alexander Hamilton in *Federalist #78*[55] and by Chief Justice Marshall in *Marbury v. Madison.*[56]

1. It is the institutional role of the judiciary to interpret and apply the law.
2. The Constitution is the supreme law of our legal system.
3. Hence, the Court must interpret and apply the Constitution.
4. Hence, if the Court determines that legislation conflicts with the Constitution, it must declare that legislation unconstitutional.

According to this rationale, it is the institutional role of the judiciary as interpreter of the law that grounds the power of judicial review.[57]

This rationale for judicial review fits nicely with a common understanding of the separation of governmental powers. Here, the separation of powers doctrine involves a separation of governmental *functions*. In our system this separation of function insists that the legislature is supposed to make law, that the judiciary is supposed to interpret and apply the law, and that the executive is supposed to enforce the law as interpreted by the judiciary. Though this account no doubt oversimplifies a more complex matter, something roughly like this division of labor has an important democratic rationale. It is thought that the legislature, rather than the judiciary, should make law, because we want our lawmakers to be democratically accountable, as, in principle, legislators are and (federal and some state) judges are not.[58] The institutional rationale for judicial review respects this division of labor. It instructs the judiciary to interpret the Constitution and measure legislation against this interpretation (interpretive review); it does not instruct the judiciary to decide if legislation is wise (noninterpretive review).[59] Indeed, whereas the separation of functions condemns noninterpretive review, it requires interpretive judicial review. It is the function of the courts to apply the law, and it is the function of the legislature to make law – subject to certain constitutional limits. Because the

Constitution is a law, it is the job of the courts to decide if the legislature has heeded its constitutional limits.[60]

The debates that interest us focus on the exercise of judicial review to protect individual rights. Whereas we want our laws to be enacted by a majority (in some cases, a supermajority) of our representatives and we want our representatives to be politically accountable, we have not accepted purely majoritarian politics. Groups can combine their electoral power to form coalitions that advance their own interests legislatively by systematically discriminating against an electoral minority within the community. This phenomenon is often referred to as *tyranny of the majority.* It presumably counts as something especially objectionable when the minority interests being ignored or harmed are especially important. Here the worry is that simple majority rule does not respect minority rights. The obvious response to this problem is to recognize institutional *constraints* on what the community can do, even with democratic support. In specifying majority rule as an appropriate law-making procedure, the constitution may also place constraints on the possible content of legislation by insisting that certain decisions cannot be taken and placing them outside the scope of majority rule. The resulting form of democracy is not pure majority rule, but rather a *constitutionally limited democracy.*

This account of the role of judicial review within a constitutional democracy explains what is wrong with the common perception that there is a tension between judicial review and democracy. In his book *Democracy and Distrust,* John Ely expresses the apparent tension this way: "Thus the central function, and it is at the same time the central problem, of judicial review: a body that is not elected or otherwise politically responsible in any significant way is telling the people's elected representatives that they cannot govern as they'd like."[61] This democratic worry misunderstands the role of judicial review within a constitutionally limited democracy. The division of labor between legislative and judicial branches of government has, as we've seen, a democratic rationale: we want our lawmakers to be politically accountable, as legislators are and as federal judges are not. However, ours is a constitutional democracy, rather than a system of pure majoritarianism; the constitutional recognition of individual rights takes certain issues off the democratic agenda. In its institutional capacity as interpreter and applier of law, it is the judiciary's job to measure democratic legislation against its interpretation of constitutional rights to see if legislation satisfies constitutional constraints.

XII. Interpretive Assumptions

One might expect a debate over the record of judicial review to concern the details of the disputed cases and of the Court's reasoning in these cases. However, the debate relies on fairly general features of these cases and assumptions about the nature of constitutional interpretation. The general features common to the various disputed cases are that they are morally and politically controversial decisions that cannot be justified by obvious inference from constitutional language or the intentions or purposes of the framers of specific constitutional provisions.

Critics of judicial review, such as Bork, see these and similar decisions by the Court as exercises of noninterpretive review in which the Court is no longer interpreting the Constitution but creating or inventing new rights. Sometimes, the complaint seems to rest on the fact that the decisions in question are morally and politically controversial. Critics may be assuming that constitutional interpretation must be *uncontroversial* or that it must be *value-free*. These two assumptions would be related if decisions based on evaluative judgments are inherently controversial. But the critics also make more concrete assumptions about interpretation. They often assume that constitutional interpretation is constrained by the *plain meaning* of explicit constitutional language or by the *intentions of the framers* of the provision under interpretation. Such assumptions can easily seem reasonable. Surely, the interpretation of any legal provision ought to be guided by the common or accepted meaning of the words in which the provision is expressed. But sometimes the meaning of express language is unclear or controversial, as it often is with general expressions, such as "due process," "cruel and unusual punishment," or "unreasonable search and seizure." At other times, application of the literal meaning of the words in which the provision is expressed to a particular case would yield absurd results; the perils of literalism suggest the interpretive need to appeal to the intentions or purposes of the framers of the provision under interpretation. These more specific interpretive constraints might be thought to fit with the more general ones. Appeal to plain or accepted meaning of explicit language will prevent interpretation from being controversial, and appeal to the intentions of the framers would seem to be a historical-cum-psychological task that does not introduce the interpreter's own evaluative beliefs.

To many, these assumptions about constitutional interpretation seem so familiar or plausible as not to require defense; they are more often taken for granted than explicitly stated, and they are more often stated than defended. Indeed, in scholarly circles, until fairly recently, these interpretive assumptions were common ground to friends and foes of the Court's record on judicial review. For instance, Michael Perry, a friend of the record of the Warren and Burger Courts, claims that "there is no point belaboring what today few if any constitutional scholars would deny: that precious few twentieth-century constitutional decisions striking down governmental action in the name of the rights of individuals — the decisions featured in the 'individual rights' section of any contemporary constitutional law casebook — are the product of interpretive review."[62] Whereas friends and foes agreed that in the cases in question the Court is no longer interpreting the Constitution but is instead applying extraconstitutional values, they disagreed over the legitimacy of noninterpretive review. Critics claimed that interpretive review is the only legitimate form of judicial review, whereas friends defended the Court's (alleged) use of noninterpretive review.

Insofar as the critics can appeal to the incompatibility of noninterpretive review with the separation of governmental functions, they have a serious complaint about the position defended by the friends of noninterpretive review. Fortunately, one can express friendship toward the record of the Warren and Burger Courts without endorsing noninterpretive review. One can and should reject the interpretive assumptions underlying their debate. Both critics and friends of the Court often act as if the issue is fidelity to the Constitution. But the real issue typically is not whether to apply the Constitution, but *how to interpret it.*[63] The real issue, then, is whether the Court's civil rights decisions reflect a systematically mistaken theory of constitutional interpretation, and this depends on what counts as constitutional interpretation. However common these interpretive assumptions are, they are deeply problematic. None of them is compelling, and they do not fit together well in an overall theory.

First, it's hard to believe that legal interpretation, in general, or constitutional interpretation, in particular, must be uncontroversial. Our interpretive theories ought to take seriously and try to make sense of our interpretive practices. But advocates, judges, and other interpreters do not drop their interpretive claims and arguments when they become controversial. Indeed, interpretive claims become most interesting, and there is greatest need for interpretive principles, precisely where it is controversial what the law requires.

Second, it's hard to see how a great deal of legal and constitutional interpretation could be value-free. A great many legal provisions employ normative categories; this is certainly true of many of the constitutional amendments whose interpretation concerns us. For instance, the First Amendment protects expressive and associational liberties; the Fourth Amendment protects people against unreasonable search and seizure; the Fifth Amendment prohibits the federal government from depriving people of life, liberty, or property without due process of law and from taking property without just compensation; the Eighth Amendment prohibits cruel and unusual punishment; the Ninth Amendment recognizes nonenumerated rights retained by the people; and the Fourteenth Amendment prohibits states from denying due process or equal protection of the laws. How could anyone interpret normatively loaded legal provisions, such as these, without making moral or political judgments?

Indeed, it's worth noting that value-laden interpretation need not be controversial if the constituent moral or political judgments are themselves not controversial. If so, not only is the constraint that interpretation be value-free implausible but also it does not follow from the constraint, itself implausible, that interpretation be uncontroversial.

To the extent that the more concrete interpretive constraints involving plain meaning and the intentions of the framers rest on these more general interpretive constraints, these more concrete constraints inherit the implausibility of the more general ones. But they may have some independent intuitive plausibility. The meaning of the language in which a legal provision is expressed is surely relevant to its proper interpretation, and it is common to appeal to the purposes of the framers of a provision to resolve apparent semantic indeterminacy or to avoid interpretive absurdity. Whereas there is something right about both of these observations, it does not support the common interpretive assumptions.

The critics (and many friends) of the Court assume that the semantic content of constitutional language cannot be controversial. On this view, the meaning of constitutional language is its *plain meaning,* that is, the descriptions conventionally associated with the language in which the provision is expressed, and the extension of constitutional language is the set of all and only those things satisfying those descriptions. On this view, any competent speaker ought to be authoritative with respect to the meaning of constitutional language; the meaning and reference of constitutional terms ought not to be a matter for theoretical dispute.[64]

But, as we have seen, this view of the semantics of constitutional language makes it difficult to understand pervasive interpretive disagreement over the meaning and extension of constitutional language. The constitutional language whose interpretation concerns us involves provisions couched in general or abstract terms such as "freedom of speech and association," "due process," "equal protection of the laws," and "cruel and unusual punishment." People disagree about the meaning of these expressions; they associate different properties or descriptions with the same constitutional categories. But if we are to represent their differences as disagreement – for instance, when one says capital punishment is cruel and unusual and another says it is not – they must use constitutional language univocally. But then we cannot simply identify meaning with the set of properties or descriptions conventionally associated with the language in question, for then they speak different idiolects. We must distinguish between conventional beliefs about the extension of constitutional categories and the meaning and extension of those categories.

Because these constitutional categories are value-laden, their extension must be a matter of which laws possess these evaluative properties and which do not. Determining the extension of such constitutional categories and the meaning of the provisions that contain them, therefore, requires substantive value judgments. Determining the semantic content of these provisions will require a correct understanding (perhaps implicit) of the values in question. For example, we cannot determine the extension of "cruel and unusual punishment" without invoking explicitly or implicitly collateral beliefs about the nature of justifiable punishment. But then, contrary to the plain meaning theory, the semantic dimension of the interpretation of constitutional provisions employing normative categories is an inherently value-laden and controversial task.

As we have also seen, it is a familiar idea that interpretation, in general, and constitutional interpretation, in particular, ought to be guided by the intentions or purposes underlying the text, as well as the meaning of the text. But, as we have also seen, this claim establishes very little until we determine the level of abstraction at which we should characterize the purposes or intentions of the framers of a law. It's clear that we must understand the appeal of the critics to the intentions of the framers as an appeal to specific intent. For only appeal to specific intent promises to represent constitutional interpretation as uncontroversial and value-free. Whereas the appeal to abstract intent requires the interpreter to rely on and defend her own conception of the proper understanding of the framers' values, ascertaining specific intent might look like a value-free task with a determinate conclusion. Moreover, precisely because the critic does not dirty her hands with detailed normative argument, only the appeal to specific intent could possibly support the sort of quick and general complaint the critic makes. For while it may be comparatively easy in many of these cases to show that the Court's decision violates or outstrips the specific intentions of the framers (i.e., the framers would not have endorsed these decisions), it would require much more argument to show that these decisions violate the best understanding of the abstract (corporate) intent of the framers.

But we argued that the interpretive focus on underlying purpose must be on abstract, rather than specific, intent. The specific intentions of the framers are often indeterminate or conflicting; the abstract language of constitutional provisions supports the dominance of abstract intent; and counterfactual evidence shows that abstract intent is more fundamental than specific intent. Moreover, we should understand appeal to the abstract intentions of the framers, not as an issue about the mental states of various individuals, but rather as an appeal to values and principles that rationalize the behavior of corporate agents.

But then the more plausible conception of the interpretive constraint exercised by the intentions of the framers also casts doubt on the common assumption that interpretation must be uncontroversial and value-free. For on this conception, judges and other interpreters must identify the abstract values underlying specific constitutional provisions and defend their beliefs about the proper conception and extension of these values.

The critics' complaint about the record of judicial review, therefore, is not compelling. Their complaint concerns the style, rather than the particular details, of a series of cases in which the Court has relied on substantive moral and political claims to declare state and federal legislation unconstitutional. Though this complaint rests on common assumptions about the nature and limits of constitutional interpretation, these assumptions reflect unexamined and ultimately implausible claims. Critics cannot express their disagreement with a decision of the Court simply by accusing it of noninterpretive review. It is no objection to the Court's decision in a hard case involving individual rights that that decision is morally and politically controversial; that's a consequence of its being a hard case. Instead, the critics must roll up their sleeves and get their interpretive hands dirty; they must identify, explain, and correct the Court's interpretation and be prepared to defend their own interpretation as the most theoretically satisfying account of the meaning and purpose of the con-stitutional provision under interpretation. These thoughts about interpretation vindicate the style, if not the content, of the Court's decisions against these common complaints. Nonetheless, we can see the significance of some of these negative and constructive claims about legal interpretation by seeing their bearing on two landmark Court cases.

XIII. *Brown*

Brown v. Board of Education invalidated segregated educational facilities as violations of the equal protection clause of the Fourteenth Amendment. In so doing, it overruled *Plessy*'s separate-but-equal doctrine, claiming that separate facilities were inherently unequal. *Brown* is usually accepted by friends and critics alike.[65] However, *Brown* is difficult to defend as a case of interpretive review on either specific intent or plain meaning theories of constitutional interpretation.

For present purposes, we might think of the equal protection clause as prohibiting unjustified or invidious governmental discrimination or as requir-ing that governmental action treat citizens with equal concern and respect. Though separate educational facilities would *now* conventionally be regarded as (invidiously) discriminatory or as inconsistent with equal concern and re-spect, this was presumably not true at the time *Brown* was decided or at the time the amendment was passed. So even if a decision today similar to *Brown* could be justified on interpretive grounds by appeal to the plain meaning theory, *Brown* cannot be so justified.

Nor, it seems, can *Brown* be justified by appeal to specific intent theory, for it seems fairly certain that the specific intentions of (at least the majority of) the framers of the Fourteenth Amendment did not include the regulation of segre-gated educational facilities. Indeed, the congressional record indicates that sponsors of the amendment specifically contemplated the case of segregated schools and assured their colleagues that adoption of the amendment would not mean that their children would have to attend school with blacks. As Raoul Berger notes

Wilson, chairman of the House Judiciary Committee and the House Manager of the Bill, who could therefore speak authoritatively, had advised the House that the words "civil rights . . . do not mean that all citizens shall sit on juries, or that their children shall attend the same schools. These are not civil rights." Wilson's statement is proof positive that segregation was excluded from the scope of the bill.[66]

We may think that the framers of the Fourteenth Amendment had the abstract intent to prohibit governmental discrimination or governmental action that violated equal concern and respect and that the correct conception of this value shows that segregated facilities violate the equal protection clause. But this would be to rely on abstract intent and our own collateral beliefs about the extension of the values expressed in that abstract intent. It seems clear that the framers of the Fourteenth Amendment held different collateral beliefs and so different specific intentions. If so, *Brown* cannot be defended by appeal to specific intent.[67]

If we accept these assumptions about the nature and limits of constitutional interpretation, we must conclude that *Brown* cannot be defended as interpretive review. By contrast, there are no such problems in accepting the legitimacy of *Brown* if our alternative interpretive claims are right. Part of interpreting the equal protection clause and applying it to *Brown* is ascertaining the meaning and extension of "equal protection." Assuming that part of its meaning is to prohibit (invidious) discrimination and to ensure that governmental action treats citizens with equal concern and respect (this may itself require appeal to abstract intent), the interpreter must rely on moral, political, and social claims in ascertaining the semantic content of the equal protection clause. Reasonable moral and political claims about the evils of discrimination and the demands of equal concern and respect together with reasonable social claims about the nature and effects of racially segregated education imply that segregated educational facilities do not fall within the extension of "equal protection." Racial segregation in public education expresses and encourages racial stereotyping that adversely affects the life prospects, opportunities, and self-esteem of racial minorities and, hence, violates central aspects of the demand that government treat its citizens with equal concern and respect. Appeal to the abstract (corporate) intent or underlying purpose of the equal protection clause of the Fourteenth Amendment would seem to point in the same interpretive direction. Something like a principle of equal concern and respect rationalizes adoption of the equal protection clause, and the same assumptions about equal concern and respect and the nature and effects of racially segregated educational facilities imply that such facilities violate the equal protection clause. *Brown* illustrates well the inadequacy of interpretive appeals to plain meaning and specific intent and the importance of a more philosophical conception of interpretation.

XIV. *Griswold*

In *Griswold v. Connecticut* the Court invalidated a Connecticut statute prohibiting the sale and use of contraceptives on the ground that this statute violated a married couple's constitutional right to privacy. Douglas, who wrote the majority opinion, admitted that the Constitution did not explicitly grant a right to privacy but claimed that the right to privacy could be found in the "penumbra" of the First Amendment (free speech and association), the Third Amendment (homeowner's right not to have his house invaded during peacetime without his consent), the Fourth Amendment (right against unreasonable search and seizure), the Fifth Amendment (guarantee of due process), and the Ninth Amendment (nonenumerated rights retained by people) and could be applied to state legislation through the due process clause of the Fourteenth Amendment.

Griswold is often thought to reflect noninterpretive review and, as a result, the judicial creation of constitutional rights. Of course, a right to privacy is, as Douglas concedes, nowhere enumerated in the Constitution. So *Griswold* cannot be defended by appeal to the plain meaning of explicit constitutional language. Equally clearly, the framers did not (specifically) intend the Bill of Rights to preclude birth control legislation. But then *Griswold* cannot be defended by appeal to the specific intentions of the framers. However, as we have seen, there is no compelling motivation for these constraints on constitutional interpretation. Determination of the meaning and extension of the provisions of the Bill of Rights and the Fourteenth Amendment protecting moral and political values will require a good deal of moral and political theory about the nature and scope of the rights recognized in those amendments. And in providing interpretations of constitutional provisions, we must appeal to corporate intent or underlying purpose as well as meaning. But it is not unreasonable to suppose, as Douglas does, that a value of privacy – really, personal autonomy – is one of the values that provide a plausible rationale for the otherwise diverse cluster of personal liberties recognized in the Bill of Rights. Of course, it would be nice to know more about the exact nature and scope of a right to privacy; that information would obviously have an important bearing on our assessment of the Court's decisions about whether privacy prevents state interference with a woman's access to abortion (*Roe v. Wade*) or with consensual homosexual relations in the privacy of one's own home (*Bowers v. Hardwick*).[68] Nonetheless, it is not implausible to suppose that a principle of personal autonomy broad enough to rationalize these disparate personal liberties in the Bill of Rights would extend to decisions about intimate association and reproduction within traditional family structures.[69]

XV. Determinacy Revisited

Having articulated a philosophical conception of interpretation and explored some of its implications for familiar and important issues in constitutional theory, we might return to issues about objectivity or determinacy, out of which our discussion of interpretation developed. For now we can see issues about the determinacy of the law as resting not just on the existence of legal rules and other standards but also on the determinacy of their correct interpretation.

We've seen reason to reject the extreme skepticism about the determinacy of the law characteristic of some strands in Legal Realism. Realist skepticism conflates the fallibility and finality of legal interpretation. The fact that some courts have the final say about how legal provisions are to be interpreted does not show that one interpretation is not correct or that decisions cannot be legally assessed in terms of their conformity to that interpretation. Easy cases appear to be cases in which one interpretation of the application of a legal provision to a situation is clearly correct and in which judicial decisions are legally mistaken insofar as they fail to conform to that interpretation.

As we have seen, a more moderate skepticism restricts indeterminacy to hard cases. Are hard cases ipso facto indeterminate? Hart accepts this more moderate skepticism, because of his claims about the open texture of legal language. Hard or controversial cases fall within the open texture of legal rules, precisely because they are cases in which reasons can be given on either side. But when a case falls within the open texture of language, Hart believes that it is legally indeterminate. Hart's view that hard cases are ipso facto indeterminate rests on the view that disagreement about the extension of legal terms to a situation implies indeterminacy in their application to a situation. It follows, on this view, that hard cases can be decided only by the application of extralegal standards.

Similar reasoning underlies claims about legal indeterminacy made within the Critical Legal Studies tradition (CLS). Some within CLS draw skeptical conclusions from the familiar observation that it is always possible for reasonable people with legal training to disagree about the correct interpretation of the law. As Roberto Unger writes, "[E]very thoughtful law student or lawyer has had the disquieting sense of being able to argue too well or too easily for too many conflicting solutions. Because everything can be defended, nothing can."[70] Because reasonable interpretive disagreement is possible, all such cases are legally indeterminate and can be decided only on extralegal normative grounds. Unger and other friends of CLS seek to expose legal indeterminacy and the inevitability of judicial legislation and to recommend judicial reliance on a normative conception of democratic equality.[71] However, the scope of such CLS skepticism is unclear. That depends on the intended domain of discourse for assessing the claim that reasonable disagreement is possible in any case. If the domain includes all cases, then the resulting skepticism is complete, as it is in verificationist strands within Legal Realism.[72] However, just as the realists were primarily judges and law professors concerned with hard cases on appeal, so too the skeptics within CLS are primarily legal academics, and, as such, may be focusing on hard cases on appeal, in which case their skepticism, like Hart's, is moderate.

But this argument for moderate skepticism rests on dubious semantic assumptions. Reasonable disagreement, we saw, would imply indeterminacy if the traditional semantic theory were true. For then legal terms would have determinate meaning and reference just so long as competent speakers by and large agree in the descriptions they associate with those terms and in the extensions they assign to those terms. However, the traditional semantic theory cannot represent disagreement and continuity of inquiry. An adequate semantic theory must (1) distinguish between the meaning and reference of terms and the beliefs of speakers about the extension of their terms, and (2) recognize that ascertaining the extension of general terms typically involves theoretical considerations of various kinds that may outstrip beliefs held by ordinary speakers. But then an adequate semantic theory implies that hard cases are not ipso facto indeterminate.

Even if hard cases are not ipso facto indeterminate, are there reasons – beyond the discredited semantic ones – for thinking that many or most hard cases are indeterminate? Some within CLS sometimes defend widespread indeterminacy, not as a direct consequence of disagreement, but as something like the best constructive interpretation of various areas of law. On this view, it's not that interpretation gives out as soon as it gets controversial; rather, the best constructive interpretation of various areas of law shows it to be deeply inconsistent. Because anything follows from a contradiction, no resolution of a case arising under conflicting legal norms could be the uniquely correct resolution. Inconsistency implies indeterminacy. Those within CLS who defend strong indeterminacy in this way often support these claims with case studies in which constructive interpretation allegedly reveals irresolvable inconsistency of principle. For instance, Unger undertakes such studies for contract law and equal protection law.[73] I'll briefly examine Unger's claims about the contradictions in contract law; I believe that his failure to pursue constructive interpretation systematically undermines his claim to have found contradiction in contract law and illustrates how CLS claims about indeterminacy in the law are unwarranted.

Unger identifies a serious inconsistency in contract law between the principle of freedom to contract and various fairness principles. Free contract presumably requires that voluntary agreements of the right sort be enforced. Unger identifies two kinds of fairness principles that he thinks are in tension with freedom of contract: (a) principles that police contracts for duress – to make sure that they do not coerce or exploit the economic necessity of one of the contracting parties – and (b) principles of reliance that require performance in the absence of a formal agreement. Unger assumes that principles of duress and reliance are inconsistent with freedom of contract. But this reflects an unimaginative constructive interpretation of freedom of contract and its relation to these fairness principles.

Freedom of contract requires that agreements be voluntary and unforced. But then freedom of contract does not require enforcing agreements reached by coercive means. By analogy, when *A* exploits *B*'s duress to secure agreement to contractual terms that *B* would not have agreed to but for his duress, it is arguable that *B*'s consent is not fully voluntary and unforced. If so, freedom of contract does not require enforcing agreements made under duress. Alternatively, we might conceive of the relevant principle as requiring the enforcement of contracts fairly made. Fairness in an agreement arguably requires both that the agreement was not coerced and that it was made in conditions of rough parity in which neither party exploits the disadvantages of the other to secure favorable terms.

Reliance principles allow for recovery of damages in the absence of a formal contract when the damaged party acted on reasonable expectations about the commitments of the other party. Unger illustrates this principle with a case in which a general contractor relies on the bid of a subcontractor.

A general contractor considers entering a bid for a job that will require him to pay a subcontractor for goods or services. To determine the amount of his own bid, he solicits bids from subcontractors. Relying upon the lowest sub's estimate, the general puts in a bid, which is accepted. Before the general can accept the sub's offer, the sub advises him that he, the sub, has made a mistake in his own calculations as a result of adding up figures erroneously or of misunderstanding the nature of the job. Can the general hold the sub to his bid?[74]

Unger's view seems to be that freedom of contract answers No, whereas reliance principles answer Yes. But we need see no conflict between reliance and freedom of contract here. There need be no contradiction between freedom of contract and reliance as long as both are treated as sufficient but not necessary conditions of contractual obligation; for then formal contract is one way to generate contractual obligation, and the right sort of reliance is another. Moreover, we might argue for further reconciliation by explaining the doctrine of reliance as a recognition of *tacit* agreement. We could then understand freedom of contract as requiring the enforcement of certain kinds of voluntary agreements, whether express or tacit.

Even if the doctrine of reliance resists capture within the intellectual net of agreement, we might well try to reconcile both reliance and freedom of contract under a broader conception of the point of contract law. Contract law is that body of law designed to establish and enforce norms of agreement that will facilitate coordination and mutually beneficial cooperation. These norms must secure predictability and so ground reasonable expectations about the behavior of partners in situations of coordination and cooperation. Enforcement of voluntary formal agreements is one obvious way to serve this goal, but holding people to abide by expectations that they have encouraged in others, when the others have reasonably relied on those expectations, is arguably another way of serving that same goal.

Though I have only sketched ways of reconciling freedom of contract and fairness demands by deriving them from common principles, there appear to be several promising strategies. And even if they are independent principles, without a common source, they need not be inconsistent provided neither aspires to be the sole determinant of contractual obligation.[75] But then it's hard to see how Unger has established a remotely plausible case for thinking that contract law contains deep inconsistency of principle.[76] If this study is, as it is intended to be, representative of CLS arguments for indeterminacy, then they provide no good grounds for expecting to find significant indeterminacy in the law.[77]

Even if CLS claims do not support significant indeterminacy, we might nonetheless wonder how much determinacy it is reasonable to expect in hard cases. Constructive interpretation is a dialectical process in which legal principles are assessed by their ability to sustain and explain existing legal materials in a way that projects to new controversies with plausible results. But not all previous decisions will track the same principles perfectly, and our initial views about what constitutes plausible resolutions of new controversies may not track a single set of principles perfectly. So we must be prepared to adjust our views about which cases have been correctly decided and what constitutes a plausible resolution of a possible controversy in light of principles that otherwise explain existing decisions and project to future controversies well. Ideally, we make adjustments in our principles, in our understanding and assessment of past decisions, and in our understanding and assessment of related controversies in response to conflicts, making adjustments here at one point and there at another, as coherence seems to require, until our interpretation is in dialectical equilibrium. Because constructive interpretation aims at dialectical equilibrium, it is an intellectual ideal that we can at best hope to approximate. As a result, the existence of preinterpretive and even reflective interpretive disagreement is no sign that legal disagreement is in principle unresolvable. The fact that the conscientious application of dialectical standards to actual interpretive controversies typically reveals comparative interpretive virtues and vices in rival views should encourage us to think that the systematic application of dialectical methods would identify the uniquely best constructive interpretation of the issues in dispute. The claim that legal disagreements are in principle unresolvable by dialectical methods is just one claim about what the results of a systematic dialectical inquiry among different interpreters would be and enjoys no privileged a priori position in relation to its nonskeptical competitors. Because of these dialectical aspects of the resolution of interpretive controversy, there can be no a priori guarantee that all disputes are resolvable in principle. But the lack of such a guarantee provides no reason to doubt that most legal issues have a best constructive resolution. Indeed, interpreters typically act as if hard cases have a best interpretation; they seek, assess, and defend interpretive claims knowing full well that other interpreters might disagree. These practices would involve no presupposition of objectivity if they were confined to parties to a lawsuit and their attorneys, inasmuch as these interpreters might have a vested interest in representing their interpretive claims in hard cases as uniquely correct, even if they were not and were not regarded as such. However, the apparent search for right answers to hard interpretive questions is not confined to interpreters with vested interests in the outcomes, but extends to judges deciding such cases and other more-or-less disinterested interpreters. Indeed, the assumption that one resolution of a case would provide a better constructive interpretation of the relevant legal materials than other resolutions appears to be a sort of regulative ideal that guides interpretive practice. The assumption of determinacy can be an appropriate regulative ideal even if it is sometimes false; if most interpretive controversies have a best resolution and it is difficult to distinguish those that do and those that don't, then it may well be reasonable to approach any interpretive controversy with the (perhaps defeasible) assumption that it has a best resolution.[78]

XVI. The Relevance of Objectivity

I have defended a fairly strong commitment to objectivity or determinacy in the law, though one that falls short of complete objectivity. It is worth considering a jurisprudential challenge to this picture that denies not so much the possibility of objectivity in interpretation as its relevance or significance. In a recent book, Cass Sunstein defends a pragmatic account of interpretation and adjudication against the sort of philosophical account that Dworkin and I have defended.[79]

Sunstein concedes that the law is rife with evaluative categories — such as, rights, responsibility, autonomy, due process, and just compensation — with the result that claims about how the law is best understood are ineliminably normative. The interesting question is how normative theorizing ought to figure in legal interpretation. He contrasts two models. The more philosophical model is epitomized by Dworkin's ultra-philosophical judge Hercules, who decides cases by appeal to philosophical first principles that can be justified in terms of their normative acceptability and their fit with previous legal materials. By contrast, the more pragmatic model is epitomized by Justice John Marshall Harlan, who, according to Sunstein, eschewed elaborate theorizing in preference for piecemeal decision making involving analogical reasoning and appeal to secondary principles that would be common to many different philosophical systems — what Sunstein calls "incompletely theorized agreements."

Sunstein mentions various reasons for preferring the pragmatic conception. First, he suggests that it is better suited to real world applications. For instance, he suggests that even if wealth maximization is an indefensible first principle, because it is only roughly correlated with factors (e.g., welfare or rights) having genuine normative significance, it may be a sufficiently reliable index of what does matter to serve as a good principle in various areas of private law adjudication. Presumably, the more philosophical conception of adjudication would eschew use of such false targets. Second, Sunstein claims that only the pragmatic conception accounts for the way in which judges and other legal interpreters engage in analogical reasoning from precedent. By contrast, the philosophical conception apparently endorses only top-down syllogistic legal reasoning from first principles or, if it can recognize reasoning from precedent, cannot treat precedents as fixed points. Third, Sunstein argues that the pragmatic conception has the advantage of allowing a convergence in outcome by partisans of different first principles and philosophical systems. By contrast, the philosophical conception seems to demand divisive examination of rival philosophical systems. In this way, the pragmatic conception might seem better suited to interpretation within a pluralist society. Interesting as these claims are, they do not give a fair picture of the comparative virtues and vices of the philosophical and pragmatic conceptions of legal interpretation and adjudication.

First, there is no reason to claim that a philosophical conception of adjudication must be ill-suited to deal with real world problems. Hercules is interested in justifying decisions in real disputes, with all their messy empirical details. Sunstein imagines that principle A might better track all the normatively relevant factors than principle B, but that principle A might be more complicated and less easy to apply reliably than principle B. If so, then even if the value of *conformity* to A is greater than that of conformity to B, B might nonetheless have greater *acceptance* value than A. The example Sunstein uses, if only for the sake of argument, of such a B-type principle is wealth maximization. But Hercules can recognize this. He can defend reliance on B as just such a second-best option, as we often defend appeal to "bright line" principles in adjudication. This sort of clear-eyed recognition of B's derivative justification seems preferable to the pragmatist's apparent refusal to recognize B's derivative justification. To recognize that B is only derivatively justified is intellectually more honest, and it allows appeal to A in contexts in which B's guidance is especially imperfect and A's guidance less liable to distortion or at such time, if any, as A's acceptance value exceeds B's. The pragmatist indifference to B's derivative justification or pretense that B is nonderivatively justified would not allow for this. In this respect, the philosophical conception seems preferable to the pragmatic one.

Second, Sunstein exaggerates the contrast between philosophical and analogical conceptions of adjudication. A philosophical conception of adjudication justifies decisions in new cases by appeal to principles that provide a good fit with existing decisions and project to new controversies with attractive results. This is how the philosophical conception understands consistency of principle. In finding principles with good backward-looking fit and attractive forward-looking implications, a philosophical conception necessarily employs a great deal of analogical reasoning. For what counts as consistency of principle with previous cases requires determining which cases are relevantly similar and how. Deciding which decision has more acceptable future implications involves foreseeing relevant analogies between a particular decision in the immediate case and more or less plausible decisions in other possible cases. It is, at least in part, by judging the acceptability of the consequences of adhering to one principle, rather than another, in other possible cases that good interpreters often decide whether that is a reasonable principle to follow in the present case.

So, although a philosophical conception of adjudication may make explicit use of principles, this is not part of some top-down or foundationalist form of reasoning; competing principles are assessed by analogical reasoning about their fit with prior decisions and their implications for future decisions. For this reason, it is quite puzzling that Sunstein writes as if a philosophical conception of adjudication does not take precedent seriously. Analogical reasoning from precedent is an essential part of consistency in principle. Of course, a philosophical conception will not treat precedents as fixed points. But any plausible view must recognize the possibility of legal mistakes. It's implausible to suppose that all existing decisions track all the relevant similarities among cases perfectly; so an analogical method must be prepared to recognize and correct legal mistakes. As we've seen, the philosophical conception of adjudication just extends the theory of mistakes in a natural way. The philosophical interpreter might decide a case according to principle A, rather than principle B, even though A requires recognizing more mistakes among previous decisions, on the ground that it projects much more plausibly to future cases than B does. This will be especially plausible, we saw, where the mistakes that A recognizes are decisions themselves interpreting some prior provision or decision and A represents the meaning or purpose of the original provision or decision more faithfully. Mistakes should not be posited lightly, but this is the sort of reasoning responsible interpretation sometimes requires, as in the Court's decision in *Brown* to overturn *Plessy*'s separate-but-equal doctrine.

Moreover, good analogical reasoning cannot avoid commitments of principle. The analogizer must decide which cases are relevantly similar and which cases are not; but to do this is just to make a determination, if only implicitly, about what principles the existing legal materials stand for. And if today's good analogies are not to be tomorrow's bad analogies, which would itself be hard to justify on analogical grounds, then the interpreter must look not only backward but forward for similarities, patterns, and principles.

Finally, I think Sunstein overrates the value of incompletely theorized agreements. To see this, we need to understand why we seek generality at all.

Normative judgments have variable generality; some concern particular cases, others concern types or classes of action, and others concern many types of actions. Generality is required to provide *guidance.* A list of discrete judgments about particular cases provides inadequate guidance. Sometimes one is uncertain what to think about a new case. A set of particular judgments about other cases will not help; one needs a general view about a class of cases under which the present one falls. Also, one might notice differences in one's judgments about apparently similar cases. By themselves, different particular judgments are not inconsistent, but they do make for inconsistency if there is no relevant difference between the two cases. Here, an appeal to more general rules would identify which differences are normatively relevant and how, and so would either remove the appearance of inconsistency or indicate how one should revise one's judgments so as to eliminate inconsistency. Moreover, even intrapersonally consistent judgments may be interpersonally inconsistent; people disagree. Appeal to more general judgments may give us leverage on our disagreement by allowing us to see how at least one of us is misapplying a shared rule or principle to the particular case. In addition to these practical reasons for ascent to more general judgments, there is an intellectual or explanatory reason. Even if all of my particular judgments were true, there would still be the question about what made them all true. What features of the cases explain the correctness of one's normative judgment about them? To answer this question is to formulate moral rules or principles. And the truth of these principles would not only explain why one's judgments are correct, when they are correct, but would also provide guidance in uncertain or contested cases. It is this sort of normative guidance that rules and principles provide and that is essential to the idea of decision according to principle characteristic of the rule of law. But similar reasoning can motivate an ascent from low-level generalizations to more general principles. I may be uncertain what to think about a particular kind of case; I may make apparently inconsistent judgments about similar kinds of cases; and I may disagree with others about the right rules. Whether or not we experience these practical difficulties, there is still the explanatory issue about why all and only these rules should be right. We can get leverage on these explanatory and practical problems by finding general principles that subsume and explain these low-level moral rules.

   This reminder about the need for normative generality suggests problems or at least serious limitations for a jurisprudence of incompletely theorized agreements. Sunstein's pragmatist eschews general principles in favor of low-level rules common to very different theoretical outlooks. Because the pragmatist eschews general principles, she cannot address the explanatory issue of why we should think these low-level rules true or plausible. But then the pragmatist can offer us no reason to think that these rules draw distinctions that are normatively relevant and an appropriate basis for decision. Even commonly accepted rules can be arbitrary or oppressive in their implications. We want some basis for thinking our common rules are legitimate, and this is the reason we seek principled justifications of our low-level rules.

Perhaps more obviously, the pragmatist offers inadequate guidance for the resolution of uncertain and contested cases. An example will help. Between *Plessy* and *Brown* the Court considered a number of equal protection challenges to segregated public facilities. For example, in *Missouri Ex. Rel. Gaines v. Canada*[80] the Court invalidated Missouri provisions for out-of-state legal education for blacks as a violation of the equal protection clause of the Fourteenth Amendment on the ground that an out-of-state legal education is inferior to an in-state one. The Court apparently followed Sunstein's pragmatist injunctions. It did not decide between *Plessy*'s conception of equality (separate-can-be-equal) and what would be *Brown*'s conception of equality (separate-cannot-be-equal); it decided that the particular provisions for blacks and whites in Missouri to attend law school were not in fact equal (separate-but-unequal). Though it reached a more egalitarian conclusion than the *Plessy* Court, the *Gaines* Court engaged in analogical reasoning from *Plessy* and reached a decision consistent with both conceptions of equality. But, however expedient the *Gaines* reasoning may have been (and this is a large empirical question whose answer should not be taken for granted), I don't take it to be the product of an adequate jurisprudence. *Gaines* is a classic case of getting the right result for the wrong reason. The out-of-state legal education for blacks that the Missouri plan provided would have constituted unequal treatment precisely because of its separation of the races, even if, contrary to fact, it offered all the other advantages of in-state legal education. For this reason, *Gaines* offers inadequate guidance; it is unable to explain why there is a violation of equal protection even when segregated facilities are equivalent but for those differences consequent only on segregation (separate-but-otherwise-equal). Agnosticism between the two conceptions of equality, even if it gets the right result in *Gaines,* does not give the right sort of guidance in the separate-but-otherwise-equal case. Indeed, analogical reasoning that treats precedents, including *Plessy,* as fixed points doesn't fail to give guidance in the separate-but-otherwise-equal case; it gives the wrong guidance. This was recognized in *Brown.* But *Brown* required giving up agnosticism between the two conceptions of equality and rejecting the *Plessy* conception. Accepting the suitably principled conception of equality in *Brown* required treating *Plessy* as a legal mistake and an inappropriate basis for analogical reasoning.

Examples might be multiplied.[81] But I think this example illustrates well some of the perils of Sunstein's pragmatic conception of adjudication that employs piecemeal analogical reasoning, which treats precedents as fixed points, and that seeks low-level generalizations that are agnostic as between competing principled justifications of those generalizations. The law – especially constitutional law – defines and constrains democratic power in terms of normative principles. Interpreters of the law must attempt to articulate those principles in ways that make best sense of existing institutions and decisions and that project onto future controversies in the most plausible way. This kind of consistency of principle is an important part of the rule of law.

XVII. Law and Morality

I would like to conclude by exploring the implications of this account of constructive legal interpretation for traditional debates between Legal Positivism and Natural Law about the relation between law and morality. As traditionally conceived, Legal Positivism and Natural Law theory represent mutually exclusive and jointly exhaustive claims about whether there is a necessary connection between law and morality.[82]

Legal Positivism, as I understand it, asserts both a thesis about the *social* nature of law and a thesis about the *separation* of law and morality.[83] The Social Thesis claims that what counts as valid law is a matter of social fact and that legal norms can be distinguished from other social norms by virtue of having the right sort of pedigree. Hart claims that every legal system contains a rule of recognition that specifies the criteria that officials of that system employ (even if only implicitly) in identifying appropriate legal behavior.[84] For instance, in the United States legal system, there is a rule of recognition that recognizes roughly three main sources of law: constitutional provision, legislative enactment, and prior judicial decision. Any norms coming from sources specified in the rule of recognition has the right pedigree.[85] Because these social sources need not be moral sources, the Social Thesis seems to support the Separation Thesis, which asserts, as Austin famously says, that "the existence of a law is one thing; its merit or demerit is another."[86] The Legal Positivist asserts that the validity of legal norms is a function of their pedigree and denies that significant moral content is a necessary condition of legality.

By contrast, the Natural Law tradition, insists on the *inseparability* of law and morality. Norms that might otherwise have the right social pedigree do not qualify as genuine laws if they do not have adequate moral content. Indeed, some versions of Natural Law go further and claim that moral content is a sufficient, as well as a necessary, condition of legal validity in the sense that all and only true moral principles are part of the law. This would be a Moral, rather than a Social, Thesis about the nature of law. Both versions embrace the Inseparability Thesis; in particular, wicked norms cannot be genuine laws.

If the law is determinate just insofar as the interpretation of legal materials yields a correct answer, the traditional debates about the connection between law and morality — whether moral content is a condition of legal validity — can be extended to legal interpretation. The traditional Natural lawyer should think that legal interpretation necessarily involves good moral reasoning and cannot represent the law as immoral to any significant degree, whereas the traditional Legal Positivist should think that legal interpretation does not necessarily conform to good moral reasoning and can deliver conclusions about what the law is that represents it as significantly morally defective.

It is important to understand that the Natural Law tradition does not win these debates because of the existence within some legal systems of laws with good moral content. Legal systems can, and fortunately sometimes do, contain laws that enforce people's moral rights and at least some of their obligations. For example, we may think that some of the provisions in the Bill of Rights have adequate moral content. Such laws do have moral content; they cannot be properly interpreted without sound moral reasoning; if so, correct interpretive claims about what the law requires in cases arising under such laws cannot represent the law as morally defective to any significant extent. However, the moral content of these laws is a happy but unfortunately contingent affair. Enacted rules with moral content need not have been enacted, and other rules with immoral content might have been enacted in their place. But then the moral content of some actual laws does not show that the law or legal interpretation necessarily has moral content. Indeed, there could be a legal system whose rule of recognition specifies morality as the source of law in the sense that all and only morally acceptable norms are valid laws within that system. Even this would be a contingent fact, would not show that valid law, as such, must be morally acceptable and, hence, would not show that significant moral content is a necessary condition of legal validity.[87]

When we are clearer about the nature of the commitments in the traditional debate between Legal Positivism and Natural Law, it is easy to suppose, as many do, that Legal Positivism wins. It just does seem that historical or social pedigree of some sort is what determines whether a social norm is a law within a given legal system, that immoral law is possible, and that morally attractive law is a precarious achievement rather than an essential feature of legal systems. Something like this had always been my view. But if we understand legal interpretation in terms of constructive interpretation, we ought to reach a somewhat different conclusion. Constructive interpretation makes possible a kind of reconciliation between Legal Positivism and Natural Law; neither view is acceptable without qualification, but each states an important element of the correct view.

Insofar as the Legal Positivist thinks that the existence of valid law is a matter of institutional fact and that laws can be distinguished from other social norms by virtue of their pedigree, she must emphasize the backward-looking aspects of interpretation that stress the interpretive fit between a particular decision in the present case and extant legal standards and previous interpretations of those standards. By contrast, insofar as the Natural lawyer thinks that the existence of valid law is a matter of acceptable moral principle and identifies the law with the demands of political morality, she must emphasize the forward-looking aspects of interpretation that stress the moral acceptability of following one principle, rather than another, in this and other related controversies. But constructive interpretation insists on *both* dimensions of interpretation; it justifies decisions in new cases by appeal to principles that provide a good dialectical fit with existing legal materials having the right pedigree and that project to new controversies with plausible results. On the one hand, if no weight is given to the forward-looking dimension of acceptability, then it is hard to see how we are trying to understand the law in a favorable light that at least tries to justify its assignment of rights and responsibilities. On the other hand, if no weight is given to the backward-looking dimension of fit, then it is hard to see how we are going to distinguish between interpretation of the law and legislation from a clean slate.

The Legal Positivist may still claim victory. For the backward-looking dimension of fit constrains eligible accounts of the principles rationalizing existing legal standards. A system of enacted law can contain rules enjoining systematic forms of harmful discrimination or nondiscriminatory but oppressive treatment of the governed. Provided the moral defects of the system are genuinely systematic, no plausible constructive account of the principles rationalizing the adoption of these provisions can represent these principles as morally defensible. Acceptable moral principles stand in no rationalization relation to the adoption of these provisions; therefore, such principles cannot be invoked as part of showing these provisions in their best light. This vindicates the positivist claims that there can be wicked legal systems and that sound legal interpretation can represent the law as morally deficient in significant ways. That may seem to establish the Separation Thesis.

However, constructive interpretation implies that we cannot completely separate the merits of the law from the correct interpretation of the law. For the best interpretation of legal provisions, even wicked legal provisions, requires articulating the most attractive principles to rationalize those provisions. As we have seen, one rationale for a set of provisions offers a better constructive interpretation than another, all else being equal, if it projects to novel cases with more acceptable results; one rationale can also offer a better constructive interpretation than another, even if it recognizes somewhat more legal mistakes, if it projects to novel cases with more acceptable results. But then even if it is true that there are or can be sufficiently wicked legal systems such that we cannot reach morally acceptable principles by the principled interpretation of its provisions, it is nonetheless true we cannot engage in principled interpretation, even of wicked legal provisions, without relying on substantive moral commitments and without preferring an interpretation that promises the most acceptable rationalization of those provisions. This makes it difficult to accept the Separation Thesis without qualification. Even though there can be wicked legal systems and the correct interpretation of its provisions can represent them as morally deficient, it is not the case that the content of the law and its merit are completely separate issues.

If interpretation requires decision according to principles that represent legal materials in their best light, then it must emphasize both the backward-looking dimension of fit and the forward-looking dimension of acceptability. This suggests a simple victory for neither Legal Positivism nor Natural Law; rather, each stresses an essential element of legal interpretation without which our conception would be incomplete.

Notes

1. Here, I understand "pedigree" broadly, so as to refer to whatever features distinguish legal norms from other sorts of social norms, such as norms of etiquette. For further discussion of the significance of this conception of pedigree for legal positivism, see §XVII (*infra*).
2. This chapter revisits themes and draws on ideas in earlier essays of mine: "Legal Positivism and Natural Law Reconsidered," *The Monist* 68 (1985): 364–387; "Legal Theory, Legal Interpretation, and Judicial Review" *Philosophy & Public Affairs* 17 (1988): 105–148; and "Semantics and Legal Interpretation (Further Thoughts)" *The Canadian Journal of Law and Jurisprudence* 2 (1989): 181–191. However, the conception of interpretation and its jurisprudential implications presented in this chapter are somewhat different than what I have defended before. In particular, my current conception brings me closer on some issues to Ronald Dworkin's views in *Law's Empire* (Cambridge, Mass.: Harvard University Press, 1986) than I had been before.
3. See John Austin, *The Province of Jurisprudence Determined* [originally published 1832], ed. H. L. A. Hart (New York: Noonday Press, 1954); H. L. A. Hart, "Positivism and the Separation of Law and Morals," reprinted in his *Essays in Jurisprudence and Philosophy* (Oxford: Clarendon Press, 1983), and *The Concept of Law,* 2d ed. [first edition 1961] (Oxford: Clarendon Press, 1994).
4. See Hart, *Concept of Law,* chap. 7.
5. See Oliver Wendell Holmes, "The Path of the Law" [originally published 1897], reprinted in his *Collected Legal Papers* (New York: Peter Smith, 1952), and John Chipman Gray, *The Nature and Sources of Law* [originally published 1909] (Gloucester, Mass.: Peter Smith, 1972). Also see Jerome Frank, *Law and the Modern Mind* [originally published 1930] (Gloucester, MA: Peter Smith, 1970), and Karl Llewellyn, *The Bramble Bush* [originally published 1930] (New York: Ocean Publications, 1960).
6. For a fuller and more sympathetic assessment of the contributions of legal realism, see Brian Leiter, "Legal Realism" in *A Companion to Philosophy of Law and Legal Theory,* ed. D. Patterson (Oxford: Blackwell, 1996), and "Rethinking Legal Realism: Toward a Naturalized Jurisprudence," *Texas Law Review* 76 (1997): 267–315.
7. Holmes, "The Path of the Law," pp. 180–184; Gray, *Nature and Sources of Law,* pp. 144–146; Frank, *Law and the Modern Mind,* chap. 13; Llewellyn, *Bramble Bush,* pp. 70–77.
8. Holmes, "The Path of the Law," p. 178.
9. Ibid., p. 179.
10. Gray, *The Nature and Sources of Law,* pp. 124–125.
11. See Holmes, "The Path of the Law," pp. 186–187, and Felix Cohen, "Transcendental Nonsense and the Functional Approach," *Columbia Law Review* 35 (1935), pp. 809–849.

12. Cf. Frank, *Law and the Modern Mind,* p. ix.

13. Percy Bridgman, *Reflections of a Physicist* (New York: Philosophical Library, 1930), p. vii.

14. (a) Holmes also defends his predictive theory as a consequence of adopting the bad man's point of view. It is true that the bad man's reasons for being interested in legal rules is derivative in a way that his interest in the decisions of courts is not; he is interested in legal rules just insofar as this affects how the court will decide his case. (Actually, he is only interested in how the court will decide his case insofar as the court's decision is a reliable but fallible indicator of how he will in fact be treated.) However, it doesn't follow that the law includes only the decisions of courts and not the legal rules unless we assume that the law is only what the bad man cares about nonderivatively. The bad man's point of view is just one potentially illuminating perspective among others (including the good man's point of view); there is no reason to privilege it as Holmes does.

(b) Holmes and Gray also defend Legal Realism as a consequence of avoiding a confusion between law and morality. See Holmes, "The Path of the Law," pp. 70–73, and Gray, *The Nature and Sources of Law,* pp. 84, 94, 308–309. The suggestion seems to be that judicial fallibility, which the realist denies, requires recognizing judicially unenforced rights and that these would have to be moral, rather than legal, rights. They offer us Realism as the antidote to Natural Law.

1. The alternative to Legal Realism is to recognize unenforced rights.
2. Unenforced rights imply Natural Law.
3. Hence, either Legal Realism or Natural Law is true.
4. Natural Law theory is false.
5. Hence, Legal Realism is true.

But the choice between Legal Realism and Natural Law is not exhaustive; we can accept Legal Positivism without endorsing Legal Realism. The culprit is premise (2). Judicial fallibility does presuppose the possibility of unenforced rights. But the fallibility in question is legal fallibility; the unenforced rights would be legal, not necessarily moral, rights. The mistake consists in a judicial failure to recognize and/or enforce entitlements recognized by legal rules, such as constitutional provisions, statutes, and precedents. An account can be given of the legal status of these rules, as both Austin and Hart do, that does not violate the separation of law and morals.

15. Gray, *Nature and Sources of Law,* pp. 124–125; also see, pp. 84, 102, 170.

16. *Concept of Law,* pp. 138–144.

17. It is, I think, recognition that precedent presupposes the model of rules that leads Frank to criticize Gray for identifying law with the *rules* laid down by courts. See Frank, *Law and the Modern Mind,* pp. 132–133, 137–138, 285.

18. See Frank, *Law and the Modern Mind,* p. xi; Karl Llewellyn, "Some Realism, about Realism" *Harvard Law Review* 44 (1931): 1239; Max Radin, "In Defense of an Unsystematic Science of Law," *Yale Law Journal* 51 (1942): 1271. Cf. Leiter, "Rethinking Legal Realism," p. 273.

19. *Concept of Law,* pp. 119–120.

20. Ibid., pp. 124, 252.

21. Ibid., pp. 128, 272–273.

22. Ibid., pp. 124, 200, 273.

23. Ibid. p. 132.

24. I am not persuaded that either the democratic worry or the fairness worry about judicial discretion is fatal. In response to the democratic worry, we might distinguish between a generalized discretion that encourages judges to make law wherever there is none and a more restricted discretion that encourages them to legislate but only interstitially, at the margins of existing legal rules. Whereas a generalized discretion would clearly offend the separation of governmental powers or functions, a restricted judicial discretion, of the sort Hart contemplates, would do so much less. In response to the fairness worry, it can be argued that retrospective legislation is unfair only where people's expectations about what they are permitted to do were reasonable. But in hard cases, where, ex hypothesi, the law is unclear, it is not clear that parties could have reasonable expectations that retrospective legislation might upset. Cf. Hart, *The Concept of Law,* pp. 273, 275–276.

25. Ronald Dworkin, "The Model of Rules" reprinted in Ronald Dworkin, *Taking Rights Seriously* (London: Duckworth, 1978).

26. 115 N.Y. 506, 22 N.E. 188 (1889).

27. 32 N.J. 358, 161 A.2d 69 (1960).

28. 115 N.Y. at 511, 22 N.E. at 190.

29. I address this question in "Legal Theory, Legal Interpretation, and Judicial Review," pp. 108–111; also see Hart, *The Concept of Law* (Postscript), pp. 259–263.

30. In "The Model of Rules" Dworkin also argues that Hart conflates a strong kind of judicial discretion that exists only when the law is indeterminate and a weak kind that exists whenever there is or can be reasonable disagreement about what the law requires (*Taking Rights Seriously,* pp. 32–33). But Hart does not simply conflate or equivocate between these two kinds of discretion; his semantic assumptions allow him to infer the stronger form of discretion (indeterminacy) from this other form (reasonable disagreement). Without addressing and rejecting Hart's semantic assumptions, Dworkin is not in a position to concede the weak form of discretion but deny the need for the strong form. See my "Legal Theory, Legal Interpretation, and Judicial Review," p. 112.

31. John Locke, *An Essay Concerning Human Understanding* [originally published 1689], ed. P. Nidditch (Oxford: Clarendon Press, 1975), book III, esp. chap. iii, sects. 12–19; Gottlob Frege, "Sense and Reference" [originally published 1892] in *Translations from the Philosophical Writings of Gottlob Frege,* tr. M. Black and P. Geach (Oxford: Blackwell, 1980), pp. 57–58; Clarence Irving Lewis, *An Analysis of Knowledge and Valuation* (La Salle: Open Court, 1946), pp. 65, 133, 150–151, 168; Rudolph Carnap, *Meaning and Necessity,* 2d ed. (Chicago: University of Chicago Press, 1956), pp. 1, 16, 19, 233–234, 242–243, 246.

32. These arguments are framed in terms of the traditional version of the descriptional theory and do not directly address versions of the descriptional theory, like Searle's, that make the meaning of a term consist, not in a single (though perhaps complex) description, but rather in a cluster or family of descriptions, some but not all of which need be satisfied in order for the term to refer. See John Searle, "Proper Names," *Mind* 67 (1958): pp. 166–173. However, like Kripke, I think that these arguments apply, with only small modifications, to the cluster theory of descriptions. See Saul Kripke, *Naming and Necessity* (Cambridge, Mass.: Harvard University Press, 1980), pp. 74–77.

33. 347 U.S. 483 (1954).

34. 163 U.S. 537 (1896).

35. See Keith Donnellan, "Reference and Definite Descriptions," reprinted in *Naming, Necessity, and Natural Kinds,* ed. S. Schwartz (Ithaca: Cornell University Press, 1977);

Kripke, *Naming and Necessity;* and Hilary Putnam, "The Meaning of 'Meaning,'" reprinted in his *Mind, Language, and Reality: Philosophical Papers,* Vol. 2 (New York: Cambridge University Press, 1975).

36. Michael Moore has made related claims about the role of semantic assumptions in discussions of legal determinacy and interpretation. See, for example, Michael Moore, "The Semantics of Judging," *Southern California Law Review* 54 (1981): 151–294, and "A Natural Law Theory of Interpretation," *Southern California Law Review* 58 (1985), pp. 277–398.

37. See Antonin Scalia, *A Matter of Interpretation: Federal Courts and the Law* (Princeton: Princeton University Press, 1997).

38. Obscene and libelous speech have been excluded from First Amendment protection; see, e.g., *Chaplinsky v. New Hampshire,* 315 U.S. 568 (1942) (upholding a state prohibition on the use of offensive language in face-to-face exchanges in public spaces). Subversive advocacy can be restricted if it poses a "clear and present danger"; see, e.g., *Schenck v. United States,* 249 U.S. 47 (1919) (upholding the conviction under the Espionage Act of 1917 of a pamphleteer urging conscripts to resist the draft), and *Brandenburg v. Ohio,* 395 U.S. 444 (1969) (striking down the conviction of a Klu Klux Klan member under the Ohio Criminal Syndicalism statute for advocating the use of terrorism).

39. Sometimes conventional beliefs, rather than our best scientific theorizing, about the extension of a legal predicate ought to determine its interpretation. For instance, we might think that the best interpretation of an environmental protection statute that prohibits all *fishing* within fifty miles of shore would apply the prohibition to the harvesting of whales and dolphins, as well as fish. (Cf. Stephen Munzer, "Realistic Limits on Realist Interpretation," *Southern California Law Review* 58 (1985), esp. pp. 469–470.) Presumably, this is the correct interpretation of the statute precisely because the evident legislative intent was the protection of all marine life or marine animals, not just fish. But we can recognize these interpretive claims; even if we have the right semantic assumptions in place, we should still reject a pure textualism. Recognizing the role of underlying intentions or purposes in interpretation allows us to get the right interpretive results here. See my "Semantics and Legal Interpretation (Further Thoughts)," pp. 186–188.

40. Scalia, *A Matter of Interpretation,* p. 23.

41. 508 U.S. 223 (1993).

42. Scalia, *A Matter of Interpretation,* pp. 23–24.

43. See Ronald Dworkin, "Constitutional Cases" reprinted in *Taking Rights Seriously.*

44. Cf. David Lyons, "Basic Rights and Constitutional Interpretation," reprinted in David Lyons, *Moral Aspects of Legal Theory* (New York: Cambridge University Press, 1993), p. 193.

45. Cf. Donald Davidson, "Actions, Reasons, and Causes," reprinted in his *Essays on Actions and Events* (New York: Oxford University Press, 1980).

46. Dworkin's preferred conception of constructive interpretation (law as integrity) assesses principled interpretations along dimensions of fit and acceptability. See Dworkin, *Law's Empire,* esp. pp. 230–232, 255–257. Despite the important affinities between my account of principled interpretation and Dworkin's account of constructive interpretation, I have some qualms about his analogy between constructive interpretation and contribution to a chain novel. For it's arguable that the contributor to a chain novel enjoys both more and less freedom than a conscientious legal interpreter. The chain novelist arguably has less freedom insofar as basic narrative consistency appears to be an important

constraint on the chain novelist but principled interpretation must allow for the possibility of legal mistakes. In this way, the legal interpreter has a kind of freedom that the chain novelist normally does not. However, it's also arguable that the chain novelist has more freedom than the legal interpreter. The chain novelist is free to introduce any new information, plot, or themes that would improve the novel provided they are consistent (in a suitably broad sense) with the prior course of the novel. By contrast, principled interpreters are not free to introduce any attractive principles that are not inconsistent (in this admittedly broad sense) with previous rulings and principles. Rather, I think they see or should see themselves as bound to provide the most attractive articulation of principles that are already present in prior law. If so, there is an important sense in which legal interpreters have less freedom than a chain novelist.

47. Cf. John Hart Ely, *Democracy and Distrust* (Cambridge, Mass.: Harvard University Press, 1980), chap. 1. My use of the labels "interpretive" and "noninterpretive" review departs from the use among recent constitutional scholars in at least one important way. These labels are standardly associated with particular assumptions about the nature and limits of constitutional interpretation – assumptions that I will be rejecting below. The labels do no harm and are, for limited purposes, useful if we do not prejudge the issue of what counts as interpretation and what does not.

48. 198 U.S. 45 (1905) (invalidating a New York statute regulating the maximum number of hours that bakery employees could work, as a violation of the liberty of contract protected by the due process clause of the Fourteenth Amendment).

49. See, e.g., *Twining v. New Jersey* 211 U.S. 78 (1908) (invalidating a state court prosecution on the ground that the Fifth Amendment right against self-incrimination is incorporated in the due process clause of the Fourteenth Amendment); *Palko v. Connecticut* 302 U.S. 319 (1937) (invalidating a state law permitting the state to appeal in criminal cases as inconsistent with the Fifth Amendment's guarantee against double jeopardy as incorporated into the due process clause of the Fourteenth Amendment); and *Adamson v. California* 332 U.S. 46 (1947) (also invalidating a state court prosecution on the ground that the Fifth Amendment right against self-incrimination is incorporated in the due process clause of the Fourteenth Amendment).

50. See, e.g., *Griswold v. Connecticut* 381 (1965) (invalidating a Connecticut statute regulating the distribution of birth control devices as inconsistent with a constitutional right of privacy); *Roe v. Wade* 410 U.S. 113 (1973) (invalidating a Texas statute prohibiting abortions during, as well as after, the first trimester, as a violation of a woman's right to privacy).

51. See, e.g., *Mapp v. Ohio* 367 U.S. 643 (1961) (declaring evidence inadmissible in criminal prosecutions if it is improperly obtained); *Miranda v. Arizona* 384 U.S. 486 (1966) (excluding coerced confessions and requiring criminal suspects to be warned of their rights and the legal significance of their disclosures).

52. See, e.g., *Baker v. Carr* 369 U.S. 186 (1962) (holding that the claim that the apportionment of the Tennessee Assembly violates the equal protection clause of the Fourteenth Amendment by diluting votes represents a justiciable cause of action); *Reynolds v. Sims* 377 U.S. 533 (1964) (holding that the system of apportionment in the Alabama legislature was inconsistent with the "one person, one vote" standard required by the equal protection clause of the Fourteenth Amendment).

53. See, e.g., *Brown and Swann v. Charlotte-Mecklenburg Board of Education* 402 U.S. 1 (1971) (upholding a court-approved school desegregation plan that involved the gerry-

mandering of school districts and student busing under the equal protection clause of the Fourteenth Amendment).

54. Critics include: Robert Bork, "Neutral Principles and Some First Amendment Problems," *Indiana Law Journal* 47 (1971): 1–35, and *The Tempting of America* (New York: Simon and Schuster, 1990), esp. chaps. 1–8; Raoul Berger, *Government by the Judiciary* (Cambridge, Mass.: Harvard University Press, 1977); Henry Monaghan, "Our Perfect Constitution," *New York University Law Review* 56 (1981): 353–396; Edwin Meese, "Construing the Constitution," *University of California Davis Law Review* 19 (1985): 22–30; William Rhenquist, "The Notion of a Living Constitution," *Texas Law Review* 54 (1976): 693–706; and Scalia, *A Matter of Interpretation.* Friends include: Thomas Grey, "Do We Have an Unwritten Constitution?" *Stanford Law Review* 28 (1975): 703–718; Paul Brest, "The Misconceived Quest for the Original Understanding," *Boston University Law Review* 60 (1980): 204–238; and Michael Perry, *The Constitution, the Courts, and Human Rights* (New Haven: Yale University Press, 1982). Ely's position in *Democracy and Distrust* mixes friendship with criticism.

55. Alexander Hamilton, John Jay, and James Madison, *The Federalist Papers* (New York: Random House, 1937), #78, paragraph 12.

56. 1 Cranch 137 (1803) (declaring §13 of the Judiciary Act of 1879, authorizing the Court to issue writs of mandamus, unconstitutional on the ground that this would expand the Court's original jurisdiction and Congress can only expand its appellate jurisdiction).

57. Skeptics about judicial review sometimes point out that the Constitution also charges the other branches of government with constitutional fidelity [Article II, §8 (the executive); Article VI, §3 (Congress)]. Cf. *Eakin v. Raub* 12 Serg. & Rawle 330 (Pa. 1825). But an obligation of fidelity to the Constitution is not the same as the institutional responsibility to interpret and apply the Constitution, which is given to the judiciary alone. By analogy, suppose that a state penal code instructed legislators and the governor to "protect" and "support" the criminal code. Surely this fact would not show that either the executive or the legislative branch had a reasonable claim to interpret and apply the state penal code or try criminal cases; nor would it undermine the judiciary's responsibility for this interpretive task.

58. See *Federalist* #78, para. 7. Sometimes, the separation of powers doctrine also stands for two theses concerning the *balance of power:* the balance of power (a) between the ruler and the ruled (#51, paras. 4, 9–10) and (b) among the rulers (#51, paras. 1, 6, 9). Insofar as the separation of governmental functions and balance of powers doctrines are related, the relationship seems to be this: the balance of power between ruler and ruled is to be secured by a balance of power among the rulers, which is to be secured by the separation of governmental functions. However, the separation of functions has importance beyond its role in the balance of powers. For the balance of powers, as such, does not require the separation of functions that we have and for which there is a democratic rationale. It requires that powers be distributed so as to prevent concentrations of political power, but this does not require elected officials to makes laws and politically independent officials to interpret the law. That division of labor may be one way to balance powers, but there is no reason to think it the only way. If we think that there is something especially compelling about our particular separation of functions, it is presumably because we find its democratic rationale compelling.

59. Cf. *Federalist* #78, para. 7.

60. Indeed, once we understand the way in which interpretive judicial review is grounded in the division of labor within a constitutional democracy, we can see why judicial review should be administered by politically unaccountable officials. For the corollary of political unaccountability is political independence. If the function of (interpretive) judicial review is to ensure that politically accountable officials have heeded constitutional constraints on democratic action, then it is important that those whose task this is not themselves be politically accountable. This is the basis of Hamilton's call for a politically independent judiciary (*Federalist* #78, paras. 8, 18–21).

61. *Democracy and Distrust,* pp. 4–5.

62. Perry, *Constitution, the Courts, and Human Rights,* p. 92. This quotation undoubtedly gives a misleading picture of contemporary consensus in the constitutional literature. But it gives a fair sense of Perry's own view and the views of many constitutional scholars a decade or so ago.

63. Compare Ronald Dworkin, "The Forum of Principle," reprinted in Ronald Dworkin, *A Matter of Principle* (Cambridge, Mass.: Harvard University Press, 1985), p. 35, and David Lyons, "Constitutional Interpretation and Original Meaning," reprinted in *Moral Aspects of Legal Theory,* p. 141. Contrast Bork, *The Tempting of America,* p. 8.

64. Because, on this view, speakers should be authoritative about the common meaning of their terms, the meaning of constitutional language ought not to be a matter for dispute. The extension of constitutional terms can be a matter of dispute, on this view, but only insofar as speakers disagree about what in the world satisfies the descriptions that they associate with these terms.

65. But see Berger, *Government by the Judiciary,* chap. 7.

66. Ibid., pp. 118–119.

67. Bork's defense of *Brown* fairly clearly appeals to abstract intent and his own conception of equal treatment and eschews appeal to specific intent. See Bork, "Neutral Principles and Some First Amendment Problems," pp. 14–15, and *The Tempting of America,* pp. 74–83. But it is hard to see how to square these interpretive assumptions with the interpretive appeal to specific intent that he needs to prop up his criticism of the Court and that he clearly employs in other contexts (e.g., *Tempting of America,* pp. 104–106). This makes it hard to avoid the conclusion that Bork understands the interpretive appeal to the intentions of the framers in different contexts in whatever way is likely to deliver the political results of which he approves. Berger's discussion of *Brown* at least has the virtue of consistency.

68. 478 U.S. 186 (1986) (upholding a Georgia antisodomy statute as applied to private and consensual homosexual sexual relations on the ground that the scope of a right to privacy does not extend to homosexual practices, even in the privacy of one's home).

69. It's worth noting that in *Bowers* the Court concludes that the right to privacy does not extend to consensual homosexual activities in the privacy of one's own home on the ground that previous privacy cases protect personal liberty only in contexts involving "family, marriage, and reproduction." But, of course, this reasoning begs the question, because the issue is precisely whether past privacy decisions exhaust the scope of a right to privacy, and the resolution of this issue requires that we identify a prior rationale for a right to privacy. *Griswold* justifies privacy as part of the rationale for a diverse cluster of personal liberties, including freedom of speech and association, a homeowner's right not to have his house invaded during peacetime without his consent, the right against unrea-

sonable search and seizure, the guarantee of due process, and various nonenumerated rights retained by people. In order for privacy to rationalize these otherwise diverse liberties, it must be fairly broad in scope and could not reasonably be limited to self-determination in matters having to do only with family, marriage, and procreation, inasmuch as a right to privacy with this narrow scope would be largely irrelevant to the justification of freedom of political or artistic speech, freedom from unreasonable search and seizure, or freedom from self-incrimination. A more plausible claim about the scope of a right to privacy, that would both show it to provide the rationale for these otherwise diverse amendments and show its philosophical appeal, is that it is roughly the freedom to make choices and pursue plans and associations central to one's conception of oneself provided that these freedoms are not exercised in ways that threaten harm to comparably important interests of others. Michael Hardwick's choice and pursuit of consensual homosexual relationships in the privacy of his own home arguably falls within the scope of *this* right to privacy.

70. Roberto Mangabeira Unger, *The Critical Legal Studies Movement* (Cambridge, Mass.: Harvard University Press, 1986), p. 8.

71. Cf. David Kairys, "Legal Reasoning," in *The Politics of Law,* ed. D. Kairys (New York: Pantheon, 1982).

72. Cf. Mark Tushnet, "Defending the Indeterminacy Thesis" in *Analyzing Law: New Essays in Legal Theory,* ed. B. Bix (Oxford: Clarendon Press, 1998).

73. Unger, *The Critical Legal Studies Movement,* chap. 3.

74. Ibid., p. 78.

75. For a discussion of the difference between conflicting and inconsistent principles, see my "Moral Conflict and Its Structure" *The Philosophical Review* 103 (1994): 215–247; cf. Dworkin, *Law's Empire,* p. 268.

76. Indeed, *Henningsen* arguably provides a better case for thinking that contract law recognizes independent principles of fairness and freedom of contract. *Henningsen* recognizes a duty to police voluntary agreements in order, among other things, to prevent certain kinds of negative externalities (e.g., automobile defects that pose dangers to other motorists and pedestrians). Negative externalities involve a fairness concern that might seem more independent of freedom of contract than either duress or reliance. However, it is arguable that both freedom of contract and concerns about negative externalities can be derived from a common concern with autonomy. And even if there is no such common source for freedom of contract and the concern with negative externalities, it would be reasonable to understand these as potentially conflicting, rather than inconsistent, principles.

77. Another illustration of CLS jurisprudential confusions about indeterminacy can be found in certain interpretations of valuable CLS historical studies. In the course of defending his claim that judges came to adopt a newly "instrumental" attitude toward the common law in the nineteenth century in his important study *The Transformation of American Law: 1780–1860* (Cambridge, Mass.: Harvard University Press, 1977), Morton Horwitz identifies various swings in the common law interpretation of the stringency of private property rights, in particular, in the adjudication of conflicts between the principles of individual control and social need or benefit. But any conclusion from these "swings" that the common law of property and contract was "riddled with contradictions" would be confused; as Horwitz's own analysis makes clear, these swings seem to reflect an

underlying principle of economic development guided by changing economic circumstances and beliefs (pp. xv–xvi).

78. Cf. Rolf Sartorius, "Bayes' Theorem, Judicial Discretion, and Hard Cases," *Georgia Law Review* 11 (1977): 1269–1275.

79. Cass Sunstein, *Legal Reasoning and Political Conflict* (New York: Oxford University Press, 1996).

80. 305 U.S. 337 (1938).

81. In particular, I think (but cannot argue here) that similar worries arise about Sunstein's preferred pragmatic disposition of privacy cases, including *Bowers*. See Sunstein, *Legal Reasoning and Political Conflict*, p. 156.

82. For fuller discussion, see my "Legal Positivism and Natural Law Reconsidered."

83. Cf. Jules Coleman and Brian Leiter, "Legal Positivism" in *A Companion to Philosophy of Law and Legal Theory*, ed. Patterson and David Lyons; "Moral Aspects of Legal Theory" reprinted in *Moral Aspects of Legal Theory*.

84. *Concept of Law*, chap. 6. It seems even Dworkin must employ something like a rule of recognition in order to explain how the legal interpreter settles on one set of interpreteds, rather than another, at the preinterpretive stage of constructive interpretation (cf. *Law's Empire*, pp. 65–66). Cf. *Concept of Law*, p. 266.

85. Here, I understand "pedigree" broadly, so as to refer to whatever features distinguish legal norms from other sorts of social norms, such as norms of etiquette. On this interpretation, a pedigree test follows from belief that there is a rule of recognition that states the existence conditions for valid law. In particular, this interpretation of pedigree does not itself preclude the possibility of a legal system that treats morality as a source of law. Without further restrictions on possible kinds of pedigree, the mere association of positivism with a test of pedigree does not require siding with so-called hard positivists, against so-called soft positivists. For some discussion of these different conceptions of positivism, see Jules Coleman, "Negative and Positive Positivism" in *Ronald Dworkin and Contemporary Jurisprudence,* ed. M. Cohen (Totowa, NJ: Rowman & Allanheld, 1983); Coleman and Leiter, "Legal Positivism"; Hart, *The Concept of Law* (Postscript), pp. 250–254; David Lyons, "Principles, Positivism, and Legal Theory" reprinted in *Ronald Dworkin and Contemporary Jurisprudence* and "Moral Aspects of Legal Theory"; and Joseph Raz, *The Authority of Law* (Oxford: Clarendon Press, 1979), chap. 3. In fact, so-called soft positivism seems to me to be the most defensible version of legal positivism, and my discussion of the reconciliation of Legal Positivism and Natural Law applies to soft, as well as hard, conceptions of positivism.

86. Austin, *The Province of Jurisprudence Determined,* lecture v, p. 184.

87. This is to side with so-called soft positivism; see note 84 *supra*.

2

Objectivity, Morality, and Adjudication

BRIAN LEITER

Two familiar features of Ronald Dworkin's theory of adjudication generate a strange predicament. On the one hand, Dworkin maintains that most cases, including most "hard" cases, have "right answers." On the other hand, Dworkin argues that to discover that right answer, judges must avail themselves of moral considerations and moral argument: a party's rights follow from the principle that explains some significant portion of the prior institutional history *and* provides the best justification for that institutional history as a matter of political morality. But if moral considerations figure decisively in determining the answer to a legal dispute, then there can only be a single right answer as a matter of law if there is a single right answer to the question of political morality. Yet if morality is, as many seem to think, "subjective" in some sense, then there may be as many right answers as a matter of morality as there are judges and thus, consequently, no single right answer as a matter of law. Here is how John Mackie put the worry many years ago:

> [W]hat the law is, on Professor Dworkin's view, may crucially depend on what is morally best – what is best, not what is conventionally regarded as best in that society. Now I would argue . . . that moral judgments of this kind have an irreducibly subjective element. If so, then Professor Dworkin's theory automatically injects a corresponding subjectivity into statements about what the law is.[1]

If, in other words, one thinks that adjudication is "objective," in the sense that there are objectively right answers to legal disputes, then it might seem a bad

I am grateful to the students in my Spring 1996 seminar on "Objectivity" at the University of Texas at Austin for help in thinking about these issues and to my colleagues in philosophy – Daniel Bonevac, Cory Juhl, and Robert C. Koons – for useful comments on an earlier draft. I also benefited from discussion of a later draft by the participants in the 2nd Annual Conference on Analytic Legal Philosophy at Columbia Law School in April 1997; I can recall helpful comments or questions on that occasion from Ruth Chang, William Edmundson, Ken Kress, David Lyons, Andrei Marmor, Thomas Nagel, Joseph Raz, Scott Shapiro, and Jeremy Waldron. Finally, thanks to David Sosa and to the students in Jules Coleman's Spring 1999 "Philosophy of Law" seminar at Yale Law School for detailed comments on the penultimate draft.

idea to make right answers in law depend on moral considerations as Dworkin does.

Dworkin has not, of course, been insensitive to these concerns; over a period of years now, he has articulated an unusual response to this attack on the "objectivity" of morality.[2] According to Dworkin, the root of the problem lies in the understanding of "objectivity" that is implicit in this attack. Once we distinguish, as Dworkin would have us do, between sensible, but defeasible, "internal" attacks on the objectivity of morality from unintelligible, and irrelevant, "external" attacks on the objectivity of morality, we see that Mackie's criticism depends on the latter, and thus reflects a misunderstanding about what is at stake in worrying about the objectivity of morality, and thus in worrying about the objectivity of law. For the only type of objectivity that matters – namely, an "internal" objectivity – Dworkin's theory faces no predicament.[3]

Dworkin's extensive writings on "external" and "internal" skepticism about objectivity have attracted little attention from philosophers or jurisprudents over the years. Indeed, I am not aware of anyone, other than Dworkin, who has found his response on this score satisfactory.[4] In Part I of this paper, I want to review what Dworkin has said about objectivity and why it has seemed to many philosophers to be wrongheaded.

But the purpose of this paper is not simply critical. Although Dworkin may not provide a suitable articulation of the point, I think there is a genuine issue about our understanding of objectivity that is at stake here. This issue, so I will argue in Part II, is best understood as involving two competing paradigms of objectivity. On what I will call the "Naturalistic Conception," objectivity in any domain must be understood on the model of the natural sciences, whose objects of study are objective in the sense of being "mind-independent"[5] and causally efficacious (i.e., in making a causal difference to the course of experience). Such a conception of objectivity informs the work of philosophers who affirm the objectivity of morality (like Boyd and Railton) as well as those who deny it (like Nietzsche and Mackie). The "Non-Naturalistic Conception," by contrast, denies that the type of objectivity found in the natural sciences is the relevant type of objectivity to aspire to in all domains; some Non-Naturalists claim this because they think Naturalistic Objectivity is unintelligible (or, at least, unintelligible as applied to domains like morality). Non-Naturalists typically have positive proposals for how to understand objectivity in domains like ethics or aesthetics. I will concentrate in Part II on only one: John McDowell's notion that objectivity in ethics is a matter of moral views being "susceptible to reasons."[6] We shall see, I think, that the grain of truth in what Dworkin is getting at in his external/internal distinction is really best understood as the difference between a Naturalistic versus a Non-Naturalistic Conception of Objectivity. Dworkin would have us, then, embrace the latter as the only type of objectivity at stake in assessing his theory of adjudication.

In Part III of this paper, however, I will argue that the Non-Naturalistic

Conception (at least the McDowell/Dworkin version) is not an adequate account of objectivity: it fails to explain basic intuitions about objectivity (even in ethics), as well as leaving us with a picture of the "objectivity" of ethics that would, in fact, be quite congenial to the noncognitivism that both McDowell and Dworkin purport to have left behind. If that is right, then the predicament remains a live one for Dworkin's theory. It is my view that the predicament has no solution and that the law is, in fact, indeterminate.[7] These latter issues are, however, beyond the scope of this paper.

Let us turn first, then, to Dworkin's response to the predicament.

I. Dworkin on Objectivity

A. Introduction

According to Dworkin, when we claim that there is an objective fact about whether one interpretation is better than another, or whether one principle is morally better than another, we are not making a claim *external* to the practice of substantive moral or interpretive argument in which these claims arise. "Slavery is objectively wrong" is simply a *moral* claim internal to the practice of argument in which we offer reasons for the proposition that "Slavery is wrong." Two thousand years of metaphysics notwithstanding, there simply are no *metaphysical* questions about value; there are only *evaluative* questions. To the extent that Protagoras, Plato, Hume, Nietzsche, G. E. Moore, A. J. Ayer, Charles Stevenson, John Mackie, Gilbert Harman, Richard Boyd, Peter Railton, Michael Smith, and Allan Gibbard thought they were answering questions of *meta*ethics, they are wrong. There is only ethics, only argument about what is right, what is just, what is good, what is evil, and the like. Here's how Dworkin has put the point over the years:

I have no arguments for the objectivity of moral judgments except moral arguments, no arguments for the objectivity of interpretive judgments except interpretive arguments, and so forth. (MP2, 171)

I have yet been given no reason to think that any skeptical argument about morality can be other than a moral argument. (MP2, 174)

Any successful — really, any intelligible — argument that evaluative propositions are neither true nor false must be internal to the evaluative domain rather than archimedean about [i.e., external to] it. (OT, 89)

Thomas Nagel, though not quite agreeing with Dworkin, characterizes the view succinctly: "the only way to answer skepticism, relativism, and subjectivism about morality is to meet it with first-order moral arguments. [Dworkin] holds that the skeptical positions must themselves be understood as moral claims — that they are unintelligible as anything else."[8]

If we aren't doing metaphysics (or metaethics) when we're worrying about "objectivity," then what are we doing? According to Dworkin, talk about the "objective" wrongness of abortion, for example, is really just disguised *moral* talk, perhaps "a slightly more emphatic form" of abortion is wrong (MP2, 171). All purportedly external statements about the status of the judgment "abortion is wrong" are really "nothing but clarifying or emphatic or metaphorical re-statements or elaborations of [the internal moral claim] that abortion is wrong" (OT, 97): "We use the language of objectivity, not to give our ordinary moral or interpretive claims a bizarre metaphysical base, but to *repeat* them, perhaps in a more precise way, to emphasize or qualify their *content*" (LE, 81).

Now at first sight these remarks seem quite obviously wrong. To claim that abortion is *objectively* wrong is, on a natural reading, not simply to "repeat" or "emphasize" that abortion is wrong, but rather to assert a certain metaphysical thesis: to wit, that there exists a property of moral wrongness, which abortion has, and which it has quite independently of what we happen to think about the matter.[9] To talk about "objective" rightness and wrongness is to talk about metaphysical or ontological issues, about what properties the world contains quite apart from what we happen to know about them. Yet this is precisely what Dworkin, in the remarks quoted above, seems to deny. To see how Dworkin motivates this counterintuitive claim, then, we need to understand a bit more about the distinction Dworkin draws between "internal" and "external" forms of skepticism about morality.

B. The "Internal" and the "External"

Internal skepticism about morality (or any other domain of discourse) is skepti-cism motivated by first-order moral (aesthetic, interpretive) argument. "The internal skeptic addresses the substance of the claims he challenges" (LE, 78), and in so doing, presupposes the cogency of moral argumentation. The internal skeptic "denies some group of familiar positive claims and justifies that denial by endorsing a different positive moral claim – perhaps a more general or counterfactual or theoretical one" (OT, 89). An internal skeptic, for example, might deny that sexual acts are moral or immoral – he might deny, that is, that they have any *moral value* – by relying on a *moral* view according to which "suffering is the only thing that is inherently bad" (OT, 91). In this sense, he would be *skeptical* about the *moral value* of sexual behavior while at the same time "presuppos[ing] the truth of some positive value judgment" (OT, 89).

It is possible, on Dworkin's view, to be (internally) skeptical not simply about the moral value of some particular behavior, but about moral value as such. Such *global* internal skepticism would itself be motivated by a *moral* view: for example, the view that God is the only plausible basis for morality,[10] conjoined with skepticism about the existence of God (OT, 91). It is crucial, says Dworkin, to recognize that the former conjunct here is itself a view "within" morality, as it were, so that even this global skepticism is generated *internal* to morality.

External skepticism, by contrast, "is a metaphysical theory, not a . . . moral position" (LE, 79); it is "a second-level theory about the philosophical standing or classification of [first-order] claims" (LE, 79–80). External skepticism is both: (1) "austere" in that "it purports to rely [only] on non-moral arguments to defeat" the ordinary or "face-value" view that moral convictions can be objectively true and false (OT, 92); and (2) "neutral" in that "it takes no sides on substantive moral controversies" (OT, 92). John Mackie is the paradigmatic external skeptic for Dworkin.[11] He purports to stand outside the practice of moral argument, appealing instead to "some transcendental metaphysical world" (LE, 78), a world that does not (claims Mackie) contain moral facts of any kind.

Before going further, we should quickly dispense with two rather facile arguments that Dworkin sometimes invokes against external skepticism in his writings. The first involves the misleading suggestion that the external skeptic is necessarily committed to the existence of a world-in-itself, a "transcendental metaphysical world." In Dworkin's recent work, in particular, the external skeptic is now accused of commitment to "archimedean skepticism" (OT, 92), of "purport[ing] to stand outside a whole body of belief, and to judge it as a whole from premises or attitudes that owe nothing to it" (OT, 88). The force of the charge becomes vivid in his claim: "We cannot climb outside of morality to judge it from some external archimedean tribunal, any more than we can climb out of reason itself to test it from above" (OT, 127).

This last claim, however, contains a revealing nonsequitur: for the reasons for thinking it incoherent to "climb out of reason itself to test it from above" – reasons familiar from Hegel and Quine, among others – have no bearing on whether we can "climb outside of morality" and assess it from some other standpoint. We can't step outside "reason" – outside our best current picture of the world – and assess it all at once, because we thereby deprive ourselves of *any* criteria by which to proceed. But we can surely assess various components of that picture – moral, religious, biological, aesthetic – from the standpoint of those other components with which we rest content at the present.

In disclaiming the ability to "climb out of reason itself to test it from above," Dworkin seems to have in mind the famous image of "Neurath's boat." But Neurath's boat is no help to Dworkin in this context. Neurath analogizes our epistemological situation to that of sailors who are trying to rebuild their ship while at sea. Since they cannot rebuild the whole ship at once – they cannot, as it were, "climb out of the ship itself" and rebuild it from scratch – they must choose to stand firm on certain planks in the ship while reconstructing others. They will, of course, choose to stand firm on those planks that work the best – a pragmatic criterion – while rebuilding those that are less dependable or useful or necessary. At a later date, the sailors may choose to rebuild the planks they had stood on previously, and in so doing they will again choose to stand firm on some other planks that serve their practical needs at that time.

Our basic epistemic situation – as Quine, in particular, has argued for many years[12] – is the same: like the sailors at sea, we can't "climb outside" our best picture of the world and rebuild it from scratch. We necessarily stand firm on certain "planks" within this picture of the world – various empirical claims, theoretical hypotheses, and epistemic norms – while evaluating other claims. Pragmatic desiderata (at least for Quine) determine which planks we choose to rest critical reflection upon, though nothing precludes the possibility that, at some later date, the claims and criteria we rely on today may themselves be subject to revision. In the Quinean picture (to which I am basically sympathetic[13]) we are committed to saying that "there is no Archimedean point of cosmic exile from which to leverage our theory of the world."[14] But a theory of *morality* is plainly just one subset of a total theory of the world, and there is nothing in the rejection of an "Archimedean point of cosmic exile" that precludes one from assessing the subtheory from *outside that particular subtheory:* "Exile" from a "subtheory" is *not* equivalent to *cosmic* exile. As Quine remarks (in a related context):

Have we . . . so far lowered our sights as to settle for a relativistic doctrine of truth – rating the statements of each theory as true for that theory, and brooking no higher criticism? Not so. The saving consideration is that we continue to take seriously our own particular aggregate science, our own particular world-theory or loose total fabric of quasi-theories, whatever it may be. Unlike Descartes, we own and use our beliefs of the moment, even in the midst of philosophizing, until by what is vaguely called scientific method we change them here and there for the better. Within our total evolving doctrine, we can judge truth as earnestly and absolutely as can be; subject to correction, but that goes without saying.[15]

But which "planks" in our boat should we choose to rest critical reflection and truth upon?

"In my naturalistic stance," says Quine, "I see the question of truth as one to be settled within science, there being no higher tribunal."[16] But science – and the norms of a scientific epistemology, that is, the implicit norms on which scientific practice relies – are the highest tribunal *not* for any a priori reasons, but because (to speak crudely, but not inaccurately) science has, as an a posteriori matter, "delivered the goods": it sends the planes into the sky, eradicates certain cancerous growths, makes possible the storage of millions of pages of data on a tiny chip, and the like. Science, for Quine, is simply on a continuum with common sense,[17] since both aim to predict and control the future course of experience – with the difference that science, unlike, say, folk psychology or economics, manages and forecasts experience with greater precision and reliability. "[W]e can never do better than occupy the standpoint of some theory or other, the best we can muster at the time."[18] For Quine, that theory is a scientific one, because that's the theory that works the best. Yet even Quine concedes that the basic norm of a scientific epistemology (namely, empiricism) "would go by the board" if, say, telepathy delivered on its claims.[19]

Let me now recap: the argument here is that while the external skeptic *might* be committed to a "transcendental metaphysical world," he need not be to worry still about the objectivity of value. He could well accept the metaphor of Neurath's boat and see the question about the objectivity of value as simply being the question: given the (ontological and epistemological) planks in our best picture of the world on which we currently stand firm, how are we to make sense of putative moral facts? This is a perfectly sensible question for an anti-Archimedean Quinean to ask, and it is the question whose intelligibility Dworkin must defeat if he is to defeat decisively the external skeptic.

There is a second distracting argument Dworkin sometimes makes. Often, he saddles the external skeptic with a commitment to "neutrality" and then accuses the skeptic of failing to be neutral. Unfortunately, this is one of those cases where Dworkin's failure to cite authors who actually hold the views that he implies some real person holds makes it easy for him to set up "straw men" as opponents.[20] Indeed, Dworkin's paradigm external skeptic – Mackie – is, by Dworkin's own admission, *not* "neutral" (OT, 113). While it *is* essential to external skepticism that its arguments against the objectivity of morality be *nonmoral* arguments (the "austerity," in Dworkin's terms, of external skepticism), it is not clear why it is essential to the position that "it take[ ] no sides on substantive moral controversies" (OT, 93). What marks the skeptic as *external* is that his attack on the objectivity of morality *is not itself a moral attack.* Whether or not this skeptical attack has *implications* for substantive moral controversies – a matter debated among moral realists and skeptics[21] – simply does not impugn the *externality* of the skepticism.

But even if the skeptic were committed to neutrality, would he have to run afoul of this constraint? Dworkin argues that he would. The external skeptic rejects the "face value" view of morality according to which moral rightness and wrongness is an "objective matter" and certain moral "opinions are true . . . and . . . people who disagree are making a bad mistake" (OT, 92). Yet the external skeptic fails to realize that this "face value" view is not some *external* thesis about the status of morality, but is itself "part of substantive morality" (OT, 93). Thus, a skeptic who rejects this view can no longer be *neutral* about morality.

The external skeptic can do no better, perhaps, than to concede this trivial point: if in fact claims about the objective status of moral judgments are internal to morality, then the external skeptic does, indeed, reject part of substantive morality. But this makes external skepticism *internal* to the domain of morality only, as it were, by stipulation: by stipulating, that is, that the claim to objectivity is in fact a *moral* claim – which is, presumably, what the Dworkinian external skeptic would want to resist stipulating in the first place. I do not disagree, of course, that ordinary people think that some moral judgments are "objectively true," but to name that a *moral* view and on that basis assail external skepticism for a breach of neutrality seems mere definitional trickery.

With these preliminary points out of the way, we can now ask what the real problem with external skepticism is supposed to be? The volume of Dworkin's rhetoric on this issue is high,[22] but the actual arguments are somewhat elusive. Dworkin's central claim, however, is quite clear: external skepticism is, at bottom, unintelligible, at least as applied to morality. "[T]he external level . . . does not exist" (P, 362) he says. The "issue of objectivity [as conceived by the external skeptic] . . . is a kind of fake" (MP2, 172). The proponent of external skepticism,

> supposes that we can distinguish between the [language-]game and the real world, that we can distinguish between the claim that slavery is unjust, offered as a move in some collective enterprise in which such judgments are made and debated, and the claim that slavery is really or objectively unjust in the actual world. . . . [But] this is exactly what we cannot do, because the words "objectively" and "really" cannot change the sense of moral . . . judgments. If moral . . . judgments have the sense and force they do because they figure in a collective human enterprise, then such judgments cannot have a "real" sense and a "real" truth value which transcend that enterprise and somehow take hold of the "real" world. (MP2, 174)

In short, the only "intelligible . . . [skeptical] argument that evaluative propositions are neither true nor false" must be an *internal* argument (OT, 89).

What are Dworkin's *arguments* for claiming that the "external" skeptic's position is essentially unintelligible? I can discern two main argumentative strategies in his work: (1) what *look* like external arguments are really *internal* arguments; and (2) the genuinely "external" arguments make either preposterous or question-begging demands on moral discourse. Let me consider the strongest representative of each argument, in order.

C. Internal Arguments All the Way Down

As noted before, a natural way of construing the debate about the objectivity of the judgment "abortion is morally wrong" is as an ontological debate "about the kinds of properties there are in the world" (OT, 103). The external skeptic says the world contains no moral properties; the "realist" affirms their existence.[23] We've already seen one facile argument that Dworkin would make against this way of understanding the debate: namely, that the external skeptic violates the "neutrality" requirement, since to deny that there are any real moral properties would be to deny that "some acts really are unjust, or some people really are good, or something of the sort" (OT, 100). But this, as already remarked, is only an interesting point against the external skeptic if (a) he is committed to neutrality, and (b) the "really" is part of substantive morality. So let us put this consideration aside.

The most common form the ontological debate has taken in recent years concerns whether "moral" properties are identical with, or supervenient upon,[24] natural properties. According to Dworkin, however, this way of framing the debate still does not take the skeptic outside substantive morality:

> Some philosophers argue that moral properties are identical with natural properties – that an act's relative rightness, for example, just is its relative power to maximize happiness. On that view, when we say that the fact that an act promotes happiness causes people to think it is right, which is often plausible, we might as well say that the fact that it is right causes people to think it is. But once again this latter claim offers the neutral archimedean no target, because he cannot reject it without rejecting the identity-of-properties claim, and that . . . is an abstract moral conviction. (OT, 104)

But is a claim about property-identity a *moral* claim? Moral realists who argue for it certainly don't do so in *moral* terms; rather it is presented as a certain sort of *semantic* or (a posteriori) *metaphysical* thesis. Peter Railton, a self-described "stark-raving moral realist,"[25] follows Richard Brandt in suggesting that we think of the identity claim – for example, the claim that morally right just means instrumentally rational from a social point of view – as a "reforming definition or an *a posteriori* statement of property identity" (NP, 157). But to give a reforming, naturalistic definition of moral rightness (or nonmoral goodness) we must, says Railton, draw on "our linguistic or moral intuitions" so as to "express recognizable notions of goodness and rightness."[26] The appeal here is to our intuitions about the use of language, not to moral argument.

Consider an analogue in the doctrine of "moon realism,"[27] that is, realism regarding talk about the moon. The moon realist holds that propositions like, "The moon has a circumference of 14,000 miles" are *objectively* true or false. But to have any idea what would count as the truth-condition for this statement, we have to have some notion what we are referring to when we talk about the "moon." We have to know, in other words, that when we make claims about the "moon" we're talking about that celestial body that stands in a certain spatial relation to the earth, and not, say, the Empire State Building: it is facts about this celestial body, and not facts about the Empire State Building, that determine the truth or falsity of statements about the "moon." To give a definition (reforming or otherwise) of some putatively cognitive predicate – whether it be "the moon" or "morally right" – is just to specify the domain of facts which constitute the locus for the truth-conditions for sentences in that domain. In specifying that domain, we can do no better than appeal to our intuitions about how the concept ("moon" or "morally right") is used. But appealing to linguistic intuitions about the use of "moon" is not an activity internal to arguments in astronomy, just as appealing to linguistic intuitions about the use of "morally right" is not an activity internal to the practice of moral argument. Thus, the external skeptic about these claims would not make a *moral* argument against the proposed definition, but a *semantic* one to the effect that the proposed identity does not, in fact, capture "recognizable notions" of moral rightness, that it omits, for example, the element of *endorsement* characteristic of moral language.[28]

Naturalistic moral realists like Railton recognize that while the reductionist tries to "capture most of the central intuitions in [the] area," he cannot do justice to all of them and thus "must do something to lessen the force of those which he cannot capture" (NP, 169). The reduction aims for "tolerable revisionism" (NP, 159) that "permits one to account for the correlations and truisms associated" with the moral predicate at issue (NP, 162). But, ultimately, the proposed claim of property-identity "must earn its place by facilitating the construction of worthwhile theories" (NP, 157), that is, theories that "locate value properties among features of the world that are accessible to us through ordinary experience and that play a role in empirical explanation" (NP, 154).[29] The claim of property-identity, then, is ultimately predicated on appeals to semantic intuitions and the desiderata of theory-construction; the external skeptic, conversely, can contest the reduction on either ground. Nowhere in this dispute does there seem to be any need for distinctively *moral* argumentation.

D. External Skepticism: Unintelligible or Question-Begging

Having ruled out the leading naturalistic attempt to make ontological sense of moral facts proves crucial for Dworkin's second main argumentative strategy against external skepticism. For Dworkin concedes that it *is* a legitimately *external* argument to deny the objectivity of morality on the grounds that it does not meet the constraints imposed by what we might call a "scientific epistemology" which says – in part, and quite roughly – that: (a) only that which makes a causal difference to experience can be known; and (b) only that which makes a causal difference to experience is real.[30] Dworkin's response is that such a demand, made about morality, is either preposterous (that is, unintelligible) or question-begging.

It is preposterous because it would commit us to what Dworkin calls "the absurd moral-field thesis" (OT, 117), the thesis that,

the universe houses, among its numerous particles of energy and matter, some special particles – morons – whose energy and momentum establish fields that at once constitute the morality or immorality, or virtue or vice, of particular human acts and institutions and also interact in some way with human nervous systems so as to make people aware of the morality or immorality or of the virtue or vice. (OT, 104)[31]

Now both the naturalistic realist and his skeptical opponent could agree that *this* thesis is, indeed, quite absurd, that it is "barely intelligible" (OT, 127). *But it is precisely for this reason that the realist wanted to identify moral properties with natural properties in the first place!* The motivation for the naturalistic reduction, in short, is to find a place for the "moral" within a scientific epistemology. Yet we've just seen that Dworkin rules out this move on the grounds that any argument for a property-identification is an essentially *moral* argument and so not sufficiently "austere" for the externalist's debate.[32] I have already contested this characterization of the debate about reduction, but since Dworkin thinks property reductions violate austerity, he is prepared to dismiss the externalist demand for conformity with a scientific epistemology on the grounds that it supposes the preposterous moral-field thesis.

But is Dworkin entitled to do this, even granting his internalist construal of the property-reduction debate? In fact, it seems he is not. If the demand that moral properties find a place within a scientific epistemology leads to the "absurd" moral-field thesis, the skeptic might well conclude that this just shows that there can be no moral facts: the "absurdity" of "morons" shows *not* that the external skeptic is misguided, but that he is right, that there is no intelligible sense in which the world could contain moral facts. What Dworkin really needs is an argument against the skeptical demand that moral facts be made to fit the requirements of a scientific epistemology. This, in a nutshell, is the *crucial* issue for Dworkin's whole position.

Now Dworkin, in fact, considers this question explicitly. He describes an "epistemological hierarchy" argument the skeptic might make according to which,

it makes no sense to suppose that acts or events or institutions have moral properties unless we have some plausible account of how human beings could be "in touch with" or aware of such properties, and if we reject the explanation offered by the moral-field thesis we must appeal to some other account of a moral faculty that would be equally occult. (OT, 117)

What Dworkin describes here is just the demand that moral facts satisfy the demands of a scientific epistemology – something they cannot do, he concedes, in a way that isn't "occult."

How does Dworkin resist, then, the epistemological argument? One argument he offers involves a familiar appeal to moral phenomenology, to the "evidence in my own experience . . . of a capacity to make moral judgments that bring conviction, that are mainly durable, that agree with the judgments of a great many others, and that are amenable to the normal logical combinations and operations" (OT, 118). Yet this is, quite transparently, a nonstarter: no one – neither realist nor skeptic – contests the *phenomenology* of moral experience and judgment. The question has always been how this experience is to be explained, whether it can be accepted at face value, or whether it must be explained in quite different terms in order to locate this experience within our best picture of how the world works. Phenomenology is simply a datum, not an argument.

This brings us to the crucial move in Dworkin's argument: the repudiation of the demand that moral experience be made to fit within a scientific epistemology. Dworkin objects that the external skeptic's

hierarchical epistemology . . . tries to establish standards for reliable belief *a priori,* ignoring the differences in content between different domains of belief, and taking no account of the range of beliefs we already hold to be reliable. (OT, 118–19)

If a scientific epistemology "does seem appropriate to beliefs about the physical world" (OT, 119), it makes no sense for moral beliefs "[s]ince morality and the other evaluative domains make no causal claims" (OT, 120). If we accept the demand that moral facts must figure in the "best explanation" of experience, it will follow that "no moral (or aesthetic or mathematical or philosophical) belief is reliable. But we can reverse that judgment: if any moral belief is reliable, the "best explanation" test is not universally sound. Either direction of argument . . . begs the question in the same way" (OT, 119). But the question is begged only if we grant Dworkin's false assumption that the demand for conformity to a scientific epistemology is really an arbitrary, a priori demand.[33] This assumption, however, reveals a complete misunderstanding of what drives the debate between external realist and skeptic about morals.

Recall Quine's posture, which assigns priority to the scientific epistemology. Quine takes science as "the highest tribunal" not for any a priori reasons, but because, as an a posteriori matter, science has "delivered the goods." Science has earned its claim to be a guide to the real and the unreal by depopulating our world of gods and witches and ethers and substituting a picture of the world and how it works of immense practical value. A scientific epistemology – predicated on such seemingly simple notions as "evidence matters" (theories must answer to experience, not simply authority) – is one of the most precious legacies of the Enlightenment, a legacy under attack from those corners of the academy where bad philosophy reigns supreme. Oddly, with his off-the-cuff slur of a scientific epistemology as *"a priori,"* Dworkin sounds more like the postmodernists he otherwise denounces with such moralistic gusto.[34]

The demand to find a place for moral facts within a scientific epistemology is neither arbitrary nor a priori, but simply the natural question to ask given the a posteriori success of science. It is not that moral claims are simply exempt from a scientific epistemology because they don't involve causal claims; it is, rather, that (crudely speaking) causal power has shown itself over the past few centuries to be the best-going indicia of the knowable and the real, and therefore it is natural to subject any putative fact to this test. Naturalistic moral realists like Boyd and Railton aren't "bad metaphysicians" (OT, 127); rather, they recognize (as Dworkin apparently does not) the epistemological pressure

generated by the success of empirical inquiry that honors a scientific epistemology. Given that we have a useful guide to the true and the real already in
hand – namely, science and its epistemic norms – why not see, these moral
realists essentially ask, whether or not "moral facts" can meet these demands
(rather than suffer the same fate as witches and the ether).

Now no one should be surprised that if we repudiate the demands of a
scientific epistemology we get a promiscuous ontology, replete with moral
facts, aesthetic facts, theological facts, and the like. But unless we are given a
good reason for repudiating this epistemology – other than the patently
question-begging reason of making room for our favorite (heretofore) suspect
facts – the real question about any putative facts is whether they can answer to
our best-going criteria of the knowable and the real.[35] This is what motivates
the debate between external realist and external skeptic. Rather than showing
their debate to be unintelligible, Dworkin has simply betrayed his misunderstanding of both *what* they are arguing about and *why* they are doing so. What
we have yet to find in Dworkin is any *argument* for insulating the domain of
morality from the demands of the scientific epistemology that has otherwise
served us well.

But perhaps there are the beginnings of such an argument in the writings
under consideration. Consider, for example, one of the ways Dworkin frames
his repudiation of the "best explanation" test of a scientific epistemology:

> Since morality and the other evaluative domains make no causal claims . . . such tests
> can play no role in any plausible test for them. We do need tests for reliability of our
> moral opinions, but these must be appropriate to the content of these opinions. That is
> why an epistemological challenge that comes to nothing more than insisting that moral
> properties are not physical properties must fail. (OT, 120)

We may get a better idea what Dworkin is, perhaps, getting at in remarks like
these by first taking a detour through a debate about the nature of objectivity
suggested by the work of John McDowell.

II. Two Kinds of Objectivity

A. McDowell on Objectivity

In a series of influential papers,[36] McDowell has advanced what he calls a
"realist" view about the objectivity of semantic, ethical, and other evaluative
facts, but one that is predicated on an explicit repudiation of a certain "scientis-
tic" view of what such objectivity must consist in.[37] We may think of
McDowell's work as a sustained attack on the idea that the conception of
objectivity we inherit from the natural sciences – what I called the "Naturalistic
Conception" – is the *only* viable conception and, in particular, that it must
apply to the domain of value. According to the Naturalistic Conception, it will

be recalled, a fact is "objective" if it: (a) is "mind-independent" (in some appropriate sense); and (b) makes a causal difference to the course of our experience.

McDowell's attack on this conception is, unfortunately, disproportionately directed at the requirement of mind-independence. Like Dworkin, he repeatedly charges the skeptic about morality with holding a certain (untenable) conception of objective reality: "how things really are is how things are in themselves – that is, independently of how they strike the occupants of this or that particular point of view" (NCRF, 141). The thrust of McDowell's critique, then, is to show that such a conception of reality is unintelligible: "We cannot occupy the independent perspective that platonism envisages; and it is only because we confusedly think we can that we think we can make any sense of it" (NCRF, 150). Famously, he thinks that the correct understanding of Wittgenstein's remarks on rule-following will reveal the problems with this conception of objective reality. Roughly, the argument proceeds as follows.

Any satisfactory philosophical account of rule-following must explain two features of the phenomenon: it must show rules to be "objective" in some sense (i.e., it can't be the case that whatever anyone thinks the rule means just determines what the rule means); and it must account for the "normativity" of rules (i.e., the fact that rules constrain conduct, that they set criteria of rightness and wrongness for those trying to follow them). The two features are connected: if rules are *not* objective, then they can't be normative. If whatever I take the rule to mean fixes the content of the rule, then there is no meaningful sense in which the rule can constrain (or serve as a yardstick) for my subsequent conduct.

Wittgenstein's remarks on rule-following are then construed as undermining one conception of the "objectivity" of rules, which McDowell calls "platonistic." Platonism involves a certain interpretation of the "mind-independence" requirement – what we might call "Strong Objectivity." A fact is strongly objective if its existence and character does not depend (epistemically) on what we do know or *could* know about it (even at the ideal limit).[38] The Strong Objectivist about rules thinks of them as "the inexorable workings of a machine . . . [which are] independent of the activities and responses that make up our . . . practice [of following the rule]" (NCRF, 151).

Such a conception of rules, according to McDowell's reading of Wittgenstein, fails for two reasons: it cannot account for the *normativity* of rules and it "always transcends any grounds there may be for postulating it" (NCRF, 147). It fails to account for normativity because it is unclear how a rule whose content is in principle unknowable by us could discharge its *normative* function.[39] ("How could something unknown obligate us?" as Nietzsche puts it.)[40] And the Platonist's version of the rule is never warranted by the available evidence, since the available evidence (past behavior, physical and mental) underdetermines the content of the rule.[41] The moral, for McDowell, is always the same: facts about what a rule means, just like moral facts and semantic facts, are all real and knowable, but only from *within* the relevant practices (of rule-following, or moral argument, or language-use); the idea that we could stand outside these practices and identify any facts is nonsensical. Here is how McDowell has put the point over the years:

(1) [I]t is only because of our own involvement in our "whirl of organism" [i.e., "the activities and responses that make up our . . . practice"] that we can understand a form of words as conferring, on the judgment that some move is the correct one at a given point, the special compellingness [i.e., normativity] possessed by [a rule]. (NCRF, 151)

(2) [I]f we are simply and normally immersed in our practices, we do not wonder how their relation to the world would look from outside them, and feel the need for a solid foundation discernible from an external point of view. (NCRF, 153)

(3) [M]oral values are there in the world, and make demands on our reason. This is not a platonism about value . . . ; the world in which moral values are said to be is not the externally characterizable world that a moral platonism would envisage. (NCRF, 156–57)

(4) [T]here is no standpoint from which we can give a sense-making characterization of linguistic practice [or moral practice] other than that of immersion in the practice. (AREU, 248).

(5) We have no point of vantage on the question what can be the case, that is, what can be a fact, external to the modes of thought and speech we know our way around in, with whatever understanding of what counts as better and worse execution of them our mastery of them can give us. (PTE, 11)

Now the hardcore realist – as opposed to the non-Archimedean Quinean realist – would want to contest this Wittgensteinian attack on the intelligibility of the "external" vantage point, on the notion of a world-as-it-is-in-itself. But I want to grant McDowell the general metaphysical point, because it is actually quite irrelevant to the debate between skeptic and realist. As we saw before in rebutting Dworkin's similar charge of "Archimedeanism," there is nothing in the skeptical position that requires the intelligibility of an "external" vantage point in the objectionable sense. One could very well think that from where we stand in Neurath's boat, it is a live question of the post-Enlightenment world how moral facts are to be squared with everything else we take ourselves to understand about the world and its processes. Or, to put this in terms of McDowell's favored metaphors: the question of how to place morality is one that arises *within* our practices, not external to them. Indeed, even within our moral practices, the issue of the objectivity of morality remains a *live* issue precisely because we find within our practices the sorts of intractable moral disagreements that invite skepticism in the first place.[42]

So the skeptic can agree with McDowell in resisting the "philosophical temptation to connect objectivity with a suitable relation to how things would look from outside" (CN, 385) and still think there is a serious issue from *within* our best-going theory of the world about what room, if any, there remains for moral facts.

McDowell, however, has another argument against the "external" skeptic, one that can be viewed as a complement to Dworkin's failed appeal to moral phenomenology. I argued earlier that moral experience is simply a datum, and that the key question (accordingly) is whether our moral experience is best explained in realist or skeptical terms. McDowell has argued that, in fact, the skeptic cannot give a *coherent* account of moral phenomenology, that he must presuppose the existence of moral facts in the very process of explaining them. The dilemma is most acute for the "projectivist," the external skeptic who holds that moral properties are simply a *projection* of our subjective responses to various features of the world onto the world. McDowell's objection to the projectivist is essentially this: the projectivist cannot identify the subjective state that is being projected without already presupposing the concept to be explained. Here is the crucial passage:

[I]t undermines a projective account of a concept if we cannot home in on the subjective state whose projection is supposed to result in the seeming feature of reality in question without the aid of the concept of that feature, the concept that was to be projectively explained. (PTE, 6)

Try, in other words, to pick out the subjective response that is projected on the world when something seems "funny" without appealing to some concept of the "funny" or "comic," and you will be at a loss. The natural subjective states to identify – "a disposition to laugh" or "to find something funny" – already presuppose the explanandum at issue.

This argument only works, however, on the assumption that one is committed to the reality of any property (e.g., "the funny" or "the morally right") simply in virtue of knowing how to apply the associated concept. But why should the skeptic agree to that assumption? The skeptical claim is an *ontological* claim about what exists. The projectivist skeptic says moral facts are not part of the world's basic furniture, that they are simply projections of various subjective states onto the world. That the projectivist must, in turn, appeal to moral *concepts* in order to characterize these responses simply does not show that he is committed to the existence of moral *facts*.

So it seems that McDowell, like Dworkin, has no good argument against the Naturalistic Conception of objectivity. McDowell's more ambitious argument from phenomenology fails to show the skeptic's position to be incoherent. And McDowell's Wittgensteinian argument attacks a metaphysical position that the skeptic need not presuppose. Moreover, in both cases the attack is only on the Naturalistic demand of "mind-independence," rather than causal efficacy. We could even grant to McDowell that moral facts are response-dependent facts in some sense[43] – that they are not robustly (or Strongly) mind-independent – and still think that they: (a) are sufficiently independent of actual human response for objectivity (in virtue of the idealization of response-conditions built in to all the current accounts of response-dependent facts); yet (b) fail to be objective because they do not figure in the causal explanation of experience. Against this latter demand, I do not see that McDowell has any direct response. Putting this problem aside, however, we can at least ask what McDowell's Non-Naturalist alternative for objectivity in ethics amounts to.[44]

McDowell speaks about "truth," not objectivity, in ethics, though the difference will not matter for purposes here. The crucial skeptical challenge to truth in ethics comes, McDowell claims, from philosophers like Alasdair Mac-Intyre and Charles Stevenson who think "we lack . . . a conception of better and worse ways to think about ethical questions" (PTE, 4). But, objects McDowell,

we do after all have at our disposal a conception of reasons for ethical thinking which is sufficiently rich and substantial to mark off rationally induced improvements in ethical stances from alterations induced by merely manipulative persuasion. (PTE, 5)[45]

What we need, then, for truth or objectivity in ethics is not that moral facts be severed from human responses, but only that ethical thought "allow[ ] for a sufficiently substantial conception of reasons" (PTE, 8). "Susceptibility to reasons" is the hallmark of objectivity in ethics, and, "The threat to truth is from the thought that there is not enough substance to our conception of reasons for ethical stances" (PTE, 9). Notice, in particular, that McDowell is *not* saying that convergence in ethical responses is enough for truth in ethics, for such convergence might simply be "a mere coincidence of subjectivities rather than agreement on a range of truths – the sort of view that would be natural if everyone came to prefer one flavor of ice cream to any other" (PTE, 8). It is the possibility of convergence *backed by substantial reasons* that demarcates genuinely objective domains from those marked by "a mere coincidence of subjectivities."

Now against the Naturalist who complains that the question about objectivity in ethics is necessarily the ontological question, McDowell simply falls back upon something like Dworkin's (mistaken) charge of arbitrary, a priori-ness. "[H]ow good are the credentials," McDowell asks, "of a 'metaphysical' understanding [of the kinds of facts the world contains] that blankly excludes values and instances of the comic from the world in advance of any philosophical enquiry into truth" (PTE, 12)? "What is missing," he adds, "is a reason to suppose that natural science has a foundational status in philosophical reflection about truth – that there can be no facts other than those that would figure in a scientific understanding of the world" (PTE, 12). Yet, once again, to the Quinean this all looks very strange. For it is not some inexplicable or accidental prejudice that privileges a scientific epistemology over all others. Rather, such a posture is the natural one to adopt (at least initially) given the tremendous success such an epistemology has enjoyed to date. To simply push the scientific epistemology aside opens the ontological floodgates to a whole pre-Enlightenment conception of the world that we seem to do better without.

B. McDowell and Dworkin

Whatever its drawbacks, I hope it is now apparent how McDowell's discussion – and the distinction between Naturalistic and Non-Naturalistic Conceptions of Objectivity – resonates with some of what we saw Dworkin trying to get at in the prior section. Indeed, there are even places in the Dworkinian corpus where he comes very close to naming the distinction at issue. For example, in a 1978 essay, he says that we should "suppose that there is something else in the world beside hard facts" (MP1, p. 138), where "hard facts" are just "physical facts and facts about behavior (including the thoughts and attitudes) of people" (MP1, p. 137) or "the sort of fact that is . . . in principle demonstrable by ordinary scientific methods" (MP1, p. 139). Moral facts and, for example, facts about the best interpretation of a story would be cases of nonhard facts, in Dworkin's view. More recently, he writes that "[m]orality is a distinct, independent dimension of our experience, and it exercises its own sovereignty" (OT, 127), and he endorses as a general epistemic "principle of tolerance" (my phrase, not Dworkin's) the following:

[T]he epistemology of any domain must be sufficiently internal to its content to provide reasons, viewed from the perspective of those who begin holding convictions within it, for testing, modifying or abandoning those convictions. (OT, 120)

As a blanket principle, of course, this could not be right. Think of the adherents of the Church of Scientology, who embrace the bizarre Hubbardian cosmology. It is natural to say that theirs is *not* an objective account of the universe, even though: (a) there are probably no reasons "internal" to the domain that would lead its adherents to abandon it; and (b) the reasons "external" to the domain – e.g., the reasons provided by physics, astronomy, and evolutionary biology – would not shake the "convictions" of the devout Scientologists.

Dworkin, however, does not mean his principle of tolerance to apply to those domains that make claims at odds with the claims of science. He explicitly says that since astrology and orthodox religion "purport to offer causal explanations" they can be subjected to the best-explanation test. But, he adds,

Since morality and the other evaluative domains make no causal claims . . . such tests can play no role in any plausible test for them. We do need tests for reliability of our moral opinions, but these must be appropriate to the content of these opinions. That is why an epistemological challenge that comes to nothing more than insisting that moral properties are not physical properties must fail. (OT, 120)

So the principle of tolerance covers those domains which don't make causal claims; for these domains we need a Non-Naturalistic criterion of objectivity.

But why suppose these domains are objective in the first place? Dworkin's central intuition – the one that undergirds, I think, the often confused attack on external skepticism discussed above – might be put as follows:

So you, Mr. Skeptic, have shown that moral properties do not figure in our best explanatory picture of the world, that they do not deserve a place in a suitably scientific ontology – that is all well and good, but it is hardly of much concern to me. For even though "moral wrongness" is not a property that slavery possesses objectively (in your Naturalistic sense of that term), it is still the case that my arguments for the wrongness of slavery are strong and persuasive ones and that you have given me no argument to cease believing that slavery is wrong. Who cares (as it were) about the ontological status of moral facts: what I want to know is whether you have a good (i.e., internal) argument that slavery is not wrong?

If this is what Dworkin's view comes to, then it is important to recognize that his real position is not that external skepticism is unintelligible, but that it is irrelevant.[46] Debate about the ontology of moral facts as much as you want, Dworkin might say; none of this affects one bit one's ability to argue for and against different moral propositions. The only objectivity that "counts," as it were, resides in the potentialities of this moral argument.

That this is the crux of Dworkin's view is suggested in various papers. He says, for example, that "[w]e do have reasons for thinking that slavery is wrong and that the Greeks were therefore in error: we have all the moral reasons we would cite in a moral debate about the matter" (OT, 122). Elsewhere, he says:

We do not say (nor can we understand anyone who does say) that . . . moral values are 'out there' or can be proved. We can only say, with different emphases, that . . . slavery is wrong. The practice[ ] . . . of morality give[s] [this] claim[ ] all the meaning [it] need[s] or could have. (LE, 83).

Similarly, in the context of discussing a dispute about an "interpretive fact" – say, the best way to make sense of certain events in the novel *David Copperfield* – Dworkin says that participants in such a discussion,

are trained to subject their responses to the disciplines of reflection and consistency, and then to make certain assertions that their training authorizes them to make on the authority of these responses so disciplined. The exercise, conducted by participants so trained, serves some purpose – perhaps recreational or cultural – other than to increase our collective knowledge of the external world . . . [The participants] certainly do not think that narrative consistency is the same sort of thing as the weight of iron, or that it is part of the external world in anything like the way the weight of iron is. . . . Whatever sense [i.e., objectivity] statements about narrative consistency may have, they are given that sense by the enterprise that trains participants to make and respond to such statements. (MP1, 140, 141)

I take Dworkin to be making essentially McDowell's point in passages like these: that objectivity in ethics is a matter of "susceptibility to reasons"; that to attack the objectivity of an ethical position is to give ethical reasons against holding it (not epistemological or ontological arguments); that the capacity for such reasoning is nurtured within certain practices of moral argumentation, and that we simply have nothing else to go on in assessing moral arguments than the sensibilities and capacities so nurtured. Dworkin, in short, should endorse McDowell's slogan that "truth in ethics [is] earned from within ethical think-ing" (PTE, 10) and could equally well agree (with certain obvious additions) that,

The threat to truth [in ethics] is from the [internally skeptical] thought that there is not enough substance to our conception of reasons for ethical stances. When we try to meet this [internally skeptical] threat, there is no reason not to appeal to all the resources at our disposal, including all the ethical concepts that we can lay our hands on, so long as they survive critical scrutiny; and there need be no basis for critical scrutiny of one ethical concept except others, so the necessary scrutiny does not involve stepping outside the point of view constituted by an ethical sensibility. (PTE, 9)

If Dworkin and McDowell are both Non-Naturalists about objectivity of roughly the same sort, it still remains the case that they have no substantial argument against the Naturalistic Conception except, perhaps, the irrelevance argument sketched above. We must consider, then, whether this argument suffices to defeat the external skeptic.

III. Against Non-Naturalism

In this section, I argue that Non-Naturalism is not a suitable conception of objectivity, even for ethics, for two reasons. First, in many cases (including ethics), we can get no purchase on the notion of a discourse being "objective" (even in the sense of being "susceptible to reasons") without implicit reliance on the Naturalistic sense of objectivity: unless there are Naturalistically objec-tive facts to which the discourse must answer we will often be unable to make sense of better and worse ways of reasoning.[47] Second, even the skeptic does not deny that people's moral views are "susceptible to reasons"; what he denies is that what is distinctively *moral* in their view is open to reasoned consider-ation. Dworkin and McDowell have done nothing to show that moral views are susceptible to reasons in this stronger sense, the sense necessary to distinguish their view from that of, say, the noncognitivist.[48]

A. Is Naturalistic Objectivity Irrelevant?

On the interpretation proposed above, Dworkin's key challenge to Naturalistic Objectivity is that it is irrelevant to moral argument in the double sense that the (Naturalistically) objective status of a moral position: (a) has no bearing on the objectivity of ethics, which is a matter of there being better and worse reasons for ethical stances; and (b) would not change anyone's first-order moral views. I propose to show that Dworkin is wrong on both counts.

Imagine there arose a practice of making arguments about the merits of different flavors of ice cream, say chocolate and vanilla. Parties to this discourse might argue for the superiority of chocolate in the following way:

What distinguishes chocolate is the richness and seriousness of the flavor, in comparison to the fleetingness of the sensation of vanilla. Chocolate grips the palate, it takes over the mouth, it washes away all the prior flavors. It is a total and encompassing taste experience, unlike vanilla. The creaminess of chocolate – that quintessential trait of great ice cream – is so unlike the creaminess of vanilla, which is hard to distinguish from mere milkiness. Chocolate ice cream is just *substantial,* in a way that vanilla could never be.

Suppose, too, that a consensus (backed by canonical forms of reasoning like the preceding) arises according to which chocolate really is the better flavor: we have, in other words, a *hegemonic* convention of reasons (call it "the Chocolate Convention") which always supports the conclusion that chocolate is to be preferred. The convention is "hegemonic" not in the sense that no other reasons can be heard or appreciated – the parties are, by hypothesis, *susceptible* to reasons – but only in the sense that everyone comes to find the reasons favoring chocolate persuasive.

According to Non-Naturalism, we should have to say that it is an *objective* fact that chocolate is better than vanilla. Ice cream flavors are, after all, susceptible to reasons in this scenario. But since there has arisen a hegemonic convention of finding the arguments for chocolate to be the strongest, there is no indefeasible *internal* skeptical attack on objectivity to be mounted. So on the Non-Naturalist picture, chocolate is objectively better than vanilla.

Now this conclusion strikes me as quite bizarre. My intuition is that the "taste" of ice cream flavors is the paradigm of a subjective property (what seems right to the judger just is right). So regardless of how compelling people find the "reasons" favoring chocolate, and regardless of how vigorously they argue, one wants to say that the parties to the Chocolate Convention are talking nonsense: there are no *objective* facts about the "tastiness" of ice cream flavors; the "tastiness" of chocolate or vanilla is merely *subjective.* But we can only articulate this intuition by appeal to an *external* conception of objectivity, by appeal to the notion that any particular discourse – no matter how robust it looks – must ultimately answer to the facts, Naturalistically conceived. The Chocolate Convention simply can't do that, since there are no objective facts about the "tastiness" of ice cream flavors to answer to.

We can generalize the point: Naturalistic Objectivity is relevant to assessing the objectivity of most domains of discourse precisely because it is always *possible* for hegemonic conventions of argumentation (like the Chocolate Convention) to grow up around nonfactual matters. The Non-Naturalist, however, has no resources for responding to this possibility, no way to say that a hegemonic convention of reasons is, in fact, not objective. Yet it seems quite implausible that objectivity should accrue to judgments solely in virtue of the fact that they are not *successfully* challenged, that they are parts of hegemonic conventions for which no *persuasive* internal skeptic can be found. The Naturalistic Conception of objectivity, then, does make a difference to how we would assess the objectivity of such domains of discourse.

McDowell, it seems, has two possible responses. First, he might deny that the Chocolate Convention is really a case of people being *susceptible* to reasons; that it is, rather, merely the facade of the kind of susceptibility to reasons that we find in evaluative discourse.[49] Unfortunately, I see no non–question-begging way for McDowell to articulate this thought. How do we know that our "moral reasoning" is, itself, not a hegemonic convention like the Chocolate Convention? Isn't that precisely what is at issue here? At least with discourses concerning matters that are objective in the Naturalistic sense, we have some way of weeding out cases of *mere* hegemony of one type of reasoning. But McDowell cannot avail himself of that consideration. What McDowell would need, but does not offer, is a robust account of "susceptibility" to reasons, one that doesn't beg the question against the skeptic about our moral discourse. I do not see such an account in the offing.

McDowell might, then, take a different line and simply "bite the bullet" and reject the intuition that the "tastiness" of ice cream is a subjective property. If, in fact, a practice of reasoning like the Chocolate Convention really were sustainable, then, the McDowellian might claim, we *should* view "tastiness" as objective.

There are two difficulties, however, with such a response. First, we must be prepared to generalize beyond this one case and claim something much stronger: namely, that it is a conceptual impossibility for a hegemonic convention of reasons to arise concerning matters that are subjective; susceptibility to reasons simply *suffices* for objectivity, even within hegemonic conventions. Yet this general claim seems too strong: surely it makes conceptual sense to think of a domain being susceptible to reasons even though it is not objective. The difficulty for the McDowellian is to account for this possibility without recourse to the "external" perspective. Second, biting the bullet seems too radical a response, compared with simply admitting the relevance of the "external" perspective. Why – except for a dogmatic commitment to Non-Naturalism – should we "bite the bullet" if an "external" perspective on objectivity suffices to account for the natural intuition that objectivity requires that reasons answer to facts about the world?

But now consider a rather different gustatory claim: namely, that chocolate ice cream is tastier than excrement.[50] Surely our *intuitions* about this case are the opposite of the prior case: we are tempted to say precisely that *this* is an objective fact about relative tastiness. Does this intuition help vindicate the McDowellian view?

The answer depends on how we go about explaining the sense in which it is an objective fact that chocolate ice cream is tastier than excrement. It does not appear that the explanation for this fact resides in the choice between chocolate and excrement being "susceptible to reasons." (To the contrary, we are inclined to think that if someone could give *reasons* for preferring excrement, that this would go no distance to changing the fact-of-the-matter.) Chocolate is surely better than excrement *intersubjectively,* that is, there is a near-universal consensus on this point. Perhaps this is all "objectivity" comes to in this context, but if so, that won't be enough to save McDowell's view. Yet chocolate might even turn out to be *objectively* better than excrement if it turns out that, in these extreme cases, the property of tastiness just supervenes upon or is identical with some cluster of chemical-physical facts about the micro- and macroconstitutions of the substances at issue and their chemical-physical interaction with the human sensory apparatus. In other words, if it is an objective (as opposed to just intersubjective) fact that chocolate tastes better than excrement, this would be objectivity in the familiar Naturalistic sense.[51]

Does external skepticism also affect one's first-order moral beliefs? I think it does, for much the same reasons that it makes a difference to one's assessment of the objectivity of hegemonic conventions of discourse. It is surely a (defeasible) norm for belief that we should believe in objective facts. According to Non-Naturalism, in the case of the Chocolate Convention there is a (Non-Naturalistically) objective fact about the superiority of chocolate to vanilla. Therefore, by our defeasible epistemic norm, we should believe that chocolate is superior to vanilla.

Now along comes the external skeptic who casts doubt on the deliverances of our hegemonic convention, for the reasons already given. But once we become skeptical about whether it really is an *objective* fact that chocolate is better than vanilla, shouldn't that affect our first-order view that chocolate *is* better than vanilla? We might, at that point, revert to an internally agnostic position or, if we were secret partisans of vanilla all along (merely swept up by the seeming force of the Chocolate Convention), we might now openly proclaim our preference for vanilla, without embarrassment.

We might sum up the general problem here in a slogan: "Talk is cheap." That we can talk about something *as though it were real,* that we can nurture a practice of giving reasons, does not suffice to underwrite the objectivity of any domain. Objective domains must generally answer to the world at some point: only then can we distinguish mere hegemonic conventions from practices of argument about genuinely objective domains. What the example of the Chocolate Convention brings out is our deeply held intuition that there is a difference between what's real and what we merely talk about as though it were real. Only the "external" perspective permits us to do any justice to that intuition.

Now it is true that Naturalistically objective domains *are* susceptible to reasons (e.g., physics). But what demarcates genuine "susceptibility to reasons," of a sort sufficient to underwrite realism, from pseudosusceptibility is precisely the possibility of the external perspective (even, to repeat, if it is still a perspective taken from within Neurath's boat).

B. *Susceptibility to Reasons*

We have already seen that susceptibility to reasons, by itself, is not sufficient to undergird our intuitions about objectivity; we also require the "external" perspective, some picture of what facts there are in the world to which genuinely objective discourses must answer. But now I want to argue that even the notion of "susceptibility to reasons" does not suffice to distance the Dworkin/ McDowell view from the view of skeptics like the ethical noncognitivist. For even noncognitivists think that moral positions are susceptible to reasons, since moral views typically depend – causally and/or logically – on various *empirical* and *factual* assumptions. Since these assumptions are "susceptible to reasons" (even for the Naturalist), it follows that people with differing moral positions have a space of reasons within which to argue.[52]

What Dworkin and McDowell want to claim, of course, is that the "ethical stance" *itself* is susceptible to reasons, quite apart from any factual assumptions. The evidence for the objectivity of ethics is supposed to reside, on this Non-Naturalist view, in what is distinctively *moral* in a moral debate being open to reasoned and critical reflection. Yet Dworkin and McDowell, quite strikingly, never make a case for this claim. Dworkin, for example, says things like: "We do have reasons for thinking that slavery is wrong and that the Greeks were therefore in error: we have all the moral reasons we would cite in a moral debate about the matter" (OT, 122). No skeptic need disagree with this, except to point out that the "error" of the Greeks lay in a set of false empirical assumptions about human beings and human potentialities. It just turns out to be false, as a matter of empirical psychology and biology, that (as Aristotle thought), "Some humans are . . . natural slaves, who altogether lack the capacity for deliberation."[53] What Dworkin needs to show is that the "error" of the Greeks lay *not* in their faulty factual assumptions, but in their distinctively *ethical* stance on this issue.

To illustrate why I think this demonstration will not be forthcoming, let me propose a pseudo-Nietzschean argument for the morality of slavery.[54] The argument is suggested by an actual passage from Nietzsche:

Every enhancement of the type "man" has so far been the work of an aristocratic society . . . a society that believes in the long ladder of an order of rank and differences in value between man and man, and that needs slavery in some sense or other. Without that *pathos of distance* which grows out of the ingrained difference between strata – when the ruling caste constantly looks afar and looks down upon subjects and instruments and just as constantly practices obedience and command, keeping down and keeping at a distance – that other, more mysterious pathos could not have grown up either – the craving for an ever new widening of distances within the soul itself, the development of ever higher, rarer, more remote, further-stretching, more comprehensive states – in brief, simply the enhancement of the type "man," the continual "self-overcoming of man," to use a moral formula in a supra-moral sense.[55]

The logic of this argument, in the hands of the pseudo-Nietzsche ("P-Nietzsche") becomes the following:

(1) Any form of socioeconomic organization that maximizes the good is itself morally valuable.
(2) The highest good is the enhancement of the "type" man, that is, the breeding or production of truly great human beings like Beethoven and Goethe.
(3) Slavery is a form of socioeconomic organization that maximizes the highest good.

Therefore, slavery is morally valuable.

Most of the quoted passage is devoted to giving empirical support to (3). Here the argument depends on a certain sort of speculative empirical psychology to the effect that nurturing greatness in a human being requires that the person be driven to want to "overcome" himself, to view his current self as unsatisfactory, to always want to become something "higher." Persons, however, only learn to be so driven by seeing mirrored in the social world a similar hierarchy between "higher" and "lower" – "greater" and "lesser" – persons. When society teaches that there are "higher" and "lower" people, this plants in the mind of the potentially great human being the idea that he, himself, may be at present a contemptible "lower" person, thus giving him the impetus to "overcome" himself and realize his greatness.

Now we can well imagine arguing with P-Nietzsche about the empirical assumptions that undergird (3). This, of course, is a debate that even the external skeptic thinks is both possible and relevant to one's ultimate moral view. But for the Non-Naturalist view to be plausible, it has to be the case that premises (1) and (2) are also susceptible to reasoned discussion. What reasoned debate might they have?

Dworkin presumably might differ with P-Nietzsche over two issues: first, that the moral value of an act is to be assessed in terms of its maximizing some value; and second, even granting the consequentialist form of reasoning, that the "highest" value is really the production of human greatness (such that this consideration trumps all competing values).

As to the first question, it is true that there has been a substantial literature arguing, for example, that deontology is irrational (an argument that won't help Dworkin),[56] or that consequentialism would lead to counterintuitive violations of individual rights. Now this latter objection, at least, won't be any help here, because it simply presupposes an answer to the basic question about value. But even the former argument – the one against deontology – is not a *moral* argument, but an argument that appeals to a certain *epistemic value,* that is, that one ought not to hold irrational beliefs.[57]

But what about someone who wants to contest that the value of producing great human beings trumps all other considerations? Is the basic ethical stance here – "the highest good is the existence of great human beings" – susceptible to reasons? What distinctively *moral* argument is there that P-Nietzsche's posture is mistaken? Is it that P-Nietzsche doesn't give enough weight to the basic happiness or well-being of the great mass of humanity? But that's no argument: it is no different than saying to the partisan of vanilla that he has failed to give sufficient weight to the creaminess of chocolate. The partisan of vanilla is neither impressed by nor interested in the "creaminess" of chocolate; so too, P-Nietzsche is neither impressed by nor interested in the happiness of most people. Is it that P-Nietzsche is just not being sensitive to the moral claim that the welfare of others has upon us? Yet this sounds more like a repetition of the disagreement, than an *argument.* (Has the partisan of vanilla just not been sensitive to the "tastiness" claim that the richness of chocolate makes upon us?) We could go on in this fashion for some time, but I do not think we would arrive at anything that looks like a *moral* reason for adopting one ethical stance over the other.

Dworkin, at least, admits as much, though perhaps without realizing how it vitiates the whole position. For sometimes, he concedes, when confronted with a moral disagreement we may simply have to say of our opponents that,

they did not "see" or show sufficient "sensitivity" to what we "see" or "sense," and these metaphors may have nothing behind them but the bare and unsubstantiated conviction that our capacity for moral judgment functions better than theirs did. (OT, 121–22)

Once we countenance this bit of posturing as a genuine response, however, we've surely conceded that being susceptible to reasons is just a figleaf for unrepentant intuitionism,[58] of the sort that Strawson demolished fifty years ago[59] and which even McDowell explicitly renounces as a serious option (cf. PTE, 5–7). Any domain can now be objective if we are permitted to fall back on our superior "sensitivity" and "sense" as vindicating the factuality of our judgments. The ontological floodgates are now thrown so wide that even a pre-Enlightenment ontology would look unduly austere.

In order to avoid this unseemly consequence, we must, I think, concede the correctness of the conventional noncognitivist view: yes, moral positions are susceptible to reasons in the familiar sense that people are typically responsive to the demands of logical consistency and factual accuracy; but once *these* are exhausted, there is nothing left but brute and opposed evaluative attitudes or "tastes." At that point, we have left the space of reasons behind.

IV. Conclusion

Dworkin's defense to the charge that his Right-Answer thesis (the claim that all, or most cases have right answers as a matter of law) is incompatible with his view that moral considerations play a decisive role in fixing the rights of litigants has turned on his insistence that his critics misunderstand the sense in which moral considerations need to be objective. At its core, Dworkin's view seems to be McDowell's: that the Naturalistic Conception of objectivity appropriate, say, for natural science, is irrelevant in the evaluative domain. What suffices for objectivity in evaluative matters is that we be able to subject our evaluative stances to reasoned discussion. I have argued that this Non-Naturalistic Conception of objectivity does not give an adequate account of objectivity, even in ethics. If I am right, and if no Naturalistic moral realist response to the skeptic succeeds, then Mackie's charge some twenty years ago stands: Dworkin's theory of adjudication "injects a corresponding subjectivity into statements about what the law is" with the result that there is no "single right answer" to questions of law.

Notes

1. John Mackie, "The Third Theory of Law," reprinted in Marshall Cohen (ed.), *Ronald Dworkin and Contemporary Jurisprudence* (London: Duckworth, 1983), p. 165.
2. Dworkin's main discussions of these issues appear in the following texts: "Can Rights Be Controversial?" in *Taking Rights Seriously* (Cambridge, Mass.: Harvard University Press, 1977) [cited hereafter as TRS]; "Is There Really No Right Answer in Hard Cases?" [cited hereafter as MP1] and "On Interpretation and Objectivity," [MP2] both in *A Matter of Principle* (Cambridge, Mass.: Harvard University Press, 1985); *Law's Empire* (Cambridge, Mass.: Harvard University Press, 1986), pp. 78–86 [cited hereafter as LE]; "Pragmatism, Right Answers, and True Banality," in M. Brint and W. Weaver (eds.), *Pragmatism in Law and Society* (Boulder: Westview, 1991) [cited hereafter as P]; and, most recently, "Objectivity and Truth: You'd Better Believe It," *Philosophy & Public Affairs* 25 (1996): 87–139 [cited hereafter as OT].
3. I am not going to be concerned with the plausibility of this latter claim here. It bears noting, however, that even if Dworkin were right about the unintelligible "external" perspective, he would still need actually to defeat all "internal" skeptical attacks to support the right-answer thesis.
4. For a representative critique, see Michael S. Moore, "Metaphysics, Epistemology, and Legal Theory," *Southern California Law Review* 60 (1987): 453–506.
5. More precisely, these objects are *epistemically* independent of human mind: what we believe, or even what we would be justified in believing, does not fix the nature of these objects. Cf. the discussion of "observer-independence" in Sigrún Svavarsdóttir, "Objective Values: Does Metaethics Rest on a Mistake?" [this volume].
6. Other adherents to the Non-Naturalist Conception of Objectivity, but not necessarily to McDowell's positive construal of it, would include Thomas Nagel, *The View From Nowhere* (New York: Oxford University Press, 1986) and Hilary Putnam, "Are Moral and

Legal Values Made or Discovered?" and "Replies to Brian Leiter and Jules Coleman," *Legal Theory* 1 (1995): 5–19, 69–80. On Nagel's views, see Svavarsdóttir's essay in this volume.

7. For a more detailed articulation of my views on this subject, see my "Legal Indeterminacy," *Legal Theory* 1 (1995): 481–492, and also my essay on "Legal Realism," in D. M. Patterson (ed.), *A Companion to Philosophy of Law and Legal Theory* (Oxford: Blackwell, 1996). For more on the realist views, to which I am generally sympathetic, see my "Rethinking Legal Realism: Toward a Naturalized Jurisprudence," *Texas Law Review* 76 (1997): 267–315.

8. Thomas Nagel, *The Last Word* (New York: Oxford University Press, 1997), p. vii.

9. Cf. David Brink, *Moral Realism and the Foundations of Ethics* (Cambridge: Cambridge University Press, 1989), p. 20 ("ethics is objective . . . [in the sense that] it concerns facts that hold independently of anyone's beliefs about what is right or wrong"); Peter Railton, "Moral Realism," *Philosophical Review* 95 (1986): 163–207, p. 164 (the issue about objectivity is the issue of "in what ways, if any, does the existence of moral properties depend upon the actual or possible states of mind of intelligent beings").

10. Dworkin assumes this is a *moral* view, but it is equally plausible understood as a metaphysical view about the aetiology of value, as David Sosa points out to me.

11. Dworkin is not always clear on this point. In one paper, he describes Mackie as "defend[ing] a kind of internal moral skepticism" (P, 366), but in a more recent paper he says (correctly, in my view) that Mackie "was an external skeptic purporting to rely only on independent, non-moral, philosophical arguments" (OT, 113).

12. For a lengthier account of how I understand Quine, see my contribution to the symposium on "Law and Truth": "Why Quine Is Not a Postmodernist," *Southern Methodist University Law Review* 50 (1997): 1739–1754.

13. Minus Quine's austere physicalism, which is detachable from his pragmatism and naturalism. See the useful discussion in Christopher Hookway, *Quine: Language, Experience, and Reality* (Stanford: Stanford University Press, 1988), pp. 63–78, 124.

14. Roger Gibson, "Willard van Orman Quine," in J. Kim and E. Sosa (eds.), *A Companion to Metaphysics* (Oxford: Blackwell, 1995), p. 427. For related discussion, see Peter Hylton, "Quine's Naturalism," *Midwest Studies in Philosophy* 19 (1994): 261–282.

15. W. V. O. Quine, *Word and Object* (Cambridge, Mass.: MIT Press, 1960), pp. 24–25.

16. W. V. O. Quine, "Comments on Lauener," in R. Barrett and R. Gibson (eds.), *Perspectives on Quine* (Oxford: Blackwell, 1990), p. 229.

17. "Science is self-conscious common sense." *Word and Object,* p. 3. "The scientist is indistinguishable from the common man in his sense of evidence, except that the scientist is more careful." W. V. O. Quine, "The Scope and Language of Science," in *The Ways of Paradox and Other Essays* (Cambridge, Mass.: Harvard University Press, 1976), p. 233.

18. *Word and Object,* p. 22.

19. W. V. O. Quine, *Pursuit of Truth* (Cambridge, Mass.: Harvard University Press, 1990), p. 21.

20. This is a long-standing feature of Dworkin's work, going back to his early articles on H. L. A. Hart's positivism, in which Hart's view is regularly misstated. See, e.g., Hart's postscript to *The Concept of Law,* 2d ed. (Oxford: Clarendon, 1994); and see also Charles Silver, "Elmer's Case: A Legal Positivist Replies to Dworkin," *Law and Philosophy* 6 (1987): 381–399.

21. See, e.g., Nicholas L. Sturgeon, "What Difference Does It Make Whether Moral Realism Is True?," in N. Gillespie (ed.), *Moral Realism: Proceedings of the 1985 Spindel Conference, Southern Journal of Philosophy* 24 Supp. (1986); Jeremy Waldron, "The Irrelevance of Moral Objectivity," in R. George (ed.), *Natural Law Theory: Contemporary Essays* (Oxford: Clarendon Press, 1992).

22. Dworkin objects "to the pointless metaphysical theater, the fierce campaigns against invented fools" (P, 382) and suggests that the challenges of external skeptics are "just bad philosophy" (OT, 139). He expresses the (aptly named) "pious hope" that "the leaden spirits of our age, which nurture [these skeptical challenges], [will] soon lift" (OT, 139). He chastises naturalistic moral realists (like Richard Boyd and Peter Railton) for "add[ing] to the confusion by accepting the [external skeptic's] challenge as sensible and trying to meet it" and dismisses them for falling prey to "the fallacy of the [external skeptics], which is to suppose that some sense can be assigned to supposedly metaphysical claims that is not itself a normative sense" (OT, 127).

23. More precisely, the full-blooded realist holds that: (a) the statements in some domain of discourse are cognitive, i.e., apt for evaluation in terms of their truth and falsity; (b) the truth-value of these statements is an objective matter (e.g., the truth-conditions of these statements are, in principle, evidence-transcendent); and (c) at least some statements in the domain are true. For a related, but slightly different, characterization, see Philip Pettit, "Embracing Objectivity in Ethics" [this volume].

24. I am convinced by Jaegwon Kim's arguments that there is no intelligible doctrine of "supervenience" intermediate between dualism and reduction. See especially Chapters 4, 5, 14, and 16 in Kim's *Supervenience and Mind* (Cambridge: Cambridge University Press, 1993). One advantage of Railton's realist program is that it deals squarely with the issue of formulating reductive identity claims between the "moral" and the "natural," rather than hiding behind the fig leaf of "mere" supervenience. See especially, Peter Railton, "Naturalism and Prescriptivity," in E. F. Paul et al. (eds.), *Foundations of Moral and Political Philosophy* (Oxford: Blackwell, 1990) [cited hereafter as "NP" in the body of the text].

25. Railton, "Moral Realism," p. 165.

26. Ibid., p. 205.

27. I've used the example before. See Brian Leiter, "Tort Theory and the Objectivity of Corrective Justice," *Arizona Law Review* 37 (1995): 45–51, p. 48.

28. See, e.g., Allan Gibbard, *Wise Choices, Apt Feelings: A Theory of Normative Judgment* (Cambridge, Mass.: Harvard University Press, 1990), pp. 10 ff.

29. For more on these issues, see also Peter Railton, "What the Noncognitivist Helps Us to See, the Naturalist Must Help Us to Explain," in J. Haldane and C. Wright (eds.), *Reality, Representation, and Projection* (New York: Oxford University Press, 1993).

30. A scientific epistemology must, of course, encompass more than a commitment to inference to the best explanation. We need, for example, a basic empiricist doctrine – the senses can be a source of knowledge – as well as certain epistemic norms that satisfy neither the empiricist nor the abductive criteria. These epistemic norms admit of only a *pragmatic* defense, as discussed earlier.

31. I take it this is what Dworkin is getting at also when he derides the external skeptic for complaining that moral claims "are not descriptions that can be proved or tested like physics" and that they are not "part of what he calls (in one of the maddening metaphors that seem crucial to any statement of his view) the 'fabric' of the universe" (LE, 79–80).

32. I take it this is the flip side of Dworkin's claim that the skeptical rejection of a naturalistic reduction of a moral predicate violates neutrality.

33. As an aside, let me point out that whether *beliefs* in general and *mathematics* in particular (as distinct from beliefs *about* mathematics) would figure in the best explanation of our experience is an open question – the latter, depending, for example, on whether or not mathematics is indispensable to science.

34. E.g.: Dworkin complains about the postmodernist "*auto-da-fe* of truth [which] has compromised public and political as well as academic discussion" (OT, 89). This strikes me as unduly melodramatic on the former count: surely "public and political" discussion was utterly compromised long before Derrida came on the scene. I would agree, though, that the fact that public discourse should have reached new lows of Orwellian doublespeak just at the time when deconstruction became all the rage in the academy (the 1980s) surely does cry out for socioeconomic explanation – though both phenomena are, I suspect, epiphenomenal.

35. Anyone who would repudiate a scientific epistemology must also provide some new, principled account of the distinction between the real and the unreal, demonstrating that while it makes room for, e.g., moral facts, it still excludes from our best picture of the world various pseudofacts.

36. See John McDowell, "Anti-Realism and the Epistemology of Understanding," in H. Parret and J. Bouveresse (eds.), *Meaning and Understanding* (Berlin: de Gruyter, 1981) [cited as AREU]; "Non-Cognitivism and Rule-Following," in S. Holtzman and C. Leich (eds.), *Wittgenstein: To Follow a Rule* (London: Routledge, 1981) [cited as NCRF]; "Wittgenstein on Following a Rule," *Synthèse* 58 (1984): 325–363; Critical Notice of Bernard Williams, *Ethics and the Limits of Philosophy, Mind* 95 (1986): 377–386 [cited as CN]; "In Defence of Modesty," in B. Taylor (ed.), *Michael Dummett: Contributions to Philosophy* (Dordrecht: M. Nijhoff, 1987); "Projection and Truth in Ethics," Lindley Lecture, Department of Philosophy, University of Kansas (1988) [cited as PTE]. McDowell's recent *Mind and World* (Cambridge, Mass.: Harvard University Press, 1994) is only indirectly concerned with these issues and could not, in any event, be thought to mark an advance in philosophical clarity over the earlier papers.

37. Cf. the attack on "scientism" in PTE, 12.

38. I borrow here from some of the discussion in my "Objectivity and the Problems of Jurisprudence," *Texas Law Review* 72 (1993): 187–209, esp. pp. 190–196.

39. For a more explicit verson of this "normativity" argument, see Crispin Wright, "Introduction," in *Realism, Meaning, and Truth* (Oxford: Blackwell, 1987), pp. 24–25.

40. "How the True World Finally Became a Fable," in *Twilight of the Idols*, in W. Kaufmann (ed.), *The Portable Nietzsche* (New York: Viking, 1954).

41. This point is related to the famous skeptical argument developed in Saul Kripke, *Wittgenstein on Rules and Private Language* (Cambridge, Mass.: Harvard University Press, 1982). Kripkenstein, however, supposes that even all the evidence available to an *ideal* knower would still underdetermine the content of the rule. McDowell's objection to Kripke, in turn, is that he construes the argument as issuing in a *skeptical* conclusion, rather than showing only that we must conceive of the objectivity of rule-following in non-Platonistic terms (in addition to purging from our account the assumption that all understanding requires *interpretation*). (I also grant, for purposes of the argument in the text, that if the content of the rule is underdetermined then belief in any particular version of the rule is not warranted; but this could be contested.)

42. This argument, it is worth noting, does not involve a commitment to verificationism, as Dworkin has misleadingly maintained at various places in his work (e.g. TRS, 281–282; MP1, 137). One need not believe that any fact must be demonstrable to be real. All one need accept is the principle of "inference to the best explanation." The skeptical argument, then, is that the best explanation for intractable moral disagreement is that there are no objective moral facts.

43. A popular proposal as of late. For versions, see Philip Pettit, "Realism and Response-Dependence," *Mind* 100 (1991): 587–626; Pettit, "Embracing Objectivity in Ethics" [this volume]; Michael Smith, *The Moral Problem* (Oxford: Blackwell, 1994); and Mark Johnston, "Dispositional Theories of Value," *Proceedings of the Aristotelian Society,* supp. vol. 63 (1989): 139–174. For a critique of the notion that moral facts are response-dependent facts, see Crispin Wright, *Truth and Objectivity* (Cambridge, Mass.: Harvard University Press, 1992).

44. McDowell would presumably contest the label "Non-Naturalist," since much of his recent work has tried to recapture a different meaning for "naturalism," one which would include his own view. Roughly, his idea seems to be that it is "natural" in some (loosely Aristotelian) sense for human beings to develop certain responsive capacities (e.g., to right and wrong, etc.), and thus there is no special problem (from the standpoint of a naturalistic worldview) about the epistemic or ontological status of the facts whose existence depends on these responsive capacities. See esp. *Mind and World,* pp. 77–86; John McDowell, "Two Sorts of Naturalism," in R. Hursthouse et al. (eds.), *Virtues and Reasons: Philippa Foot and Moral Theory* (Oxford: Clarendon Press, 1995). (For penetrating criticism of this account, see Crispin Wright's review, "Human Nature?" *European Journal of Philosophy* 5 (1996): 235–254.) McDowell, though, is certainly a Non-Naturalist in my sense, i.e., someone who rejects the Naturalistic Conception of objectivity.

45. This point echoes a familiar complaint about emotivism, first broached by Richard Brandt in "The Emotive Theory of Ethics," *Philosophical Review* 59 (1950): 305–318.

46. I confess that this would be a somewhat strange complaint for Dworkin to make, since for external skepticism to be "relevant" would be for it to be nonneutral, which, as we've seen, Dworkin claims it must not be.

47. I hedge here because of the case of mathematics, a paradigmatic objective domain. At least parts of mathematics – those parts that are indispensable to scientific practice – can, in theory, have their objectivity vindicated in conventionally naturalistic terms; but other parts of mathematics present a more difficult case. There are several possible lines of response: (1) we might suppose that the objectivity of math (and, say, logic) is simply conventional, so that math is not, appearances to the contrary, robustly objective in the way the objects studied by the natural sciences are; (2) we might think there is some Humean story to be told about why creatures like us experience the compulsion of the mathematical and logical "must" or "ought" ("2 + 2 *must* elicit the response 4") – indeed, such a story might be conjoined with a version of the conventionalism suggested under (1); (3) finally, we might concede that math and logic are objective, even though this objectivity cannot be explained naturalistically, but question whether the features that warrant our confidence in their objectivity (the cross-cultural, and often timeless, quality of mathematical and logical truths) really give us reason to think that morality will also turn out to be objective in some Non-Naturalistic way. (I am grateful to Ed Stein and Jules Coleman for help in thinking about this question.)

48. By "noncognitivism," I mean a view about the *semantics* of moral discourse to the effect that the meaning of moral language is its role in *expressing* certain noncognitive attitudes. Universal prescriptivists (Hare), normexpressivists (Gibbard), crude emotivists (Ayer), and sophisticated emotivists (Stevenson) all differ about the attitudes expressed but agree about the basic semantic thesis. They also agree with the skeptical ontological thesis that there are no moral facts. Mackie accepts this latter thesis but rejects the semantic one: he construes moral language as *cognitive* – i.e., as apt for evaluation in terms of its truth and falsity – but, given his ontology, thinks all moral statements are false. Mackie's error theory has the drawback of making it puzzling why anyone should engage in moral discourse: what could be the point of a putatively fact-stating discourse that states no facts? Noncognitivists are moved by the same ontological considerations to try to find a way to preserve the point of moral discourse by proposing a revisionary semantics.

49. Thanks to C. J. Summers for pressing this line of response.

50. I owe this challenge to Rob Koons, who put it in slightly more colorful terms.

51. The same should be said about, e.g., the taste of wines. To the extent that there actually are objective reasons concerning the quality of wines, this too is surely because there is an underlying naturalistic story to be told about the microconstitution of wines, and their physico-chemical interaction with the human sensory apparatus. Of course, this would have to be argued on a case-by-case basis. Often it may turn out that questions of taste that purport to be part of domains in which reasons prevail are really better explicable in debunking sociological terms. See, e.g., Pierre Bourdieu, *Distinction: A Social Critique of the Judgment of Taste,* trans. R. Nice (Cambridge, Mass.: Harvard University Press, 1984).

52. At one point, Dworkin does make the following rather striking (Nietzschean!) claim: "No matter what we learn about the physical or mental world, it must remain an open question, and one that calls for a moral rather than any other kind of judgment, how we ought to respond" (OT, 127). This way of putting the point, however, simply conflates *moral* value with all other kinds of value (including, especially, *epistemic* value). No one need disagree that *norms* figure in all judgments, including judgments about uncontroversially *factual* matters. But I take Dworkin's potentially interesting thesis – to which most of his work on this question is devoted – to be that *moral* norms are always implicated in moral skepticism. This is the claim Dworkin argues for and which I have been arguing against.

53. C. C. W. Taylor, "Politics," in J. Barnes (ed.), *The Cambridge Companion to Aristotle* (Cambridge: Cambridge University Press, 1995), p. 255. It is true, of course, that some people – e.g., those suffering certain forms of mental retardation – lack the ability to deliberate, and it is also true that we know some normal adults who tend to act on impulse and instinct and so seem to be poor deliberators. But these are *not* the special situations Aristotle has in mind. Moreover, the empirical claims are embedded in a larger claim: to wit, that the "natural slaves" are better off being slaves, under the direction of masters. Yet this is far from being obvious, to put the matter gently.

54. Although Nietzsche makes ambiguous remarks about slavery, I don't actually think there is any support for thinking he had a political program that required the institution of slavery. Nietzsche, in my view, is an "esoteric" moralist, addressing his remarks to select individuals who suffer from the "false consciousness" of thinking that the dominant morality is really *good for them*. For more on these issues, see my "Morality in the

Pejorative Sense: On the Logic of Nietzsche's Critique of Morality," *British Journal for the History of Philosophy* 3 (1995): 113–145, and my "Nietzsche and the Morality Critics," *Ethics* 107 (1997): 250–285.

55. Friedrich Nietzsche, *Beyond Good and Evil,* ed. & trans. W. Kaufmann (New York: Vintage, 1966), Section 257.

56. See, e.g., Samuel Scheffler, "Agent-Centered Restrictions, Rationality, and the Virtues," *Mind* 94 (1985): 409–419.

57. Skepticism about *moral* value need not go hand-in-hand with skepticism about all kinds of value: it depends on the sorts of arguments being advanced for skepticism. In the case of the moral skepticism at issue here, it is motivated precisely by accepting first certain *epistemic* values for essentially pragmatic reasons, as discussed earlier.

58. Do all forms of intuitionism require repentance? Perhaps not. The type one finds in Aristotle and Sidgwick, for example, does not seem to depend on the now discredited perceptual metaphors, that Dworkin invokes here. I do not venture an opinion on this large and difficult question.

59. See P. F. Strawson, "Ethical Intuitionism," *Philosophy* 24 (1949): 23–33.

3

Objectivity Fit for Law

GERALD J. POSTEMA

Tomatoes, plump and fresh from the vine, are wonderful. I love them! Linda won't touch them. And when our neighbor, Mr. Pickett, proudly presents her with a dozen of his best, she admires them, thanks him graciously, and promptly hands them to me. Mr. Pickett also collects glass bottles; he'll talk enthusiastically about them to anyone who will listen, but he rarely has an audience. I confess, I could never see much point in the hobby.

Kevin is absolutely smitten with Meredith, even though none of us can understand what he sees in her.

Seinfeld's Kramer is really funny, and Linda agrees, although she never laughs quite as hard as I do when we watch him. I once played a trick on my mother, and my friends and I laughed very hard. When my father heard about it, he said it was just not funny and made me apologize to her.

Shannon Miller got a score of 9.89 on her balance beam routine in the recent Olympic games. Alicia and I were watching basketball. I thought the replay showed that it wasn't a charging foul, but Alicia said it clearly was. We agreed that it wouldn't have made a difference to the outcome, since UNC was far ahead.

I told Linda that I just heard thunder, but she said no, it was only an airplane going over. New evidence shows that significant reductions of iron in the blood of American males can reduce their likelihood of suffering a heart attack by up to 50 percent. Depletion of ozone in the atmosphere has significantly contributed to global warming.

Jackie Joyner-Kersey earned the bronze for the long jump with a final jump of 16 ft. 11 3/4 in. Yesterday, the stonemason called and said that he must have made a mistake the first time he measured the marble, because it is only 54 in. long and so it's not long enough for the countertop.

Food, hobbies, love, humor, sports, perception, medicine, science, measurement – we make assertions and express our views in lots of different contexts and others of us accept or reject or qualify them. On the basis of these views we make decisions and act in ways that materially affect our lives and the lives of others. In some of these contexts we are content to give de gustibus free rein. Our differences don't lead us to think that one of us has made a mistake. Sometimes this leads to frustration or conflict, as when I want to go out for Greek food and Linda wants Thai. Still, we often regard the freedom manifest in this state of affairs to be a good thing. We even celebrate it. However, in other contexts our differences look more like disagreements, and it makes sense (however impolite it may be) to say the other party has made a mistake. We do not expect objectivity everywhere, but sometimes we demand it or at least hope for it, and regard the demand, if not the hope, as reasonable.

Moreover, reflection on the above examples suggests that the kind of objectivity we expect – or perhaps better, the standards of objectivity we apply – can vary across domains of discourse. There is a prevalent tendency, especially in debates over the objectivity of normative and evaluative judgments, to treat science as the measure of all objectivity. Yet, we may have second thoughts once we cast our gaze intently over the whole range of contexts in which it seems to make sense to expect objectivity of our judgments.

Objective judgments are independent, constrained judgments and in that independence we find warrant for the hope that others will affirm them as well. Since subject matter and modes of inquiry vary across domains, it is reasonable to expect the kind of independence called for to differ somewhat.[1] In view of the nature of the discourse and aims of inquiries pursued in it, the demand for independence may be articulated in different ways. We might expect such differences especially to appear between domains of practical reasoning like morality and law, on the one hand, and domains of theoretical reasoning like natural science, on the other. The latter seek to describe causal relations in a world existing apart from our beliefs about it, whereas the former seek to articulate reasons for action independent of, for example, self-interest or immediate inclinations. It is prima facie reasonable to suppose that the nature of the constraints of objectivity in a given domain will depend on its nature or the subject matter of that domain and on the reasons why objectivity is important in it.

The thesis orienting my exploration of objectivity of legal judgments in this chapter is that objectivity is moderately domain-specific. I postpone further defense of this assumption to the concluding section of this chapter, but I shall briefly clarify the thesis here. A radical domain-specificity thesis holds that for every domain of discourse there is a conception of objectivity tailored to it and valid for it. This thesis empties the notion of objectivity of all significance. Some domains do not claim objectivity for themselves and others may have no right to claim it. There must be some criteria for judging proposed claims of and standards for objectivity in a given domain. If anything goes, objectivity goes. In this chapter I assume *moderate* domain-specificity. According to the moderate thesis, there is no single dominant notion or standard of objectivity that holds for all areas of thought, judgment, and discourse. It also assumes that while it is possible for specific conceptions of objectivity to differ, they share certain generic, structuring features. My project in this chapter is to articulate and defend the conception of objectivity that I believe is at work in the domain of law – objectivity fit for law.

Although the term "objectivity" has a garden variety use (or uses), its roots are sunk deep in a long tradition of philosophical reflection, and philosophers are more than a little inclined to take a proprietary interest in its explication. In view of the (moderate) domain-specific character of objectivity, however, we ignore the practical context of the legal objectivity debate at the price of irrelevance. So, before I set out to defend a conception of objectivity fit for law, I must locate my philosophical discussion in this context.

I. Rhetoric, Reaction, and Reality

Law claims legitimacy for itself. It claims the allegiance of all citizens, even conscientious citizens who disagree with it and judge it to be mistaken or misdirected. It rests this claim, in part, on the objectivity of characteristic modes of reasoning and the normative judgments they produce. Yet the claim of legal – or, more precisely, adjudicative – reasoning to objectivity is currently under heavy attack.[2] There is nothing new in this, of course. In the Anglophone jurisprudential tradition, the main themes of this attack were sounded loudly already in Bentham's early critique of eighteenth-century common law practice and possibly earlier.[3] It would not surprise me if a similar lineage could be traced in other major jurisprudential traditions as well. However, in recent years the critique has acquired a radical edge not immediately evident in earlier versions. The notion of objectivity itself is under attack, not just law's title to wrap itself in the mantle of objectivity. Not only is the law parading under false pretenses, it is argued; the pretended status is itself incoherent and pernicious.

1.

Recent critics of objectivity in American legal theory have been remarkably sensitive to the rhetoric and pragmatics of the language of objectivity – to what is done in and through claiming objectivity for one's reasoning, judgment, or decision. The language of objectivity is a mask for class, race, or gender power, they argue.[4] It speaks coercively for everyone,[5] stopping dissent in its argumentative tracks.

[T]he search has been for an approach to the real on which to base arguments and conclusions that will make one's point of view unquestionable and unanswerable, immortal and definitive to the last word, regardless of time, place, or person. Its thrust has been to end diversity of viewpoint, so that there can be no valid disagreement over what knowing is right knowing. . . . Objectivity has been its answer, its standard, its holy grail. When it speaks and there is silence, it imagines it has found it.[6]

This is surely a caricature. It turns the notion of objectivity on its head. Objectivity is never achieved for a judgment in the act of *claiming* it, no matter how loudly, or forcefully, and no matter what its source. Yet, there is no doubt that the caricature fits – it fits not the notion of objectivity itself, but its frequent use in contexts where serious matters are contested.

Like Proudhon who declared that property is theft, objectivity critics call attention to hypocrisy in the pious rhetoric of the day. Patricia Williams, for example, says that "so much of what is spoken in so-called objective, unmediated voices is in fact mired in hidden subjectivities and unexamined claims."[7] And Kimberley Crenshaw maintains that "the authoritative universal [objective] voice" is too often just "white male subjectivity masquerading as non-racial, non-gendered objectivity."[8] MacKinnon, again, puts the point most vividly: The male point of view, she maintains,

is the standard for point-of-viewlessness, its particularity the meaning of universality. When [the state] is most ruthlessly neutral, it is most male; when it is most sex blind, it is most blind to the sex of the standard being applied. When it most closely conforms to precedent, to "facts," to legislative intent, it most closely enforces socially male norms and most thoroughly precludes questioning their content as having a point of view at all.[9]

This form of argument, or rather the form of social and legal criticism implicit in these comments, has been used to great effect especially in feminist literature.[10] Critics focus on a practice, rule, or norm that is alleged to be objective (or "neutral") and find implicit in that claim a commitment to a deeper standard. They then show that the practice, rule, or norm fails when judged by that implicit standard. Thus, for example, rules defined in terms that make no explicit reference to gender may still express deep gender bias if they take circumstances determined historically by the needs or interests of men as normal circumstances against which deviations are measured. Hence, subjectivity masquerades as objectivity, and the particular limitations of a private individual or class perspective are represented as transcendence of all limitations, as objective "point-of-viewlessness" itself.

This is a valuable form of criticism, but it is easy to overstate its implications. There are at least two ways to understand the force of this kind of argument. The more radical is to see it as a kind of *reductio ad absurdum,* an internal critique that displays the incoherence of the very notion of objectivity (or the incoherence of striving for objectivity). Alternatively, one can see it as calling attention to a deeper standard of objectivity in view of which alone the surface standard could plausibly claim our allegiance, and then showing how that deeper standard is, in fact, violated in the cases under consideration. This would amount to a reduction to *hypocrisy,* not absurdity.

Viewed in the latter way, the argument understands the claim of objectivity to be open to critical assessment, and it holds that claim up to the harsh light of experience. Of course, in doing so, the critic must often reinterpret that principle, give it new persuasive meaning. The critique may be contentious, not just because established interests are at stake, but also because what is proposed is in fact a new conception, a new understanding of objectivity. This is a valuable form of criticism and its use is often defensible and devastating to comfortable illusions. Some critics, however, press the criticism further and insist on the more radical reading. The only appropriate response to the internal conflict between explicit and implicit standard, they argue, is to reject objectivity entirely. Apparently in this spirit, MacKinnon concludes, "Disaffected from objectivity, having been its prey, but excluded from its world through relegation to subjective inwardness, women's interest lies in overthrowing *the distinction itself.*"[11]

2.

Members of the Critical Legal Studies movement also sometimes draw this radical conclusion from their familiar "indeterminacy critique" of liberal jurisprudence. In outline, the argument goes as follows.[12] Liberalism makes objectivity of adjudicative reasoning an essential condition of legal and political legitimacy.[13] For this purpose, the objectivity of judicial decision making must not only be free of arbitrary whim and personal idiosyncrasy, but must also be manifestly "nonideological." That is, extralegal political principles or judgments that are broadly in contention in the society at large must not influence adjudication. They argue that for purposes of objectivity-secured legitimacy it is not enough to show that judges are constrained by craft and profession to avoid enacting strictly personal moral views into the law of the land. The problem is that the strictures of craft and profession themselves embody the very political forces in contention in society at large. Objectivity requires that adjudication is demonstrably above politics, but that is not possible because of the indeterminacy of legal rules and norms. The indeterminacy to which Critics point is not causal; their claim is not that it is not possible reliably to *predict* the decisions of judges. The indeterminacy, rather, is rational: the legal materials with which judges must work do not entail a single outcome or decisively point deliberation in a single direction for decision.[14] For any truly contested, and so politically sensitive case (that is, any case in which the question of the objectivity and legitimacy of adjudication is in the foreground), nearly any outcome can be defended publicly as derived from, or consistent with, the law. And this indeterminacy immediately undermines the claim of adjudicative reasoning to objectivity. Objectivity is an empty promise, since indeterminacy leaves the door wide open for just the external, political influences that objectivity promised to exclude. In the face of law's ineradicable indeterminacy, objectivity is a sham.

Now this argument rests on a mistake that several critics have pointed out, most notably, perhaps, Ronald Dworkin.[15] The kind of indeterminacy of legal reasoning to which Critics point, namely, "epistemic indeterminacy"[16] — widespread disagreement amongst lawyers about the implications of legal materials for a given contested case — does not imply that the law is rationally indeterminate. Lawyers may be *uncertain,* either as individuals or as a group, about what the law actually implies, but uncertainty is not indeterminacy. So, the argument rests on an illegitimate inference. This criticism is narrowly correct, but ultimately offers no challenge to the Critics' attack on objectivity. For their argument does not depend ultimately on the premise about the rational indeterminacy of law. It only needs the weaker premise of epistemic indeterminacy. The Critics only need to show that in such cases the legal materials demonstrably dictate no single outcome or decision.[17] For objectivity, as they have construed it, calls for *manifest, demonstrable* lack of influence of politics and the weaker, epistemic indeterminacy is all they need for that. Thus, criticisms of the indeterminacy critique that stress the difference between rational indeterminacy and uncertainty or evident disagreement among competent professionals fail to challenge fundamentally the indeterminacy critique.

However, the upshot of the indeterminacy critique, like that of the earlier feminist critique, is ambiguous. Does it challenge the accepted notion of objectivity in the name of, or making way for, a deeper, more appropriate conception, or does it represent a challenge to the very notion of objectivity? Critics, I suspect, disagree, but the radical, rejectionist conclusion is familiar enough. Joseph Singer, for example, maintains that since "legal reasoning is internally contradictory and therefore indeterminate, there are no objective limits on what judges or other governmental officials can do. The goal of constraining government or regulating interpersonal conduct by previously knowable general rules seems impossible."[18]

Paradoxically, however, this radical reading can actually produce a quietist effect. After all, if objectivity is not worth striving for, it is no great loss if judges fail to achieve it or even fail to pretend to strive for it. Would we not be better without it? What then of law's legitimacy? Should we be glad to give it up, too? Some might say yes, because law's pretense to legitimacy would thereby be exposed. Of course, it is not clear what we should say, and more importantly what we should do, once we accept this thought. Others, however, are inclined to think that law's legitimacy is thereby more firmly established, because its claim on our allegiance is more honest (if also more "contingent" and "political"), and we get more contextually sensitive adjudicative reasoning in the bargain.

The issues raised in the critiques of objectivity from these different quarters are many and complex, but two are at the center: the coherence of the notion of objectivity for adjudicative reasoning, and the relationship between objectivity and law's legitimacy. I shall argue that the discontent with the notion of objectivity in this context is due to an inadequate understanding of objectivity. I shall not undertake to defend the objectivity of legal reasoning, because I believe that is still an open question. I will, however, defend a conception of objectivity that is coherent, plausible, and appropriate for law. I will try to show that practical objectivity conceived in this way defines a standard to which it is worth holding our officials and ourselves.

II. Structuring Ideas of the Concept of Objectivity

Earlier I called attention to the fact that we demand objectivity in some domains of experience and discourse but not in others; and even where we demand it, our demands may be tailored to some degree to the domain. Subject matters and modes of inquiry vary across domains. So, it is reasonable to expect that the kind of constraints that objectivity imposes in a given domain will depend on the nature or subject matter of that domain and on the reasons why objectivity is important in it. Of course, certain structuring features of the concept of objectivity are common to all the domains in which it is in demand, yet we can expect to find variations in conceptions of objectivity across domains. That is, objectivity is moderately domain-specific.[19]

My project, as I have said, is to defend a conception of objectivity fit for law, for the domain of legal discourse. The concept of objectivity sets the agenda for this domain-specific project. So, I will proceed from the general to the specific, considering, first, structuring features of objectivity, and our reasons for thinking it matters, which appear to be common to all domains where it is in demand. Then I will refine the notion of objectivity to fit the special tasks of adjudicative reasoning.

1.

In its typical modern use, the distinction marked by the terms "subjective" and "objective" is defined relative to a thinking, perceiving, knowing, or judging subject and the object of thought, perception, or judgment. I will focus our attention primarily on the objectivity of claims, assertions, and assessments, all of which I will lump under the term *judgments*.[20]

Ordinarily, to say that a judgment is objective is to say that the person making the judgment is open in an appropriate way to the subject matter of the judgment.[21] It is to say something about the relationship between the judging subject, the judgment, and its subject matter, and, in view of that relationship, to vouch for the credibility, if not necessarily the truth, of the judgment. It is also to hold it eligible for certain kinds of assessment and criticism. We can isolate three structuring features of this generic concept of objectivity.

First, *independence*. If a judgment is objective, its claim on our regard transcends the subjectivity of the judging subject. She is properly open to the subject matter and bases her judgment on it and not on factors peculiar to her. This is to say, at minimum, that the judgment is not the product of improper factors; but also, typically, it is to suggest that it is the product of proper factors. Both negative and positive determinations are important, for as Arthur Ripstein reminds us, "some influences make us . . . better judges, while others make us worse, and the total absence of influences would leave us as no judges at all."[22] In virtue of this independence, the judgment may not be dismissed as merely the expression of the arbitrary, idiosyncratic whim of the subject. The claim of objectivity opens a welcome gap between the subject's attitude or experience and her expression of them, on the one hand, and some more ideal version of them on the other.

This feature of the concept of objectivity poses, but does not itself answer, two critical questions. First, we must ask, *from what* is independence sought? Which features of the judging subject's circumstances or subjectivity are inappropriate influences on her judgment, and which are appropriate? Any adequate conception of objectivity for a given domain of discourse must supply a defensible answer to this question. We can expect that answer to be determined in large part by the nature of that domain and its subject matter and not by the concept of objectivity in general.[23] Of course, we may find features common to different domains, but we should not be surprised to find significant variations as well. This is one important reason why we should be especially wary about borrowing conceptions that are appropriate to one domain for use in another without careful attention to the distinctive features of the domains and our reasons for demanding objectivity in them.

Second, we must ask what exactly is the *nature* of this independence? What makes it possible – that is, intelligible or plausible – for us to claim such independence for a judgment? To answer this question we can take one of two fundamentally different approaches. One focuses on the *subject matter* of the judgment, or of the discourse of which it is a part, and defines independence in terms of the nature or status of the objects of that discourse. On this view, judgments are objective in virtue of the fact that the entities or facts they are about exist independently of our judgments of them. Judgments are objective just when the facts to which the judgment refers are objective. Let's call this the "semantic" approach.[24] The alternative approach focuses on the judging *subject*. It proposes to understand independence in terms of characteristics of the judging process, features of the point of view from which it is made, or constraints on the process by which it is reached. Let's call this the "methodological" approach. In distinguishing these two approaches I do not mean to suggest that conceptions that adopt one of them have nothing to say about the matters on which the other focuses. Typically, they will address both of them, but with different emphases and in different orders of priority.

It is especially important to keep in mind that the choice between them is not to be made at the transdomain level. It is not settled by appeal to the generic concept of objectivity, but rather, again, by appeal to specific features of the domains that demand objectivity. They represent two different interpretations (or interpretation schemata) of the basic idea of independence at the core of the concept of objectivity, two different models for the development of domain-specific conceptions. The eligibility or appropriateness of one or the other of these interpretations depends on the nature of the domain of discourse for which the conception is being developed. It is tempting to think that we should be able to decide the question of which approach to adopt on the basis of general metaphysical considerations, but I think this would be a mistake for two reasons. First, our reflections on the metaphysical status of the objects of any given domain of discourse must be based solely on the best overall understanding of the domain, its nature, structure, subject matter, and modes of inquiry. Thus, metaphysics comes into play only after we have done the work of characterizing and defining independence, and hence objectivity, for the domain. Second, metaphysics itself is a domain of discourse. While it looks to other domains to provide it with its subject matter, we cannot assume that the concerns of metaphysical theory are the same as the concerns of those other domains. Until we look more closely at those other domains, we cannot assume that the conception of objectivity with which metaphysics concerns itself is the same as that fit for some other domain. This is not to say that "metaphysical objectivity" is never relevant to our understanding of objectivity in other domains, but just that it is relevant only upon invitation.[25]

2.

The second structuring feature of the concept of objectivity is that objectivity makes room for assessments of the *correctness* or *validity* of judgments. The independence secured by objectivity must secure the basis for a distinction between something's *seeming* to be so (someone's *thinking, believing, taking* it to be so) and its *being so*. So the independence must open a gap between the judgment and one's acceptance of it. Correctness or validity of a judgment implies that it is *worthy* of acceptance or endorsement. Thus, to say that a judgment is objective is to say that there are standards by which the judgment can be assessed, that these standards are not met merely by the fact that one believes or holds that they are, and that the judgment meets them. (This must be true on either the "semantic" or the "methodological" interpretation of independence.)

This has three important implications or corollaries. First, it must be possible to fund a notion of *mistake,* to maintain intelligibly that the judgment is mistaken. Second, judgments are located in a framework of reasons. They are seen as conclusions that can be reached on the basis of reasons or evidence, after reflection and discussion.[26] Hence, third, where judgments are objective both *disagreement* and *agreement* are intelligible, and there is some ground for hope of moving from one to the other on the basis of the reasons that support the judgments. Objectivity makes possible, or presupposes, that expressions not only can coordinate or conflict, but also can be in agreement or disagreement, and that this agreement or disagreement can be pursued, articulated, discussed, deliberated about in virtue of genuine joinder of issue on the matter in question. Where objectivity resides it is reasonable to hope that reasoning can move subjects to agreement. By the same token, it is an important mark of objectivity that consideration of reasons for judgments in an objective domain can move subjects from agreement to disagreement. In the absence of objectivity, conflict and opposition are possible, but disagreement is not. Opposition can be mute, but disagreement must be articulate, discursive. It requires thought, reasons, and reasoning. Both agreement and disagreement play crucial roles in objective domains of discourse, although the proper mix of the two is likely to vary across domains.

3.

A third key component of the concept of objectivity – some think it the most important – is *invariance across judging subjects.*[27]

The importance of intersubjective invariance can be seen clearly by considering two cases, one a possibly limiting case of objectivity, the other lying just beyond the limit. In *Objectivity and Position,* Amartya Sen recently urged a distinction between subjectivity and what he called "positional objectivity": "Positional variability does not necessarily provide counterevidence to the objectivity of observational statements. If I say that the moon looks small from where I am, I need not be accused of deep subjectivity – another person seeing the moon from where I am could confirm that observational *fact.*"[28] In "Positional Objectivity" he added:

The subject matter of an objective assessment can well be the way an object appears from a *specified* position of observation. What is observed can vary from position to position, but [if the judgments made from them are to be regarded as objective] different people [must be able to] conduct their respective observations from similar positions and make much the same observations. The position parameters need not, of course, be only locational (or related to any spatial placing), and can include any condition that (1) may influence observation, and (2) can apply parametrically to different persons.[29]

The limit of positional objectivity is the limit of the specificity of the parameters of the position from which such observations are made. We may be inclined to call them "subjective" or relativized judgments, but there is an important difference. Consider Greg Currie's claim that "by relativizing, we may transform a highly non-objective notion into an objective one, though what we get is not always very interesting."[30] His point seems to be close to Sen's, but it is not the same. At least it is not the same if he means to say that we can transform any subjective notion into an objective one by relativizing it. Read in this way, the claim is incorrect for two reasons. First, if we mean by "relativize" making the parameters that define a position more and more specific, thereby increasingly narrowing the definition of the "position," then sooner or later that "position" will be indistinguishable from the peculiar features of the judging subject. When we cross that line, we no longer have a (possibly limiting) case of objectivity, but simply a case of subjectivity. Second, of course, we can even regard subjective judgments as expressive of a fact of the subject's experience. This fact can be regarded as *objective*. But note, what is objective is the fact of the subject having this experience, not the judgment issuing from it. The judgment is not objective, precisely because the experience is, by hypothesis, not available to and so not confirmable by other subjects. Sen writes, "An observation may be inevitably position-dependent, but it would lack something in credibility if others viewing the object from the same parametric position could not see what this subject sees. The demands of objectivity . . . have to go beyond relying entirely on personally peculiar observations that others cannot reproduce even when they share the same position."[31] What makes positional judgments, even those at the limit, plausible candidates for objectivity is the possibility in principle of other subjects taking up the position and confirming them. Where such intersubjective confirmation (or disconfirmation) of the judgment is ruled out, so too is objectivity.

Like the notion of independence we just considered, the notion of positional objectivity raises some important questions. What are the appropriate position parameters for objective judgments? What is the limit of specificity of such parameters? How wide must the scope of intersubjectivity be – alternatively, how narrow can it be without undermining a judgment's claim to objectivity? Again, like the questions raised by independence, these questions cannot be answered wholesale. They are inevitably dependent on the nature, tasks, and modes of inquiry of particular domains of discourse. The important general point to record here is that it must be possible for other subjects to assess a judgment, and confirm or disconfirm it, if it is to count, even at the limit, as objective in principle. In principle intersubjective confirmation is a mark of objectivity.[32]

Thus, to claim objectivity for a judgment is to claim an authority for it that implicates other subjects as well. It calls on them to assess it according to standards of correctness, to judge it as worthy of endorsement, not only by the original judging subject, but also by them, for the reasons on which the judgment properly depends.

4.

Kant illustrates nicely the core features of the notion of objectivity and the distinctions it employs. Speaking primarily of theoretical reason in a late section of his *Critique of Pure Reason,* he distinguishes between mere "persuasion" and true "conviction," and introduces the test of objectivity to enable us (from our inevitably "subjective" point of view) to distinguish them. Truth in the theoretical realm, he argues, "depends upon agreement [of the judgment] with the object." However, "[t]he holding of a thing to be true is an occurrence in our understanding which, though it may rest on objective grounds, also requires subjective causes in the mind of the individual who makes the judgment. . . . So long, therefore, as the subject views the judgment merely as an appearance of his mind, persuasion cannot be subjectively distinguished from conviction." Of course, we cannot escape our "subjective" conditions to verify the agreement of the judgment and its object, but we can establish its objectivity and hence distinguish persuasion from mere conviction. For, since (according to Kant) truth depends on agreement with the object, and not on conditions peculiar to any particular subject, the judgment of each subject must be in agreement with each other.

The touchstone whereby we decide whether our holding a thing to be true is conviction or mere persuasion is therefore external, namely, the possibility of communicating it and of finding it to be valid for all human reason. . . . The experiment . . . whereby we test upon the understanding of others whether those grounds of the judgment which are valid for us have the same effect on the reason of others as our own, is a means . . . of detecting any merely private validity in the judgment.

Thus, "If the judgment is valid for everyone, provided only he is in possession of reason, its ground is objectively sufficient, and the holding of it to be true is entitled conviction."[33]

Kant understands objectivity of judgments as intersubjective validity demonstrated by the agreement of all those possessed of reason. He distinguishes objectivity from truth. Objectivity is not a *guarantee* of truth, on his view, it is the "touchstone" whereby we assure ourselves, from where we are, that our sense of the truth of judgments we accept is not idiosyncratic, but has validity independent of our acceptance of them. We are assured that the reasons we take as sufficient grounds for the judgments are indeed sufficient. Intersubjective validity – "the possibility of communicating [the judgment] and of finding it valid for all human reason" – is probative of truth, but constitutive of objectivity.

Kant, of course, sharply distinguishes practical from theoretical reason. For practical reason, the notion of the truth or correctness of a judgment is different, according to Kant, because in this realm the notion of agreement of judgment with its object is not appropriate. This is not, however, because of the *metaphysical* nature or status of moral entities (values, norms), but because of the centrality of autonomy in morality, as Kant understood it. Autonomy, for Kant, requires that there exist no order of moral objects given prior to and determining moral first principles. In view of the nature of moral agents (as rational, free, and equal agents), and the categorical demands of morality, moral obligations and the right can only be understood as grounded in rational, *self-legislated* norms.[34] Despite these differences, however, the notion of objectivity at work in Kant's account of practical reason remains essentially the same as that described in the passages from the *Critique of Pure Reason* quoted above. Moral judgments or norms are objective if they are rationally inescapable, and they are rationally inescapable if they meet the tests supplied by practical reason itself, namely, necessity and universality. Objectivity, again, is measured by the possibility of intersubjective validity.

Kant, it appears, articulates for both theoretical and practical reason a methodological account of objectivity. On this account we can infer the objectivity (i.e., the independence) of the matters judged of from the fact of intersubjective validity. This would not satisfy partisans of the semantic approach, of course. They insist that this independence is not sufficient for objectivity. Kant's intersubjective validity can only assure us that idiosyncratic features of judges do not bias the judgments in question. It does not show that the matters judged of are independent of judges or judging per se. Thus, semantic objectivity accounts do not reject the above three conditions, but they regard them as insufficient and derivative from a more fundamental concept of objectivity.[35]

5.

I conclude this brief survey of core features of the concept of objectivity with several related comments. First, we need to recognize an important, but often ignored, distinction between two ways of looking at a judgment when saying of it that it is objective. We may mean to say that a certain *type* of judgment, of which the judgment in question is an instance, is objective, or we may mean that this particular judgment regarded in itself is objective. For ease of reference, let's call the former "type objectivity" and the latter "token objectivity." Take, for example, the judgment "James is not the father of Baby Doe." This judgment is type objective because (or insofar as) its truth can be established by objective procedures. There is evidence that could objectively settle the matter of whether or not James is Baby Doe's father. The judgment would be token objective if it were made on the basis of such evidence after reliable tests for paternity were performed and evaluated.

In both cases, we assess the judgment in question, but if we have type objectivity in mind, that judgment's objectivity is derivative, because it is borrowed from the objectivity of the type – usually, the domain of discourse – to which it belongs. *Type objectivity* treats the particular judgment as objective in virtue of the objectivity of the system, or domain of discourse of which it is a part, or the mode of inquiry that has produced it (or, in some cases, could or might produce it). Objectivity of this sort is an *eligibility* notion. To claim that a judgment is *type objective* is to claim that it is assessable by standards relevant to the domain of discourse in view. *Token objectivity* is a *success* notion and expresses a direct, conclusory assessment of the judgment. If one has this notion in mind, one claims not only that the judgment is eligible for member-ship in the system, but that it actually meets its standards, at least minimally.

Second, it follows from our discussion of the structuring features of objec-tivity that neither a claim of type objectivity nor a claim of token objectivity is properly regarded as an "argument stopper." On the contrary, to claim objec-tivity of either sort is in effect to issue an *invitation* to reasoned argument. For to claim objectivity for a judgment is to locate it relative to standards of assessment and to invite rehearsal of reasons regarding both the judgment itself and the standards by which its correctness is assessed.[36]

Moreover, neither claim implies that the judgment is correct or true or fully justified. Correctness and objectivity, as we have already seen, are closely related concepts, but they are logically distinct. One can make an incorrect objective judgment and one's judgment can be correct, while failing standards of objectivity relevant to the domain to which it belongs. This is an entirely general point about the notion of objectivity, but, as we shall see, it is espe-cially important where, as in law's domain, there is hope that the objectivity of a judgment can secure its legitimacy in the face of deep disagreement over its truth or correctness.[37]

Finally, the objectivity of a judgment can provide one with a reason to accept or endorse that judgment, but it does not provide a reason *for the judgment itself*. The judgment's objectivity is not one of the reasons on which the truth or correctness of the judgment depends. If we are debating some contested thesis, we may reject certain considerations offered on behalf of it because they are biased or purely subjective, and we will be forced to take seriously in our deliberations and discussion those with a genuine claim to objectivity. But we cannot weigh the objectivity of the thesis on one side of that debate. It is not one of the reasons supporting the thesis, and a fortiori not the clinching reason.

Deflationists regarding objectivity have made a lot of this conceptual fea-ture of objectivity. But it is possible to take the point too far. It is a mistake to say that to claim objectivity of a judgment is not to say anything of substance about the judgment at all, and so it can never give one any reason to accept it. On the deflationist view, to say a judgment is objective, is merely to give a certain emphatic boost to the judgment, express one's conviction regarding it with a special ardor. This is correct to the extent that it reflects the fact that a judgment's objectivity is not one of the reasons for its truth or correctness. However, a warranted assessment of objectivity is not rationally or epistemo-logically inert either. If the (token) objectivity claim is itself warranted, then the activity of contending over the correctness of the judgment with rational arguments has a point. Moreover, we have some reason for confidence in the judgment, and in some cases we have some reason to accept and act on the judgment. In this respect, objectivity seems to operate epistemologically like theoretical (as opposed to practical) authority, in that it can provide a kind of second-order rational support for judgments. Like theoretical authority, the reason is indirectly related to the reasons there are for the judgment. Just how they are related is best answered by asking the next question on our agenda: why do we demand objectivity in those domains where we do?

III. Why Objectivity?

1.

We do not demand objectivity in all areas of life and experience, and we do not always find its absence something to be regretted. Why, then, do we demand it in some domains and why do we think that compromising or jeopardizing it in these domains is regrettable?

It is possible to give a satisfying albeit general answer to this question, an answer that is true at this very general level concerning all domains that demand objectivity. This answer, of course, is not sufficient in itself; its value lies in enabling us to focus more sharply the questions why we seek objectivity in this or that domain. In this section I sketch briefly the general answer, and in subsequent sections I look more closely at our reasons for demanding objectivity in law.

Very simply, objectivity is important to us because "it make[s] a difference to the ends, methods, or progress of our forms of inquiry," as Paul Seabright put it.[38] Domains of discourse that aspire to objectivity provide us with modes of inquiry, argument, and judgment, not merely modes of self-expression or communication. We engage in them with others on the shared assumption that we address and participate in a common world. We take it as common knowledge (or at least common belief) that this world is sufficiently stable and invariant across participants to enable us to engage together in intelligible discourse and that our reasoning can be held to standards of good performance. We assume that there is a difference between badly conducted inquiries and well-conducted ones.[39] Objectivity assures us that this assumption is well founded, that the inquiry "is not in some major way misleading or off the rails."[40] Often, such modes of reasoning and inquiry call for large personal and social investments. Objectivity assures us that they are worthy of the investment.

2.

This assurance of the integrity of our modes of reasoning and judgment is especially important in domains of normative discourse. Perhaps some practi-

cal domains do not demand objectivity. We are willing to accept, and sometimes even celebrate, idiosyncrasy in choices and decisions that concern certain areas of private life. Even there, though, we have developed canons of
rationality, relativized to particular agents to be sure, by which we assess the
private decisions and choices of others. Yet, we hold that acknowledging the
rationality of another person's private decisions does not commit us to the same
decision in similar circumstances. Neither does it bind us to respect them as we
would respect proper and reasonable moral decisions. If we are bound not to
interfere with the private decisions of others, it is not out of respect for their
rationality, but out of respect for the autonomy of those who make them.
However, in the domains of morality, politics (by which I mean political
morality), and law, we demand more. We demand something like common
modes of practical reasoning.

When we engage in moral or legal discourse, we assume that there are
common issues between us, that ours is a discourse of judgments, a discourse
that attracts reasoned practical argument. And we assume that our differences
will respond to such argument. We assume that our judgments are vulnerable to
reasoned challenge by appeals to evidence, principles, common experience,
and standards of sound reasoning. We assume, that is, that there is a difference
between better and worse arguments, and that when we engage in better arguments we can reasonably hope to make progress in our inquiry – progress that
involves at the very least narrowing our differences and more often approaching some measure of agreement. At least, we assume that these things are true
often enough for us reasonably to think that there is a point to engaging in the
practice on its own terms (as opposed to pretending to engage in it, or engaging
in it ritualistically for extrinsic reasons). We look to the objectivity of the
product and the process of moral and of legal reasoning to assure us that we are
not broadly deceived in this respect.

We demand objectivity of our moral and our legal discourse for very fundamental practical reasons, reasons that are very general but nevertheless normative in nature. We expect moral and legal norms to guide action and through
this guidance inter alia to coordinate our social interaction. Yet, it is qua norms
(practical judgments, rules, and principles) that we expect morality and law to
accomplish this task – that is, qua reasons addressed to our deliberative faculties. It is important to morality and law as we practice them that their norms
be addressed to us as rational agents capable of grasping their requirements on
our actions and the grounds of their claims to reasonableness, legitimacy, or
authority. These reasons and norms are supposed to guide our actions and help
us anticipate the decisions and actions of our fellows. They also offer us a basis
for vindication of our actions and our claims on each other. That is, we look to
these norms not only for guidance and coordination, but also for justification,
or at least legitimacy. The assurance of the integrity and intersubjective validity
of our modes of practical reasoning provided by objectivity gives point to the

aim of practical normative guidance and legitimacy. This is why we demand objectivity of our moral and legal discourse. It is not merely a welcome side-benefit of objectivity; it is objectivity's raison d'être.

Someone might object at this point that this argument makes the objectivity of morality and law dependent on certain practical, normative concerns. To this charge I boldly plead guilty. What the objector points out is a consequence of the domain-specific character of objectivity. Objectivity for any given domain gets its specific content, the definition of its parameters, from the nature, objectives, and tasks of that domain. It is entirely to be expected, then, that we would look to practical concerns of moral and legal discourse to give shape to conceptions of objectivity fit for each of them.

3.

In the words of Justice Brandeis, we look to law to help us govern ourselves because we want "deliberative forces [to] prevail over the arbitrary" in our society and its government.[41] Objectivity, I argue, assures us of the integrity of the deliberative forces we put in place. In law, objectivity matters because legitimacy matters.[42] Let me fill out the argument of the preceding section focusing more sharply on law.

Law is an institution of political society, and the conditions of its legitimacy are a function of the characteristic needs of political society and the role of law in it. For purposes of this chapter, we can focus our attention on the needs of modern, western, industrial societies and the distinctive tasks of law in them.[43] Modern, western political societies are usually large, territorially bounded social groups and membership in them is for all practical purposes nonvoluntary. Moreover, relations amongst citizens typically are distant, nonintimate, and nearly unidimensional. Common experience, where it exists, is mediated through participation in a wide variety of social, economic, and political institutions and associations. More important for citizens of political societies than the texture of personal relations are the structures of social interaction and mutual dealing, the coordination of the efforts of large social groups, the institutionalized constitution of power, and the modes and limits of its exercise. Also, modern political societies tend to be morally and culturally heterogeneous to a high degree. Modern political societies tend to gather under a single roof a wide array of traditions and moral visions, all competing for space, resources, standing, and especially power. Because of this pluralism, conflict in modern political societies tends to involve not only conflicts of interest, but also deep and pervasive conflict of vision and principle. Political societies must continually work to *create* unity in the face of rival claims, unequal power, and conflicting interests, principles, and moral visions. Finally, political societies are pervasively coercive. Behavior, relationships, arrangements, and institutions are coercively enforced or at least underwritten by coercive institutions. Hence, politics operates in an environment of power and is always concerned, explicitly or implicitly, with a struggle over the exercise of power and over the standards by which this exercise is justified.

In these societies, citizens demand justice of their institutions and social arrangements; yet, they disagree deeply over what justice requires. In view of such disagreement, it may be too much for an individual to demand now that political and social institutions meet his best judgments regarding the requirements of justice. Still, he can reasonably demand that these institutions take justice for their governing aspiration and at least that they meet minimum conditions of legitimacy. I have argued that these conditions are met only through political institutions of deliberative democracy,[44] for only through such institutions can citizens participate in the struggle for common definition of their social arrangements while being held to the aspiration of justice. Key to this process are not only democratic legislative institutions but also a process for periodic open and public assessment and reassessment of the legal norms governing society. Equally important, for legitimacy under the above conditions, is a structure of reasoning in the administration of these norms that preserves and enhances the public deliberative conditions of their adoption and reassessment.

The practice of reasoning and deliberation within the law must meet certain conditions of rationality, reasonableness, and publicity for several reasons. For one, the directives and judgments of officials can hope to earn legitimacy only if they can vindicate their decisions in terms that they can reasonably hope will be recognized as relevant and appropriate by most citizens. Moreover, such reasoning is a means of holding our officials publicly accountable for the decisions and actions they take under color of law. It is also important that the adjudicative process provides a forum for the systematic articulation, exploration, challenge, and defense of the norms by which citizens and their institutions are governed, and so for the articulation and criticism of the arrangements by which they live.

Why, then, do we demand objectivity of legal reasoning? Because we want law to make good on its offer to provide a forum and a language for, and a structured and disciplined practice of, public practical reasoning in conditions of coercive pluralism of modern political societies. The stakes are high. Without a credible claim to objectivity, we could not hope to sustain the legitimacy of law and the modern political society it serves.

IV. Objectivity as Publicity

I have outlined features of the concept of objectivity and I have argued that we have good reasons to demand objectivity of law. These reasons, combined with some sense of the defining features of law and the practice of legal reasoning, will guide our construction of a conception of objectivity fit for law. For reasons that will soon become clear I will call this conception "objectivity as publicity."

1.

Objectivity as publicity is a methodological conception of objectivity. It is defined relative to a particular notion of correct normative judgments. This notion of correctness has an important procedural component built into it. It cannot be separated from the process of deliberative judging.

Broadly speaking, a judgment is correct, on this view, if it is backed by sound reasons that are or can be articulated and assessed publicly. More precisely, a judgment is correct if but only if it is maximally supported by the arguments and the balance of reasons available for articulation and assessment by reasonable and competent persons in a fully public deliberative process. On this view, correctness of judgments is a direct function of the arguments that can be offered publicly in support of them.

Notice two essential features of this conception of correctness. First, correctness is a property of propositions, or rather it is a relation between propositions and arguments or reasons that support them, and this relationship is embodied in the activity of making and assessing arguments offered in support of the proposition. Thus, to say that a proposition is correct is to assess it in terms of standards of argument drawn from the normative discourse in question. Second, the process of offering and assessing arguments for judgments is regarded as essentially interpersonal, public. Correctness is manifested in the process of reasonable persons offering reasons to *each other.*

Let me expand briefly on the first of these two features. This conception of objectivity rests on the observation that normative judgments make claims to correctness and those claims are redeemed deliberatively, that is, by offering the reasons and arguments that support them. To hold that a judgment is correct is to make an *evaluative assessment* of the merits of arguments for the judgment. Thus, claiming that a judgment is correct invites a demonstration of the strengths of the reasons and soundness of the arguments available for it.

It is tempting to dress this point in metaphysical robes. For example, one might think, "To say that the correctness of a judgment is a matter of the best arguments for it, commits us to the view that *there is* a best argument, if there are any correct judgments. And to claim that there is a best argument is to make a metaphysical claim. It commits us to the view that there is a fact of the matter, and *that's what makes it the best argument.* Of this fact we can ask what exactly is its nature? Is it dependent on our minds, for example; that is, is this *fact* objective?" We must resist the temptation to go down this road. I do not reject the kind of metaphysical inquiry suggested here as pointless or unintelligible or intellectually suspect. But I do believe that to dress the notion of correctness at work in everyday normative discourse in this metaphysical uniform makes it into something different from what it is and claims to be. Metaphysical objectivists are mistaken to insist that the notion of correctness here in play must be, or necessarily depends on, a metaphysical one. Correctness, on the view in question, is understood in terms of best (or maximal) arguments; but the claim that a certain set of arguments is "best" relative to a judgment is redeemed by offering further arguments of essentially the same kind. To say there is a conclusive argument for this normative judgment is to make a normative judgment, not an ontological one. Standards for assessing it are normative, not metaphysical.[45]

2.

Objectivity as publicity understands objectivity in terms of this notion of correctness. Objectivity, on this view, defines the standard to which the deliberative process is held. Objectivity of judgments is a function of, or defined in terms of, the objectivity of the deliberative process by which they are (or, by extension, could be) formed and defended. The objectivity of the deliberative process is defined in terms of two standards. (1) Participants in the deliberative process conduct their deliberation only with normatively relevant reasons and arguments in view and assess the merits of the arguments only by normatively relevant standards; and (2) their participation is governed by the overarching aim of achieving reasonable common formation of judgment on the basis of the reasons and arguments publicly offered.[46] These two broad standards define schematically the parameters of objectivity for the discourse in question. That is, they define schematically the parameters of the "position" or "point of view" from which judgments qualifying as objective in this domain are to be formed. This point of view, while in certain respects ideal, is nevertheless one that ordinary reasonable participants in the discourse can occupy. This perspective is defined by certain constraints on the formation of judgments, holding participants to standards of deliberative reasoning governed by a certain discipline.

Let me say a few words about these two standards. They govern, respectively, the materials and the methodological aim of the deliberative process. The first standard holds that the deliberation must focus on normatively relevant evidence, reasons, and arguments, and standards of the merits of them, and not be distracted or materially influenced by factors other than them. The process is objective to the extent that the reasons, evidence, and arguments that are deliberated upon and that bring participants to judgment are the relevant ones. This, of course, leaves the definition of the parameters of objectivity incomplete. It can be completed only with substantive argument from *within* the normative discourse in question. Objectivity is, thus, a normatively substantive matter.[47] The parameters of objectivity are themselves contestable and must be determined by the same deliberative process as all other substantive judgments in the normative domain. Thus, in the case of law, criteria of objectivity are fixed by substantive argument within law regarding the boundaries of its domain. There is, inevitably, an element of circularity here. The only way in which disputes over the relevance of certain kinds of reasons or evidence can be resolved is through accepting for the time being the relevance of other reasons and evidence.

The second standard prescribes the securing of agreement among all participants in the domain as the governing *project* of the deliberative process. Consensus is not the precondition of objective deliberation, on this view, neither is it the regularly anticipated outcome (far from it). It is, rather, its *regulative ideal.* This ideal exerts its influence on the deliberative process and participants in it through the distinctive discipline that it imposes on them. The project is to justify one's judgments *to others,* showing to them that the judgments are reasonable and responsible in terms one sincerely believes all can recognize and affirm. Normative deliberation is regarded as a process of publicly offering public reasons – reasons which are not merely reasons *I personally* find persuasive, nor reasons I believe that *you* would find persuasive (but I could not endorse), but reasons *we share,* or after conversation and argument, we *could come to share.*[48]

This regulative ideal yields a discipline that makes demands on the deliberative process and its participants. The discipline consists of attitudes that participants must adopt when they engage in public deliberation and certain constraints on the manner in which they carry on the deliberation.[49] The most obvious procedural constraint is that (1) discourse in this domain is restricted to deliberative reasoning regarding reasons and arguments that are normatively relevant to the domain. The reasoning may, of course, also involve articulation and assessment of considerations and arguments with an eye to testing their relevance, as well as considerations and arguments bearing on settling the standards of relevance themselves. The main point here is that the discursive process is first of all a reflective reasoning process, and judgments are to be formed on the basis of reasons and arguments articulated and assessed in this process. The aim of this process is not individual (or collective) self-expression or clarification of conviction; neither is it conquest or conversion of other participants. The process is discursive and deliberative, and it goes beyond bargaining and negotiation. Its aim is to uncover, explore, and assess grounds for judgments or norms that all reasonable participants could accept (or at least could not reasonably reject).[50] Other constraints can be seen as corollaries of this primary constraint. Among them we find the following. (2) All reasons uttered publicly must be accessible to and assessable by all participants. (3) Proposals for judgments and norms and arguments for them must be advanced sincerely, as arguments one endorses, or at least as arguments one advances to assess whether they are worthy of one's endorsement. Closely related to this, (4) participants must accept the implications of the norms and judgments they endorse, and the arguments they advance, and are bound to fit them into a reasonably coherent scheme. And (5) all proposals must be regarded as defeasible and open to criticism from other participants.

The attitudes required of participants by the discipline of public practical reason are related directly or indirectly to the general attitude of a willingness to seek mutually satisfactory grounds for common judgments. The discipline, for example, calls for (1) seriousness of purpose – that is, seriousness about the issues at stake and commitment to the public process of deliberation as a means of collectively addressing them. This involves willingness to engage in the process in good faith with the hope that others are also engaging in good faith. It also calls for (2) willingness on the part of each of the participants to reconsider their views and arguments, to admit error where error is reasonably shown; (3) a willingness to avoid premature leaps to judgment or interpretation of proposals or arguments of other participants, or to defensive justification of one's own; and (4) a willingness to stick with the process even when it appears to be faltering or communication has broken down.

Certain constraints are also imposed on the *structure* of the process itself. For example, (1) participation must not be arbitrarily limited and ideally it should extend to all competent members of the relevant community. Similarly, (2) all parties must have fair equality of opportunity to participate in the process. (3) Ideally deliberative reasoning should go on until agreement on the basis of publicly articulated and assessed reasons is reached. However, if premature closure is necessary for practical reasons, closure is permissible, on condition that there are opportunities, resources, and structures for reopening the issue for further deliberation later.

Finally, all features of the discipline and constraints on the structure of the process are subject to a general *reflexivity constraint.* All such conditions are subject to the governing regulative ideal and must be justifiable in public in deliberations governed by that ideal.

3.

Objectivity as publicity puts the notion of consensus, or agreement based on public argument, at the center of the notion of objectivity. Yet, the relationship between objectivity and consensus is very complex. We need to explore some of these complexities before we can assess the suggestion that objectivity as publicity provides us the best understanding of legal objectivity.

First, the notion of agreement on which objectivity as publicity is based is not mere coincidence or convergence of opinions or judgments. Rather it aims at common formation of judgment on the basis of the reasons and arguments on which it rests, explored and assessed in a public deliberative process. Objectivity as publicity sets as its ideal wide intersubjective agreement of judgment *based on* a full and open public articulation and assessment of all relevant reasons and arguments. Let's call this "strong deliberative consensus."

Second, consider the relationship between consensus and correctness, as understood in this conception. We have seen that correctness and objectivity, on this conception, are distinct concepts (as they must be if this account is to be consistent with our earlier discussion of the concept of objectivity). Objectivity is defined in terms of a deliberative process aimed at agreement of judgment based on reasons uttered in that process, and correctness is defined in terms of maximally supportive arguments, arguments that take shape in a public deliberative process. Correctness, however, is not constituted by agreement, even agreement that is the product of the deliberative process operating ideally. Agreement of rational, reasonable, and competent deliberators, resulting from an ideally operated deliberative process, may be our best mark of correctness of the judgments in question; but that agreement does not make the judgment correct. That is not the fact in virtue of which the judgment is correct. In this point, objectivity as publicity fits Kant's view that we considered earlier. Recall, Kant argued that if the judgment is valid for everyone who is in possession of reason, then its ground is objectively sufficient. This is sufficient for objectivity, but not for correctness ("truth" in his discussion). Objectivity, understood as intersubjective validity demonstrated by the agreement of all those possessed of reason, does not *constitute* correctness (indeed, he maintains even more strongly that it does not even *guarantee* it), but it provides the "touchstone" whereby we assure ourselves, from where we are, that our sense of the truth of judgments we accept is not idiosyncratic, but has validity independent of our acceptance of them. We are assured that the reasons we take as sufficient grounds for the judgments are indeed sufficient.

Third, the relationship between consensus and objectivity needs to be clarified and in particular the place of dissensus and disagreement in this conception. I broached the question of the relationship between objectivity and disagreement briefly earlier. It would be helpful to pause for a somewhat closer look now that we have a more richly articulated conception of objectivity in view.

4.

To begin, recall that, on the conception on offer, agreement defines a *regulative ideal*. It does not take actual consensus as a precondition of objective deliberative reasoning, nor does it warrant the expectation that it will be the actual outcome of any piece of deliberative reasoning. This governing aim or project of the deliberative process exerts its influence through imposing a discipline and constraints on participants and process. This leaves room for recognizing not only the possibility of, but also a positive role for, dissensus in a deliberative process that can legitimately claim objectivity. I shall argue for the importance of disagreement in objectivity at two levels, first, as integral to the conception of objectivity as publicity, and, second, as integral to law and the demands of legitimacy on it.

First, consider the place of disagreement and dissensus in objectivity as publicity. The idea integrating dissensus into a conception defined in terms of the regulative ideal of consensus is simple. Structured opportunities for dissent, disagreement, and challenge are in fact functionally necessary if deliberations of ordinary reasonable persons are satisfactorily to approximate this regulative ideal. That is, opportunities for challenge, and so structured arrangements for disagreement and dissent, and a willingness to unsettle and disrupt an existing consensus are essential features of the deliberative process aimed at consensus as a regulative ideal. Recall that objectivity sets as its ideal *strong deliberative consensus* – that is, wide intersubjective agreement of judgment *based on* a full and open public articulation and assessment of all relevant reasons and arguments. This is an exacting standard. Not just any consensus, even if it is deep and stable, automatically meets it. Agreement may be too complacent, too narrow; it may be the product of systematic bias, limited or unequal or inappropriately exclusive participation, or various forms of false consciousness. We who are citizens of pluralistic societies tend to be impressed with the difficulty of achieving agreement on important moral or political matters. But objectivity as publicity is equally keenly aware that consensus can be too easy or brought about by the wrong kind of forces. Consensus can be a sign not of deliberative success but of dysfunction, not of objectivity but of complacent and uncritical acceptance of received views.[51] Objectivity as publicity does not value consensus for its own sake. Consensus that is not the product of the deliberative process, properly governed by the discipline and constraints of publicity, has no intrinsic appeal according to this conception. (By the same token, conflict is not welcomed just for its own sake. Recall, what is important is disagreement, not mere opposition.) Challenge, vigorous dissent, and articulate, dogged disagreement, these are the analogues of tough love in practices and institutions governed by the ideal of strong deliberative consensus. *De moribus,* we might say, *est disputandum.*[52]

Defenders of law's objectivity sometimes blame skepticism with regard to objectivity on the practice of public judicial dissent, especially at the appellate level.[53] Objectivity as publicity holds, on the contrary, that structured opportunities for public disagreement and dissent are essential if a deliberative process is to make a credible claim to (approximate) objectivity. Good faith participation in a public deliberative process approximating the constraints mentioned above is no guarantee that personal or systemic biases will not distort appreciation of relevant reasons and arguments, nor will it necessarily block entirely the influence of inappropriate factors. Salvation, however, lies in the demand of reflexivity and a correlative requirement of alertness on the part of all participants in the deliberative process to the influence of distorting factors and a willingness to entertain challenges from others that may expose the objectivity failures of existing processes or their products. Reflexivity, openness of every aspect of the deliberative practice – from the most mundane to the most abstract, including critical challenges to the standards of relevance of reasons and scope of participation in the deliberative process – is essential to the integrity of the process and its claim to objectivity. But reflexivity is an empty promise unless there are places to stand, models to follow, and resources to draw on to mount challenges. Opportunities, resources, and spaces for challenge of even the most well-settled principles of a domain, fund the hope that the deliberative process is self-correcting.

Second, Dworkin has recently argued that "diversity of opinion in some intellectual domain has skeptical implications . . . only if the best account of the content of that domain explains why it should."[54] By the same token, diversity of opinion may invite no skeptical conclusions if the best account of the domain explains why diversity is important to that domain. Toleration of diversity of opinion is not constant across domains of discourse that demand objectivity of their modes of inquiry. Objectivity is not a direct function of the amount of disagreement a domain tolerates. Practices of measurement and weighing are not "more objective" than the scientific enterprise that makes use of them, even though the former tolerates far less disagreement. Indeed, such cross-domain comparisons of "quantities" of objectivity seem, on reflection, to make little sense. Of course, as we have often remarked, standards of objectivity may vary across domains and they may vary in the amount of disagreement they tolerate, but one domain is not "more objective" in virtue of being less tolerant of diversity of opinion. There are limits to the tolerance of diversity that objectivity can accept. On the conception we have been considering, these limits are defined by the demands of strong deliberative consensus regarded as a regulative ideal. Within those limits, toleration of diversity is determined by the nature of the domain, its subject matter, and its basic tasks. For example, although morality is governed by something like the ideal of public practical reason lying at the heart of objectivity as publicity, there are important *substantive moral* reasons for acknowledging an important role for disagreement and dissensus in the structure of moral life and moral reasoning.[55] These arguments may be faulty, and the values they draw on may have been misunderstood or mistakenly characterized, but if we reject their conclusions, our reasons for doing so will also be moral arguments. A notion of moral objectivity ignores these features of the moral life at the price of being irrelevant to experience and the mode of inquiry for which it is designed.

Arguments of a similar general nature can be mounted to account for the existence and importance of disagreement and conflict in legal reasoning.[56] I will briefly sketch here just two arguments, one drawn from structural features of institutionalized legal reasoning (adjudication) and the other from conditions of law's legitimacy.

First, consider certain structural features of legal reasoning. Law is a distinctive form of practical reasoning. Distinctive of this form is the fact that it anchors the public justification of decisions and actions of officials and citizens alike to past decisions and actions of the community.[57] Moreover, the form and structure of legal reasoning are decisively shaped by the fact that it is, in principle, designed to be presented in a public forum in which it is assessed and open to critical challenge. Legal arguments typically take the form of reasons for extending or delimiting a rule used and established by a past decision. The reasons are developed through the exploration of analogies with competing lines of cases (and relevant hypothetical cases). Public matters, then, are decided, and disputes in the present are resolved, by arguments drawn from analogies to past decisions. It is a highly refined device for the exploration and exploitation of the guidance provided by these past decisions.

Essential to this process and its claim to legitimacy is the fact that, before a decision is officially and authoritatively extended or dramatically restricted, competing cases are extensively explored in a fully public forum. Recall Edward Levi's classic description of the common law process of argument:

The law forum is the most explicit demonstration of the mechanism required of a moving classification system. . . . [This forum] requires the presentation of competing examples. The forum protects parties and the community by making sure that the competing analogies are before the court. The rule which will be created arises out of a process in which if different things are to be treated as similar, at least the differences have been urged.[58]

Vigorous presentation of competing analogies and vigorous competing interpretations of past decisions are essential to the proper progress of this form of reasoning. Clashes in public over the proper and reasonable understanding of past decisions are not signs that "anything goes" and that standards of sound argument and rational deliberation have been abandoned. Rather, they are signs that products of the system can claim the right to be taken seriously as products of a credible structure of public practical deliberation. As Christopher Kutz has observed,

ineradicable conflict and divergence in a complex legal system is not a sign that things have gone awry, but that things are going well, that the legal regime is taking seriously plural claims of value. Vigorous dissents and weak doctrines of stare decisis, so long as they do not undermine the general stability of the legal regime, represent an important form of dialectical engagement with the conflicting normative claims the regime incorporates. . . . Divergence [of opinion and argument] . . . signals that the techniques of reason and argumentative insight are playing a vigorous role in the law.[59]

Second, the possibility of vigorous, reasoned disagreement over the interpretation, application, extension, and even the validity of legal norms is essential to the claim of legitimacy that law makes for itself. Law not only provides publicly identifiable norms, sufficiently enforced to motivate reasonably reliable compliance on the part of a majority of citizens, but it also provides opportunities for citizens to articulate challenges to those norms in a publicly recognized language. This is critical for law's claim to legitimacy. For the task of law is not merely, in Hume's words, "to cut off all occasions of discord and contention,"[60] but to manage it and to enable public deliberation about matters of fundamental concern to the society, especially about matters of justice, where there is deep disagreement of moral vision, even disagreement about what justice itself requires.

An institutionalized tradition of dissent is, thus, an essential structural condition of law's legitimacy. Moreover, far from representing a challenge to objectivity, it promotes it. Toleration of diversity of opinion in a domain of discourse does not threaten its claim to objectivity if it still makes sense, in the face of such diversity, to regard the domain as committed to strong deliberative consensus as a regulative idea. This is possible if the diversity plays a crucial role in securing or promoting that kind of consensus. This is exactly why I have argued for (some forms of) dissensus in the practice of legal reasoning. It creates spaces, both literally and figuratively, in which forms of bias, prejudice, exclusion, and unreason can be publicly exposed and challenged. Our hope for objectivity in law rests not just in the norms governing legal reasoning itself, or in the training of those entrusted with the administration of justice through its means. It rests also, and critically, on the institutions in which officials and citizens practice the art of public practical reasoning.

5.

This, then, is objectivity as publicity. It provides an appropriate understanding of the objectivity claimed for legal discourse. The following comments will prepare the ground of my argument for it by setting in relief certain salient features of this conception.

First, objectivity as publicity offers a methodological conception of objectivity. Objectivity, on this view, attaches in the first instance to a deliberative process. A deliberative process is objective to the extent that it meets, or approximates, the conditions of publicity mentioned above. Judgments are type-objective – objective in the "eligibility sense" – if they are candidates for examination and assessment in such a system. Judgments are token-objective – objective in the "success sense" – to the extent that they have been subjected to a process of reflective deliberation meeting or at least sufficiently approximating conditions of objectivity as publicity. As we have seen, objective judgments, on this view, are not necessarily correct judgments. For judgments are objective if they are formulated, or at least defended, under objective conditions of deliberation, but they can be objective and yet open to challenge as incorrect.

There is perhaps another derivative sense in which we might claim objectivity for a judgment, or at least not summarily deny it the honorific. Some judgments or norms, while not themselves ever subjected to full scrutiny in the deliberative process, nevertheless have become settled and operative in the practice. Until challenged, we may wish to accord them a kind of derivative objectivity. Not only are they eligible to scrutiny within the system and so type-objective, but in addition they borrow a degree of legitimacy from the place they have in a practice governed by a deliberative process that can rightly claim to approximate objectivity. These judgments or norms enjoy only a derivative and somewhat tenuous objectivity, however, for not only are they, like all judgments and norms of the domain, subject to challenge as mistaken and inadequately supported by argument, but their very claim to objectivity is vulnerable to challenge. For when subjected to scrutiny they may prove to be the product of nothing more than systematic personal or class biases.

Second, we saw in Part I that critics often associate objectivity with abstraction, disengagement, and detachment. However, according to objectivity as publicity, objectivity is achieved not by abandoning one's experience or perspective and taking up an alien one, but by expanding the circle of one's interlocutors. Objectivity, on this view, does not call for disengagement or detachment, but rather a specific kind of engaged, self-critical reflection on one's own experience and in the experiences of others. Similarly, according to this conception, objectivity does not encourage privileging of one's own perspective or ignoring the perspectives, experiences, or insights of others. On the contrary, it demands that we constantly listen to the voices of others for challenges to our own judgments and the arguments we offer for them. It also demands that we articulate our reasoning and arguments in terms that others, even those very different from us, can find intelligible and can ultimately affirm. To claim objectivity for a judgment *is* in a way to claim to speak for all, but this is not an exercise of verbal coercion. It is, rather, the expression of a hope, the very uttering of which opens it to challenge. Perhaps the most important thing one learns from uttering such a claim in a public deliberative process is the scope of the claim one makes in saying "we."[61] Of course, the claim is pretentious and coercive when those for whom it purports to speak are not empowered to participate in the deliberative process. But this is a failure not of the notion of objectivity, but of the deliberative process, a challenge to its claim to objectivity.

Finally, we saw in Part I that there is a strong tendency in the writings of legal theorists to equate legal objectivity with the requirement that legal reasoning be "nonpolitical." It is now possible to see both the attractions of this view and its mistake. Taken as a proposal for a conception of legal objectivity, the suggestion is not strictly speaking incompatible with objectivity as publicity; it is just more specific. It focuses on one part of that conception, the "relevant arguments" standard, and specifies (or rather presupposes a specification of) "relevance" for adjudicative reasoning. On this view, only strictly "nonpolitical" reasons and arguments are appropriate grounds for legal judgments. From the point of view of objectivity as publicity, this is not mistaken, it is merely incomplete. It is incomplete both because it specifies only one class of factors that are allegedly not permitted to influence the formation of legal judgments and because it ignores the role of consensus as a regulative ideal for legal discourse. Objectivity as publicity regards the specification of the criteria of argumentative relevance to be a matter of substantive argument within the domain of discourse (in this case legal theory). Thus, the question about the defensibility of this (partial) account of legal objectivity is a question about the fundamental aims of law and legal reasoning and central to this argument, of course, is the notion of legitimacy.

However, this suggestion for specifying the notion of legal objectivity, while it might get in the door, will not be at ease in the house that our conception of objectivity builds for law. Not only do the reasons of legitimacy that call for objectivity militate against equating objectivity with strictly and demonstrably nonpolitical argument, but so too does the core notion of strong deliberative consensus that lies at the heart of objectivity as publicity. As we saw in the previous section, diversity of opinion, disagreement, and dissent are not necessarily signs of objectivity dysfunction, but rather can be welcome *and necessary* signs of systemic health.

V. Is Law Objective?

1.

My thesis is that objectivity as publicity offers a conception of objectivity that is intellectually appealing and uniquely fitting to serve as the standard of legal objectivity.[62] It is a conception of objectivity fit for law.

The case for the appropriateness of the conception for law is straightforward. Legal reasoning is an historically situated, institutionalized form of deliberative, normative discourse regarding public matters and purporting to bind everyone in its jurisdiction, at least in part, by virtue of its being able to speak for all of them. It seeks to guide citizens and coordinate their interaction through publicly articulated and defended norms addressed to their practical deliberative faculties. Its legitimacy depends on the actions and decisions of officials, and the norms they apply and enforce, being defensible in terms of reasons and arguments that are in an important sense public. Legitimacy of the norms and judgments depends crucially on the integrity, credibility, and accountability of the deliberative process that produces them. Objectivity as publicity seems tailor-made for this deliberative practice. It provides the standards by which the process is judged and its legitimacy is secured. Objectivity as publicity articulates the conditions that the practice and its institutions must seek to achieve if it is to make good on its offer of a disciplined practice of public practical reasoning suited to the conditions of modern pluralistic societies.

2.

I have said that the practice of legal reasoning can be regarded as a form of public practical reasoning, but the notion of deliberation on which objectivity as publicity relies is highly idealized. The practice of legal reasoning can be regarded as an institutionalization of that idealized notion, adjusting it to meet specific conditions of modern political societies. A full defense of the appropriateness of objectivity as publicity to law awaits a fully articulated theory of public practical reason and the relationship of law to it. I cannot provide that here.[63] Instead of developing this theory here, I will close by considering some important, more practically minded, objections to my thesis.

Critics might argue that legal practice falls far short of the ideal of objectivity as publicity. It is just false, for example, that participation in the practice of legal reasoning is widely open to all members of society on anything like a fair and equal basis. This surely threatens law's claim to objectivity. Other sources of distortion seem to have roots in features of law that do not appear to be merely accidental. For example, while purporting to provide exemplars of public deliberation and a language for public practical reason, as law gets relentlessly more technical, its language and its modes of reasoning become less and less accessible. Moreover, the cadres of official and private functionaries create elites that mediate between the law and the citizenry, but they do so largely on their terms, terms that often reflect the interests and concerns, the norms and the agendas, of the legal class. While these interests are not crassly idiosyncratic, they are no less "sinister," as Bentham would say.

These features and trends are truly worrisome, and I suspect that they are due to factors that can never be wholly eliminated from law, without eliminating law itself. But they can be better managed, and their objectivity-distorting effects ameliorated. It would be premature to draw any radically skeptical conclusion from these critical observations. There are strong reasons for thinking objectivity as publicity provides the appropriate measure of legal objectivity. While existing legal practice falls short of its demands in several respects, in some perhaps dramatically, we still have reason to demand that it do a better job, rather than to give up on objectivity altogether. Objectivity is not a fact to be established or demonstrated, it is an ideal to aspire to. The failure of our actual legal practice to meet the measure objectivity lays down is no reason to abandon the aspiration and give up the project. It is, rather, strong reason to redouble our efforts to meet it. After all, law's claim to legitimacy is only as good as its efforts to achieve objectivity.

VI. Metaphysics and Objectivity

1.

Throughout the argument above I have said very little about the metaphysical status of law or of the facts of legal practice. This has been intentional. Objectivity as publicity has no metaphysical pretensions or commitments. This is not to say, however, that it takes a *skeptical* view of the metaphysics of the discourses to which it applies. It simply regards the metaphysical issues as orthogonal to the central questions of the objectivity of the discourse. Objectivity as publicity is a methodological conception of objectivity. Its only metaphysical rivals are those semantic accounts that insist on a conceptual and practical priority over all alternative proposals for the legal domain. Metaphysical objectivity viewed in this way is, in my view, mistaken. The mistake lies in thinking that we can settle the metaphysics of the discourse prior to settling the practical question of the nature of the demand for objectivity within that domain and, more generally, in insisting on a single conception of objectivity for all domains of discourse and reasoning.

Of course, it will not do merely to assert the moderate domain-specificity thesis on which this chapter has rested, for it is precisely this thesis that critics challenge. In the remaining pages of this chapter I will say a few words in defense of the moderate domain-specificity thesis, recognizing that the topic is larger than treatment in these pages permits. I do not deny completely the relevance of metaphysics to questions of objectivity in normative domains like law and morality, but I will argue that there are good reasons to question the alleged priority of metaphysical objectivity for such domains.

2.

To begin, I acknowledge that alongside the project of this chapter, there is another, *metaphysical,* inquiry in which the philosophical terminology "objective" and "subjective" are at home. The difference between these two inquiries emerges from consideration of the following attempt of Jules Coleman to motivate the metaphysical project for law.

The truth of legal assertions depends on what the legal facts are. . . . Take a sentence like, "Coleman is liable for all and only the foreseeable consequences of his negligence." It makes perfectly good sense for someone to ask you whether that sentence is true or not. Suppose you answer that it is true. It then makes perfectly good sense for your questioner to ask you why you say that it's true: by that he means to be asking you something like what *makes* it true. You answer that it's true because it reports what the law is on that matter. But then he asks you to tell him whether, when you say that it's what the law is, you mean that it is what a judge says is the law, or what most judges say is the law, or would say if asked, or whether it is the law no matter how a judge or all judges and lawyers regard (or would regard) it. He is asking you whether the (legal) fact that makes the sentence true . . . is objective or not. Your inquirer is asking you to specify something about the metaphysical status of legal facts.[64]

If we read this passage in one entirely natural way, the last sentence comes as a complete surprise. Surely, the truth of legal assertions depends on the legal facts – the considerations that figure properly in any sound argument offered in defense of their truth. It makes sense, too, to ask whether among these legal facts is the fact that the judgment is said or believed to be law by a judge, or by most judges, and the like. That is, we can ask whether among the relevant arguments for the correctness of a legal judgment we might find appeals to the beliefs or decisions of other judges or lawyers. Yet, as I understand it, this is a practical inquiry into the kind of considerations that properly figure in legal arguments, an inquiry that depends at least in part on substantive normative considerations within, as it were, first-order legal theory. In the view of objectivity as publicity, it is one of the crucial questions that must be asked if we are to specify the standard of objectivity for legal judgments. What, then, makes this inquiry an inquiry into "the metaphysical status" of legal facts? Is "metaphysics" here just a fancy word for the kind of inquiry I argued earlier is essential to defining the parameters of objectivity as publicity? If it is, then all along we have been speaking metaphysical prose without knowing it.

However, Coleman and others who defend (and those who reject) the metaphysical enterprise think it is not merely a name for the project pursued in this chapter.[65] Its aim, I take it, is to explore the nature of legal facts regarded as the objects of legal discourse. This is regarded not as a practical, normative inquiry into the kind of considerations that properly figure in legal argument (a question of the normative theory of this discourse), but rather as a theoretical inquiry into the nature of the *objects* of judgments of the discourse. It asks whether there are facts or objects to which legal assertions correspond (or at least refer) and which in virtue of this relationship "make the assertions true." It asks whether these facts or objects are mind-dependent, and if so, in what way or to what extent they are mind-dependent. Of course, as we have just seen, these cannot be facts on which participants in the practice of legal reasoning do, would, or could rely in their deliberation, for then these facts would be assayed for relevance like all the usual kinds of legal (normative) facts which legal arguments deploy.

3.

It is tempting to argue that, if there is such an inquiry, its results are simply *irrelevant* to legal objectivity, for no claim produced by metaphysical theory could ever, by hypothesis, figure in any argument for the truth or correctness of any legal judgment.[66] But this does not identify the problem correctly. While it is true that no metaphysical thesis, no claim of metaphysical objectivity, could clinch a disputed point in law, the same is true for *any* claim of objectivity whether it is given a metaphysical gloss or a methodological one. This "irrelevancy" is a function not of the special character of metaphysical theories of objectivity, but of the notion of objectivity in general. It is a general feature of the role of appeals to objectivity in practical discourse. We look to objectivity, not to clinch the case for this or that legal judgment in the course of debate about its correctness, but to give us the assurance we need to carry on with the argument for its correctness with others who persist in disagreement. This, then, is not a special problem for metaphysical objectivity. Indeed, it may pose no problem for metaphysical theories at all, if they make no pretense to address the practical concerns that underlie our demand for legal objectivity. That is, the metaphysical project can be understood as entirely independent of the practical project, raising its own questions, or raising what look like the same questions in very different ways, and looking for very different kinds of answers.

Of course, legal theorists who look to metaphysics are usually not content with this view of the metaphysical enterprise. They believe that the claims of legal authorities to legitimacy of their judgments and decisions depend in a crucial way on answers to the metaphysical inquiry.[67] They agree with the thesis I argued earlier: adjudicative objectivity matters because it matters to us that our adjudicative processes, and the judgments issuing from them, make credible, legitimate claims to authority. They insist, then, on a practical relevance for their theories. However, in view of the difference between the practical and the metaphysical projects, and the resulting "gap" between the results of metaphysical inquiry and actual legal argument, metaphysical theorists must give us some reason for thinking the results are systemically relevant. And there are reasons to doubt this alleged relevance. One might argue, for example, that no assurance that our modes of legal inquiry and argument are worthy of the respect they demand of us can come from knowing what *kind of facts* correspond to the true or correct legal judgments. For, once we have distinguished this question from the practical question of which kinds of arguments may properly figure in legal arguments, there seems to be no practical work for this account of the facts or objects of legal discourse to do.

To this the metaphysical objectivity theorist might reply that a proper conception of the *kind* of facts that make legal assertions true determine the standards of objectivity of the enterprise. Methodology presupposes metaphysics.[68] How exactly does metaphysics make a difference? The answer cannot be that it will tell us whether the judge can rely on his own attitudes or beliefs, or those of other judges and lawyers, or the like. That confuses the metaphysical inquiry with the substantive one. It assumes that the facts in question are facts that might figure directly in legal argument, and, by hypothesis, that is not what we have in mind. Suppose that it is true that the metaphysical facts are facts about the attitudes of judges and lawyers, and the like. Does this threaten legal deliberation, or make it less than it claims for itself? Would knowing that the facts are complex facts about judicial attitudes under ideal conditions calm these worries? Strictly speaking, these accounts have no implications for our view of this deliberative process, because nothing follows from them about the possibility of standards of good and bad argument, the integrity of reasoning or inquiry, or like matters at the heart of our concern for legal objectivity. Moreover, if we have strong reason to think the deliberative process can support such standards, then our metaphysics will have to make room for an account of standards of good argument, and the like. Our *metaphysics,* however, will not tell us whether and how to construct such an account.

Of course, the conviction that we can distinguish good from bad arguments in a domain is not self-justifying. We can be wrong in our assessment of the objectivity of a domain of discourse. But serious challenges cannot be launched from a metaphysical quarter alone. Metaphysics is only a subcontractor in the project of constructing a coherent account of the objectivity of law. In the face of strong and apparently reasonable convictions of objectivity we will quite reasonably reject an inconsistent account of the metaphysics before we will abandon our conviction of its objectivity. This is surely the right approach to take to so-called error theories in ethics.[69] This theory attributes a strong, Platonist metaphysics to moral reasoning, and then objects that the theory is radically implausible, and concludes we must reject morality's claim to objectivity. Yet, with all the power of *modus tollens,* this argument drives us to search for a more plausible metaphysics, rather than to abandon moral objectivity.[70] The argument puts a lever in the hands of the moral philosopher, but it is easier and more reasonable to move the metaphysics than from this metaphysical quarter to dislodge our convictions regarding the objectivity of moral reasoning.[71] This does not *demonstrate* the subjection of the metaphysical to the practical enterprise in normative domains. But it does suggest that, if we have reason from within a discourse to take its demand for objectivity seriously, then we are inclined to give it greater importance than our metaphysical speculations and to allow them to be directed by our sense of the objectivity of the discourse.

4.

Still, one might ask: Why adopt a methodological approach to objectivity for a given domain unless one is already committed to a version of antirealism for that domain?[72] The adoption of the methodological approach appears reactive, even defensive. It looks like a way to preserve a semblance of objectivity, or perhaps the illusion of objectivity, in the face of a metaphysical view that whispers tempting skeptical doubts. It is difficult to resist the suspicion that we turn to politics only when metaphysics fails.[73] Rawls's pragmatic rejection of metaphysics, and his notion of objectivity in search of stable social union of free and equal moral persons, may seem to reinforce rather than to silence this suspicion.

However, these suspicions notwithstanding, the case for a methodological approach to objectivity in law does not depend on antirealism (or any other metaphysical thesis) regarding the normative realm. It depends, rather, on the domain-specific nature of the notion of objectivity. This, of course, is precisely what partisans of metaphysical objectivity reject. In their view, there is only one credible conception of objectivity. According to this view, *facts* are objective in virtue of being causally independent of minds, and *judgments* are objective in virtue of being judgements about objective facts. In its current and perhaps its most powerful version, the only credible notion of objectivity is that funded by "scientific epistemology." According to this Naturalistic Conception, a fact is objective if it is mind-independent and makes a causal difference to the course of our experience.[74] As Leiter takes pains to point out,[75] this view does not assume any transcendental metaphysical world, but only the familiar world of experience as described and explained by natural science. Likewise, it does not assume that there is some Archimedean place to stand outside all beliefs and all exercises of reason from which to judge them. It assumes only that we assess any particular set of beliefs or exercises of reason from the temporary vantage point of other beliefs or parts of our experience. This conception of objectivity, underwritten by scientific epistemology, provides a test – the only viable and reliable test – of the real.[76] If normative judgments wish to claim objectivity, they must find a place in the picture of our world provided by scientific epistemology.

Metaphysical objectivity, and especially this Naturalistic version of it, insists that objectivity demands that our beliefs and judgments be anchored in the real (that is, the *empirical*) world – that they be, in Bernard Williams's words, "world-guided."[77] From this follows the requirement that the objects, or facts, to which our judgments refer make a causal difference to our experience. They must be able to figure materially in causal explanations of our making the judgments and holding the beliefs we do. This contrasts sharply with what we might call the "rationalist" bent of methodological accounts of objectivity. On the latter, what is critical is that our judgments are *reason*-anchored, *reason*-guided. In its strongest versions, this requires that our judgments be rationally inescapable. In weaker versions, it calls for their being substantially, perhaps publicly, reason-based.

According to the Naturalistic Conception, being reason-anchored is not sufficient for objectivity worthy of its name and reputation. Furthermore, it is argued, any approach to objectivity in a given domain that focuses exclusively on methodology betrays insecurity about its metaphysical foundations. But why should we accept the hegemony of the Naturalistic Conception? In his chapter in this volume, Leiter offers two important arguments. First, he argues,

"Science has earned its claim to be a guide to the real and the unreal by depopulating our world of gods and witches and ethers and substituting a picture of the world and how it works of immense practical value."[78] This is an a posteriori, pragmatic argument for the hegemony of Naturalistic Conception. On this Conception, objectivity is the objectivity of, and underwritten by, natural science. Scientific epistemology provides the test of the real, because *it succeeds,* "it delivered the goods."[79] Second, we get no purchase on the notion of discourse being objective without implicit reliance on Naturalistic Conception: "unless there are Naturalistically Objective facts to which the discourse must answer we will often be unable to make sense of better or worse ways of reasoning."[80] Thus, if we abandon Naturalistic Objectivity, we have no way to block clearly nonobjective modes of discourse from claiming objectivity with impunity. We should not be surprised to find that "if we repudiate the demands of scientific epistemology we get a promiscuous ontology, replete with moral facts, aesthetic facts, theological facts, and the like. . . . To simply push the scientific epistemology aside opens the ontological floodgates to a whole pre-Enlightenment conception of the world that we seem to do better without."[81] Reject this solid, pragmatically proven test of the real and the unreal, Leiter argues, and Pandora's box is opened. We will have no way reasonably to challenge the Church of Scientology or the "Chocolate Convention" (Leiter's hypothetical practice of debating and determining the "objective" tastiness of chocolate).[82] We have only two choices, according to Leiter, the Naturalistic Conception of objectivity and radical domain-specificity, which, in effect, abandons objectivity.

These arguments are, to my eye, unpersuasive. Consider, first, the pragmatic argument. The hegemony of the Naturalistic Conception is said to follow from the "success" of natural science and the "immense practical value" of its picture of the world. This is a non sequitur. Grant that the criteria implicit in the argument in terms of which scientific epistemology is judged a great success are of immense practical value. Nothing follows about the relevance of the notion of objectivity associated with this epistemology to other areas of experience, judgment, reasoning, and discourse. Some argument must be given for thinking that the validity of this conception of objectivity can be generalized. For we have reason to resist the generalization, since the "success" of natural science depends at least in part on the fact that it self-consciously brackets, and thus remains silent about, large portions of human experience (notably the normative dimensions of that experience). Moreover, normative discourse does not deal in the base currency of natural science – causal explanations; why, then, should we accept that success in charting the world organized under the category of causation gives license to determine the tools for reasoning our way around the practical world? This pragmatic argument for the hegemony of the Naturalistic Conception may not be vulnerable to Dworkin's charge of a priori bias in favor of scientific epistemology, but the a posteriori argument made in its behalf begs the very question at issue.

The Pandora's box argument is also a non sequitur. No reason is given for the claim that, if we abandon the Naturalistic Conception, there *is no* basis for distinguishing pseudo-objective from genuinely objective discourse. It only follows that we cannot look to that conception and we must look elsewhere. I think the argument is more plausibly seen as a challenge. One might argue that, if we abandon science, which provides a proven, relevant, and effective test of the real, we need some other test of at least equal power to put in its place. This puts a challenge to any methodological account that proposes to do without the resources of the Naturalistic Conception. The argument correctly throws suspicion on alleged self-validating standards of objectivity. Domains that cannot provide some cross-domain grounds for recognizing the standard of objectivity claimed for them surely earn our suspicion. As Leiter puts it, "Talk is cheap. That we can talk about something *as though it were real,* that we can nurture a practice of giving reasons, does not suffice to underwrite the objectivity of any domain."[83]

However, this revised Pandora's box argument still assumes the success of the pragmatic argument, for if we have no reason to think that the Naturalistic Conception can provide a relevant test of good and bad reasoning in a given discipline, then abandoning it puts us in no worse a position. The argument provides no support for its claim to hegemony. The argument also faces a more serious problem. It appears that the claim of objectivity of scientific inquiry, or large parts of it at least, may fail by the standards of the Naturalistic Conception and the revised Pandora's box argument. By hypothesis, the Naturalistic Conception is bottomed on scientific epistemology. No cross-domain, cross-disciplinary confirmation is available, as the Pandora's box argument requires. Moreover, we have reason to doubt whether scientific epistemology can pass the Naturalistic Conception's causal explanation test. Warren Quinn has argued that the claim that we can give causal explanations of our beliefs and judgments about matters of natural science (e.g., of physics or even biology) in terms of the truth of those beliefs and judgments is largely unsubstantiated. These causal explanations presuppose a link between the domains of these basic sciences and the domain of psychology that simply does not exist. He writes,

The accounts that cognitive psychology provides of our beliefs and perceptions are to a considerable extent indifferent to the precise nature and cause of these external stimuli. These accounts would go through whether, for example, elementary particle physics turns out one way or another, even where the alternatives are of the very greatest importance to physics. If this is right, then our scientific belief that the world is one way (represented by one possible development of elementary particle physics) rather than another (represented by an alternative development) will not be confirmed by its contribution to the explanation of our beliefs and perceptions.[84]

Thus, it appears that, by the Natural Conception's causal explanation tests, our best basic science is of dubious objectivity. Alternatively, we might conclude that the Natural Conception is not an apt model of objectivity even for this domain. As Quinn observes, although it does not pass the causal explanation test, our basic science is "confirmed by the experimental methods of physics itself – as part of the best theory of physical events around us."[85] But this means that our conception of the physical world has a different claim to objectivity, namely, that "it is the conception of the world that good scientists, conscientiously applying scientific method in order to understand the world around them, have converged upon."[86] If this is correct, then our confidence in the objectivity of basic science rests not so much on the conviction that it is *world*-guided, but rather on the conviction that it is appropriately *reason*-guided.

However, the Pandora's box objection still challenges claims to reason-guided objectivity, although now it appears that this challenge applies not just to morality and law but even to inquiries in the natural sciences. The challenge is a worthy one. We may not rest content with radically domain-specific claims of objectivity. Our only hope is to find some cross-disciplinary test or tests. I have no specific test to offer. I can only suggest three broad considerations that will have to be taken into account. First, any domain-specific conception of objectivity must articulate faithfully and reasonably the generic features of the concept of objectivity. Second, any such conception should also be checked by demands of reason and reasonableness common to cognate domains. And, third, no such conception may validate a domain the main propositions of which cannot be integrated plausibly into an account of human experience as a whole. These are stringent, albeit vague, constraints. Definitive judgments about the viability of standards of objectivity in a given domain are probably premature, but we can perhaps make interim judgments about various domains as they mature: natural science, morals, law, scientology, and the "chocolate convention." The case against some of these may be overwhelming and pretty strong in favor of others. However, we have no a priori reason to suppose that any one domain will prove foundational whether it be theology or natural science.

We have good reason, then, to resist the claim to hegemony made on behalf of the Naturalistic Conception and, thus, reason to think that a reason-guided, methodological conception of objectivity proposed for normative domains is not merely the product of metaphysical bad faith. These reasons rest ultimately on the thesis that there is a fundamental difference between theoretical and practical reasoning and inquiry. Of course, the distinction between theoretical and practical domains is in one sense of the word "metaphysical": it concerns the basic categories of thought in terms of which we organize experience. So, it cannot be said that the argument for objectivity as publicity has avoided metaphysics entirely. However, while the distinction between the theoretical and practical is categorical, it is not *ontological,* and it is in the latter sense that my argument takes no particular metaphysical position.

Thus, the moderate domain-specificity on the basis of which I have sought to articulate a conception of objectivity fit for law presupposes the distinction between theoretical and practical thought and reasoning. This, distinction, however, is truly fundamental. It concerns the most basic categories in terms of which we seek to understand and negotiate our common world. I know of no convincing argument to offer one who truly rejects the distinction, but equally I cannot imagine a plausible reason for rejecting it. Both theoretical discourse and practical discourse are modes of thought, involving, when they are in good working order, reason-guided movements of thought. The difference between them lies (a) in that which reasoning in each domain seeks to do, (b) in that by which the movements of thought are assessed, and most importantly (c) in the set of concepts or categories that organize and give structure to the reasoning. Since practical reasoning is concerned not only with the way the world is, or is likely to be, but also with the reasons rational agents have to act and interact in it, practical reasoning depends essentially on normative notions that, for all we now understand, are not reducible to nonnormative notions. These modes of reasoning and inquiry are distinct because the categories in terms of which they proceed and are assessed are categorically distinct. To insist on this distinction in no way jeopardizes objectivity in one or the other domain, because it is a distinction that is more fundamental than the notion of objectivity. In its terms objectivity must be understood. It is a mistake, then, to think that objectivity appropriate to one side of this categorical divide should provide the sole appropriate test of objectivity on the other side. By the same token, radical specificity of the criteria of objectivity would fly in the face of the fact that both theoretical discourse and practical discourse are modes of reasoning. The only plausible working assumption to make is that of moderate domain-specificity of the concept of objectivity.

5.

Reflecting on the progress of his long argument in the *Critique of Pure Reason,* Kant remarks, "We have found, indeed, that although we had contemplated building a tower which should reach to the heavens, the supply of materials suffices only for a dwelling-house, just sufficiently commodious for our business on the level of experience, and just sufficiently high to allow of our overlooking it."[87] Kant sought to corral the inclination to metaphysical speculation, to teach us to be satisfied with a more restrained view of the power of reason. His motive was, in one sense of the term, "deflationary." I mention

Kant's reflections at the conclusion of this chapter to highlight the very different attitude that I believe should accompany acceptance of objectivity as publicity as the conception of objectivity fit for law. We have no reason to think that we are forced to "settle" for this approach, in view of the absence of a robust, metaphysical account. We have no reason to regret the metaphysically modest pretensions of objectivity as publicity. By the same token, we are not encouraged to embrace this conception of objectivity for merely pragmatic reasons – merely for "political purposes," as Rawls would put it. We are encouraged to accept it for the best reason there is: it is the one that best accounts for our demand for objectivity in law.[88]

Notes

1. Arthur Ripstein, "Questionable Objectivity," *Noûs* 27 (1993): 355–372, pp. 358–359.
2. My subject is the alleged objectivity of legal reasoning, that is, reasoning within the law, as opposed to reasoning about what laws we should have or make for ourselves. In legal theory this is often called adjudicative reasoning. There is good reason for this. Courts are, for better or worse, exemplars of such reasoning. But they are only exemplars; they are not the only users of this form of reasoning. I will also speak of adjudicative reasoning, but with the caveat that I am not speaking solely of the reasoning of judges, or even of lawyers, but also of citizens generally.
3. See G. J. Postema, *Bentham and the Common Law Tradition* (Oxford: Clarendon Press, 1986, 1989), chap. 8.
4. For example, see C. MacKinnon, *Toward a Feminist Theory of the State* (Cambridge, Mass.: Harvard University Press, 1989), pp. 116, 121–122.
5. Angela P. Harris, "Race and Essentialism in Feminist Legal Theory," in K. T. Bartlett and R. Kennedy (eds.), *Feminist Legal Theory* (Boulder: Westview Press, 1991), pp. 236–237.
6. MacKinnon, *Feminist Theory of the State,* pp. 106–107.
7. P. J. Williams, *The Alchemy of Race and Rights* (Cambridge, Mass.: Harvard University Press, 1991), p. 11.
8. K. Crenshaw, "Demarginalizing at the Intersection of Race and Sex," in Bartlett and Kennedy (eds.), *Feminist Legal Theory,* p. 67.
9. MacKinnon, *Feminist Theory of the State,* pp. 116–117, 248.
10. Katharine Bartlett refers to this as "the Woman Question." See K. Bartlett, "Feminist Legal Methods," in Bartlett and Kennedy (eds.), *Feminist Legal Theory,* pp. 371–376. See also M. Minow, "The Supreme Court 1986 Term-Foreword: Justice Engendered," *Harvard Law Review* 101 (1987), p. 10, and *Making All the Difference* (Cambridge, Mass.: Harvard University Press, 1990).
11. MacKinnon, *Feminist Theory of the State,* 120f (author's emphasis).
12. See, for example, Joseph Singer, "The Player and the Cards: Nihilism and Legal Theory," *Yale Law Journal* 94 (1984): 1–70, p. 1; Mark Tushnet, "Following the Rules Laid Down: A Critique of Interpretivism and Neutral Principles," *Harvard Law Review* 96 (1983): 781–827.
13. On the relationship between law's indeterminacy and legitimacy, according to Critical

Legal Studies, see Ken Kress, "Legal Indeterminacy," *California Law Review* 77 (1989): 283–337, pp. 283, 285–295.

14. The distinction between causal and rational determinacy/indeterminacy is drawn clearly by Brian Leiter. See Brian Leiter, "Legal Indeterminacy," *Legal Theory* 1 (1995): 481–492, at pp. 481–483; and Jules Coleman and Brian Leiter, "Determinacy, Objectivity, and Authority," *University of Pennsylvania Law Review* 142 (1993): 549–637, at pp. 559–564.

15. For a recent version of his argument see R. Dworkin, "Objectivity and Truth: You'd Better Believe It," *Philosophy & Public Affairs* 25 (1996): 87–139, at pp. 129–137.

16. Ken Kress, "A Preface to Epistemological Indeterminacy," *Northwestern University Law Review* 85 (1990): 134–147, at pp. 139ff.

17. That is, they need only show that no decision is regarded to be so dictated by most competent lawyers who know the materials and assess the implications of those materials for the case at hand in good faith.

18. Joseph Singer, "The Player and the Cards," p. 6.

19. I defend this assumption below in Part VI.

20. Two points of clarification are in order. First, the term "judgment" can be used to refer either to acts of judging or their products. For the time being, I wish to leave this ambiguity unresolved. Second, in an ecumenical spirit, I take judgments for my point of departure in this Part. Some philosophers, of course, prefer to speak of the objectivity of *facts* rather than the objectivity of judgments. On what I call below the "semantic" approach to objectivity, judgments are said to be objective in virtue of the objectivity of the facts to which they are semantically related. In this Part, I discuss generic features of the concept of objectivity shared by such "semantic" and epistemic (I call them "methodological") accounts of the concept. Later, I will develop an account of objectivity that does not put the objectivity of facts at its center, but at this point in the discussion I do not wish unduly to prejudice the present discussion in favor of such a view. Nonetheless, I suspect that partisans of the semantic approach will not be entirely happy, since the concessions to the methodological approach evident in this Part will seem to unduly compromise the concept of objectivity as they see it.

21. According to the *OED*, ordinary linguistic usage here follows modern philosophical usage. It is interesting to note, however, that a dramatic reversal in philosophical usage seems to have occurred during the eighteenth century. Constant across this shift was the idea that the terms "subjective" and "objective" were defined relative to that which is regarded as the "subject." But in the modern period, the conception or locus of the subject shifted and with it the contrast marked by these two terms. In scholastic philosophy, that which pertained to things *subjective* pertained to them as they are in themselves, as subjects; whereas that which pertained to them *objective* pertained to them insofar as they were presented to, or objects of, consciousness. When European thought began to think of the thinking, perceiving, judging consciousness as subject, the terms reversed meanings.

22. Ripstein, "Questionable Objectivity," p. 359.

23. Ibid., pp. 358–361.

24. I use the term "semantic" here as a term of art.

25. In this chapter I try to avoid talking about reflections "inside" or "outside" a practice or domain and, in particular, the suggestion that metaphysics is "outside" and "above"

thought, reasoning, and judgment in other domains. These metaphors have led to unfortunate confusions and mistakes. As I see it, metaphysics is one form of reflection among many others, distinctive for being highly abstract and taking as its primary subject matter broad categories of thought and, secondarily, certain broad features of other domains of discourse (hence its "meta" status). If we must use spatial metaphors, metaphysics stands along side these other domains, dependent in a way on them, as they are, perhaps, aided by it, but also pursuing its own theoretical agenda. I return below in Part VI to the relationship between "metaphysical objectivity" and the practical conception of objectivity I shall defend for law.

26. See J. Rawls, *Political Liberalism* (New York: Columbia University Press, 1993), p. 110.

27. As will soon be apparent, I mean here invariance of judgment across suitably situated, competent subjects.

28. Amartya Sen, *Objectivity and Position* (Lawrence: University of Kansas Press,, 1992), p. 2 (author's emphasis).

29. Amartya Sen, "Positional Objectivity," *Philosophy & Public Affairs* 22 (1993): 126–145, at p. 127 (author's emphasis).

30. G. Currie, "Interpretation and Objectivity," *Mind* 102 (1993): 413–428, at p. 413.

31. Sen, *Objectivity and Position,* pp. 283–284.

32. Note, the claim here is that intersubjectivity is a mark of *objectivity,* not either of truth or correctness. See above Part II.2 and below Part IV.1 and Part IV.3.

33. All quotations in this paragraph are taken from Immanuel Kant, *Critique of Pure Reason,* trans. Norman Kemp Smith (London: St. Martin's, 1965), pp. 645f (A 820, 821/B 848, 849).

34. In this paragraph I follow Rawls's interpretation of Kant's moral theory. See John Rawls, "Kantian Constructivism in Moral Theory," *Journal of Philosophy* 77 (1980): 559–572.

35. For further discussion see below Part VI.4.

36. Thus, the radical critics' discussion in Part I mistakenly rejects the concept of objectivity as fraudulent upon a showing of the hypocrisy of its use.

37. On this point see, for example, Owen Fiss, "Objectivity and Interpretation," *Stanford Law Review* 34 (1982): 739–763, at pp. 748–749.

38. Paul Seabright, "Objectivity, Disagreement, and Projectibility," *Inquiry* 31 (1988): 25–51, at p. 44.

39. Ibid., 44–45.

40. Bernard Williams, *Ethics and the Limits of Philosophy* (Cambridge, Mass.: Harvard University Press, 1985), p. 135.

41. *Whitney v. California,* 274 U.S. 357, 372 (1927) (Brandeis concurring).

42. I paraphrase here for my own purposes a comment made by Kenneth Kress regarding the determinacy of law. See Kress, "Legal Indeterminacy," p. 285.

43. I follow here my discussion in "Public Practical Reasoning: Political Practice," in I. Shapiro and J. Wagner DeCew (eds.), *NOMOS XXXVII: Theory and Practice* (New York: New York University Press, 1995), pp. 362–363.

44. See ibid., 366–378.

45. I discuss the issues raised in this paragraph in greater detail in Part VI of this essay.

46. Rawls's conception of the objectivity of political morality is similar to the approach taken here. He writes, "To say that a political conviction is objective is to say that there are reasons, specified by a reasonable and mutually recognizable political conception,

. . . sufficient to convince all reasonable persons that it is reasonable." Rawls, *Political Liberalism,* p. 119.

47. Ripstein, "Questionable Objectivity," pp. 359–361.

48. For an articulation and defense of this notion of public reasons and public justification, see my "Public Practical Reasoning: An Archeology," *Social Philosophy and Policy* 12 (1995): 43–86, and "Public Practical Reasoning: Political Practice," pp. 345–385.

49. The list set out here is based on my discussion of the "discipline of public practical reason" in "Public Practical Reasoning: Political Practice," pp. 356–361, although I have expanded the list in certain respects and shortened it slightly in others. The list, in basic outline, is defended in that essay, so I will not repeat the argument here.

50. There is, of course, an important difference between these two formulations, but this is not the place to decide which is the preferred interpretation. See Thomas Scanlon, "Contractualism and Utilitarianism," in A. Sen and B. Williams (eds.), *Utilitarianism and Beyond* (Cambridge: Cambridge University Press, 1982), pp. 110–115; Rawls, *Political Liberalism,* pp. 48–54.

51. Christopher Kutz, "Just Disagreement: Indeterminacy and Rationality in the Rule of Law," *Yale Law Journal* 103 (1994): 997–1030, at p. 1029.

52. The phrase is Viktor Vanberg's, although he put it to a very different use. See Viktor J. Vanberg, *Rules and Choice in Economics* (London: Routledge, 1994), p. 51.

53. "Part of the doubt about judicial objectivity may be a product of the fact that the courts protest too much." R. W. Bennett, "Objectivity in Constitutional Law," *University of Pennsylvania Law Review,* 132 (1984): 445–496, at p. 445.

54. Dworkin, "Objectivity and Truth," p. 113.

55. I argue there that we make room for disagreement because (1) it is required by the radical plurality of value to which human appreciation is susceptible and to which human life and imagination can be directed; and (2) it is required by recognition and respect for individual moral autonomy. See "Public Practical Reason: Political Practice," pp. 353–355.

56. We should admit up front, however, that some reasons for disputes and disagreements within the law that can be traced to systemic features of legal practice may nevertheless be perverse and provide no occasion for celebration. At the same time, we should not take the existence of such perverse incentives as reason to treat all causes of conflict and dissensus as similarly perverse. How are we to distinguish perverse from healthy causes? A full answer lies in the best overall account of the nature and fundamental tasks of legal reasoning.

57. See Gerald Postema, "Integrity: Justice in Workclothes," *Iowa Law Review* 82 (1997): 821–855, at pp. 851ff; see also R. Dworkin, *Law's Empire* (Cambridge, Mass.: Harvard University Press, 1986), p. 93. This is a pervasive feature of legal reasoning, true not only for common law reasoning, but also for much legal reasoning dealing with statutory or constitutional materials. For purposes of illustration I will consider only common law reasoning.

58. E. Levi, *An Introduction to Legal Reasoning* (Chicago: University of Chicago Press, 1949), pp. 4–5.

59. Kutz, "Just Disagreement," pp. 1028–1029.

60. David Hume, *A Treatise of Human Nature,* Selby-Bigge, ed., P. H. Nidditch, 2nd ed. (Oxford: Clarendon Press, 1978), p. 502.

61. See Postema, "Public Practical Reason: Political Practice," p. 377.
62. Of course, as I have noted earlier, the conception sketched above is incomplete in certain respects. In particular, it leaves for further argument determination of the criteria of relevance of materials available to participants in the process of legal deliberation.
63. I have sketched the basic outlines of the theory in papers mentioned earlier, especially, "Public Practical Reason: An Archeology," "Public Practical Reason: Political Practice," and "Law's Autonomy and Public Practical Reason," in R. P. George (ed.), *The Autonomy of Law: Essays on Legal Positivism* (Oxford: Clarendon Press, 1996), pp. 79–118.
64. Jules Coleman, "Truth and Objectivity in Law," *Legal Theory* 1 (1995): 33–68, at pp. 33, 45, 57 (author's emphasis); see also Coleman and Leiter, "Determinacy, Objectivity, and Authority," p. 559.
65. Coleman and Leiter make a point of distinguishing the metaphysical project from the project of accounting for objectivity in "procedural" or "epistemic" terms in Coleman and Leiter, "Determinacy, Objectivity, and Authority," pp. 594–601.
66. As Leiter observes, Dworkin succumbs to this temptation in "Objectivity and Truth." See Brian Leiter, "McDowell and Dworkin" in "Objectivity, Morality, and Adjudication," this volume. Note that this is a broader claim of irrelevance than the one defended by Jeremy Waldron in "The Irrelevance of Moral Objectivity," in R. P. George (ed.), *Natural Law Theory* (Oxford: Clarendon Press, 1992), pp. 158–187. Waldron there is arguing against strong realist metaphysics, not against the metaphysical project itself.
67. See, e.g., Leiter, "Objectivity, Morality, and Adjudication"; M. Moore, "Law as a Functional Kind," in George, *Natural Law Theory,* pp. 228–231; Coleman, "Truth and Objectivity in Law," pp. 36–37. Coleman and Leiter accept that liberal political theory is committed to objectivity, and that the objectivity in question is metaphysical, see "Determinacy, Objectivity, and Authority," pp. 553, 559, 594–595, 597–598.
68. I am grateful to Brian Leiter for this objection.
69. See J. L. Mackie, *Ethics: Inventing Right and Wrong* (New York: Penguin Books, 1977), chap. 1.
70. The same motivation, I suspect, drives Coleman and Leiter to explore alternatives to strong, platonist accounts of the metaphysics of law in "Determinacy, Objectivity, and Authority."
71. A similar story can be told about the development of more sophisticated projectivist and expressivist theories of ethics in response to objections that earlier emotivist theories failed to account for the possibility of logical relations among moral assertions (the so-called Frege-Geach problem).
72. This objection was also pressed on me by Brian Leiter.
73. "Politics is what men do when metaphysics fails." Benjamin Barber, *The Conquest of Politics* (Princeton: Princeton University Press, 1988), p. 209.
74. Leiter, "Two Kinds of Objectivity" and "McDowell on Objectivity" in "Objectivity, Morality, and Adjudication," this volume.
75. Ibid., "The 'Internal' and the 'External.'"
76. Ibid., "External Skepticism: Unintelligible or Question-Begging."
77. Williams, *Ethics and the Limits of Philosophy,* chap. 8.
78. Leiter, "External Skepticism," in "Objectivity, Morality, and Adjudication," this volume.
79. Ibid.
80. Ibid., "McDowell and Skepticism."

81. Ibid., "External Skepticism: Unitelligent or Question Begging" and "Is Naturalistic Objectivity Irrelevant?"

82. Ibid., "McDowell and Dworkin" and "Is Naturalistic Objectivity Irrelevant?"

83. Ibid., "Is Naturalistic Objectivity Irrelevant?" emphasis in the original.

84. Warren Quinn, "Reflection and the Loss of Moral Knowledge: Williams on Objectivity," *Philosophy and Public Affairs* 16 (1987): 195–209, at p. 200.

85. Ibid.

86. Ibid.

87. Kant, *Critique of Pure Reason,* p. 573 (A 707/B 735).

88. Ideas and arguments expressed in this chapter have been presented in lectures and seminary at the University of Erlangen, the University of Bayreuth, the Australian National University, the University of Melbourne, the Triangle Ethics Group in Chapel Hill, and Columbia University Legal Theory Workshop. I am grateful to audiences and patient colleagues for comments and criticism, especially Brian Leiter, Joachim Hruschka, Ulrich Metschl, Julian Roberts, Joseph Raz, Jeremy Waldron, Michael Smith, Richard Holton, Rae Langton, Geoffrey Sayre-McCord, Thomas Hill, Jr., and Thomas Powell. Some of the key ideas in this chapter were first sketched out in one of my Wittgenstein Lectures at the University of Bayreuth. A substantial draft of the chapter was written during my stay as a Visiting Fellow at the Research School for Social Science at the Australian National University. I want to thank my hosts at these two wonderful institutions, especially Ulrich Metschl at the University of Bayreuth and Philip Pettit and Geoffrey Brennan at ANU.

4

Objective Values

Does Metaethics Rest on a Mistake?

SIGRÚN SVAVARSDÓTTIR

It is fairly standard in the contemporary literature to distinguish between moral cognitivism and moral realism. The former position takes a stand only on the semantics of moral language and the nature of the mental activity crucially involved in moral evaluation, while the latter position also takes on certain metaphysical (and possibly epistemological) commitments. Cognitivism holds that moral terms function semantically as predicate expressions: that is, their semantic values are properties.[1] Corresponding to them are genuine moral concepts employed for forming moral beliefs and judgments that truly or falsely represent the object of evaluation[2] as having the designated properties.[3] The contrasting view is noncognitivism which maintains that moral terms, though having the syntactic distribution of predicate expressions, semantically function as mood indicators: that is, they signal a grammatical mood typically used for expressing certain affective or conative attitudes toward the object of evaluation under *a nonmoral* mode of presentation. Moral judgments[4] are identified with or regarded as manifestations of such attitudes and are consequently not subject to semantic evaluation in terms of truth and falsity.[5] The disagreement between cognitivists and noncognitivists thus centers on how it is best to interpret moral language and thought. It is not a metaphysical disagreement. Realism is commonly taken to presuppose cognitivism but adds at least the metaphysical claim[6] that there are facts – independent of our opinion in the matter – as to which objects and events instantiate the properties that are ascribed by moral judgments; that is, there are objective facts that render some of our moral claims true and others false.[7]

Famously, J. L. Mackie rejects the metaphysical thesis that lies at the core of moral realism, although he accepts a cognitivist interpretation of moral discourse and thought.[8] The upshot is his error theory, according to which every single moral judgment incorporates a mistaken ontic commitment to sui generis moral properties and is, therefore, strictly speaking false.[9] Many anti-realists have found it more attractive to favor noncognitivism and thus avoid construing moral discourse and thought as embodying a pervasive metaphysical error. According to them, moral discourse and thought is not correctly understood as ascribing any sort of properties to the object of evaluation and, hence, the metaphysical issue dividing realists and error theorists does not even arise: namely, whether these properties exist or have any actual (even possible) instantiations.

I hasten to add that the disagreement between Mackie and realists need not reflect a deep disagreement about what sort of facts there are. Admittedly, this sounds paradoxical, given that I have just claimed that Mackie rejects the metaphysical thesis that lies at the core of realism. But Mackie rejects this thesis because he thinks that conceptual analysis reveals that the properties ascribed by moral judgments are of such a peculiar kind that they could not be instantiated and, hence, there could be no facts rendering some moral claims true. Realists who accept this claim about the results of an analysis of moral concepts will have a deep metaphysical disagreement with Mackie: they will endorse ontic commitments that Mackie rejects. This realist position is commonly referred to as Non-Naturalism, since the only facts Mackie is willing to acknowledge are those that belong to the natural order of things, accessible to us through empirical observation aided by inductive and deductive reasoning.[10] But realists need not accept Mackie's claim about the results of an analysis of moral concepts. They may argue that conceptual analysis reveals that the properties, ascribed by moral judgments, are of a sort that Mackie himself does not hold suspect. Or they may maintain that conceptual analysis cannot reveal about what sort of properties moral concepts enable us to think and talk, but that we have some other grounds for believing that these are of a sort that Mackie himself does not find problematic. These versions of realism may be referred to as analytic naturalism and nonanalytic naturalism, respectively.[11] Proponents of the former view may, for example, argue that an informative conceptual analysis will reveal that moral concepts enable us to think of the dispositional property of the object of evaluation to affect humans in a certain way under certain conditions. And advocates of the latter view may remind us that conceptual analysis could, for example, never have revealed that the concept of heat enables us to think of the property of having a certain mean molecular kinetic energy. The disagreement between Mackie and such naturalistic realists would not really be metaphysical in nature but would rather center on the nature of moral concepts and the semantics of moral language. Of course, there will be a partial agreement among them on these issues, namely, they will all agree that moral thought and discourse is best given a cognitivist rather than a noncognitivist interpretation. But there is much room for disagreement among cognitivists about the exact nature of moral concepts and the exact meaning of moral terms.

Mackie's view can, therefore, come under attack from three different directions. The noncognitivist will dispute his moral cognitivism. Some fellow cognitivists will dispute that conceptual analysis of moral thought and discourse will turn up any ontic commitments that Mackie would find objectionable. And finally, Non-Naturalistic realists, who agree with him about the ontic commitments incurred by employing moral concepts, will dispute Mackie's skepticism about the corresponding properties and their instantiations. Prima facie, this exhausts the theoretical possibilities for his opponents, although there is much to disagree on within these three camps.[12] However, Thomas Nagel has mounted an opposition to Mackie that appears not to fit into any of these three categories, although it is supposed to come from a realist direction.[13] Indeed, the sense I get from Nagel's writings is that Mackie's skeptical position depends on framing questions about the reality of values in the wrong way, and that the right strategy is to upset the sort of framework that dictates the above three approaches to attacking his account of moral thought and discourse. If this is right, Nagel's true target is much broader than Mackie's skepticism; for much of contemporary metaethical discussion takes place within the framework under attack.

In this chapter, I put Nagel's challenge to Mackie – and possibly much of contemporary metaethics – under scrutiny. I find it very difficult to get a clear conception of Nagel's moral realism, and as a consequence the chapter is largely devoted to finding a coherent interpretation of his view as presented in *The View from Nowhere.* The exploratory nature of my discussion may frustrate some readers. But I frankly do not see the value of focusing all philosophical discussions on setting up and solving neat dilemmas or other riddles, or on setting forth and defending yet another position in logical space. It can also be worthwhile just to explore the terrain from a new angle. That is my purpose in writing this chapter. The focus on Nagel's challenge provides my new angle on the semantic and metaphysical issues sketched above. I am afraid that my excursion will end back home in the mundane landscape of contemporary metaethical discussions rather than in some more exotic and elevated territory. But that hardly means that the trip has not been worth taking. My interest in undertaking this journey is augmented by the fact that Nagel's response to Mackie comes in the context of an extensive discussion of objectivity. This is not surprising given that Mackie's preferred statement of his moral antirealism comes in the form of a denial that there are any objective values. Indeed, Nagel's quarrel with Mackie has much to do with their different conceptions of objectivity. And that gives me the opportunity to examine how the issue of objectivity in morals relates to the semantic and metaphysical issues sketched above. My hope is that this chapter will deepen our understanding of these issues.

A road map might be helpful: I start by examining more closely Mackie's skeptical thesis and his conception of objectivity. I argue that he is operating with two distinct notions of objectivity: one is normative, the other is metaphysical. The discussion then moves to Nagel's conception of objectivity, which is epistemic, and his response to Mackie. The response raises puzzles about how to understand Nagel's moral realism. An attempt to do so (section V) provides the forum for examining the metaphor of externality and the notion of mind-dependence, which figure prominently in discussions of realism and of objectivity. A second attempt (section VI) provides the occasion for distinguishing between two different notions of value. This explorative discussion culminates, at the end of section VI, in the intermediate conclusion that Nagel's moral realism is to be understood as a position reached within value inquiry rather than as the metaethical position characterized above. Moreover, Nagel rejects the dispute over the metaethical position as radically misguided. In section VII, I examine Nagel's grounds for dismissing the metaethical debate and conclude that Nagel is objecting not so much to the metaethical enterprise as to the naturalistic methodology that many metaethicists employ. At this point, the question arises whether Nagel is after all committed to some metaethical view. Although somewhat inconclusive, the discussion of this issue (section XIII) leads to a closer examination of the realist claim that the nature of the facts that render moral judgments true or false are independent of our opinion in the matter. In the final section, I take issue with Nagel's extreme (methodological) antinaturalism and articulate my tentative view of meta-ethical – and more generally, philosophical – inquiry and its relation to scientific inquiry.

I. Mackie's Skeptical Thesis

Mackie opens his *Ethics: Inventing Right and Wrong* with the provocative claim that there are no objective values. Two paragraphs into the first chapter, Mackie comments on his opening statement as follows:

> The claim that values are not objective, are not part of the fabric of the world, is meant to include not only moral goodness, which might be most naturally equated with moral value, but also other things that could be more loosely called moral values or disvalues – rightness and wrongness, duty, obligation, an action's being rotten and contemptible, and so on. It also includes non-moral values, notably aesthetic ones, beauty and various kinds of artistic merit. (*Ethics*, 15)

From this restatement of his claim, it is clear that Mackie is making an ontological claim concerning the properties that evaluative judgments prima facie ascribe to objects or events (e.g., goodness and beauty) and the relations that some such judgments prima facie assert to hold between an agent and an action under a specific description (e.g., being someone's duty or obligation). And the claim is that these properties and relations are not objective in the sense of not being "part of the fabric of the world."

This picturesque phrase suggests that it is best to model our understanding of Mackie's rejection of objective values on the stronger claim – found in the literature on properties – that there are no objective properties. Such an outright rejection of objective properties is usually understood as a rejection of the view that the world has a certain structure independently of how we carve it up in thought or language.[14] And such a view of properties is usually accompanied with the idea that, when developing the classificatory schemes we employ in thinking and talking about the world, we are trying to capture this thought- or language-independent structure of reality. Indeed, it is the structure of reality that validates one of the many competing classificatory schemes as the right one: the one which best captures that structure. Mackie does not reject this view of properties in general. On the contrary, he accepts it. But if his rejection of objective values is best modeled on the rejection of objective properties as understood above, then he is denying that values – that is, the properties evaluative judgments prima facie ascribe to the object of evaluation – are part of the structure of the world conceived of as being independent of human thought and language. Put differently, he holds that there is a language- and thought-independent structure to reality but denies that there is anything in that structure which corresponds to evaluative concepts in such a way that it can validate one of the many competing theories of any given type of value as the correct one.

This way of understanding Mackie is supported by his insistence on keeping conceptual and ontological questions apart:

But there are also ontological, as contrasted with linguistic or conceptual, questions about the nature and status of goodness or rightness or whatever it is that first order statements are distinctively about. These are questions of factual rather than conceptual analysis: the problem of what goodness is cannot be settled conclusively or exhaustively by finding out what the word "good" means, or what it is conventionally used to say or to do. (*Ethics,* 19)

We cannot settle questions about what properties actually exist by examining our concepts or the meaning of the predicates in our language. This presupposes that the qualitative structure, of which actual properties are part, is independent of the classificatory structure found in our language and conceptual scheme. Indeed, if conceptual analysis could reveal what properties there are, it would, according to Mackie, establish that there are objective values:

If second order ethics were confined, then, to linguistic and conceptual analysis, it ought to conclude that moral values at least are objective: that they are so is part of what our ordinary moral statements mean: the traditional moral concepts of the ordinary man as well as of the main line of western philosophers are concepts of objective value. (*Ethics,* 35)

But Mackie argues that this only goes to show that the content of all our moral judgments is infested with a mistaken ontic commitment and all moral judgments are, therefore, strictly speaking false. This is his error theory of moral thought and discourse.[15]

A closer examination of the error Mackie claims to detect in moral thought and discourse will reveal, however, that the above construal of Mackie's opening statement needs to be further refined: "But the denial of objective values will have to be put forward not as the result of an analytic approach, but as an 'error theory', a theory that although most people in making moral judgements implicitly claim, among other things, to be pointing to something objectively prescriptive, these claims are all false" (*Ethics,* 35). The error involved in moral thought is to presume that there is something "objectively prescriptive." One way of understanding this diagnosis of the error is that moral judgments involve the assumption that there is something prescriptive *and* objective in the sense of being part of the language- and mind-independent structure of the world. This would be completely in line with the above construal of Mackie's opening statement. However, a slightly different understanding of Mackie's diagnosis of the error is suggested by his remark about how his skeptical thesis relates to Kant's claim that moral requirements are categorical imperatives of reason: "So far as ethics is concerned, my thesis that there are no objective values is specifically the denial that any such categorically imperative element is objectively valid. The objective values which I am denying would be action-directing absolutely, not contingently . . . upon the agent's desires and inclinations" (*Ethics,* 29). This passage suggests that when Mackie denies that there are objective values, he is denying that there is anything in the language- and mind-independent structure of the world which is "action-directing absolutely, not contingently . . . upon the agent's desires and inclinations." And this in turn suggests that the error he detects in moral thought and language consists in an implicit claim to the effect that when making moral judgments we are successfully referring to something that is action-directing absolutely. That is, the error of assuming that moral judgments succeed in referring to something objectively prescriptive is the error of assuming that they succeed in referring to something that is action-directing irrespective of what concerns the agent has. But then "objectively prescriptive" should not be read as "objective and prescriptive," but rather as designating a peculiar prescriptive status. The error involved in moral thought is to presume that something that is *objectively prescriptive exists objectively* in the sense of being part of the thought- and language-independent world.

I am in fact suggesting that "objective" is being used differently in Mackie's initial statement of his claim – namely, "there are no objective values" – and in his restatement of the claim – namely, "values are not objective, are not part of the fabric of the world." When "objective" is predicated of a value it is not to be understood as conferring to the value a language- and thought-independent mode of existence, but rather as conferring to it a certain mode of prescriptivity: namely, that of directing people to take certain actions irrespective of what their concerns are.[16] When "objective" indicates such a prescriptive status, let's talk about *normative objectivity;* and when it indicates an ontic status, let's talk about *ontic objectivity*.[17] A concept of an objective value is a concept of a value that is normatively objective rather than of a value that exists objectively, although the exercise of that concept (at least in nonhypothetical contexts) commits one to there being such properties (or, at least, to there being instantiations of such properties). Mackie's claim is that properties that are normatively objective do not have ontic objectivity.[18]

I believe that such a shift in Mackie's use of "objective" occurs throughout the first chapter of his book and is worth noting. It implies that there are two different issues concerning objectivity in morals as far as Mackie is concerned. The first is whether our moral concepts are, indeed, concepts of values that are objective in the sense of directing people to act in certain ways irrespective of their ends. The second is whether moral concepts enable us to think and speak of properties, which are objective in the sense of being part of the language- and thought-independent structure of the world. Mackie answers the former question in the affirmative and takes that to require a negative answer to the latter question. It is easy to discern the relation between the issue of objectivity in morals and the issue between realists and antirealists, given Mackie's conception of these issues. His rejection of the idea that moral concepts enable us to think and speak of ontically objective properties implies the core claim of antirealism: namely, that there are no facts, independent of our opinion in the matter, as to that objects and events instantiate the properties which are ascribed by moral judgments. There are no such objective facts, according to Mackie, because such properties do not exist objectively.

II. Nagel on Objectivity and Values

Nagel appears to be straightforwardly contradicting Mackie, when he confidently declares that there are objective values. But things are not that simple because Nagel is employing a markedly different notion of objectivity than either one of Mackie's. Nagel talks about objectivity as "a method of understanding" (*Nowhere,* 4) and even as "a human faculty" (*Nowhere,* 7). As a method of understanding, objectivity involves "step[ping] back from our initial view of [some aspect of life or the world] and form[ing] a new conception which has that view and its relation to the world as its object" (*Nowhere,* 4). This process of "stepping back" involves forming a conception of the world and life that reflects less and less our particular position within space and time, our peculiar sensory, motivational, and emotional endowments, and other idiosyncratic or species-specific features of our psychology: the result is a more and more "impersonal" and "detached" conception of life and the world, which can be shared by an increasing number of rational thinkers.[19] Such a method, Nagel contends, has been particularly effective for expanding our understanding of the physical world. In that domain of inquiry, the method involves causal reasoning as well as ongoing revision of the conceptual resources used to represent our physical environment (*Nowhere,* 14). This revision consists in eliminating certain concepts commonly employed in perceptual experience, which yield representations of the world that reflect the spatial location and the sensory endowments of the perceiving subject. (Paradigmatic examples of such concepts are, presumably, *in front of, to the left,* and secondary quality concepts.) Nagel uses "objective" to describe the beliefs formed in this way, the representation they give of the world, and the parts of reality that can be thus understood. He warns us not to take objective reality to be all the reality there is (*Nowhere,* 26–27), since it would amount to using an "epistemological criterion of reality" (*Nowhere,* 141): a certain type of understandability would be taken as definitive of what there is. Thus, Nagel is employing an epistemic notion of objectivity that is distinct from either one of the two that we have encountered in Mackie's writings: it marks a mode of understanding and understandability rather than a mode of existence or of prescriptivity.

Nagel contends that the process leading to detachment from our personal perspective on life and the world must be different depending on whether we are trying to gain an understanding of the physical world, mental phenomena, or values. But he tells us disappointingly little about what is involved in any of the three cases. It is, however, clear that the main challenge in value inquiry is to neutralize the effects of our interests and desires on how we conceive of life and the world.[20] And he recognizes as natural, though ultimately unwarranted, the worry that should we achieve this – should: "we push the claims of objective detachment to their logical conclusion, and survey the world from a standpoint completely detached from all interests, we discover that there is *nothing* – no values left of any kind: things can be said to matter at all only to individuals within the world. The result is objective nihilism" (*Nowhere,* 146). This is not Mackie's worry. Mackie does not suggest that our employment of value concepts is keyed to our desires and interests in such a way that if we succeeded in neutralizing the effects of the latter on our conception of life and the world, we would cease to employ value concepts in our representations of the world. His worry is rather that – regardless of the conditions under which we can use such concepts – so long as these are concepts of normatively objective values, nothing in the language- and thought-independent world can be truthfully represented with their aid. This is based on an ontological worry that Nagel thinks is radically misplaced. But before examining Nagel's response to Mackie, let's complete our discussion of Nagel's conception of objectivity in value inquiry.

Nagel's reaction to the above natural worry is revealing: "And indeed, when we take up the objective standpoint, the problem is not that values seem to disappear but that there seem to be too many of them, coming from every life and drowning out those that arise from our own" (*Nowhere,* 147). Why is the problem that "there seem to be too many [values], coming from every life and drowning out those that arise from our own"? Bear in mind that the view of life and the world that is formed by the detachment process has the initial view – affected by the thinker's idiosyncratic and species-specific psychology – and its relation to the world as its object (*Nowhere,* 4). The detached view treats the initial view as consisting of appearances. Moreover, the detached view has not only the initial view of the thinker as its object but also the personal perspectives of other cognizers. All appearances are of equal interest for gaining an objective understanding of the world. Now, in our inquiry into the physical, we try to go beyond these appearances by understanding what sorts of things caused them, via physical impact on our bodies, and how these things causally interact among themselves (*Nowhere,* 14). The goal is to form a representation of this causal realm that is not affected by the mode in which it appears to us in sensory experience. Within this project, we are interested in our experiences only as starting points for understanding their physical causes. But in an inquiry into the mental, they interest us in their own right. They are seen as an interesting part of the world of which we need to gain a more impersonal understanding, without losing sight of their subjective and perspectival character. In order to do so, we must be able to conceive of our own initial point of view as just one among many subjective perspectives on the world and be able to conceive of these diverse loci of appearances as parts of the world. The attempt to gain such an impersonal understanding of diverse experiences is an attempt to form an understanding of minds within the world that could be shared by other cognizers. One's own personal perspective cannot be privileged as the prototypical subjective standpoint, if this effort is to succeed. Nagel seems to suggest that such an endeavor can never be completely successful, but successive approximations to such an impersonal understanding of subjective experiences are possible (*Nowhere,* 17–18). And such approximations – if I understand Nagel correctly – are involved in the detachment process integral to value inquiry. Now we can begin to understand why Nagel claims that the problem is that when we go through the detachment process, there *seem* to be too many values "coming from every life and drowning out those that arise from our own" personal standpoints.

The point is not merely that we come to realize that it is possible to desire and value other things than we ourselves happen to desire and value. We come to appreciate this "from inside," so to speak: part of the impersonal understanding is an understanding of the various perspectives qua perspectives on the world. Insofar as we are successful at obtaining an objective understanding of the mental, we appreciate *what it is like* to see value in all sorts of activities and qualities we would not count among our values. Indeed, from the objective standpoint we would make no distinction between the values we prereflectively embrace and those that others prereflectively embrace. All the various value possibilities are grasped from the objective standpoint as if the thinker were able simultaneously to take on the various possible perspectives generated by entirely different sets of desires and interests. But at the same time he does not fully occupy any of them because he is equally "detached" from all these desires and interests, and hence he views the various values seen from the different subjective perspectives as apparent values. However, Nagel maintains that when we occupy this standpoint, certain things will come or continue to be seen by us as values rather than mere appearances of values: "When we take the objective step, we don't leave the evaluative capacity behind automatically, since that capacity does not depend on antecedently present desires. We may find that it continues to operate from an external standpoint, and we may conclude that this is not just a case of subjective desires popping up in objective disguise" (*Nowhere,* 143). We have the capacity to form evaluations even when we have neutralized the effects of our desires and interests on our conception of life and view the subjective perspective, affected by these desires and interests, as on a par with the many other subjective perspectives affected by the various possible clusters of desires and interests. It is things that are seen as values from such an impersonal perspective that deserve to be regarded as objective values.

Thus, it appears that Nagel's claim that there are objective values should be understood as the claim that there are things that will be recognized as values from the objective standpoint. At play is an epistemic notion of objectivity rather than a normative or a metaphysical one. But perhaps values that can be appreciated from a standpoint unaffected by one's desires and interests should be regarded as normatively objective, that is, as directing people to take certain actions irrespective of what their concerns are.[21] But need such values be ontically objective? Prima facie the answer would have to be in the affirmative in order for Nagel to have a successful response to Mackie's challenge. However, we will see in the next section that it is far from clear whether this is the correct answer and whether Nagel's response hangs on its being so.

III. Nagel's Puzzling Response to Mackie

I have already noted that Nagel is operating with a notion of objectivity that marks a mode of understanding or understandability rather than a mode of existence or of prescriptivity. In other words, he is employing an epistemic notion of objectivity. This is certainly a familiar notion that we operate with in moral, scientific, and other types of inquiry. We use it to describe the method of inquiry, the process of inquiry, the inquirers, and the results of inquiry. It signifies that the output of the method – if correctly applied – or of the actual process of inquiry is not affected by distorting factors, especially the prior opinions, expectations, wishes, and biases of the inquirers. This sort of objectivity will be a matter of degree: the output, method, inquiry, and inquirer will be more or less objective depending on how well the method or the inquirer succeeds in neutralizing the effects of distorting factors on the results of inquiry. Indeed, even if we can never attain complete objectivity, it can function as an ideal to strive toward and approximate.[22]

In value inquiry, we want in particular to neutralize the effects of such factors as paranoic tendencies, insecurities, wishes, self-interest, care for loved ones, and loyalty to friends. Insofar as we are honest inquirers, we will attempt to check the influence of such psychological factors. The most effective way is typically to converse with others, but various other strategies are open to us as well: we may, for example, imagine what it is like to see the situation from the vantage point of someone else or try to uncover how exactly, say, a care for a friend is affecting one's perspective on the situation. Such efforts may be described as a process of detachment or of stepping back from our initial personal perspective. And certainly such efforts may alter our assessment of what is of value. However, it is questionable to assume that such a process tends toward the neutralization of the effects of all idiosyncratic and culturally conditioned, let alone species-specific, psychological features of the inquirer. And it is highly speculative and controversial that such a process will tend to culminate in an understanding and evaluation of social interactions that will be shared by all rational thinkers who go through a similar process whatever their starting point is.

Mackie, in particular, is likely to dispute this. He offers an argument – the so-called argument from relativity – for his skeptical thesis that relies on an observation of wide cultural variations in moral evaluation as well as persistent moral disagreements within cultures. It is unlikely that Mackie is simply refer-ring to actual disagreements; more plausibly he has also in mind the apparent absence of a (noncoercive) method for solving them. Nagel cannot, therefore, rest his response to Mackie on the undefended assumption that there is such a method. More interestingly, even if Nagel turned out to be right on this score, it is far from obvious that he has the material for successfully responding to Mackie's challenge. To see why, let's waive the above worries and simply grant Nagel that there is a method for neutralizing the effects of our idiosyn-cratic, culturally conditioned, and even species-specific psychological features on our understanding and evaluation of our social transactions, which will yield the same conception of what is of value for any inquirer whatever his subjective starting point is like. (For convenience, I will refer to this as *the Nagelian method.*) Nagel finds it incredible that this process – if correctly carried out – would at its ideal limit yield a conception of life from which values have disappeared. Let's grant him this as well.

Mackie's argument from relativity takes the form of an inference to the best explanation. He argues that the best explanation of persistent and intractable moral disagreements will trace them to differences in the social background of the parties to the dispute rather than to distorting factors that obscure the parties' ability to discern accurately ontically objective values (*Ethics,* 37).[23] If the Nagelian method is available in value inquiry, persistent and intractable moral disagreements are, indeed, resolvable. However, the existence of the Nagelian method does not go far in establishing that the best explanation of these disagreements will trace them to distorting factors that interfere with the parties' ability to discern accurately ontically objective values. Granted the existence of the Nagelian method, the best explanation of persistent and intractable moral disagreements is likely to trace them to factors that interfere with the parties' ability to form an objective – in Nagel's sense – evaluative conception of the matter in dispute. But it is unclear that this has anything to do with these factors obscuring the parties' ability to discern accurately ontically objective values. It is open to doubt whether forming an objective evaluative conception amounts to discerning values whose existence and nature is ontically objective. The only thing that is clear at this point is that this conception ex hypothesi will not be affected by mental states or traits that are not shared by all rational inquirers. But do the mental states and traits that can be shared by all rational inquirers render an accurate representation of ontically objective reality? Indeed, why are they more likely to yield such a representation than mental states and traits that cannot be universally shared by all rational inquirers?

The availability of an objective method for settling disagreements in an area of inquiry hardly suffices for establishing the ontic objectivity of its subject matter. If you doubt this, bear in mind that we have a perfectly objective method for determining any disagreement that can be formulated in terms of a question that has only two possible answers: "no" or "yes." Flipping a coin is the perfect method for neutralizing the effects of our idiosyncrasies on such queries. But it hardly implies that all such disagreements concern an ontically objective subject matter. Of course, the objective method Nagel believes is available to us in value inquiry relies on much more substantial mental operations than the method of flipping a coin. There is the process of detachment that neutralizes the effects of our interests and desires on how we conceive of life, the process of coming to understand what it is like to see value in all sorts of activities and qualities, and finally the exercise of the evaluative capacity under such conditions of detached understanding of all the possible personal perspectives. Perhaps a story can be told that makes it plausible that the output of such mental processes gives us insights into a realm of ontically objective facts.[24] But that is by no means obvious, and Mackie's challenge stands until that has been done. Or what?

The skeptical questions I have been raising about the maximally objective conception of values – assuming it is in principle obtainable – could equally be raised about the maximally objective conception of mental and physical phenomena. I have, admittedly, served as the mouthpiece of the radical skeptic who indiscriminately targets the results of any type of inquiry. But certainly, Mackie's challenge is supposed to be distinct from the radical skeptic's and apply specifically to our conception of (objectively prescriptive) values. So, perhaps Mackie's challenge could be met even in the absence of the sort of story for which I advertised above: that is, without laying to rest the doubt that even our maximally objective conception of values accurately represents a realm of ontically objective facts. Indeed, notice that accepting this worry as inescapable would not amount to an acceptance of Mackie's skeptical thesis. Mackie's skeptical position goes beyond a mere *doubt that* objectively prescriptive values have an objective existence: his claim is that objectively prescriptive values *could not* be ontically objective. It is open to Nagel to argue that Mackie has no good grounds for making such an *assertion,* even if the skeptical worry can never be laid to rest. Indeed, if the Nagelian method is the best one we have in value inquiry and it yields a conception of life that depicts certain things as being of value, then we have no good grounds for denying that values are part of the ontically objective world, although that might not stop us from intelligently worrying whether it could, indeed, be the case.[25]

Curiously, this is not the response that Nagel offers Mackie. Instead, he maintains that Mackie's skeptical worry rests on a mistaken assumption about the ontic commitments incurred by value realists:

> Mackie . . . denies the objectivity of values by saying that they are "not part of the fabric of the world," and that if they were, they would have to be "entities or qualities or relations of a very strange sort, utterly different from anything else in the universe." . . . He clearly has a definite picture of what the universe is like, and assumes that realism about value would require crowding it with extra entities, qualities, or relations, things like Platonic Forms or Moore's nonnatural qualities. But this assumption is not correct. (*Nowhere,* 144)

Nagel is, obviously, distancing himself from Non-Naturalistic realism. However, the whole tenor of Nagel's writing suggests that he would equally reject naturalistic realism. But what does his realism about values then come to? Nagel rather unhelpfully tells us that realism is committed to the view that there are real values, which is the view that real values are real values and nothing else: "The view that values are real is not the view that they are real occult entities or properties, but that they are real values: that our claims about value and about what people have reason to do may be true or false independently of our beliefs and inclinations" (*Nowhere,* 144). Of course, any realist will claim that real values are real values and nothing else. But that does not foreclose that we can at least partly elucidate the nature of values and even identify them as entities we can also conceptualize under an entirely different mode of presentation.[26] If these entities are real values, it will make them no less of real values, or something else than real values, that they can be presented in thought in a different way. A realist may, however, take the view that there is no elucidation or different mode of presentation to be gotten of these entities. Such a realist may be either a nonanalytic naturalist or a Non-

Naturalist. But it seems like Nagel is not even endorsing this view; for he objects to any talk of values as entities.[27]

All he does is to equate the fact that pain is objectively bad with the fact that there is a reason for anyone capable of viewing the world objectively to want to stop it (*Nowhere*, 144). In general, Nagel equates questions of values with questions of reasons for action. Realism about values, indeed, gets elucidated as realism about reasons to act:

> Here as elsewhere there is a connection between objectivity and realism, though realism about values is different from realism about empirical facts. Normative realism is the view that propositions about what gives us reasons for action can be true or false independently of how things appear to us, and that we can hope to discover the truth by transcending the appearances and subjecting them to critical assessment. What we aim to discover by this method is not a new aspect of the external world, called value, but rather just the truth about what we and others should do and want. (*Nowhere*, 139)

This quote gives us direct evidence that Nagel holds a cognitivist view of judgments about reasons for action: they express propositions about what gives us reasons for action that are, of course, true or false. And there are plenty of suggestions in the text to the effect that claims about values amount to claims about reasons for action. But taken at face value, the proposition that c gives s a reason to f represents a three-place relation as obtaining between c, s, and f.[28] Now, one would have thought that if this proposition is true "independently of how things appear to us," then this triadic relation (let's call it "the reason-relation") holds between c, s, and f, and that fact is part of the language- and thought-independent world. But why then the disclaimer that confirmation of reason-claims does not amount to a discovery of "a new aspect of the external world"?[29] It does not help to be told that what we discover is "just the truth about what we and others should do and want." Maybe that is just what we discover, but why does that not amount to discovering an aspect of the ontically objective world, if such claims have propositional content and their truth-values are determined independently of how we represent things in thought and language?

Nagel presumably wants to resist conceding this point. On it hangs his response to Mackie. For his response is not simply that Mackie has no good grounds for declaring the properties and relations of which moral claims speak as too mysterious to be part of the language- and thought-independent structure of the world. Rather, he claims that Mackie's skeptical worry is misplaced since realism about values and reasons does not commit us to any properties or relations beyond those on which we base our evaluation. It is not that his skeptical challenge can intelligibly and somewhat reasonably be mounted but then plausibly met. This is of a piece with Nagel's contention that there is no room for skeptical worries about the maximally objective evaluative conception of life:

The connection between objectivity and truth is . . . closer in ethics than it is in science. I do not believe that the truth about how we should live *could* extend radically beyond any capacity we might have to discover it (apart from its dependence on nonevaluative facts we might be unable to discover). . . . [T]he only thing I can think of to say about ethical truth in general is that it *must* be a possible result of this process [of seeking objective evaluative conception of life], correctly carried out. (*Nowhere,* 139; italics mine)

In this passage, Nagel is not merely expressing optimism about our ability to correctly discern what is of value; rather he is unequivocally advocating the view that there is no room for a mistake – and, hence, no room for a skeptical worry – in value inquiry so long as we have correctly followed the procedure for obtaining an objective understanding of values. But surely we need a story to back up this claim and the debunking response to Mackie. The burden is on Nagel to explain how claims about reasons and values can express propositions – that is, be representational and truth-evaluable – but still their truth does not require that the object of evaluation have any distinctive feature or enter into a distinctive relation with other things, natural or nonnatural. Do they not represent the object of evaluation as being one way or another? And why can we not ask at every stage of value inquiry – including the ideal final stage – whether the object exists objectively the way it is represented to be?

IV. Nagel on Representation and Epistemic Justification

The answers to these questions are not to be found in Nagel's general view of representation. Significantly, Nagel maintains that the skeptical worry can never be laid to rest in an inquiry into the nature of physical reality (*Nowhere,* 67–68): "The search for objective knowledge, because of its commitment to a realistic picture, is inescapably subject to skepticism and cannot refute it but must proceed under its shadow. Skepticism, in turn, is a problem only because of the realist claims of objectivity" (*Nowhere,* 71). In this context, Nagel conjures up the standard realist imagery: there is an ontically objective world of which we are part, and our subjective experiences of this world result from our interactions with the rest of it (*Nowhere,* 68). A commitment to that picture, Nagel contends, makes us continually question to what extent our understanding of the world is distorted by the constitution of our own mind. We strive to have our representation of the world as little affected as possible by our peculiar location within that world; by our peculiar physiological and psychological capacities, which provide us cognitive and epistemic access to this world; and by any other psychological feature peculiar to ourselves. In other words, a commitment to the realist picture makes us seek an objective, in Nagel's sense, understanding of the world. But at no point can we fully satisfy ourselves that our understanding of the world is not distorted by the constitution of our mind. That worry will be alive even at the ideal limit of inquiry when we have obtained a maximally objective understanding of the world. That is why the commitment to realism dooms us to live under the shadow of skepticism. The flip side of the search for an objective understanding of the world is the skeptical question about the maximally objective representation of the physical world. Both are unavoidable concomitants of a commitment to the realist picture.

It is instructive to note how Nagel departs on this point from Bernard Williams, whose notion of the absolute conception of the world is a precursor to Nagel's notion of the maximally objective conception of the world. The former is presented in the context of Williams's elucidation of the distinction between primary and secondary qualities in Descartes.[30] Williams suggests that crucial to understanding this distinction in Descartes's system is to realize how "it associates together . . . the notion of the material world as it may be scientifically understood, and the notion of that world as it really is" (*Descartes*, 239). The latter notion involves the contrast with the notion of the world as it seems to us. Williams suggests that the contrast between "the world as it really is" and "the world as it seems to us" is to be understood as a contrast between two types of conceptions or representations of the world. The difference lies largely in the conceptual resources employed. The representation associated with the notion of the world as it really is employs concepts "which are not peculiarly ours, and not peculiarly relative to our experience" (*Descartes*, 244); whereas the representation that is associated with the notion of the world as it seems to us employs anthropocentric concepts "which reflect merely a local interest, taste or sensory peculiarity" (*Descartes*, 245). Furthermore, the former has to be explanatory of both events in the material world and of how the latter, anthropocentric representation of the world arises – that is, why the world seems to us the way it does – as well as how it itself can arise (*Descartes*, 244–266). The representation that employs maximally neutral concepts and has the greatest explanatory power of the relevant sort, Williams refers to as *the absolute conception of reality*. It yields the understanding of the world that lies at the ideal limit of scientific inquiry (*Descartes*, 244). According to Williams, there is merely a verbal difference, firstly, between talking about the world as it really is and about the world as depicted by the absolute conception and, secondly, between talking about the world as it seems to us and about the world as it is depicted by the anthropocentric conception.

The affinity between Williams's absolute conception of the world and the representation that Nagel envisions as the final output of the method of physical objectivity should be obvious. But given Williams's understanding of the distinction between the world as it really is and the world as it seems to us, it makes no sense to ask whether the absolute conception accurately represents the world as it really is. In other words, there is no room for the skeptical worry at the ideal limit of (scientific) inquiry. But Nagel – rightly, I believe – rejects any such redrawing of the distinction between the real and the apparent: "I want to resist the natural tendency to identify the idea of the world as it really is with the idea of what can be revealed, at the limit, by an indefinite increase in objectivity of standpoint" (*Nowhere,* 91). Nagel contends that it is possible that reality extends beyond our cognitive powers such that: (1) there might be aspects of reality about which we cannot have more specific thoughts than *something that exists* or *part of reality;* (2) there might be aspects of reality to which we are related in such a way that, although we can think various thoughts about them and can thus speculate about them, we cannot occupy an epistemic position from which we can know or be reasonably justified in believing anything about them; (3) there might be aspects of reality which are such that, although we are justified in believing various things about them, we are so unfortunately positioned vis-à-vis them that our most justified beliefs about them are inaccurate and hence we know nothing about these parts of reality. Thus, the absolute conception of the world may possibly be an incomplete and even an inaccurate representation of the world as it really is.

Obviously, Nagel is committed to a very strong realist position about physical phenomena: what physical reality is like does in no way depend on how anyone experiences it, how anyone thinks about it, or what anyone justifiably believes about it. He is also committed to strong views about the nature of representation and of epistemic justification that, first of all, allow that we can coherently frame the thought that there are things about which we cannot frame any more specific thought; that, secondly, open up the possibility that we think thoughts we could never be in a position to credit or discredit with our methods of justification; and that, thirdly, open up the possibility that we can frame thoughts which, even if credited with our method of justification under optimal epistemic conditions, might still be misrepresentations of reality. This is not the place to examine the underlying metaphysical, epistemological, and semantic views. But it is important for us to appreciate that Nagel is committed to such views about the nature of representation and epistemic justification.[31] It makes it all the more puzzling that Nagel maintains that there is no room for skeptical worries about the maximally objective evaluative conception of life, while expounding the cognitivist view that claims about reasons and values express propositions. Nagel clearly thinks that in scientific and value inquiry there is a radically different relation between a commitment to realism, the pursuit of objective understanding, and the skeptical worry about the resulting conception of the world.[32] But why would there be such a difference between these two areas of inquiry? Why would a commitment to realism about values not give rise – at every stage of value inquiry, including the ideal final stage – to the question whether our evaluative conception is distorted by the constitution of our own mind such that we are misrepresenting what is really of value, independently of our or anyone else's opinion in the matter? Alas, Nagel's conception of value realism continues to elude us.

V. The External World, Mind-Dependence, and Nagel as a Non-Naturalist

It may be thought that the answer to our puzzles lies in a proper understanding of Nagel's claim that in value inquiry we are not aiming to discover "a new aspect of the external world" (*Nowhere,* 139). I am not so sure about that. Nonetheless, an examination of his claim will be worthwhile, since it forces us to think hard about the metaphor of externality, which is commonly used to characterize realism about any discourse, as well as about the notion of mind-dependence, which figures prominently in discussions of ontic objectivity.

Realists are said to accept that the discourse is about facts that are "out there" or part of "the external world." If taken literally it might be thought that realism is committed to an image of the relevant facts as existing at a spatial location different from those occupied by us. More plausibly the allusion to spatial location is treated metaphorically, and "out there" or "the external world" taken to refer to the part of the world that does not contain anything mental. If Nagel intended these expressions in either of these two ways, his disclaimer that confirmation of reason-claims does not amount to a discovery of "a new aspect of the external world" would be readily understandable and *uncontroversial.*[33] For the facts in question – facts about something giving someone a reason to act – involve the subjects who have reasons: these facts are instantiations of the reason-relation by (besides two other things) cognitively sophisticated enough beings to count as rational agents. Thus, these are facts of a world that includes rational agents and, hence, will not be part of a world that is void of minds; nor do these facts actually obtain at spatial locations none of us occupy. This is not because the truth-values of propositions about instantiations of the reason-relation depend on how these facts appear to us, but simply because one of the relata has to be a rational agent. This cannot be the appropriate understanding of the metaphor. Surely, realists intend the metaphor (the same goes for Mackie's metaphor of "among the furniture of the world") to be understood as alluding to the idea that the subject matter of inquiry is not ontologically dependent in any way on the area of thought, discourse, or inquiry in question: that is, it is not language- and thought-dependent in the sense discussed in section I. To understand it differently is simply uncharitable. But if Nagel means the metaphor this way, then it is difficult to reconcile his disclaimer with his characterization of normative realism as "the view . . . that our claims about value and about what people have reason to do may be true or false independently of our beliefs and inclinations" (*Nowhere,* 139).[34]

Some remarks are in order about the difference between the claim that a relation could not be instantiated in a world void of minds and the claim that the relation does not exist or isn't instantiated in the language- and mind-independent – that is, the ontically objective – world. At stake are two radically different ways for the instantiation of a relation (or a property) to be mind-dependent. I find it easiest to explain the difference by focusing on intentional actions. Of course, intentional actions are the sort of events they are because they ensue from mental states (i.e., they are individuated at least partly in terms of the mental states from which they ensue). And because of this, they are in one sense mind-dependent: there would (of conceptual or metaphysical necessity) be no intentional actions unless there were agents with intentional states of mind. Let's call this *existential mind-dependence*.[35] An entity is existentially mind-dependent if and only if it would not exist in the absence of minds or mental activity. This is, however, not the sort of mind-dependence that we have been excluding when referring to the structure of the world as thought- and language-independent. Mackie is certainly not implying that mental states and properties – obviously existentially mind-dependent entities – are not part of the language- and thought-independent world. The language- and thought-independent world as far as he is concerned contains physical, psychological, and sociological properties and instantiations of them (whatever the relations between these may be). To say that they are language- and thought-independent is to claim that their nature does not depend on how *observers of them* conceive of, talk about, or conduct inquiries *about them*. To remind us of this, as well as for the sake of elegance, from now on I will use the expression "observer-independent" (interchangeably with "ontically objective") instead of the more longwinded "language- and thought-independent."[36]

It is maybe easiest to understand my point by considering the intentional activities of people of a culture alien from ours. The nature of their intentional actions depends on what sort of intentional mental states they have and from which their actions ensue. In that way, their intentional actions are existentially mind-dependent. Now, imagine that we are struggling to make sense of the behavior of these strangers. Of course, we cannot but use our current conceptual repertoire for doing so. Say that we have come to an interpretation of what is going on that is coherent and seems plausible to ourselves. The claim that the intentional actions of the strangers are part of the observer-independent world implies that our interpretation may nonetheless be mistaken.[37] We might not have gotten right from what sort of mental states the actions ensued and hence what type of actions they are. What sort of actions these are does not depend on how we or any other observers carve up the psychological reality underlying them; it simply depends on what that psychological reality is. Indeed, the agents themselves might at times be mistaken in their reflective claims about what sort of actions they have been undertaking (e.g., in the case of self-deception), although they are less likely than other observers to be thus mistaken.

Returning now to Nagel, his disclaimer that reason-claims amount to a discovery of "a new aspect of the external world" is uninteresting and uncalled-for, if he means to be referring to the world that does not contain minds or existentially mind-dependent entities. But if he means to be referring to the observer-independent world in its entirety (whatever it contains), then the claim is puzzling insofar as he is a cognitivist and furthermore a realist about reason-claims. Fortunately, our examination of Nagel's conception of objectivity may contain the clue to understanding his resistance to the description of the subject matter of value inquiry as something "out there" or "in the external world." Nagel might have in mind a very different reading of the metaphor of externality than those we have considered. On this new reading, the metaphor gestures at whatever is epistemically accessible to us by relying only on our five senses and our capacities for inductive and deductive reasoning. The contrast is with the part of reality to which we cannot gain epistemic access without relying on our first-person access to subjective experiences of the world.[38] Notice that external reality, thus understood, need not be coextensive with physical reality. Even Nagel – who thinks that much of psychological reality cannot be fully understood without first-person access to mental states – would have to admit that some psychological processes are part of the world that is external, in the relevant sense. For example, many of the psychological processes involved in the comprehension of a lecture are of such a kind. We have no first-person access to them. Assuming that we have epistemic access to them, it has to be through psychological research that gives, in general, insight into the information and language processing of humans. More importantly, external reality, on this reading of the metaphor, is not to be equated with observer-independent reality. Whatever we can come to know only by relying on first-person access to conscious life need not metaphysically depend on how we conceptualize or theorize about it. To take a paradigmatic example: pain is certainly something that Nagel would claim is not part of the external world, as understood above. But it comes into existence, persists, and is of the kind it is whether or not the subject undergoing the pain focuses his attention to it, whether or not he manages to pin down its location, whether or not he or anyone else can adequately describe it, etcetera. Even if it were of the essence of phenomenological qualities to be felt and even if epistemic access to them came only through first-person access, they would not be observer-dependent in the sense that has interested us in this chapter: their existence or nature does not depend on our opinion of them.

If this is how Nagel is understanding the "external"-metaphor, his resistance to the image of the subject matter of value inquiry as something "out there" or in the "external world" is of a piece with his view of the difference between the nature of scientific and value inquiry. Recall that he maintains that in scientific inquiry we pursue an objective understanding of the world, that is, by engaging in causal reasoning to construct a representation of the reality with which we perceptually interact. We are exclusively occupied with the domain of reality that is accessible to us from the third-person perspective, that is, through our five senses aided by inductive and deductive reasoning. In contrast, we pursue objective understanding of mental life and of values by relying on our first-person access to what it is like to experience the world and life in a certain way, while appreciating that different individuals experience it in different ways and giving one's own personal perspective no more significance than any of the other possible personal perspectives. In this way, ethical thought crucially relies on first-person access to mental life and, unlike the sciences, is not an examination of external (in the sense explained above) reality. Thus, Nagel's rejection of the image of values as being "out there" can be seen as tantamount to rejecting the idea that value inquiry is occupied with the domain of the world that is accessible to us through sensory experience aided by inductive and deductive reasoning. It need not be a rejection of the realist idea that values are part of the observer-independent world: they just have to be part of the observer-independent world to which we can gain access only by relying partly on our first-person knowledge of what it is like to perceive, experience, feel, comprehend, master, take interest in, find worthwhile, value, pursue, act, and so forth.

This seems like a satisfying construal of Nagel's claim that in value inquiry we do not seek to discover "a new aspect of the external world"; his point is that the subject matter of ethics is part of reality that lies outside of the domain of science. But notice that this just is the central claim of Non-Naturalistic realism. Moral Non-Naturalists – as I understand their position – accept Mackie's analysis of moral concepts and, furthermore, agree that their semantic values could not be "natural" properties, but must rather be sui generis "nonnatural" properties. Now, the only account I know of this natural–nonnatural distinction is that natural properties lie within the domain of science, whereas the nonnatural do not and have to be accessed by a distinct method. Certainly, this is in line with how G. E. Moore drew the distinction originally.[39] Non-Naturalists are unfazed with Mackie's bafflement at what this distinctive method could be or at there being different sorts of properties than those that we can access by the scientific method. They meet Mackie's incredulous stare ("Weird properties!!!") with an incredulous stare ("Weird properties???"). Now, Nagel can easily be read as having adopted the Non-Naturalist position, but gone beyond the "Weird properties???"-response by diagnosing the source of Mackie's bafflement in a philosophical mistake. He would maintain that it is only because Mackie is comparing these entities to those accessible by the scientific method that he declares them "utterly different from anything else in the universe" (*Ethics*, 38). And although Nagel will, undoubtedly, accept that observation, he would reject it as grounds for concluding that values do not exist. He would argue that the assumption that only the type of entities that we can discover by the scientific method could exist involves the mistake of adopting an epistemic criterion of reality.

Recall, however, that in his explicit response to Mackie, Nagel distances himself from Moore's Non-Naturalism. He claims that Mackie's skepticism relies on the assumption that value realists are committed to "extra entities, qualities, or relations, things like Platonic Forms or Moore's nonnatural qualities" (*Nowhere*, 144) and responds by rejecting this assumption. But perhaps, he did not mean to speak that strongly. Or perhaps, his rejection of Non-Naturalism rests on a different understanding of that position than I have. He might, for example, take more seriously than I do some of the extravagant metaphors that are often employed to describe the position and may seem to suggest that Non-Naturalists regard moral reality to be some faraway region to which we may travel in thought on the wings of rational intuition.[40] Perhaps Nagel is ready to own up to Non-Naturalism on a more sane construal of that position.[41]

However, I hesitate to treat Nagel's renouncement of Non-Naturalism lightly. Whereas in his discussion of realism about the physical, Nagel offers us an imagery of an observer-independent world of which we are part and of which we have subjective experiences that result from our interactions with the rest of it (*Nowhere*, 68), the picture he offers us to go with realism about values or normative realism is of entirely different kind: "The picture I associate with normative realism is not that of an extra set of properties of things and events in the world, but of a series of possible steps in the development of human motivation which would improve the way we lead our lives, whether or not we will actually take them" (*Nowhere*, 140). Here he seems to go beyond the claim that in value inquiry we do not aim to discover new aspects of "the external world" (the domain of science on the reading suggested above) to suggesting that the subject matter of value inquiry does not include any "extra set of properties of thing and events in the world." The picture that emerges is that Nagel's realism about values has something to say about the motivational potentials of the evaluators rather than about properties of the objects of evaluation: a picture that does not sit well with Non-Naturalistic realism.

If Nagel's realism were of the Non-Naturalistic sort, it would also be difficult to see why he insists that the shadow of skepticism does not hang over value inquiry like it does over inquiry into physical reality. If values and reasons belong to an observer-independent realm of reality, why would it not be possible to be mistaken about what is of value (or what there are reasons for or against doing), even when we have succeeded in neutralizing the effects of our idiosyncrasies on our inquiry? Why this asymmetry between value inquiry and inquiry into physical reality? Certainly, we are owed some sort of an explanation here, and it is not provided by simply telling us that an epistemic access to this realm – unlike to the physical realm – relies on our first-person knowledge of what it is like to be an experiencing subject. If realism about values commits us to seek an objective understanding of such a realm of reasons and values, we should continuously question to what extent our conception of this realm is distorted by the constitution of our own mind – even when we have obtained the sort of objectivity appropriate to the subject matter. Even Moore would accept this, I believe. Although Moore refers to the content of the intuitive judgments about moral values as self-evident, he does not think they are infallible, even under optimal conditions. Their self-evidence is a matter of their warrant being independent of their inferential relations to other judgments.[42] Unlike Nagel, he thinks that we can be mistaken in moral matters, even under optimal epistemic conditions.

VI. A Preposterous Suggestion

Our assessment of the Non-Naturalist reading of Nagel has been somewhat inconclusive. One of our main puzzles continues to be that Nagel thinks that he can accept value realism without owing any account of the metaphysical commitments he thereby incurs. Perhaps this is because Nagel employs not only a different notion of objectivity than Mackie's but also a different notion of value. Mackie makes clear that when talking about values, he is talking about the properties that evaluative judgments prima facie ascribe to objects or events: properties like moral goodness and moral rightness. Certainly, this accords with a familiar talk of an object's value – be it economic, aesthetic, moral, or some other kind. But we also talk about a person's values in which case we are not talking about his merits, but rather about what he values. Literature, athletic excellence, honesty, and economic equality may, for example, be among his values. But even if one specifies someone's values by listing the things he values – just like one may specify his beliefs by listing the propositions he believes – these values, much like beliefs, are really part of the person's mental stance: he has and forms these values and that is a matter of his having or acquiring a mental attitude. Although there might be a relation between the notions of an object's value and a person's values, it is by no means obvious what it is. (If you doubt this, think of the economic value of an object; how does it relate to how any particular person values it?) Now, there are some reasons for thinking that Nagel is using the latter notion of value rather than the former, which might explain his disregard for the metaphysical implications of his view.

This interpretive idea is suggested by a contrast Nagel draws between the output of the method of objectivity in scientific and evaluative inquiries:

> In theoretical reasoning objectivity is advanced when we form a new conception of reality that includes ourselves as components. This involves an alteration or at least an extension of our beliefs. In the sphere of values or practical reasoning, the problem is different. As in the theoretical case, we must take up a new, comprehensive viewpoint after stepping back and including our former perspective in what is to be understood. But here the new viewpoint will be not a new set of beliefs, but a new or extended set of values. (*Nowhere,* 138–139)

The above passage suggests that the starting point and the endpoint of the detachment process is different in scientific (or more generally, theoretical) and evaluative inquiries. In the former, we move from one set of beliefs to another set of beliefs, while in the latter the starting point and the endpoint of the process is a set of values. Values are contrasted with beliefs rather than with nonevaluative properties of the object of evaluation, which makes it reasonable to think that the mental state we reach at the ideal limit of value inquiry is a constellation of attitudes of valuing rather than of beliefs. This type of mental attitude would surely be conative. Valuing involves various motivational dispositions.[43] A person would, for example, not value truth telling unless she were typically somewhat inclined to refrain from lying, to esteem truth tellers, and to scorn liars. This accords nicely with a second passage in which Nagel contrasts the output of the method of objectivity in scientific and evaluative inquiries: "Objectivity is the driving force of ethics as it is of science: it enables us to develop new motives when we occupy a standpoint detached from that of our purely personal desires and interests, just as in the realm of thought it enables us to develop new beliefs" (*Nowhere*, 8). And it makes sense of Nagel's description of "the process of ethical thought" as "one of motivational discovery" (*Nowhere*, 148): by engaging in the process of detachment and undergoing the resulting motivational development, we would – in a firsthand way – learn something about our own motivational potentials.

Nagel's disregard for the metaphysical implications of his view would, however, not have been explained unless we also ascribed to him the view that attitudes of valuing, though yielding an evaluative outlook on life, do not represent their objects as having a property, called value. The contrast he draws between beliefs and values may, indeed, be taken to support this ascription. This suggests that Nagel's claim that there are objective values should not be understood as the claim that there are evaluative properties that are objectively understandable or whose instantiations will be recognized from the objective standpoint. Rather it should be understood as the claim that we will continue to value certain things – that is, have values – after going through the process of detachment. These would be attitudes of valuing that all rational evaluators could share and are appropriately ascribed as objective: "It is beliefs *and attitudes* that are objective in the primary sense" (*Nowhere*, 4; italics mine). It is only in a derivative sense that we speak of their objects as objective values.

This interpretation of Nagel is in many ways satisfying. It makes sense of his remarks about the output of value inquiry and his insistence that moral discourse does not import any new ontic commitments as well as his contention that skepticism is not the unavoidable concomitant of realism in value inquiry as it is in scientific inquiry. Indeed, given that the search for objectivity – to which a commitment to realism supposedly drives us – yields conative attitudes rather than beliefs in value inquiry, we should be more surprised at Nagel's claim that it yields truth than at his claim that it could not yield falsehood. On this interpretation, Nagel holds an essentially noncognitivist view of the mental states that yield the evaluative outlook on life: they are not beliefs that represent the object of evaluation as having a property, called value, but rather attitudes of valuing these objects. True, these attitudes manifest themselves in some sort of a subjective outlook on the object, but it does not involve a representation of the object as having such and such an evaluative property. Consequently, there is no room for worrying that this outlook is radically false. Mackie's skepticism and error theory is, thus, undermined in the standard noncognitivist manner.

A noncognitivist interpretation of Nagel flies, of course, in the face of Nagel's explicit commitment to value realism. And some readers will undoubtedly be quick to point out that his characterization of the output of evaluative inquiry as motives is consistent with his acceptance of moral cognitivism. Nagel has famously defended the view that ethical (as well as prudential) beliefs are motivating irrespective of what the agent's prior desires are like.[44] Granted that view of moral motivation, a progress in our *understanding* of moral values will be reflected in motivational development. And hence ethical inquiry will be a process of motivational discovery. However, the motivational discovery is a mere correlate of value discovery, since moral beliefs affect our motivations. It may, indeed, be significant that Nagel says that a commitment to realism about values "leads us to seek a detached point of view from which it will be possible to correct inclination *and* to discern what we really should do" (*Nowhere,* 140; italics mine). This suggests that there are two correlative mental developments rather than a single one: discerning what we really should do is not simply a matter of developing new motivations, even if it results in motivational development. To this it may be added that Nagel explicitly reaffirms his anti-Humean view of motivation in *The View from Nowhere.* As I noted in section III, Nagel characterizes normative realism as the view "that propositions about what gives us reasons for action can be true or false independently of how things appear to us" (*Nowhere,* 139). And later he claims that "[s]ometimes a desire appears only because I recognize that there is reason to do or want something" (*Nowhere,* 151). Moreover, there are numerous references to moral beliefs, real values, moral truths, discovery of real values through reasoning, and answers to questions of values that are correct "in virtue of something independent of our arriving at them" (*Nowhere,* 149). It may be argued that the existence of such realist imagery throughout the text as well as an appreciation of Nagel's anti-Humean view of moral motivation should drive away the specter of noncognitivism that some isolated passages may raise.

It is right to note that Nagel accepts an anti-Humean view of motivation that allows him to hold that ethical inquiry is a process of motivational discovery, even if it is also a process of a development in belief or understanding. However, it is striking that in crucial passages the emphasis is constantly on the motivational development and that Nagel goes, indeed, so far as to contrast the output of the detachment process in scientific and value inquiry not by identifying it as, respectively, motivationally inert and motivating beliefs, but rather as, respectively, motives and beliefs. This would be a highly misleading way of drawing a contrast between nonmotivating and motivating beliefs. Add to this that Nagel explicitly contrasts discerning what we really should do with discerning features of reality (*Nowhere,* 140) and discloses that he does not associate with normative realism the picture of "an extra set of properties of things and events in the world" (*Nowhere,* 140). In general, we cannot ignore the questions these remarks raise about Nagel's commitment to cognitivism and realism, notwithstanding his realist rhetoric and claimed commitment to value realism. Certainly, there is a tension in Nagel's work between his realist rhetoric and everything he says to defuse skeptical worries about values.

Recent noncognitivists have argued that they can earn their right to realist rhetoric: although moral judgments are not subject to *semantic* evaluation in terms of truth and falsity, the trappings of language that appear to respect relations between truth-values of sentences expressing these judgments and the application of the truth-predicate to these sentences can be explained as convenient devices for expressing nontruth-functional relations between these judgments and a nonsemantic evaluation of them.[45] Perhaps we should take our cue from such noncognitivists and attempt to reconstruct Nagel's realist imagery within the framework of the above interpretation. However, this approach to understanding Nagel is, I believe, questionable. As much as there is to be said for the above noncognitivist interpretation, we should not ignore Nagel's charge that certain brands of antirealism – including noncognitivism – are built on the mistake of approaching the task of understanding evaluative practice by employing the method of detachment characteristic of scientific inquiry. I'll reconstruct below how Nagel would run this line of argument specifically against noncognitivists.[46]

Nagel would maintain that the noncognitivist account of the evaluative act only seems credible if we seek an objective understanding of our evaluative practice by employing the method of detachment characteristic of scientific inquiry, that is, if we seek to understand evaluative practice as a psychological and sociological phenomenon. When we do so, we continue to see people as having values and expressing those in evaluative language, but we do not continue to engage in evaluation from that standpoint and no longer recognize any values or disvalues in the world. A noncognitivist or some other antirealist account of moral language and thought may then seem inviting. But Nagel thinks it is a mistake to settle the dispute between realists and antirealists by seeking such an objective understanding of our evaluative practice. One of his central tenets is that not all of reality is accessible to us by employing the objective method of science. And another one is that it is futile to use the objective method of science for approaching the question whether there are real values; for values lie outside the purview of the sciences. This does not mean that we must give up the search for an objective understanding of values, but we must "seek a form of objectivity appropriate to the subject" (*Nowhere,* 142). Recall from Section II that this form of objectivity supposedly requires that we rely on our first-person access to what it is like to experience the world and life in a certain way, while appreciating that different individuals experience it in different ways and giving one's own personal perspective no more significance than any of the other possible personal perspectives. The question whether there are real values has to be settled by employing this method of inquiry. And our conclusion at the ideal limit, Nagel confidently assures us, will be that there are real values.

But what sort of claim will we be making when articulating this conclusion? Nagel will dismiss our query as misguided so long as we are interested in the reality of values: as arising simply because we have slipped into a search for the sort of objective understanding of evaluative practice that cannot help us to determine whether or not there are real values to which that practice is responsive. That issue – the issue between realists and antirealists about values – has to be settled from the only perspective from which it can be addressed: the objective perspective distinctive of value inquiry. It is in value inquiry, not scientific or any other type of inquiry, that we can hope to figure out whether there really are any values and if so which they are. In this inquiry, our gaze is fixed on the object of evaluation rather than on the mental attitudes that sustain that gaze, so the question whether these mental attitudes are representational simply does not rise. Once that question has been raised, we are no longer conducting an inquiry that can reveal anything about whether there are real values to be pursued in life and, hence, we have lost track of the issue dividing realists and antirealists.

Notice that this suggests that Nagel would dismiss the cognitivist and realist positions described in the introduction to this chapter for the same reasons he dismisses noncognitivist and other antirealist accounts: they are developed and defended by engaging in the same sort of inquiry about evaluative practice as noncognitivists do. Nagel's value realism is a position reached within ethical inquiry and simply advances the claim that there are real values. It is not to be confused with moral realism understood as consisting of the claims that moral thought and language employ distinct conceptual resources and that certain aspects of observer-independent reality render some moral representations true and others false. It is not that Nagel wants to deny such claims, rather he maintains that the sort of inquiry that begets them – as well as their contradictories – has lost track of the issue whether there are real values. If I understand Nagel right, this is the problem he sees with contemporary meta-ethical discussions.[47]

VII. Ethical Inquiry and Metaethics

This reading of Nagel cries out for a comparison with Simon Blackburn's quasi-realism.[48] Blackburn wholeheartedly agrees that the only way of pursuing questions about values is to engage in ethical inquiry. While engaging in such an inquiry, he claims that wanton cruelty is really wrong and rejects out of hand the claim that its wrongness depends on our disapproving of it. He is confident about this but wonders whether other aspects of his moral view are correct. Of course, he hopes that his view is fairly close to true and that he is pursuing what is really of value and fulfilling his real obligations. Blackburn does not question such realist rhetoric so long as it appears within evaluative discourse. However, he sees nothing against asking what we are doing when making such claims and, thus, stepping out of the evaluative mode and reflecting on the activity of evaluation. And here he comes to noncognitivist conclusions: all claims made within evaluative discourse – including claims about the mind-independence of values, the existence of real values and obligations, moral truths, and mistaken moral views – express conative attitudes.[49] I have my doubts about his noncognitivist interpretation of moral discourse but will resist reconstructing or evaluating it here. Suffice it to say that if his interpretation were successful, Blackburn would have eased any tension there might appear to be between a noncognitivist account of evaluative thought and language and the sort of realist rhetoric we have found in Nagel. Yet, he considers himself to have accepted antirealism about moral thought and discourse. This is not because he would deny that there are real values. Blackburn agrees with Nagel that such a claim has place only within evaluative discourse, and like Nagel he thinks it will not be the conclusion of evaluative inquiry. However, the noncognitivist view of the evaluative act "deserves to be called anti-realist because it avoids the view that when we moralize we respond to, and describe, an independent aspect of reality" (*Quasi-Realism,* 157). The antirealist conclusion is reached as we reflect on the nature of our activity of moral evaluation and will, therefore, be couched in nonevaluative language.

Nagel formulates the point at issue between realism and antirealism in evaluative language: Are there any real values? He then argues that this question can only be settled within evaluative inquiry; no light can be shed on it by reflections on evaluative thought and its relation to the world. Now, one may concede that point as Blackburn has done but still insist that it is of interest to reflect on what we are doing when engaging in value inquiry and on how moral thought relates to the world. This is, indeed, what metaethicists take themselves to be doing. And within that discussion, we have the crucial division between cognitivists and noncognitivists as well as between realists – who maintain that there are observer-independent states of affairs that render some moral claims true and others false – and antirealists, who either deny this or preempt this metaphysical issue by accepting moral noncognitivism. Conceived of in this way, the issue between moral realists and antirealists rises at the level of reflection on moral inquiry rather than at the level of moral inquiry. And surely, that is the debate into which Mackie means to enter. He is not tackling the issue Nagel formulates within value inquiry. If Nagel is exclusively concerned with that issue, one may wonder whether Nagel has any response to Mackie's skeptical challenge.

Nagel seems to resist this attempt to relocate and reformulate the issue between moral realists and antirealists – or put differently, the attempt to distinguish between two moral realist–antirealist debates, one at the level of moral inquiry and the other at the level of philosophical reflection on moral thought. One possibility is that Nagel is advocating a form of quietism about value discourse and thought: it is utterly misguided to think that after reaching, within value inquiry, a conclusion regarding the issue whether there are real values, there is some further question to be answered about what we are doing when expressing this conclusion and whether in reaching this conclusion we are responding to any independent aspect of reality. There is no legitimate vantage point – the quietist continues – from which we can raise and pursue such questions.[50] Since Mackie's skepticism about values stems exactly from raising such questions, it can be safely ignored. His skeptical answer should not be opposed in any of the three ways offered by rival metaethical positions, instead his questions should be rejected as misplaced. If this is, indeed, Nagel's theoretical stance, he is opposing the whole framework within which metaethical discussions are typically conducted. Indeed, he could be seen as dismissing the whole field of metaethics, understood as the subfield of philosophy that addresses questions about the meaning of moral language, about the nature of the mental activity involved in moral evaluation, and about whether any aspects of reality are the truth makers of moral claims.

I find it somewhat difficult to read Nagel as holding this quietist view. He would, certainly, be a quietist who finds it difficult to keep quiet about the nature of moral thinking. For example: after a passage filled with realist rhetoric including claims to the effect that we often perceive that there are reasons for action (or values), Nagel distances himself from a perceptual model of moral thought:

Again let me stress that this is not to be understood on the model of perception of features of the external world. The subject matter of our investigations is how to live, and the process of ethical thought is one of motivational discovery. The fact that people can to some extent reach agreement on answers which they regard as objective suggests that when they step outside of their particular individual perspectives, they call into operation a common evaluative faculty whose correct functioning provides the answers, even though it can also malfunction and be distorted by other influences. It is not a question of bringing the mind into correspondence with an external reality which acts causally on it, but of reordering the mind itself in accordance with the demands of its own external view of itself. (*Nowhere,* 148)

Here, Nagel himself seems to be reflecting on what we are doing when engaging in value inquiry and how moral thought relates, at least, to the external world (understood as explained before). He does not hesitate to speculate that a distinctive evaluative faculty is in operation as well as to comment on the relation between the states of mind it produces and external reality: according to him, it is at least not the correspondence relation.

Nagel clearly joins Blackburn in rejecting "the view that when we moralize we respond to, and describe, an independent aspect of reality" (*Quasi-Realism*, 157), so long as the reality of which Blackburn speaks is restricted to "external" reality or the domain of science. Nagel seems quite ready to venture that far into metaethics. But how can he then defensibly stop there and refuse to engage further in the debate between realists and antirealists as Blackburn has reformulated and relocated it at the level of reflection on moral inquiry? The obvious suggestion is that Nagel would declare the debate futile, since not all of reality is accessible to us from such a reflective standpoint on our evaluative activity. We could never be in the epistemic position of either affirming or dismissing "the view that when we moralize we respond to, and describe, an independent aspect of reality" (Blackburn, *Quasi-Realism*, 157), which lies beyond the purview of science. But if this is Nagel's point, he is not so much resisting Blackburn's relocation and reformulation of the issue between moral realists and antirealists as arguing that the epistemic position from which it can be settled is unavailable to us. There are legitimate questions here, but they are bound to remain open, at least for creatures with our epistemic powers. Metaethicists are not debating pseudoquestions, as quietists would maintain, but rather wasting time in a futile attempt to answer intractable – though perhaps profound – questions.

This position would commit Nagel to agnosticism about the issues that typically interest metaethicists. And it is not clear that it is any easier to read Nagel as an agnostic than as a quietist. Again, he just ventures too far into metaethical discussions to be a consistent agnostic. It would, indeed, be hard to see about what he remained agnostic. For he seems to have dismissed moral noncognitivism, naturalistic realism, Non-Naturalistic realism, and error theory as we have already discussed. Here, we are running into a general problem in our attempt to give a coherent interpretation of Nagel's overall view concerning the issue between moral realists and antirealists. On the one hand, Nagel seems likely to resist Blackburn's reformulation of this issue at the level of reflection on our evaluative activity. On the other hand, he himself seems to have too much to say about our evaluative thought and its relation to our environment to be able to take the position that it is in any way misguided to reflect on this matter. I see only one way out of this quandary. Nagel would, I suspect, claim that he is engaging in a certain type of reflection on evaluative activity that grows out of and is continuous with value inquiry itself, while objecting to attempts to account for our evaluative thought and its interplay with reality that proceed on the terms set by empirical science. I cannot point to any passages in *The View from Nowhere* where this idea is clearly and explicitly set forth and developed, but it is, I believe, in the spirit of that work. I will briefly consider a direction in which Nagel might take it.

Let's first consider the type of reflections on our moral thought and discourse that Nagel is likely to condone and engage in himself. These reflections would, I submit, be on how we proceed in our quest for a discovery of the right values and how we hold ourselves accountable to certain methodological standards. However, we will not be approaching this task as amateur anthropologists observing what we actually do while engaging in ethical inquiry, but rather as participants of that practice who are trying to render explicit the methodological ideals under which we labor while engaged in ethical inquiry. Nagel would have to claim that it is as a result of such reflections that he has come up with his account of the method of objectivity appropriate to ethical inquiry as well as his idea that in ethical inquiry we call into operation an evaluative faculty whose operations and outputs do not depend on what prior desires or interests we have. Also, an examination of how we hold each other's ethical deliberations to methodological standards would have to be cited in favor of his claim that this faculty may function more or less correctly. To this Nagel would presumably add that as participants of ethical inquiry, we can attest to its being a process of motivational discovery: the discovery that as a result of exercising our evaluative faculty, we can be motivated in ways that are not conditioned by the desires and interests we had before embarking on the process of detachment. Nagel would, moreover, have to claim that such reflections on evaluative inquiry will reveal something about the interplay between our ethical thought and the world in which we are embedded. He could, first, observe that a minor reflection on ethical thought reveals that it is sensitive to various features of our social and natural environment. Our evaluations target social phenomena and take into consideration their social dimensions. Economic equality is, for example, instantiated (to greater or lesser extent) by politico-economic systems. In order to assess whether or not it is a value, we have to consider how stable these various systems would be, what other (non-moral) features they would have, and more generally what it would be like for humans to live within them. But to this Nagel would have to add that when, on the basis of such considerations, we judge that economic equality either is or is not a value, we are not mentally registering some social ramifications of instantiations of this property. This I take to be the force of Nagel's claim that ethical thought does not involve "bringing the mind into correspondence with an external reality which acts causally on it" (*Nowhere,* 148). The support for this view, I presume, is supposed to come from an examination of the aims and methodological standards of ethical inquiry: they reveal that it is not plausible to think that this is what we are doing when discovering that economic equality is or is not of value. I suspect that Nagel will even go further and claim that the discovery of real values reveals that we are capable of coming into contact with real values and reasons – "the world of reasons" (*Nowhere,* 140) – through ethical inquiry, just as the discovery of a type of subatomic particle in physics reveals that we are capable of epistemically accessing such particles by the method of physics.

Certainly, metaethicists have to engage in such reflections on the aims and methodological ideals of ethical inquiry in order to address questions about the nature of moral thinking and its relation to reality. But it seems doubtful that we can responsibly draw any conclusions about these matters merely on the basis of such reflections. Although the methodological constraints and ideals under which we labor must reveal something about what we are doing when engaging in moral thought, they may also embody unrealizable aspirations of that practice and reveal very little about the actual interplay between our moral thought and the world in which we are embedded. We should, for example, be cautious in claiming on the grounds of such reflections that moral thinking is not a matter of mentally registering any facts about the social dimensions of the object of evaluation. True, the aims and methodological standards of ethical inquiry may be so different from those of sociological inquiry that it seems implausible to think that we are performing the same type of mental act, when coming to a conclusion in these two areas of thought. But that does not preclude that both acts relate to certain aspects of the social order in such a way that they can both be regarded as mentally registering or representing, in a full-blooded sense, the latter, even if this relation could not be discerned solely on the basis of an examination of the methodological standards of moral thought. The conclusions of ethical and sociological inquiry may be different types of mental acts because they employ different concepts or modes of presentation, but they nevertheless represent the same social phenomena because the concepts or modes of presentation they employ are different concepts or modes of presentation of the same phenomena.[51] Needless to say, I take myself to be pointing out an epistemic possibility; for all I know it may be precluded by the nature of mental representation. But given our limited understanding of mental representation at this point in time, we have to consider this possibility. Another epistemic possibility – Mackie as well as Blackburn would be eager to point out – is that our evaluations do not relate to any aspect of reality in such a way that they can be regarded as representing them.

It is these sorts of queries about moral thought and its relation to reality that Nagel wants to rule out of court and thereby block the realist–antirealist dispute that preoccupies much of contemporary metaethical discussions. The drift of his thought suggests that the problem he has with these reflections is that they will push the discussion of what we are doing in moral inquiry from the reflective stance of the participants on their endeavor to the stance of the amateur anthropologist who treats the practice as a sociological phenomenon to be scientifically understood. To employ a familiar metaphor: Nagel objects to moving the metaethical discussion from an *internal* to an *external* investigation of our ethical thought.[52] Now, it is fairly easy to see why he thinks that this sort of shift in approach has to occur as we address the questions I broached in the last paragraph. If we are not simply to rely on the method employed in value inquiry and an analysis of that method in contemplating the nature of moral thought and its relation to the world, the question arises what other method we can use to examine the matter. And the obvious answer – at least, in this time and age – identifies the method we use in the social sciences for examining the nature of human activities and practices. This is, indeed, where a number of metaethicists have turned, although they have not exactly crossed disciplinary boundaries to join ranks with social scientists. A number of them have engaged in some form of speculative theorizing about our moral thought and its evolution, which is clearly continuous with some branch of the scientific study of humans.[53]

But why exactly does Nagel find this approach objectionable? Presumably, he thinks that it is hopeless to conduct our inquiry into the relation moral thought bears to reality with a method that gives us access to only a limited part of reality. Indeed, he claims that this approach presupposes an epistemic criterion of reality (*Nowhere,* 141): the thought must be that the approach presupposes that a certain type of epistemic accessibility is definitive of what there is. Whatever is to be said about this objection (a question considered in the final section of this chapter), it should be clear by now that Nagel's position is a form of antinaturalism. The naturalism Nagel is opposing is not naturalistic realism, but rather what Peter Railton has called *methodological naturalism,* which may be accepted by noncognitivists and error theorists as well as naturalistic realists. As Railton formulates the position, it consists in the Quinean claim that "philosophy does not possess a distinctive, *a priori* method able to yield substantive truths that, in principle, are not subject to any sort of empirical test. Instead, . . . philosophy should proceed *a posteriori,* in tandem with – perhaps as a particularly abstract and general part of – the broadly empirical inquiry carried on in the natural and social sciences."[54] Railton himself has, of course, proceeded like this in his attempts to give an account of nonmoral and moral value. I would think that Nagel rejects the first claim and maintains that philosophy possesses a distinctive a priori method for discovering substantive truths. And he certainly believes that the scientific method is not the only available one. According to him, value inquiry employs a distinctive method for arriving at substantive truths about values. Moreover, he holds that it is disastrous to reject this method in favor of the scientific method, if the subject of reflection is values or our evaluative practice. Thus, it is methodological naturalism that is Nagel's primary target rather than metaethics per se. It is worth noting in this context that at one point he admits that it "is not clear whether normative realism is compatible with the hypothesis that all our normative beliefs can be accounted for by some kind of naturalistic psychology"

(*Nowhere,* 145). Interestingly, the moral he draws from this is not that normative realism may be suspect, but rather that there may be serious limits to "naturalistic" psychology (presumably, the branch of psychology that is committed to the experimental method developed within the natural sciences). This brings out crisply how strong his antinaturalistic stand is.

It might be helpful to summarize at this point my conclusions about how to understand Nagel's value realism in *The View from Nowhere.* At the end of the last section, I concluded that Nagel is not to be seen as defending the realist position characterized in the introduction to this chapter. His value realism is a position reached within ethical inquiry. Rather than giving an account of moral thought and discourse, it advances and defends the evaluative claim that there are real values. From now on I will refer to this position as *normative realism.* I have been wondering in this section how Nagel could resist Blackburn's reformulation of the issue between moral realists and antirealists at the level of reflection on our evaluative activity. Call these *meta-realism* and *meta-antirealism,* respectively. And the suggestion I have finally come up with is that Nagel does not object to attempts to say something about the nature of our evaluative thinking and its relation to our environment, but thinks that such reflections have to grow out of evaluative inquiry and employ its method as well as an analysis of that method. Moreover, he objects to the naturalistic endeavor of supplementing such reflections with speculations about moral practice and its evolution, which essentially rely on the approach of social science to human activities. For he holds that such a naturalistic take on value inquiry restricts in advance to what sort of facts moral thought and discourse could be seen as responsive.

VIII. Reconsidering Nagel's Value Realism

I will critically assess Nagel's antinaturalistic stance in the next and final section of this chapter. In this section, I want to revisit the conclusion of Section VI, namely, that Nagel does not take any stand on the issue between realists and antirealists as it rises at the level of reflection on value inquiry. If I am right that it is methodological naturalism rather than metaethics per se that is the target of Nagel's criticism, we should reconsider whether his numerous remarks about the output of value inquiry after all commit him to a metaethical position about the nature of judgments about values and their relation to the reality in which we and our evaluative activities are embedded.

It certainly appears that Nagel's defense of the antinaturalistic stance serves to clear the ground for Non-Naturalistic meta-realism. Given that he rejects methodological naturalism as based on the mistaken assumption that all of reality is epistemically accessible by the scientific method, Nagel is easily read as hankering after the idea that the subject matter of ethics is part of reality that lies out of the domain of science. In Section V, I discussed the considerations for and against this interpretation, and I do not think that anything new has come to light. But we now have grounds for reconsidering the noncognitivist interpretation. Although it is a historical fact that noncognitivists have been ardent methodological naturalists,[55] naturalism is not an essential ingredient in noncognitivism as characterized in my introduction. The central tenet of moral noncognitivism is that moral judgments manifest affective or conative attitudes toward the object of evaluation under a nonmoral mode of presentation: they do not truly or falsely represent the object as having any moral features and hence moral discourse does not bring with it any unique ontic commitments. Now, noncognitivists who embrace methodological naturalism will seek a scientific or naturalistic understanding of the relevant affective or conative attitudes as well as other aspects of moral practice. But nothing bars a noncognitivist from accepting antinaturalism and refusing to engage in such a query about moral psychology. This raises the question whether Nagel is after all best interpreted as a noncognitivist of an antinaturalistic stripe.[56]

In Section VI, we saw that there is surprisingly much to be said for interpreting Nagel as taking a noncognitivist view of the evaluative act. Prima facie, there is, however, a tension between the elements in Nagel's thought that support such an interpretation and his commitment to realism, although we are now in a position to see that the tension is not as stark as one might think. The conclusion of Section VI was that Nagel's value realism is meant to be a position reached within ethical inquiry and is not to be confused with meta-realism. It consists in the evaluative claim that there are values to be pursued in life. Prima facie this opens up the possibility that Nagel's value realism could be reconciled with noncognitivism about evaluative claims. However, this would require that all his realist rhetoric be understood as taking place at the level of value inquiry. And although that might be feasible with respect to his talk about moral beliefs, moral truths, and discovery of real values through reasoning, such an interpretation becomes a bit strained when we encounter his characterization of "[n]ormative realism [as] the view that propositions about what gives us reasons for action can be true or false independently of how things appear to us, and that we can hope to discover the truth by transcending the appearances and subjecting them to critical assessment" (*Nowhere*, 139).

Perhaps we can reconcile Nagel's commitment to moral cognitivism with reading him as holding that the evaluative method yields conative attitudes of valuing that do not represent the object of evaluation as having a property, called value. Perhaps it has been a mistake on my part to think that Nagel conceives of evaluative judgments as expressing the sort of mental states that are the outputs of the method of detachment. Perhaps evaluative judgments express instead beliefs to the effect that certain things would be objects of the attitude of valuing yielded by the detachment process at the ideal limit. In other words, claiming that x is a value is not to express the attitude of valuing x; rather it amounts to judging that x would be valued by (i.e., be among the values of) any rational inquirer who has succeeded in fully neutralizing the effects of his desires, interests, and other idiosyncrasies on his values. In that case, the content of judgments to the effect that such and such is a value ensures that under the conditions of full detachment we are infallible judges of what is of value, assuming that we are infallible judges of what we value at the actual time of judgment. This reading of Nagel – let's call it the dispositional reading – would, therefore, make sense of why he thinks that the conclusions at the ideal limit of value inquiry – unlike those at the ideal limit of scientific inquiry – are not open to radical doubt.[57]

The dispositional reading of Nagel is arguably superior to the noncognitivist reading. The noncognitivist reading requires that we interpret Nagel's realist rhetoric as belonging entirely at the level of evaluation rather than at the level of reflection on evaluative activity, whereas the reading just proposed amounts to interpreting him as siding with cognitivists and meta-realists about the nature of evaluative judgments. At the same time, it allows us to understand why Nagel explicitly commits himself to the view that evaluative judgments do not incur any distinctive ontic commitments: the ontic commitments of evaluative discourse are the same as those of a discourse about what rational evaluators would value if they had fully neutralized the effect of their idiosyncratic psychological features on the faculty of evaluation. The advantages of the dispositional reading over the noncognitivist are that it allows us to take at face value the passages in which Nagel seems explicitly to commit himself to cognitivism about the evaluative act, while at the same time make sense of the passages that have made us wonder whether he is in fact committed to noncognitivism.

I hasten to add that one may have worries about the claim that on this interpretation Nagel would not ascribe to evaluative discourse any distinctive ontic commitments. For what are the ontic commitments of a discourse about what rational evaluators would value under conditions of full detachment? It depends at least in part on how "rational" is understood here: is it meant to contrast with "irrational" or "arational"? If the former reading is intended, the view – call it *IR-dispositionalism* – gives us a reduction of a discourse about values to a normative discourse about the rationality of evaluators, a discourse about what sort of evaluative dispositions a person must have in order to count as rational rather than irrational. The "must" is normative: it spells out conditions for rational assessment of evaluators. Thus, if Nagel is an IR-dispositionalist, his meta-realism about value discourse would depend on meta-realism about a discourse about the rationality of evaluators. But this, of course, takes us back to square one as far as understanding his claim that normative discourse does not have any distinctive ontic commitments.

I suspect that this is where our exploration of Nagel's view should properly end: back on square one. But I want to consider the dispositional reading, when "rational" is understood as contrasting with "arational" – call this *ar-*

dispositionalism. Ar-dispositionalism gives us a reduction of a discourse about values to a discourse about the evaluative dispositions of beings sophisticated enough to be subject to rational assessment. One worry about this interpretation is that it would make Nagel out to be a naturalist, both substantive and methodological. If judgments about values are tantamount to judgments about what certain types of cognitive beings would value at the ideal limit of the detachment process, it may seem that they are about mental dispositions and can be verified by studying scientifically our evaluative dispositions, assuming that we are the only examples of such beings in the actual world.[58] But recall that we are dealing with a philosopher who is ready to accept that scientific psychology may not be equipped to study normative beliefs (*Nowhere,* 145). I for one would not be surprised to learn that Nagel holds that scientific psychology is not equipped to study the detachment process and its output. He might hold that the only way of verifying judgments to the effect that rational inquirers would value, say, economic equality at the end of ethical inquiry is to go through the detachment process ourselves. Hence, our best evidence for what is of value is what our values are under the most detached perspective we have already attained. But we can always ask whether our values are the real values which is tantamount to asking whether we have yet attained full objectivity in ethics. And since full objectivity is a methodological ideal that we are unlikely to attain, that question will continue to be with us, even if it would be misplaced at the ideal limit of ethical inquiry. If this were the correct reading of Nagel, he would be advocating a new brand of Non-Naturalism. On this view, the subject matter of ethics lies beyond the purview of science, even if the ontic commitments of the position pertain to the mental realm rather than a distinct value realm. This might, indeed, provide us with the most satisfying understanding of why he seeks to distance himself from Moore's Non-Naturalism.

Another worry is that on this interpretation Nagel would not be a meta-realist. He would, of course, be a cognitivist: for example, the judgment that economic equality is a value would be true just in case rational evaluators would value economic equality under conditions of full detachment. Moreover, he clearly holds that there is a fact in the matter. But it is less clear whether this fact meets the independence condition of meta-realism (as characterized in my introduction): Do the facts that determine the truth values of evaluative judgments, according to this view, obtain independently of our evaluative opinions?[59] These are facts about what values rational inquirers would have under conditions of full detachment. Whether such facts obtain depends on neither our current values nor our current opinion about what rational evaluators would value under conditions of full detachment (assuming realism about intentional states). But it does depend on what the evaluative dispositions of rational evaluators, including ourselves, are like: for example, whether rational evaluators would value economic equality under conditions of perfect detachment. So, there is a dependence here on the evaluative attitudes of rational inquirers, including ourselves, under certain counterfactual conditions. Does that violate the independence requirement? The answer is unclear pending a more precise formulation of the condition.

So far I have interpreted the independence condition as requiring that the subject matter of a realistically construable discourse is observer-independent in the sense explained in Section V. On this interpretation, ar-dispositionalism meets the independence condition, assuming that the evaluative dispositions of ourselves and other rational inquirers are what they are independently of what we might think they are like.[60] But I do not think that the above worry should be dismissed so lightly. I have grave doubts about construing the issue between meta-realists and meta-antirealists about values as concerning simply whether value judgments are about observer-independent subject matter. If that were the case a view that maintains that value judgments are effectively judgments about what the majority of people in our society values would count as a meta-realist view so long as the relevant psychological facts are observer-independent. Of course, "meta-realism" (and "realism") is a term of art and it is possible to introduce it to cover any view according to which the subject matter of value judgments is observer-independent. But it would at least be my preference to use the term in such a way that the debate between meta-realists and antirealists would be recognizable as addressing a crucial worry of reflective people about the grounds for their value judgments. I suspect that the appropriate worry pertains not only to the observer-independence of the subject matter of value inquiry, but also to its relation to the attitudes on which value judgments function as critical checks: the question is whether value judgments have correctness conditions that allow them to function as critical checks on our values, and hence our conduct, under all actual and counterfactual conditions. If this is right, the independence condition should be formulated as requiring that the facts that determine the truth values of evaluative judgments be such that these truth values do not depend on what we value under any actual or counterfactual conditions. Ar-dispositionalism would prima facie not meet that condition.

A possible response is that the counterfactual conditions in question are the optimal conditions for forming values and, hence, it should not worry anyone that value judgments cannot provide any critical check on our values under these conditions. If we want to tailor our use of the labels "realism" and "antirealism" within metaethics such that realist views lay to rest the above worry while antirealist views show it to be warranted, it may seem that the independence condition has to be formulated such that the dispositional view under question comes out as a realist view. But this suggestion is, I believe, misguided. For notice that on this view the reason that conditions of full detachment are optimal for forming values is not that they are the optimal *epistemic* conditions for forming judgments about the values of objects or events. On this view, we need some entirely different account of why conditions of detachment are optimal for forming values. And I suspect that the distinction between realism and antirealism is best drawn within metaethics in such a way that realists not only lay to rest the above worry, but also do it in such a way that the explanation of why certain conditions are optimal for forming values is that they are *epistemically* optimal conditions for discerning the facts that render value judgments true. But perhaps Nagel would have no qualms about his view not meeting the latter condition.

The above discussion has been highly speculative, and no definite conclusion has been drawn about whether Nagel's remarks about the output of value inquiry commit him to Non-Naturalism, noncognitivism, IR-dispositionalism, or ar-dispositionalism. The examination of these four interpretive options has more served the purpose of casting these positions in a new light than of increasing our understanding of Nagel's view. I doubt there is a fuller understanding to be gained of Nagel's metaethical position: it is underdeveloped, which is not surprising given his ambivalent attitude toward the metaethical enterprise.

IX. A Critique of Nagel's Antinaturalism

I would like to end this chapter with a few remarks about Nagel's methodological antinaturalism. It seems reasonable to refuse to give science the position of an ontological *arbitrator* on the grounds that it would amount to accepting an epistemic criterion of reality: whether something is accessible by scientific methodology is not *definitive* of whether it exists. But if the authority accorded to science in matters of ontology is merely epistemic, the objection loses its bite.[61] Those who take such a stand readily admit that reality might not be quite like the best possible scientific theory claims: it may get things wrong or at least not encompass all of reality. However, they will maintain that our best shot at discovering what really exists is to adhere to the method of science. This is certainly Railton's stance and, I suspect, that of most methodological naturalists. This position does not wield an epistemic criterion of reality. Undoubtedly, Nagel would reject it nonetheless; for he is confident that we have a distinctive and adequate method for discovering values and that we better use it, if we want to learn about all of reality. So, even if methodological naturalists are not guilty of wielding an epistemic criterion of reality, they are – Nagel would charge – unnecessarily making themselves blind to certain dimensions of reality.

This brings us back to worries about Nagel's position that were, in Section III, set aside for the purposes of this chapter. Many will be skeptical of Nagel's claim that value inquiry is conducted by a distinctive method that – if correctly applied – will bring consensus among rational beings and, indeed, bring them to the truth in moral matters. For one thing the intractability of major moral disagreements suggests otherwise. Nagel, of course, anticipates and tries to deflect such objections by reminding us that strong interests are typically at stake in ethical inquiry, which may make us particularly bad at sticking to the objective method and reaching consensus in that area of thought. And he points out that most people would dismiss similar worries about hotly contested biological, psychological, and sociological matters that bear on important interests (e.g., various issues having to do with possible differences in psychological capacities between the genders or the races). The apparent irresolvability of such disputes fails to show that there is no truth in these matters, nor does it show that the scientific method is in principle inadequate for discovering that truth. By the same token, the intractability of moral disagreements fails to show that the method of ethical inquiry is inadequate or that there is no truth in the matter (*Nowhere,* 148).[62] This point is well taken. However, we cannot ignore that our confidence in the scientific method builds on the remarkable success we have had in applying it, at least, in the natural sciences. Our rapidly growing knowledge of physical phenomena – not only of microparticles, but also of astronomical, geological, meteorological, oceanographical, and biological phenomena – and the technology it sustains are truly impressive. It is not clear that there is any comparable success within value inquiry to build confidence in its method in the face of deep and intractable moral disagreements.

It is of interest to note in this context that at least one methodological naturalist – namely, Railton – uses the same strategy as Nagel for deflecting objections to moral realism that build on the observation that many important moral disagreements are persistent and seemingly intractable.[63] However, Railton does not use this argumentative move to build confidence in some distinctive method for value inquiry; instead, he merely uses it to resist the antirealist conclusion that there are no facts in moral matters. He does not think there is a method that, if correctly applied, will unavoidably lead to consensus among rational evaluators. Indeed, he does not even believe that the scientific method rationally commands consensus on empirical matters, although he maintains that this does not distract from it as a truth-conducive method of inquiry.[64] But Railton, I suspect, would have doubts about the truth-conduciveness of the intuition-driven method commonly employed in ethical inquiry. Indeed, he has been toying with the idea that truth in moral matters is best pursued by the a posteriori method used in empirical inquiry. In his writings, Railton has attempted to lay the groundwork for a good explanatory account of what is going on in evaluative practice, which has the upshot of providing a defense in the same breath, so to speak, of both naturalistic realism and a specific substantive moral view. In other words, we have the suggestion that our best chance at discovering real values is to proceed like methodological naturalists. Certainly, Nagel would question this project, but he could not dismiss it on the grounds that Railton is wielding an epistemic criterion of reality. We would need some other principled reasons for rejecting this project as a nonstarter.

My general point is that sophisticated forms of methodological naturalism cannot be dismissed as easily as Nagel dismisses them. There are difficult methodological issues both in ethical and in philosophical inquiry that need to be discussed in depth before coming to any sweeping conclusions about this form of naturalism. I am, however, quite sympathetic to the view that philosophical inquiry is radically different from sociological or anthropological inquiry of our practices. I am attracted to the view – which I have tentatively attributed to Nagel – that in philosophical inquiry we approach reflections on moral thought and practice as participants, trying to make sense of their own activity, rather than as amateur anthropologists, observing what we actually do while engaging in ethical inquiry.[65] Philosophical reflections are, I submit, conducted by participants of the practice under consideration. They take off from an exploration of a conceptual space and methodological ideals by those who live and think within that space and underthose ideals.[66] Such an examination does not depend on surveys or observations of how people use the relevant concepts or evoke the relevant ideals. Rather it depends on conversations that trigger and test the participants' intuitions about what moves are *correct* and *incorrect* within that practice. Philosophical reflections are in certain ways analogous to self-reflection. Even if self-reflection involves thinking about one of the organisms inhabiting this world, it still proceeds from the first-person perspective and is the thinking of the introspecting self. Similarly, philosophical reflections on a practice proceed from the perspective characteristic of that very practice, that is, it presupposes competence with the concepts and conventions under examination as well as an insider's knowledge of how that practice is played out in real life. The starting point of philosophical reflections on a practice is as different from the anthropologist's and sociologist's as the starting point of self-reflection is from the behavioral psychologist's.[67]

But even if I am drawn to this conception of philosophy, it is far from clear to me that philosophy employs forms of reasoning that are radically different from those characteristic of scientific methodology. The starting point and the emphasis of philosophical reflections might be very different from that of scientific inquiry, but is their methodology radically different? Do we not use deductive and inductive reasoning both in science and in philosophy, although we proceed more experimentally in the former? And certainly what anthropologists and sociologists have to say is of interest to the philosopher: it may deepen her understanding of the practice under consideration just like various findings of empirical psychology may prove illuminating for understanding oneself. I am, in fact, deeply bothered by the apparent extremity of Nagel's antinaturalistic stance. It is not only that he opposes the claim that the scientific method is the only good method available for us to discover the contours of reality. If I understand him correctly, he opposes any attempt by metaethicists to understand our evaluative practices by proceeding "*a posteriori,* in tandem with – perhaps as a particularly abstract and general part of – the broadly empirical inquiry carried on in the natural and social sciences" (Railton, "Naturalism and Prescriptivity," 155–156). This opposition, I submit, is entirely misguided. Whether or not we confer to science supreme epistemic authority, we have – in our philosophical reflections – to consider how our evaluative practice could be scientifically understood.

This is not only because the sciences can give us valuable insights and ideas to explore in our philosophical reflections. The fact is that we are all participants both of moral and scientific practice,[68] and that calls for philosophical reflections on whether we can make sense of our being committed to both of them at the same time. These practices involve different conceptions of ourselves and the world that may appear to be at odds with each other. One may even worry that the conception of ourselves, our activities, and our environment integral to science undermines moral practice, given its own standards of legitimacy for moral evaluations. When faced with such worries, we cannot simply shrug our shoulders and claim that the methods they employ give us access to different parts of reality. Philosophical reflections par excellence attempt to reconcile two apparently incompatible conceptions of ourselves. They proceed from the perspective of the participant of both practices: of a person who conceives of humans both as biological organisms and as moral agents, and who thinks of certain events both as belonging to the natural order and as being subject to moral assessment. The philosopher struggles with the question whether one can coherently be committed to both perspectives, or whether there is a problematic relation between these two ways of thinking about ourselves and the world.[69] And in order to do so, she has to consider how our evaluative practice could be scientifically understood, regardless of whether she treats science as authoritative in matters of ontology.[70]

Notes

1. It may be thought that this characterization of cognitivism implies that nominalists cannot be cognitivists. But talk of properties in this context should be understood as pretheoretical relative to the debate between nominalists and realists about properties. Nominalists would have to provide a translation of this talk of properties into a language acceptable to them. Thanks to Brian Leiter for raising this worry.

2. Of course, the object of evaluation need not be a particular. More often, especially if the evaluation is moral, it is a type: a type of conduct, quality of mind or character, type of institution, etc.

3. The cognitivist camp includes as diverse thinkers as: Richard Boyd ("How To Be a Moral Realist," in G. Sayre-McCord [ed.], *Essays on Moral Realism* [Ithaca: Cornell University Press, 1988]); David Brink (*Moral Realism and the Foundations of Ethics* [Cambridge: Cambridge University Press, 1989]); J. L. Mackie (*Ethics: Inventing Right and Wrong*

[New York: Penguin, 1977]); John McDowell ("Projection and Truth in Ethics," re-printed in S. Darwall et al. [eds.], *Moral Discourse and Practice: Some Philosphical Approaches* [Oxford: Oxford University Press, 1997). G. E. Moore (*Principia Ethica* [Cambridge: Cambridge University Press, 1903]); Peter Railton ("Moral Realism," *Philosophical Review* 95 [1986]: 163–207); Michael Smith (*The Moral Problem* [Oxford: Basil Blackwell, 1994]); N. Sturgeon ("Moral Explanations," in D. Copp and D. Zimmerman [eds.], *Morality, Reason, and Truth* [Totowa: Rowman and Allenheld, 1985]); and D. Wiggins ("A Sensible Subjectivism?" in his *Needs, Values, Truth: Essays in the Philosophy of Value* [Oxford: Blackwell, 1987]).

4. "Moral judgment" has become a term of art in the metaethical literature. It is used to refer to the mental and speech acts central to moral evaluation, whatever their nature may be.

5. Within the noncognitivist camp we can find the emotivist view of A. J. Ayer (*Language, Truth, and Logic* [London: Gollancz, 1946], chap. 6) and C. L. Stevenson ("The Emotive Meaning of Ethical Terms," *Mind* 46 [1937]: 14–31); R. M. Hare's prescriptivism (*The Language of Morals* [Oxford: Clarendon Press, 1952]); Simon Blackburn's quasi-realism (*Spreading the Word* [Oxford: Oxford University Press, 1984], chap. 6; *Essays in Quasi-Realism* [Oxford: Oxford University Press, 1993]); and Allan Gibbard's norm expressivism (*Wise Choices, Apt Feelings: A Theory of Normative Judgment* [Cambridge, Mass.: Harvard University Press, 1990]).

6. Deflationism or minimalism about truth, fact, and property requires, I believe, a restatement of the issue between realists and antirealists. For an attempt to formulate the issue between realists and antirealists without relying on the notion of truth, see Crispin Wright, *Truth and Objectivity* (Cambridge, Mass.: Harvard University Press, 1992).

7. In addition to the semantic and metaphysical theses mentioned above, moral realists are plausibly thought to be committed to the epistemological thesis that we have epistemic access to the facts that render moral judgments true or false. Most philosophers would certainly be unhappy about advancing the thesis that there are certain types of facts, while denying that we have epistemic access to such facts; for that would amount to admitting that one's metaphysical position is unwarranted. But we should not expect moral realists to agree on moral epistemology beyond the minimal thesis that we have fairly decent epistemic access to moral facts. Some may also want to build into moral realism the nonreductivist thesis that moral properties and facts are sui generis, but I will not do so. With the exception of Mackie, all the cognitivists listed in note 3 are realists of some stripe or another.

8. See Chapter 1 of his *Ethics: Inventing Right and Wrong.* I will refer to this work parenthetically in the text as *Ethics.*

9. One may worry that the error theory cannot be coherently stated. After all, it claims that both "P" and "not P" are false, when "P" is a moral sentence. I am fairly confident that the position can be formulated such as to avoid this worry and will, therefore, waive it here.

10. I will discuss the natural–nonnatural distinction in more detail in section V.

11. Most or all naturalists accept a reductive view of moral properties and facts (but not necessarily of moral concepts), assuming a broad conception of the reductive relation as including metaphysical relations like supervenience and constitution as well as identity. Thus, most or all versions of naturalism would not count as realist, if we built a nonreductivist thesis into the characterization of moral realism. But I have not done so. For a defense of nonanalytic naturalism, see Boyd, "How To Be a Moral Realist"; Brink,

Moral Realism; Railton, "Moral Realism"; and Sturgeon, "Moral Explanations." The best example of analytic naturalism within the contemporary literature is probably David Lewis's dispositional theory of value. See his "Dispositional Theories of Value," *Proceedings of the Aristotelian Society,* supp. vol. 63 (1989): 113–137. G. E. Moore is, of course, the quintessential nonnaturalist.

12. The disagreement could be about issues specific to ethical discourse: naturalistic realists may, for example, disagree on the analyzability of moral concepts. Or the disagreement may be about more general issues that affect the arguments for or the development of these metaethical positions: for example, a disagreement about the nature of truth, representation, or properties in general.

13. See his *The View from Nowhere* (Oxford: Oxford University Press, 1986), p. 144. I will refer to this work parenthetically in the text as *Nowhere.*

14. See, for example, David M. Armstrong's discussion of realism and nominalism about universals in *Universals and Scientific Realism,* vol.1 (Cambridge: Cambridge University Press, 1978).

15. There are other versions of error theory around. Stephen Schiffer has, for example, argued for an error theory of moral discourse, against the background of a deflationary (or pleonastic) conception of properties. He does not deny that there are moral properties corresponding to moral concepts, but rather claims that these properties are necessarily uninstantiated. Stephen Schiffer, "Meaning and Value," *Journal of Philosophy* 87 (1990): 602–614.

16. Some ethicists who write on objectivity in ethics seem to be exclusively interested in this prescriptive status. See, for example, Jonathan Lear, "Moral Objectivity," in S. Brown (ed.), *Objectivity and Cultural Divergence* (Cambridge: Cambridge University Press, 1984).

17. These labels were suggested by Brian Leiter. I will also use "objective prescriptivity" and "objective existence" to mark the same distinction.

18. This leaves open the possibility that some values exist objectively; namely, values that are not objectively prescriptive. It is, e.g., possible to agree completely with Mackie on moral concepts and the ontic commitments of moral thought, but hold that the concept of a person's good or well-being is not a concept of a value that is objectively prescriptive and see no problem with thinking that there is a thought- and language-independent property that corresponds to this concept. Indeed, this might be Mackie's position. The discussion of mind-independence in Section V will make it clearer why this is prima facie a coherent possibility.

19. The following quote is revealing: "What really happens in the pursuit of objectivity is that a certain element of oneself, the impersonal or objective self, which can escape from the specific contingencies of one's creaturely point of view, is allowed to predominate. Withdrawing into this element one detaches from the rest and develops an impersonal conception of the world and, so far as possible, of the elements of self from which one has detached" (*Nowhere,* 9).

20. Nagel seems to think that there is just one type of value inquiry, even if it may yield a recognition of different types of values: e.g., personal, prudential, moral. He identifies the search for objectivity in value inquiry with ethical thought. Objective values are values recognized at the limit of ethical thought as legitimate; they may be either agent-relative or agent-neutral values. I am more inclined to defend the view that there are different sub-areas of value inquiry, guided by different methodological norms, that yield

conclusions about different types of values. However, I will not focus on this aspect of Nagel's view here. I will also assume for the purpose of this paper that there is no interesting distinction to be drawn between morality and ethics; I will use "moral" and "ethical," as well as other cognate terms, interchangeably.

21. If values' directing agents to act in a certain manner is a matter of the recognition of them motivating agents to undertake a certain action (as Mackie and many others seem to think) and if the recognition of values from a detached standpoint is motivating (as Nagel surely maintains – see next section), then values recognized from the detached standpoint are, indeed, normatively objective. I do not accept this conception of the action-directiveness of values, but I will not discuss that matter here. See my "Moral Cognitivism and Motivation" *Philosophical Review* 108 (1999): 161–219.

22. Here, I am largely following Gideon Rosen, who also distinguishes this epistemic notion of objectivity from metaphysical notions of objectivity. He dubs the former "methodological objectivity." See pp. 283–285 of his "Objectivity and Modern Idealism: What Is the Question?" in M. Michael and J. O'Leary-Hawthorne (eds.), *Philosophy in Mind* (Dordrecht: Kluwer Academic Publishers, 1994). Richard N. Boyd offers a different take on the objectivity of scientific methodology as "its capacity to lead to the discovery of *theory-independent reality*" (Boyd, "How To Be a Moral Realist," p. 191). On Boyd's conception of methodological objectivity, a method that makes the inquirers heavily rely on their own emotional responses is objective so long as their emotions happen to be reliable indicators of what is going on in the part of the ontically objective world under investigation. This seems to be a radical departure from common understanding of the objectivity of a method and fits better as an elucidation of the notion of truth-conduciveness of a method. We should, I submit, maintain a distinction between the truth-conduciveness and the objectivity of a method. It is an interesting question whether and why objective methodology tends to be truth-conducive. But perhaps there is a close connection between these two features, when the subject of inquiry is ontically objective. The objectivity of a method requires that the output of the method or the actual process of inquiry is not affected by distorting factors. Obviously, for any type of inquiry we need some grounds for distinguishing between factors that are distorting and those that are not. Perhaps the only way of doing so, when the subject of inquiry is ontically objective, is to refer to the features of the subject of inquiry in such a way that the objectivity and truth-conduciveness of the method are, in these cases, essentially linked.

23. Some comments on the argument from relativity are in order. First, Mackie writes as if the realist explanatory hypothesis has to be that moral judgments are "perceptions, most of them seriously inadequate and badly distorted, of objective values" (*Ethics*, 37). But certainly this is not right. The realist need not offer a perceptual model of moral evaluation. However, this does not seriously affect his argument. Second, there is certainly some room for disputing Mackie's assessment of the explanations in the offing. Nagel, e.g., raises reasonable objections to it, which I will briefly discuss in the final section of this chapter. But here I do not want to evaluate Mackie's argument. Instead, I want to examine the consequences of granting that the Nagelian method is available in value inquiry.

24. Thanks are due to Frances Kamm for suggesting that perhaps such a story could be told.

25. It is worth noting that this response to Mackie is not fully secured by what we have already granted Nagel. We have waived any worry we might have about the availability of the Nagelian method in value inquiry and the assumption that it will yield an evalua-

tive conception that will be shared by all rational inquirers, whatever their subjective starting points are. But that does not quite amount to granting that it is the best method for discovering what is of ontically objective value, and that is what is needed for countering Mackie's antirealist position. Indeed, it is not obvious that an inquiry into any aspect of ontically objective reality is best conducted by neutralizing the effects of *all* our psychological features that we do not share with all possible rational inquirers. For it is at least possible that some psychological features specific to a subset of all rational inquirers make them better equipped than any of the others to uncover, understand, and represent certain features of the ontically objective world. Gideon Rosen makes a similar point with respect to Bernard Williams's view ("Objectivity and Modern Idealism," p. 307).

26. I use "entities" to refer to the members of any ontological category: properties, relations, individuals, events, etc.

27. In conversation, Nagel has clarified that he was rejecting any form of reductivism. This suggests that he is a Non-Naturalist about values, but it is far from obvious how to reconcile that with his explicit response to Mackie. However, in Section V and again in Section VIII, I suggest different ways in which that could be done.

28. Somewhat less plausibly, the three-place relation represented may be taken as holding between c, s, and r_f, when r_f is an entity designated by "a reason to f."

29. In Section V, I examine more closely how to understand this expression.

30. See his *Descartes: The Project of Pure Enquiry* (New York: Penguin, 1978), pp. 237–245. I will refer to this work parenthetically in the text as *Descartes*.

31. In thinking about this part of Nagel's *Nowhere,* I have benefited from reading an unpublished manuscript ("Realism and Its Reasons") by Carsten Hansen.

32. Christopher Peacocke also notes this in his review of *The View from Nowhere.* See his "No Resting Place: A Critical Notice of the View from Nowhere, by Thomas Nagel," *Philosophical Review* 98 (1989): 65–82.

33. Recall from Section III that Nagel equates talk about values with talk about reasons for action. And Nagel makes the claim under discussion in the context of talking about propositions about reasons for action.

34. Should we perhaps put an emphasis on "new" when reading "a new aspect of the external world," and understand Nagel as allowing that we are discovering, under a new mode of presentation, aspects of the world to which we have already access under a different nonevaluative mode of presentation? But in that case, we would be attributing to Nagel some form of naturalistic realism, which surely goes against the spirit of the text. Thanks to Barry Loewer for raising this question.

35. I borrow this term from Rosen, "Objectivity and Modern Idealism," p. 288. Compare Bruce W. Brower's notion of constitutional independence. See his "Dispositional Ethical Realism," *Ethics* 103 (1993): 221–249.

36. Put in a possible-world-speak, the difference between existential mind-independence and observer-independence is as follows: An entity is existentially mind-independent iff it exists at a world in which there are no minds or mental activity. An entity x is *observer-independent* iff for any subject S and condition C, x exists and has the same nature in at least two worlds which differ with respect to the opinions which S under condition C has of x or there are at least two worlds which are exactly similar with respect to what opinion S, under condition C, has of x, but which are dissimilar with respect to the existence or nature of x. Since these notions of mind-independence are supposed to be metaphysical, the possible worlds would have to represent metaphysical possibilities.

37. This is evocative of Brower's notion of epistemic independence. Thanks to Brian Leiter for pointing this out to me. An entity is epistemically independent, in Brower's sense, just in case our beliefs about it, "even with adequate justification, could be false." Brower, "Dispositional Ethical Realism," p. 244. Brower's terminology suggests that this is an epistemic notion of objectivity. However, Brower appears to be drawing attention to an ontic status of constituents of the world similar to the one I refer to as observer-independence, i.e., it appears to be a metaphysical notion of objectivity.

38. Notice that this notion of the external world is, like Nagel's notion of objectivity, epistemic: the external world is the part of the world of which we can gain knowledge in a certain way. This raises the question whether some part of reality could be fully accessible to us through the five senses, while we have also an alternative way of experiencing or understanding it through first-person access. Nagel seems to think that this is not possible because if first-person access can contribute to our understanding of the thing in question, then there is some aspect of it that is not accessible through the five senses, aided by inductive and deductive reasoning. I am not convinced that this is right.

39. Moore identifies *nature* as the domain of the natural sciences; see p. 40 of his *Principia Ethica* (Cambridge: Cambridge University Press, 1903). I shall cite this work as *Principia*. However, he also claims that natural properties are "parts of which [natural objects are] made up" and can exist independent of these objects, whereas nonnatural properties are "mere predicates which attach to" the natural objects (*Principia*, 41). This is too obscure to be a helpful characterization of the distinction.

40. There is an enormous tendency to caricature Non-Naturalistic realism. It is instructive to bear in mind that the actual and possible particulars that instantiate moral properties also instantiate various physical, psychological, and sociological properties. So, moral facts — assuming a fact has as constituents a *n*-adic property and an *n*-tuple of particulars that stand in the relation of instantiation to each other — share at least one of their constituents with physical, psychological, and sociological facts. The Non-Naturalist maintains that they share only one constituent (the *n*-tuple of particulars), since moral properties are sui generis and not to be identified with physical, psychological, or sociological properties. Now, this hardly makes moral reality somehow radically disjoint with — let alone spatially separate from — the natural and social order. Of course, it is an enormously difficult question in metaphysics how we are to think of the existence and nature of properties in general. I venture the claim that properties of any kind exist in space and time only in the sense of being instantiated by spatially and temporally located individuals. Literally speaking, there is no faraway place where properties of any kind are stored safely away from the world of birth and decay. Certainly, Moore and other reasonable Non-Naturalists are not committed to any such nonsense.

41. Notice that Nagel would at least have diverged from Moore's position in giving a very different sketch of what sort of method is needed for discovering real values: he would have rejected Moore's intuitionist epistemology in favor of the method of objectivity. It is worth noting that Moore does not think that we can simply sit back and intuit what the good is. In order to elicit trustworthy intuitions we need to engage in the sort of thought experiments that are common in normative ethics. See his discussion of "the method of isolation" on p. 94 of his *Principia*.

42. See *Principia*, p. 143.

43. Some philosophers will claim that valuing reduces to believing: believing valuable. See, for example, Michael Smith, *The Moral Problem* (Oxford: Blackwell, 1994), pp. 147–

151. I myself suspect we need to distinguish between the mental attitudes of valuing (cherishing, holding dear) and of judging or believing valuable.

44. See his *The Possibility of Altruism* (Oxford: Clarendon Press, 1970).

45. I have in mind Allan Gibbard and Simon Blackburn (Gibbard, *Wise Choices, Apt Feelings;* Blackburn, *Spreading the Word,* chap. 6, and *Essays in Quasi-Realism*). In the next section, I discuss further Blackburn's quasi-realism.

46. I rely mainly on the discussion on pp. 141–142 in *Nowhere.*

47. The view I am teasing out of *Nowhere* is echoed in Nagel's recent claim that "we can defend moral reason only by abandoning metatheory for substantive ethics." *The Last Word* (New York: Oxford University Press, 1997), p. 125. Ronald Dworkin advances a similar view in his "Objectivity and Truth: You'd Better Believe It," *Philosophy & Public Affairs* 25 (1996): 87–139.

48. The following characterization of Blackburn's moral view is gathered from his books cited above, especially from remarks on pp. 128, 152, 157, 173 of *Quasi-Realism.*

49. This view is perhaps most explicitly stated on pp. 168–169 of *Quasi-Realism.*

50. Dworkin's view is a form of quietism. Dworkin, "Objectivity and Truth." Blackburn has responded to Dworkin on the web at *Brown Electronic Article Review Service* (posted November 11, 1996) (http://www.brown.edu/Departments/Philosophy/bears/ 9611blac.html). Quietism is also found in at least some of John McDowell's work in metaethics. See especially his "Non-Cognitivism and Rule-Following," in S. Holtzman and C. Leich (eds.), *Wittgenstein: To Follow a Rule* (London: Routledge & Kegan Paul, 1981). For a critical discussion of quietism, see the last chapter of Crispin Wright's *Truth and Objectivity.* And for a critical discussion of Dworkin's and McDowell's take on metaethical issues, see Brian Leiter's "Objectivity, Morality, and Adjudication" in this volume.

51. Another possibility would be that the difference is in the force of the judgment rather than in its content. Also, regarding the possibility considered in the text, the suggestion need not be that there is a nonevaluative simple predicate or simple concept corresponding to each moral concept. The concept employed in the sociological judgment may be highly complex and expressed by a complex rather than a simple predicate.

52. This is evocative of H. L. A. Hart's criticism of "the predictive theory of obligation" in *The Concept of Law* (Oxford: Oxford University Press, 1961), pp. 77–80. The predictive theory treats statements of obligation as predictions of chances of incurring punishment. Hart objects that this account cannot accommodate how rules, whose existence is implied by statements of obligation, appear from the "internal point of view": the point of view of those who accept and use the rules as guides to conduct. The predictive theory captures only what can be said about statements of obligation from an extreme "external point of view" on rule-governed activity: the point of view of the observer who does not accept the rules as guides to conduct and sees the rule-governed activity only as a regular pattern of observable behavior. But obligation and statements of obligation cannot, according to Hart, be properly understood from such a standpoint. Thanks are due to Brian Leiter for drawing my attention to this aspect of Hart's work.

53. For obvious examples of this see Gibbard's *Wise Choices, Apt Feelings* and Peter Railton's "Moral Realism." Gibbard uses both sociobiological thinking and anthropological thinking when developing his noncognitivist or expressivist view of moral judgments, while Railton uses more of a sociological approach to clear the ground for his naturalistic realism.

54. Peter Railton, "Naturalism and Prescriptivity," *Social Philosophy and Policy* 7 (1989): 151–174, at pp. 155–156.
55. Strictly speaking they might not be methodological naturalists, given Railton's Quinean characterization of the position as rejecting the idea that there is any distinctive a priori philosophical method. For they may hold that philosophy is in command of such a method for examining the meaning of linguistic expressions and our linguistic conventions. However, they are certainly methodological naturalists in a weaker sense; they accept that philosophy has to a large extent to "proceed *a posteriori,* in tandem with . . . the broadly empirical inquiry carried on in the natural and social sciences" (ibid.).
56. Notice that if Nagel is a closet noncognitivist, he would have another important disagreement with other fellow noncognitivists. The Humean view that beliefs are motivationally inert has traditionally played an important role in arguments for moral noncognitivism. Noncognitivists have joined this Humean thesis with the internalist view that moral judgments are intrinsically motivating to rule out the cognitivist claim that moral judgments manifest genuine moral beliefs. Now, Nagel is one of the more famous anti-Humeans about motivation, so he would not defend noncognitivism in this way. Indeed, I am not sure what resources he would have for justifying the distinctive claims of noncognitivism.
57. For an illuminating discussion of dispositionalism about values see papers by Michael Smith, Mark Johnston, and David Lewis in the symposium "Dispositional Theories of Value," *Proceedings of the Aritotelian Society,* supp. vol. 63 (1989): 89–174.
58. In that case, Nagel's position would have a strong affinity with David Lewis's position in "Dispositional Theories of Value."
59. Nagel obviously aspires to meet this condition; for he claims that answers to questions of values are correct "in virtue of something independent of our arriving of them" (*Nowhere,* p. 149). The question whether (naturalistic) dispositionalist theories of value meet the independence condition is discussed by both Lewis ("Dispositional Theories of Value") and Brower ("Dispositional Ethical Realism").
60. Brower makes essentially the same point in defense of the claim that his nonanalytic dispositionalism about values is a realist position. Brower, "Dispositional Ethical Realism."
61. I am drawing attention to the important difference between, on the one hand, taking science to have authority in matters of ontology that is strongly analogous to the authority an arbitrator has in a dispute and, on the other hand, taking science to have epistemic authority in matters of ontology. The arbitrator's authority is a matter of having the right to decide what is or will be the case; whereas epistemic authority is a matter of deserving doxastic trust due to having superior knowledge of the relevant matters or due to superior past performance in attaining or producing knowledge about similar matters. (I use "doxastic trust" primarily to refer to trust one has in someone's beliefs or theories and secondarily to refer to trust one has in a method for arriving at beliefs or theories.)
62. This is Nagel's response to Mackie's argument from relativity. See Section III of this chapter.
63. See, for example, p. 195 of his "Moral Realism."
64. See, especially, his "Facts and Values," *Philosophical Topics* 14 (1986): 4–31. Needless to say, Railton is working with a very different conception of rationality than Nagel is.
65. There is certainly an affinity here with Hart's view of philosophical legal theory. See fn. 52 above. Thanks to Brian Leiter for pointing this out to me.

66. I would not go so far as to claim that we can only reflect, philosophically, on our own practices, but we would, at least, have to be familiar with what it is like to live and think within the relevant conceptual space and under the relevant methodological ideals. In other words, we would have to be familiar enough with the practice to master its distinctive concepts and methodology.

67. It may be objected that I am mistakenly assuming that anthropologists and sociologists need not have the sort of familiarity with the practice that I claim is necessary for philosophical reflections on it. But I would, at least, venture that social scientists could rely more on informants than philosophical reflections do.

68. I am not limiting my audience to trained scientists and ardent moralists. For I do not construe scientific practice narrowly as the activity of those directly engaged in scientific research; nor moral practice as the activity of those on a moral crusade. As far as I am concerned, anyone is a party to scientific practice who, directly or indirectly, consults the meteorologist, the seismologist, the engineer, the physician, the pharmacist, or any other scientist. And anyone is a party to moral practice who periodically thinks of the human predicament in moral terms and recognizes that such thoughts bear on action. Undoubtedly, there have been, are, and will continue to be, humans who could not plausibly be said to be participants of either practice. The "we" I so freely use is exclusive of these people. But that does not bother me. The nature of philosophical reflections sets this limit. Since philosophical reflections proceed from the perspective of the practice that they target, we cannot hope to involve others than competent users of the concepts and conventions of the practices under consideration. I do not think this distracts from the value of philosophy. Self-reflection is valuable, although it can only be conducted by a single person. It most immediately enriches the life of that person, but can also more indirectly enrich the lives of those with whom she shares the results of her self-examination. Similarly, philosophical reflections are valuable, although one cannot hope to engage in them with people who do not master the concepts and conventions under consideration. They amount to an extension of the practice within which they take place; and they both modify and enrich that practice. The more thoroughly the practice is woven into the cultural fabric, the greater interest philosophical reflections on it command. And it certainly need not be feared that scientific and moral practice are peripheral to our culture.

69. There is certainly an affinity here with Wilfrid Sellars's discussion of the aim of philosophy and of the relation between "the manifest image" and "the scientific image." See his "Philosophy and the Scientific Image of Man," reprinted in Wilfrid Sellars, *Science, Perception, and Reality* (New York: Humanities Press, 1963). Thanks are due to Carsten Hansen and Brian Leiter for pointing this out to me.

70. Thanks are due to Daniel Bonevac, Carsten Hansen, Cory Juhl, Frances Kamm, Robert Koons, Brian Leiter, Barry Loewer, Thomas Nagel, Peter Railton, Stephen Schiffer, and David Velleman. I would also like to thank a small group of undergraduates in my 1996 class on metaethics where I tried out some of the material in this chapter; from that group, Adrienne Martin deserves special mention. Finally, I would like to acknowledge that the original version of this chapter was written when I was on a Goddard Fellowship, awarded by New York University, spring term 1996.

5

Notes on Value and Objectivity

JOSEPH RAZ

I. The Long Route

A. Introduction

It is natural that we should be interested in the nature of objectivity in general and in the objectivity or otherwise of practical thought in particular. In one of its senses objectivity is a precondition of knowledge. It also demarcates a type of thought[1] that is importantly different from others.

In this chapter our interest is in one way in which various types of thought differ. They are subject to different disciplines. Suppose, for example, that I say "I will be a good teacher" and you tell me: "But you have tried and failed for years," "I may reply by saying: "So what? That does not stop me from daydreaming," a response that is inappropriate if the thought expresses a belief. This is but one example of one aspect of what I called the different "disciplines" to which a thought or the holding of a thought can be subjected, a difference that marks the distinction between classes of thoughts and of ways of holding them. These disciplines determine whether my thought and yours, which have the same content, belong to the same type.

Of some thoughts, for example, it is possible to say, "They were mistaken," whereas of others this is inappropriate. A closely connected mark is that having or holding some thoughts can constitute knowledge. I mean that the fact I think that a general election was held in Italy yesterday is part of what makes it true that I know that a general election took place in Italy yesterday.

We mark this distinction between classes of thoughts that can constitute knowledge and can be mistaken and those that cannot by calling the first objective and the others subjective. When we ask whether practical thought is objective or subjective we are asking whether it is subject to one type of discipline or another. So the inquiry is natural and important. In the first part of

I am grateful to Peter Hacker and especially to Brian Leiter for comments on an earlier draft.

the chapter ("The Long Route") I will say something in general about the way we can characterize and explain objectivity in abstract terms. Parts II and III attempt to allay certain doubts about the objectivity of practical thought. Part II deals with the fact that practical concepts are parochial and not universally accessible to all. Part III deals with the social dependence of practical concepts.

B. *Some Senses of the Objective/Subjective Contrast*

The objective/subjective distinction originates in philosophy. With time its uses multiplied. People, beliefs, sometimes even facts are said to be objective or subjective, not only thoughts. And the suspicion is strong that more than one distinction is drawn by the use of these words. Here, to illustrate the point, are a couple of senses of the "objective/subjective" contrast: In science it is some-times said that an experiment is subjective if its results cannot be mechanically replicated. "Objective" here has something to do with intersubjectivity, when the intersubjective standard assumes the very strict form of a more or less mechanical process of experimentation whose results can be established by relying on little more than simple perception (assuming, of course, a rich background knowledge). A much more common use of the contrast, and a much less interesting one, is that by which any mental states are subjective, meaning belonging to a subject, and statements about mental states are subjec-tive simply in virtue of being about mental states.

More relevant for our purpose is a third common sense in which the distinc-tion is used. In what I will call *the epistemic sense* people are objective about certain matters if they are, in forming or holding opinions, judgments, and the like, about these matters, properly sensitive to factors that are epistemically relevant to the truth or correctness of their opinions or judgments, that is, if they respond to these factors as they should. Their views or beliefs may be wrong or mistaken, but there are no emotionally induced distortions in the way they were reached, or the conditions under which they are held. That means, for example, that people are objective in this sense if they form their opinions and judgments on the basis of the relevant evidence available to them, mindful of whether or not they are in circumstances that might affect the reliability of their perceptions or thought processes, and when their selection of information as relevant and their evaluation of it are sensible and not affected by such emo-tional or other psychological distortions. Opinions and beliefs are objective if they are reached or held in an objective manner. Sometimes people are said to be objective if they are capable of being objective in the sense just explained.

A related sense is that of objectivity as *impartiality*. People are impartial if and only if, in matters affecting others as well as possibly themselves, they act on relevant reasons and shun irrelevant ones, in particular if they shun irrele-vant considerations that favor themselves or people or causes dear to their hearts, and if their evaluation of the situation is not distorted by the fact that such people or causes are dear to them.[2] Epistemic objectivity as a capacity to avoid bias, or other emotional distortions, requires impartiality as one of its constituent conditions, and this condition by itself is sometimes taken to make a person an objective judge of a certain matter. But the impartiality sense of objectivity reaches beyond these cases. It is the most important sense of objectivity in practical matters, objectivity in action (e.g., when the objectivity of judges or of officials is in question, usually impartiality is meant). Not infrequently official action is based in part not on the beliefs of the officials concerned, but on the basis of propositions that are accepted by them as a reasonable basis for action in the circumstances of the case. Objectivity as impartiality can characterize deliberation and decisionmaking based on accepted – rather than believed – premises as well. This requirement of objectivity is a requirement of impartiality in all the stages of the decision-making process.

Our interest is in a different distinction drawn by the objective/subjective contrast. I identified it at the outset as the sense of objectivity in which it is a condition of the possibility or perhaps of the conceivability of knowledge, and a condition for the applicability of the notions of mistaken or correct (true) thoughts. Intersubjectivity, albeit in a weaker sense than that required by the scientific usage that I mentioned, and the possibility of holding views that are not influenced by bias, or by similar cognitive distortions, are among the general conditions for the possibility of knowledge. But equally clearly we have not yet identified the core sense that is relevant for our purpose. For lack of a better word, I will sometimes refer to *domain-objectivity* when wishing to distinguish this sense of objectivity from others. Primarily it is domains of thoughts, propositions, or statements that are objective in that sense.[3] By natural extension, single propositions, statements, and thoughts are objective if they belong to an objective domain, and so is whatever they are about.

It is not easy to describe what makes domains of thought objective. The difficulty is that in trying to do so one enters disputes about the nature of what there is, the nature of reality, and about the structure of thoughts or of propositions about how things are. A proposition is objective if it is about an object of a nonempty kind, that is, such that there are objects belonging to it, some writers suggest.[4] But what counts as an object and how do we determine what kind it belongs to? Worse still, how do we determine what propositions are about? Consider, for example, propositions like "The African lion lives to be 23 years old and fathers 3.7 cubs"; "There are two types of energy, static and kinetic." Both are objective propositions. That is not in dispute. But is it because they are about objects such as the African lion and energy? Or are they about lions, all the lions bred in Africa, and all the objects in the world? To resolve these questions we need to come to a view regarding the status of universals, of dummy objects, and of the conditions for the existence of objects in general. We may also have to enter into the morass of determining what propositions are *about.* And there are further difficulties in store.

David Wiggins seems to sidestep these problems when he says that "A subject matter is objective (or relates to an objective reality) if and only if there are questions about it (and enough questions about it) that admit of answers that are substantially true – simply and plainly true."[5] The qualification "substantially true" puts us on our guard, however. It would seem that in order to gain an understanding of objectivity we need to resolve issues concerning various kinds of truths.[6]

Trying to sidestep these issues as well I suggested at the beginning of this article that a domain is objective if it is capable of being the object of knowledge, if propositions that belong to it can state what one knows, thoughts that belong to it can manifest what one knows. If only true propositions can be known, and only true thoughts can express one's knowledge, domains are objective in this sense only if thoughts, propositions, and statements that belong to them can be true or false. But problems are to be found here too. If there can be aspects of reality that it is logically impossible for us (but who are "us"? The human race? Or all agents capable of knowing something? Or each one of us?) to know anything about, then while the objectivity of a domain is a precondition of knowledge, the reverse is not the case. We cannot say that a domain is objective only if it can express knowledge, that is, express what is knowable. There may be (objective domains of) propositions that state how things are regarding matters of which it is impossible to have any knowledge. This is one reason why I will not try to define domain-objectivity or to give necessary and sufficient conditions for the objectivity of domains. Rather I will attempt to elucidate the notion by considering a number of conditions that partially characterize it.

While the epistemic and domain senses of objectivity are obviously interrelated, they differ in important respects. When judging someone or some opinions to be epistemically objective (or lacking objectivity), one presupposes that the matter which is so judged is domain-objective. In other words, domain-objectivity marks the fact that we are dealing with a domain about which one can be objective in the epistemic sense, and statements that are domain-objective are those that *can* also be epistemically objective.

One way in which the two clusters of senses differ is in the responsibility[7] of people who are or are not, or whose opinions are or are not, objective in the various senses. People should be epistemically objective and their opinions should not be epistemically subjective. They are responsible for failing to be as they should, for such failures are due to biases and other distortions of their cognitive functioning for which people are held responsible. Their responsibility for their failures of epistemic objectivity does not assume that knowledge is a good that they should pursue. It only means that they should not form judgments that are tainted by bias. Even though in some of its variants noted above epistemic responsibility is a matter of ability rather than performance, it is an ability the presence or lack of which can only be established by performance. Hence those who lack it are those who are lacking in performance.[8]

The only responsibility that can arise if an area of inquiry or judgments about it are domain-subjective is responsibility for failure to realize that the domain is subjective. There can be, of course, no responsibility for these matters or judgments being subjective. This is just how things are. Nor for that matter can people be responsible for treating matters subjectively in these cases, for there is nothing else they can properly do.

It is crucial to notice that in no sense is objectivity identified with truth, though in all of them it is related more or less indirectly to truth. Thoughts that are objective can be the subject of knowledge, and they are expressed in propositions that can be true or false (or correct or incorrect). People who are epistemically objective judges of certain matters are not free from error in those matters. They are merely free from errors arising out of biases and an emotionally blinkered inability to respond to the evidence and evaluate it. Statements and opinions that are epistemically objective are those that are neither reached nor sustained through biases of this kind. But obviously they can be false or mistaken for other reasons. Epistemic objectivity is closely associated with rationality. It is a condition of being a rational judge of certain matters that one is epistemically objective regarding them. Being objective is not, however, sufficient to make one a rational judge. Various inabilities may undermine one's rationality that do not arise out of bias but are a result of cognitive incompetence, hastiness, and like defects that do not undermine one's objectivity.

C. Some Conditions of Domain Objectivity

Given our interest in the objectivity of practical thought, we can leave the epistemic sense on one side and concentrate on the question of the objectivity of the domain of practical or evaluative thought. What exactly is domain-objectivity? How is it to be explained?

Possibly there is no short answer to the question. A domain of thought is objective if and only if thoughts belonging to it satisfy a whole range of criteria. They define the discipline to which objective thoughts are subject. We have already encountered a few of them:

1. THE POSSIBILITY OF KNOWLEDGE CONDITION. Only if a domain is objective can it express knowledge or be said to be about something that one can have knowledge of.

2. THE POSSIBILITY OF ERROR CONDITION. A domain is objective only if thoughts that belong to it obey the distinction between seeming and being, that

is, only if the fact that I think that things are so and so does not constitute their being so and so (some self-referential thoughts are the exception).[9]

3. THE POSSIBILITY OF EPISTEMIC OBJECTIVITY. Only if a domain is objective can one be an objective or a subjective judge of matters in this domain. Similarly, only then can one's opinions about it, or the way one forms them, be objective, et cetera.

This last condition is in some sense a subsidiary of the first two. But another condition central to our understanding of the objective is:

4. THE RELEVANCE CONDITION. Thoughts are objective only if there can be facts or other considerations that are reasons for believing that they are or are likely to be true or correct.

The second condition allows us

i. to talk of thoughts as being correct, true, or as being errors and mistakes.[10]
ii. to admit that two views are contradictory and therefore that there are logical relations among thoughts
iii. to talk of changing one's mind (with the implication that one was in error then, not only that one now wants something different), et cetera.

The fourth condition allows us to apply the distinction between what is relevant to the truth of a thought and what is not, and the whole terminology of support and confirmation. The reasons for holding a thought to be true are of a large variety of kinds. They may be evidential (there are heavy clouds, therefore it will rain), or legal (it has been approved by the Queen in Parliament, therefore it is a valid law), or moral (it shows disrespect, therefore it is wrong), or semantic (he is your uncle's son, therefore he is your cousin), and many others. Reasons for believing that a thought is true need not be available to the person who has it, or at least need not be available to him as reasons for the thought. This caveat covers, among other cases, the case where belief is direct and not based on reasons. A person looking at a red bus and thinking "This is a red bus" does not have reasons for his belief. But there are reasons to think his belief correct, for example, that he was in an advantageous position to judge the character and color of the object he saw.

The objectivity of a domain does not presuppose that anyone can have either a priori or self-evident or incorrigible understanding of what relevant reasons are like or of the rules of reasoning in this domain. It only presupposes that the thoughts belonging to an objective domain (a) allow for the application of judgments based on reasons. Schematically, it allows for beliefs of the kind "This thought is unjustified for the reason that . . ." where the reason adduced – even if it is a bad reason, and even if it is of a type that cannot but be a bad reason – is one that can intelligibly be thought of as a reason in this context. And (b) they allow that there can be reasons of an appropriate kind, that is, reasons whose existence makes such beliefs true.

Two further important conditions derive from Bernard Williams's discussion of the absolute conception of reality (about which more will be said below). In advancing the absolute conception Williams was concerned with the conditions for the possibility of knowledge. His discussion is therefore relevant to objectivity understood as a mark of domains of thoughts that could constitute knowledge. Williams introduces the discussion by saying: "If knowledge is what it claims to be, then it is knowledge of a reality which exists independently of that knowledge. . . . Knowledge is of what is there *anyway.* "[11] This thought yields the condition of objectivity which can be formulated as follows:

5. THE INDEPENDENCE CONDITION. Thoughts are objective only if they are about a reality[12] that exists independently of them, that is, whose truth is independent of the fact that those thoughts are entertained.[13]

If there are exceptions to this condition they are marginal and degenerate cases. Trying to refine the condition to accommodate them need not detain us. Williams follows the above quotation with a complex statement introducing several ideas, one of which can be called the single reality condition.

6. THE SINGLE REALITY CONDITION. The domain of objective thoughts is subject to the constraint that thoughts constitute knowledge only if they can all be explained as being about a single reality.[14]

The condition is intended by Williams to allow for the acceptance of apparently conflicting claims of knowledge, provided they can be reconciled as claims about a single reality (e.g., by representing it in different but intertranslatable schemes of representations), but to exclude claims whose apparent conflict cannot be thus reconciled. In particular he is keen to rule out suggested reconciliations that relativize claims of knowledge: "p is true from my perspective, or relative to me, or from point of view x, even while not-p is true from your perspective," and so forth. It is a rejection of isolationism, of claims that every domain of thought must be judged by its own standards of truth, knowledge, and objectivity, which may be very different from those of any other domain.[15] The single reality condition, while allowing for different perspectives and different domains of thoughts, each with its own standards of evidence, et cetera, insists that they must all be reconcilable within one conception of reality. They must be shown to be not only consistent with each other but also perspectives or domains that can be seen as being about different aspects of one world — not an easy condition to spell out,[16] but one that is worth retaining, as it bears on a variety of subjectivist and relativist claims.

We could go on drawing out the implications of these conditions and adding others to them. I call this approach the "long route" to an explanation of objectivity, for it does not yield a comprehensive set of conditions, the satisfaction of which is necessary and sufficient for a domain to be objective, and that provide an adequate explanation of objectivity beyond the need for further refinement and adjustment. Any set of conditions, however successful they may be in answering the questions and concerns that led to their formulation, will need to be refined as new problems emerge. It is in principle impossible to circumvent the long route by providing a set of necessary and sufficient conditions that will never call for revision and refinement and from which all the other necessary features of objectivity can be deduced. It is not possible to argue for this impossibility here. It depends, first, on the fact that propositions are open to somewhat different interpretations, that they are all inherently vague and therefore, even if true, may call for further refinement to meet the needs of new puzzles and hitherto unexplored questions.[17] It depends, second, on the ever-present possibility that new questions will emerge forcing us to notice and articulate new conditions of objectivity. Perhaps the following could serve as an example of another condition that does not follow from the above and that may illustrate how more and more may emerge with emerging reasons to think of them:

7. THE POSSIBILITY OF IRRATIONALITY CONDITION. That is, that it is possible to endorse propositions belonging to the domain out of wishful thinking, self-deception, et cetera.[18]

Even if the "additional conditions" that may emerge with time apply to the same domain already delineated by previously spelled-out conditions, they are not redundant. An explanation of objectivity aims to do more than mark the boundaries of objective domains. It aims to explain puzzles about objectivity. The point I am pressing home here is that as new puzzles arise new conditions may be noticed which help to explain them away.

D. Defending the Approach

Is this "long route" to explaining objectivity adequate? Some may say that while it brings out necessary conditions of objectivity, it is never going to get to the real hard questions: are there really things or properties like "rights," "tastefulness" or "beauty"? Is it in principle possible for them to exist?

The problem with the approach I outlined, these people might say, is that it considers only internal criteria of objectivity. Basically it regards thoughts as objective if we treat them as objective or if the concepts and sentences employed to express them meet certain conditions, which show that they are treated as expressing thoughts that can be true or false, and so forth. But we cannot, so the objection goes, make a thought objective just by treating it as objective. Whether or not it is objective is not up to us. It depends on how things are in the world.[19] In classifying thoughts as objective we are saying that they constitute beliefs, that to hold such thoughts is to have certain beliefs, and that means that these thoughts can be true or false and that holding them can in principle amount to knowledge. This shows, the argument proceeds, that whether they are objective cannot just be a matter of how we treat them. It is a question of what the world really is like, a question about how things are in the world.

Here is my problem: Domains of thought are objective, I suggested at the outset, only if they are subject to disciplines that make them capable of constituting knowledge, and so on. The charge against the way I explained this route to an explanation of objectivity was that it led to an articulation of what we take to be the conditions of knowledge, rather than what really are the conditions of knowledge. It may seem that the only way to justify my position is to deny that the two can differ. But that would imply that we cannot be wrong about the conditions of knowledge, which seems too strong a claim. In fact it is not needed. All I need to argue for is that, necessarily, our knowledge or understanding of the conditions of objectivity depends on our knowledge or understanding of the conditions of knowledge. If our knowledge or understanding of one of these concepts is imperfect so is our knowledge or understanding of the other.

Whether our thoughts are true or not is immaterial to their objective character, but they must, among other things, be capable of being true or false, of bearing a truth-value. Therefore, they cannot amount to knowledge unless they are about how things are anyway, about the world as it is independently of these thoughts. That means (given that the character of domains of thought depends on the disciplines to which we subject them) that they cannot be about reality unless we treat them as about how things are independently of thought about them.

As so far stated, these considerations do not show more than that satisfying the conditions spelled out above, and others derived in like manner, is necessary for a domain of thought to be objective. But their implications reach further:

First, it is not the case that this approach allows that what is objective is "up to us." That would mean that we can choose whether to regard matters of taste or morality as objective. But the account I suggested has no such consequence.

Second, notice that these conditions do more than point to surface syntactical features, for example, that the thoughts are expressed in indicative sentences, allow embedding, et cetera. They assume the practices that Wright regards as underlying what he calls "the minimalist" account of truth.[20] Wright's account has convinced some writers that nothing of substance depends on allowing that propositions and utterances can be true or false, given the minimalist account of truth.[21] The condition of relevance, however, takes my explanation of objectivity beyond the conditions that, according to Wright, have to be satisfied for a truth predicate to apply to a domain.

Third, the condition of relevance makes the objectivity of a domain dependent on the existence of criteria that support or undermine beliefs within that domain. These criteria could in appropriate circumstances warrant the conclusion that all beliefs within the domain are false or lacking in truth-value (because a presupposition of their having truth-value fails). Thus this approach allows in principle for an error theory[22] that while admitting that a domain is the subject of objective thought establishes that there can be nothing in it, that there can be no rights, no tasteful or beautiful objects, and so forth.

Fourth, the approach allows for the possibility that a domain that appears objective is not in fact objective, even though it is taken by everyone to be objective. This can happen if discourse involving it collapses into contradiction or incoherence, or if it fails to cohere with other established beliefs.

Fifth, the approach allows that our concepts of knowledge, truth, and objectivity may themselves be defective and in need of revision (more on this in Section IIE below).

Sixth, externalist accounts are the better accounts of knowledge. According to them, whether or not one's belief is justified depends, in part, on how things turn out in the world, and not merely on satisfying criteria that the agent is aware of.

The third, fourth, and fifth points establish that the approach I delineated is not essentially a conservative one, that it is open to challenges that can force revisions in, or even the abandonment of, established aspects of common discourse and thought. The last point is but one additional way in which the criteria of objectivity, derived from the essential properties of knowledge, are not "too internal."

This six-point reply to the objection may only prompt some of those who suspect the long route of being too internal to raise another charge. I seem to have an answer, they would say, because I conflate and confuse a number of different issues: metaphysical, epistemic, and semantic. The possibility of error condition concerns semantics, the relevance and the possibility of irrationality conditions are explicitly epistemic, and the independence and single reality conditions are metaphysical.

At one level I have no defense against this charge. The list of criteria of objectivity does include criteria that can readily be classified as semantic, metaphysical and epistemic, as well as some that may defy such a classification. Nor do I wish to raise any doubts about the legitimacy of separating issues into semantic, metaphysical and epistemic. In many cases such a separation is useful, and in some it is essential. But not all concepts can be readily separated in this way, and to my mind the attempts by some writers[23] to define separate semantic and metaphysical senses of objectivity miss the point that the two are interdependent, and at the most fundamental level these stipulated concepts are not useful.

Take the relevance condition. It is epistemic in nature, but not exclusively so. Someone who does not know anything at all about what may count as evidence in favor of the proposition that Gubaidulina is a great composer, or that this chair is not comfortable, or that Everest is the highest mountain on earth, does not really know what it is to be a composer or a mountain, and so forth. If upon hearing the claim that Gubaidulina is a great composer someone replies, "Oh yes? Does she eat fish?" then, barring a peculiar sense of humor, his remarks reveal that he has not understood what he was told. Such misunderstandings are often used in popular humor to expose the ignorance and pretense of social climbers. Examples like this would show that part of understanding any concept is having some grasp of what counts as relevant evidence showing that it applies or does not apply.

At the same time, the fact that one thing or another is evidence for the existence of something, or for its possession of some property, tells us something about the nature of these existences: material things are those whose existence and properties can be established one way, mathematical objects and properties are those that are established in very different ways, et cetera. In sum, the relevance conditions straddle the divide between the semantic, epistemic, and metaphysical. It requires more than knowledge of connections among concepts. It requires knowledge of the way things are in the world is relevant to the application of concepts.

The interdependence of the different aspects (semantic, metaphysical, and epistemic) reveals itself in the way arguments regarding problem cases proceed. There is a striking correlation between those philosophers who think that there are "Non-Naturalistic" moral properties and those who believes that moral predicates refer to such properties. Mackie is the only philosopher who believes that moral predicates refer to nonnatural properties, but that there are no such properties, nor can there be. Apart from him, those who believe that moral statements are "semantically objective" also believe that there are moral properties, and – some argue – since there are no nonnatural properties, moral properties must be natural properties. Those who believe that there are no moral properties opt for a noncognitive interpretation of moral utterances and so on. The same is true regarding secondary qualities. Even Mackie does not offer an error theory of secondary qualities or of mathematical properties. In all these cases one's view of the nature of the properties that exist and one's view of the semantics of the relevant range of predicates go hand in hand. They are interdependent and, needless to say, so are the relevant evidential criteria. That is why I claimed that domain-objectivity combines semantic, epistemic, and metaphysical criteria.

The interdependence of the semantic and metaphysical is recognized and explained by Crispin Wright. He argues that, if one believes, as error theorists like Mackie and Field do, that even though propositions asserting the existence of ethical (or mathematical or other) properties are false, we need not radically change our use of them for they serve some other valid purpose, then one has to explain why not accepting that truth in that domain is constituted by serving that purpose. In his words: "why insist on construing *truth* for moral discourse in terms which motivate a charge of global error, rather than explicate it in terms of the satisfaction of the putative subsidiary norm [what I called "the valuable purpose"], whatever it is? The question may have a good answer. . . . But I do not know of promising argument in that direction."[24] That is the sort of consideration that led me to claim that domain-objectivity combines semantic, epistemic, and metaphysical criteria.

In spite of these points doubts are likely to linger. While not being conservative, the criteria I mentioned are all in some sense internal to the ways we treat thoughts in the domain in question. Is there no possibility that a domain will meet these criteria and yet fail to be objective simply because of how things are? In principle the answer is affirmative. Since the long route deals with problems as they are encountered, and denies the feasibility of producing a definitive list of necessary and sufficient conditions for objectivity, the (epistemic) possibility that factors may emerge that defeat the objectivity of domains of thought that meet the above conditions cannot be ruled out. All we can do is examine specific doubts regarding the objectivity of practical thought. The rest of this chapter consists in dispelling two specific sources of such doubt that have attracted considerable attention.

II. The Role of Parochial Concepts

A. Is Parochial Knowledge Possible?

A couple of terminological stipulations will help us along: "Perspectival knowledge" is knowledge that can only be expressed with the use of parochial concepts. "Parochial concepts" are concepts that cannot be mastered by all, not even by everyone capable of knowledge. "Nonparochial" concepts can be mastered by anyone capable of knowing anything at all. Any concepts possession of which requires having particular perceptual capacities (such as color concepts) and not merely the possession of some perceptual capacity or another, are parochial concepts. For different reasons concepts whose mastery presupposes interests or imaginative or emotive capacities that are not shared, nor can be shared, by all creatures capable of possessing knowledge are parochial concepts. We come to understand interests we do not share by relating them to interests we do share. If an interest is remote from any of ours, and if its role in the life of the people who have it is ramified and unlike the role of any interests we have, or know about, then explanation has to be supplemented with simulation or real habituation before we can understand it or the concepts that presuppose its understanding. But our capacity for simulation or habituation is limited. Interests that will evolve only in the future, for example, cannot be understood in that way, and often they are interests that it is in principle impossible for us to understand. By the same token, many of our interests were beyond the reach of people in previous generations, and so were the concepts mastery of which depends on understanding these interests.

The impossibility of acquiring concepts that presuppose interests remote from those we have and that do not yet exist (and therefore cannot be mastered or discovered by simulation) is sufficient to show that practically all concepts that can be acquired only by people who understand some nonuniversal interests are parochial concepts. Regarding all of them, there was a time when they were beyond the reach of people living at that time. There is, however, yet another type of limitation on people's ability in principle to master such concepts: habituation and simulation are demanding and relatively slow processes. You often have to immerse yourself in an alien culture, understand its concerns, religious and other beliefs, come to understand how people normally react in many (to them normal) situations, share – at least in imagination – their hopes, fears, and aspirations. All these factors mean that even if there is no interest-dependent concept one cannot acquire, it is in principle possible for any person to master only a relatively small number of such concepts and hence, given the length and diversity of human history, impossible in principle for anyone living today to master more than a fraction of the interest-dependent concepts that pertain to different human societies now, or did in the past, even if we leave aside the future.[25]

If interest-related concepts are parochial, so are evaluative or normative concepts, for they are all interest-related (not, of course, in "serving" the interests of the agent, but in the fact that mastery of the concept requires understanding some interests or others). This is evident when we consider relatively specific, so called thick, concepts, like the excellence of an opera or a novel. But the same is true of our abstract normative concepts such as those designated by the terms "duty," "obligation," "ought," "a right," "valuable," "good," "beautiful," "person," "happiness," "pleasure." The history of these terms, and the attempt to find terms of comparable meaning in other languages, show how their meaning mutated over time and how different languages differ in their abstract normative vocabulary. It is reasonable to conclude that abstract normative concepts too are parochial.

Doubts have been cast on the objectivity of parochial concepts, on the possibility of knowledge that depends on their possession and cannot be reformulated without their use. I will examine some grounds for such doubts.

B. Nagel on the Objective and the Subjective

Thomas Nagel regards parochial concepts as subjective but does not deny that they enable us to acquire knowledge that cannot be obtained without them. In most respects my views are consonant with his. The most striking apparent difference is due to the special sense in which he uses the objective/subjective distinction, which differs from any I have mentioned so far. "A view or form of thought is more objective than another if it relies less on the specifics of the individual's makeup and position in the world, or on the character of the particular type of creature he is."[26] In other words, Nagel calls a view or thought subjective if it essentially depends on employing parochial concepts for its expression. The greater its dependence on parochial concepts the more subjective it is.

For Nagel "objectivity is a method of understanding."[27] It seems to be a method of understanding reality with different aspects of reality being understood depending on the degree of objectivity attained in the method of understanding them: "We may think of reality as a set of concentric spheres, progressively revealed as we detach gradually from the contingencies of the self" (*Nowhere,* 5). This sentence may suggest that the more objective our method of understanding the more of reality we come to know and understand. But this is not Nagel's meaning, or at least it is only part of his meaning. While some aspects of reality reveal themselves only as they are objectively investigated, others are lost except when understood through subjective methods. "The attempt to give a complete account of the world in objective terms . . . inevitably leads to false reductions or to outright denial that certain patently real phenomena exist at all" (*Nowhere,* 7). In particular, "[t]he subjectivity of consciousness is an irreducible feature of reality" (ibid.), which presumably means that it can only be fully known and understood with the use of subjective methods, including the use of parochial concepts. Nagel seems to think that only the mental requires parochial concepts for its understanding.

Although there is a connection between objectivity and reality – only the supposition that we and our appearances [this seems to mean here: how things appear to us, not how we appear to others – JR] are part of a larger reality makes it reasonable to seek understanding by stepping back from the appearances in this way – still not all reality is better understood the more objectively it is viewed. Appearance and perspective are essential parts of what there is, and in some respects they are best understood from a less detached standpoint. Realism underlines the claims of objectivity and detachment, but it supports them only up to a point. (*Nowhere,* 4)

But how can we know that no other aspect of reality requires parochial concepts for its understanding? Perhaps the thought is that since the mental is subjective it requires subjective concepts for its understanding. But that thought is guilty of the fallacy of equivocation: Thought is subjective in the psychological sense that means simply that it is mental. The "method of subjectivity" as a method of knowledge does not mean knowing in a way which involves mental states, dispositions, or capacities. All knowing involves the mental in these ways, be it knowledge obtained by more or less objective methods. "The method of subjectivity" means knowledge that can only be obtained by the use of parochial concepts. To avoid equivocation the thought should be: parochial concepts, and thoughts involving them, can only be under-stood with the use of parochial concepts. That amounts to claiming that paro-chial concepts cannot be eliminated. If they are necessary for knowledge of certain matters, then those matters cannot be known "objectively." *That* would not justify the conclusion that only the mental can be understood by the use of parochial concepts.

Perhaps I am wrong to identify Nagel's understanding of the objective/subjective distinction with reliance on and the use of concepts that are more or less parochial? Perhaps all he means is that the mental can be understood only with the use of psychological concepts? He certainly believes the latter, but that is not all he is claiming.

The more objective our understanding the more detached it is from our specific situation, specific capacities, et cetera. To quote Nagel again: the more objective the thought the less it relies "on the specifics of the individual's makeup and position in the world, or on the character of the particular type of creature he is." These specifics constitute what he calls the special perspective of that creature. Objective knowledge, like any other knowledge, is obtained within that perspective, but it does not rely on it. It can be shared by people whose perspectives are different. Subjective knowledge cannot be shared in this way. It is available only to those who share the same perspective.

My suggestion is that perspectives can be identified by the range of con-cepts that those who inhabit them can possess. This does not exhaust the differences between perspectives, but the others follow from the inability of those who inhabit a perspective to possess certain concepts. The possession of concepts, let us remind ourselves, involves certain mental abilities, certain perceptual abilities, and certain experiences. For example, inability to master mathematical concepts makes one incapable of possessing a whole range of scientific concepts, the lack of sight makes the understanding of color concepts incomplete, and those who never desired anything cannot understand what it is to want something.

So the more objective knowledge is the less does its possession presuppose. It presupposes fewer common mental abilities, fewer common perceptual abil-ities, and fewer common experiences. If that is so we can understand why knowledge of the nature of thought is more objective than knowledge of the nature of Christianity. To understand the nature of thought one needs to have the capacity for thought, but other things being equal, this capacity is available to anyone capable of thinking. These may include Martians, automata, and others, besides humans. Knowledge of Christianity requires concepts such as salvation, redemption, and love that need not be available to all who are capable of knowledge. Hence it is more subjective.

This line of thought can explain some aspects of Nagel's position. But it does not seem to explain some of its basic tenets. First, it does not explain why all knowledge of the mental is more subjective. Since only people with a mental life are capable of knowledge none is excluded from the perspective that involves at least some mental concepts. Second, it does not explain why only the mental defies complete objectivity. It does not answer the question: Why should we assume that there are no aspects of reality that can be known or understood only by creatures with specific capacities and experiences, that are incompatible with the capacities needed to understand other aspects of reality? Nagel seems bereft of an argument which will limit his "subjective method" of knowledge to the mental only.[28]

C. Williams and the Priority of Nonparochial Concepts

Williams in discussing secondary qualities introduces the requirement that all knowledge must be capable of being expressed without the use of parochial concepts. I will call this the *priority condition,* meaning the condition that a thought is objective only if it can be expressed without the use of parochial concepts. Here is his argument:

Can we really distinguish between some concepts or propositions which figure in the conception of the world without observers, and others that do not? Are not all our concepts ours . . . ? Of course; but there is no suggestion that we should try to describe a world without ourselves using any concepts, or without using concepts which we, human beings, can understand. The suggestion is that there are possible descriptions of the world using concepts which are not peculiarly ours, and not peculiarly relative to our experience. Such a description would be that which would be arrived at, as C. S. Peirce put it, if scientific enquiry continued long enough; it is the content of that "final opinion" which Peirce believed that enquiry would inevitably converge upon, a final opinion . . . independent not indeed of thought in general, but of all that is arbitrary and individual in thought.[29]

The scientific representation of the material world can be the point of convergence of the Peircean enquirer precisely because it does not have among its concepts any which reflect merely a local interest, taste or sensory peculiarity. . . . This extended conception would then be that absolute conception of reality.[30]

And Williams contrasts this view with that of a critic who maintains that "scientific theories are a cultural product which it would be senseless to suppose could be freed from local relativities."[31]

The motivating concern leading to the priority condition seems to be the need to establish the credentials of our knowledge claims and of our concepts. We need to know that through our concepts we can understand the world as it is independently of us, that our thoughts are no mere shadows cast by our own concepts. Therefore, any view or thought that claims to be knowledge must meet a test that is concept-independent, or – given the impossibility of thought without concepts – that is at least independent of any concepts that are not accessible to everyone. That test is the Peirceian convergence of all those who are engaged in pure inquiry. In the nature of things if the convergence is to encompass all those capable of knowledge, then it must exclude thoughts that essentially depend on parochial concepts for their expression. Such parochial thoughts will not be available to all inquirers and therefore will not be able to be subjected to the test of convergence.

The priority condition has been criticized as incoherent and inconsistent with its aim of establishing some limited credentials of knowledge that relies on parochial concepts.[32] In later writings Williams abandons it and concedes that the understanding, as well as the explanation, of knowledge relying on parochial concepts cannot be accomplished without such concepts.[33] This entails also abandoning the ideal convergence condition in Peirce's version that Williams endorsed earlier. There is knowledge regarding which no convergence of all competent inquirers is possible. "Alien investigators," to use his phrase, may be unable to understand our perspective, even those aspects of it that yield knowledge, if that knowledge is dependent on parochial concepts.[34]

Convergence is in any case a suspect condition.[35] A degree of convergence is entailed by the fact that agreement in meaning presupposes a degree of agreement in judgment. This does indeed vindicate testing agreement in meaning by looking for agreement in judgment. But the convergence that test entails is limited to those who share the same meanings. This cannot be a requirement of a Peirceian convergence of all competent inquirers, since, by definition, they do not share understanding of parochial concepts. Within local communities who share parochial concepts, such as "inflation," "chivalry," and their like, there will indeed be a degree of convergence in judgment. But not enough to eliminate disagreements and disputes. In particular, beliefs whose justification typically involves complex reasoning regarding a diverse range of considerations will always be liable to disagreement even among those who share the same meaning and a similar environment (and therefore a similar evidential starting point).

Most theorists who recommend convergence as a criterion of objectivity emphasize that it is the convergence of competent inquirers that is achieved when they follow the relevant reasons. The required convergence can never be the convergence of all. But who is competent is not a neutral question, independent of one's other epistemic claims. Rather, it is defined by competence to understand and apply the criteria of objectivity and, in particular, the condition of relevance. Therefore, if parochial concepts are essential to some knowledge, then convergence may possibly be attainable, but it will be confined to those who can master these concepts, not the Peirceian convergence of all competent inquirers. Ideal convergence cannot be a requirement that rules out parochial concepts or removes them to a lesser status. Rather settling the question of the status of parochial concepts is necessary before one can establish what sort of convergence is necessary.

There is another, perhaps more radical, limitation on any convergence requirement. Would the criterion of relevance meet a convergence requirement limited to those who master the relevant concepts? Not quite, it would have met the requirement but for the fact that it allows for indeterminacy of reasons that may lead rational inquirers, even when they share the same premises, to diverge in their conclusions on those occasions where it would be rational to believe a certain proposition and also rational to doubt it. The manifestations of the underdetermination of reasons are widespread and familiar. For example, two people hear the same testimony and one believes it while the other does not. In many (though not in all) everyday situations like this both have to admit that the other is not irrational, while insisting, of course, on the rationality of their own stance. Common as underdetermination by reason is, it has not received adequate attention in epistemology. This is not the occasion to discuss it in detail,[36] though I will return to the point later.

D. The Siren Call of Epistemic Absolutes

Why does Williams think that parochial concepts are more suspect than non-parochial ones? They are concepts "which reflect merely a local interest, taste or sensory peculiarity." What is it for a concept to reflect merely a local interest? It has become an oft-repeated philosophical example that the Innuits have more terms designating types of snow than are known to any other language. Are the concepts of types of snow they have an example of concepts of a "mere local interest"? This is how Putnam understands Williams, for he thinks that "grass" is similarly a local concept.[37] They may well be concepts that not every inquirer can master. Their mastery may well presuppose familiarity with some minutiae of Innuit life, which give their ways of distinguishing types of snow their point, and which are beyond the comprehension of Martians. As mentioned earlier, perceptual concepts are another class of parochial concepts. Since not all people possess the same sense organs not all of them can master the concepts possession of which requires perceiving the world through particular senses.

It is not my purpose to argue that scientific theories are likely to find concepts like "grass" or "sweet" particularly useful.[38] Suppose that they do not. Is that relevant to the preconditions of knowledge or to the nature of reality or the world? Accountants have no more use for the notion of quarks than physicists for the notion of inflation. Does it follow that inflation is a mere illusion? Clearly not. The interest of Innuits in snow may lead to the emergence of a range of parochial concepts, which are no use to the rest of the world. But *that* does not show that they do not pick out real features of the real world. In fact it is hardly conceivable that they could express local or, indeed, any tastes or interests if they did not. The same considerations apply to perceptual concepts. That certain creatures lack a certain perceptual capacity may prevent them from becoming aware of certain aspects of the world that can be known only by those who have that capacity. It does not show that those who have those senses are not able through them to perceive how things really are, thus acquiring (perceptual) knowledge the others lack.[39]

Clearly some concepts have no use in formulating any true thoughts about how things are (other than about what use people made of those concepts). The credentials of concepts are not beyond question. But I doubt that parochial concepts need more defense than nonparochial ones. "Ether," "alkahest," and other scientific or pseudoscientific concepts, nonparochial if any are, fail the test. They are no help in acquiring knowledge. Some of these concepts are empirically empty. Others are conceptually incoherent or inconsistent with basic scientific laws.

Nonparochial concepts, because they are in principle accessible to all, have one obvious advantage. When they can be used to test parochial concepts and parochial epistemic principles, then they can be used to test whether those parochial concepts and principles are free of local biases. Such taints will be exposed once the concepts and principles that incorporate them are judged by principles that are accessible to people not blinkered by those interests, and whose vision is not distorted by the peculiarities of any specific perceptual capacity or alleged capacity.

It does not follow that all parochial concepts or principles can be thoroughly tested in this way. Moreover, pointing out this advantage is very different from giving nonparochial concepts and principles special priority, a special status among the conditions for the possibility of knowledge.[40]

It seems to me that the thought that they could play such a criterial role is a mutation of a Cartesian ideal. Not that Williams's absolute conception involves a commitment to self-evident knowledge, but it is committed to the thesis that the objectivity of thought is underpinned by an epistemic principle stating that under ideal conditions knowledge is undisputed and clear for all to see. Two ideas combine here, one explicit and one implicit: The first is that under ideal conditions there will not be any deep disagreement. (If a disagreement occurs it will be quickly resolved – by looking at the evidence as it were). The second is that in the ideal conditions epistemic tests will not lead us astray. In the real world, it is acknowledged, we are at the mercy of epistemic luck. We may often be epistemically justified, indeed required, to accept beliefs that are in fact false. But under ideal conditions this will not happen.

These ideal conditions may never be realized, but only an epistemology that subjects itself to this test, that accepts that what is true will be recognized as such under ideal conditions, can underpin a claim to objectivity. Only domains of thought that can stand this test (i.e., that out of the thoughts which belong to them, under ideal conditions competent inquirers will necessarily converge and accept the same thoughts and reject the same thoughts) are domains of objective thought. While we acknowledge, the thought is, that in real life we are at the mercy of epistemic luck since we may be rationally justified in accepting false propositions as true, no domain of thought is objective if it is necessarily always subject to epistemic luck, if there are no circumstances in which the gap between justified belief and true belief is closed.

There is no cogent reason to accept this yearning for freedom from epistemic luck. In all areas of knowledge there are limits – imposed by conditions of intelligibility – to the possibility of error. But beyond that we are at the mercy of epistemic luck. This is an inevitable result of the fact that (again with the same exception already mentioned) epistemic justification is path-dependent. This means that what is rational for one person to accept (given his situation and history) may well be rational for another person to reject (given his situation and history). It follows that whether or not they have knowledge depends, for both of them, on the luck of their situation. There is no reason to think that this path-dependence can be overcome by everyone occupying the same starting point. There are good reasons to think that it is not possible for everyone to occupy the same starting point (this will involve, e.g., time travel, changes in perceptual organs, as well as complete change of culture). There are also good reasons to think that there is no starting point such that those who can occupy it can know everything that can be known. If some knowledge is parochial then that possibility is ruled out. If people must diverge in their epistemic baggage then path-dependence is a necessary feature of human existence. One that cannot be overcome under any conditions, however ideal. There is therefore no reason to make submission to a luck-free ideal test a condition of objectivity.

E. Epistemic Anxieties and the Long Route

I suggested that domains of thought are objective if they meet conditions like the possibility of error, the relevance condition, the possibility of irrationality, the independence condition, and the single reality condition. The list can be extended indefinitely. The method of the "long route" consists in tracing various truisms associated with the logic of truth and knowledge. We seek them out as the need arises, that is, as we encounter questions and doubts they help to answer.

I raised a doubt about this method, namely, that it is "too exclusively internal." We can agree that whatever meets its conditions is *thought by us* to be objective, but is it necessarily so in reality? The thought that this method is "too internal" is the thought that there are, or at least that there could be, preconditions for anything being capable of being true or false that are due to how things are and are not reflected in the logic of our concepts.

The quest for ideal convergence, or for the testing of parochial concepts by nonparochial ones, which are available to all, are manifestations of the same anxiety. They are attempts to break out of the inner and to connect with how things really are in the world. They do so by claiming that knowledge must be anchored in the universal, in those concepts all can have and those claims of knowledge round which all competent inquirers will converge in ideal conditions. By replying that the worry is illusory, that by exploring the preconditions of our concepts of knowledge and truth we are willy-nilly exploring features of reality I was navigating a middle course. On the one hand is the Scylla of denying that the nature of reality, knowledge, truth, and objectivity are just what is revealed through use of the concepts we happen to have of them, and requiring some absolute test satisfaction of which by a concept or a principle guarantees that they reach to reality "as it really is."[41] Against this is the Charybdis that denies that we can ever have any concepts of reality, knowledge, or truth different from those we happen to have, or that the nature of reality or knowledge can be different from what these concepts (our concepts of them) reveal. Our concepts are what we measure by. A thought that is not a thought (i.e., does not conform to our concept of a thought) is not a thought. Knowledge that is not knowledge (i.e., not an instance of our concept of knowledge) is not knowledge.

The middle road allows that our concepts can be subjected to rational evaluation, which may lead to revision. But it denies that the evaluation is in the light of any absolute test, like the tests of convergence. We judge our concepts in light of our concepts and beliefs. While it is necessary that in general they will be vindicated, some of them, some aspects of even the most basic of them, may turn out to be incoherent or unsustainable, given whatever else we know. If we are lucky we improve our understanding of reality and of knowledge. But we do not do so by satisfying one or several master tests. Similarly, some of our epistemic procedures may be misguided. What is taken to be good or adequate evidence for a class of conclusions may turn out to be inadequate. Considerations taken to be good reasons for certain positions may be irrelevant, or confused, or just insufficient to justify them.

The history of the practice of science provides examples of how epistemic standards change, often in the light of rational reflection and criticism, but without any master test that is held constant and governs the changes. Various people have suspected that concepts such as the divine, the supernatural, time travel, miracle, action at a distance, beauty are not all that they seem to be. Arguments have been put forward to show that their use has to be abandoned because they are incoherent, or that they have to be reformed in some fundamental ways.

If that is so then even the necessary features of our concepts of objectivity and knowledge may stand in need of revision and can be revised through reasoning that follows the long route. To deny that is to assume that while the use of these concepts can reveal difficulties with concepts like "beauty," that pressure is one-sided: Our concept of "beauty" comes under pressure for being in tension with the presuppositions of knowledge, but our concept of knowledge is not under pressure for being in conflict with necessary features of "beauty." But there is no reason to think that. So long as we remain holistic in our approach to the clarification of the structures of thought the possibility of a need to revise our notions of knowledge and truth remains.[42] I am not saying that they need revising, only that it is possible that they do.

To acknowledge this possibility is to acknowledge the possibility that there are preconditions for anything being true or false, or capable of being known, which are not reflected in our concepts, that is, our concepts as they are. Therefore, the long route is not "purely internal" and self-vindicating. I conclude that it may be that the long route is all we need.

As doubts about the objectivity of this or that domain arise we inquire and – if successful – we establish conditions that settle the issue one way or another. In other words we need a focus for an inquiry. The focus establishes which results might be relevant and helpful. There is no way of producing an exhaustive list of such conditions, for we can never anticipate all the doubts that can arise concerning the objectivity of this or that domain.

Put it another way: there is no interesting comprehensive theory of objectivity. But there can be fruitful inquiries into the objectivity of one area or another when specific doubts arise regarding their status.

III. The Illusion of the Authority of the Social

A. Thick Concepts and the Social Connection

In elaborating on his absolute conception Williams adds another condition to those mentioned so far. It is set out in the words I italicize in the following: "If knowledge is what it claims to be, then it is knowledge of a reality which exists independently of that knowledge, *and indeed (except for the special case where the reality known happens itself to be some psychological item) independently of any thought or experience.* Knowledge is of what is there *anyway.* "[43]

So far as I know Williams does not develop this extension of his idea, but in one form or another it is a common condition in many discussions of realism. It is often set out in its strong form: knowledge must be of what is there anyway, independently not only of the thoughts and experiences of the agent, but of any thought or experience of anyone. This condition would rule out the possibility of knowledge of many properties of artifacts and of many socially constituted persons (organizations, cities, etc.), facts and events.

Think of an existing chess club,[44] with its rules and customs. They are not merely created through acts involving thoughts and experiences, they are also maintained in existence through the continued intentions of the club's members to carry on with their participation in the club. To be sure, some people would want to say that such clubs, or their rules and customs, do not form a part of what is really real. But if they are right there must be other reasons for that view. It does not follow from the idea that knowledge is of what is there anyway.

Williams's condition fares no better if it is narrowed down to saying that knowledge must be of a reality that exists independently of any thoughts or beliefs about its existence. The example of the chess club refutes this condition as well, since the existence of the club depends on some people believing (or having believed) that it exists.

Objects of knowledge can sometimes even depend on the agent's own prior thoughts and experiences. The motivation for the condition of independence, namely, that knowledge is of what is there anyway, does not justify the blanket exclusion of all cases of this kind. For example, yesterday the chairperson of the chess club may have passed a regulation binding on the club. Its existence and content depend on his intentions in passing it. They also depend on his beliefs about what he was doing, that is, his belief that he is making a rule for the club. There is nothing in that to disqualify him from having knowledge of the existence or content of rules he made any more than there is reason to deny that other people can have that knowledge. Moreover, his knowledge of the regulation is not knowledge of his own thoughts and intentions. It is knowledge of a rule of the club. Nor need it derive from his memory of his own thoughts. He may have forgotten that it is his regulation, and learn about it from colleagues. He, like anyone else, can have knowledge of the regulations of the club. The underlying rationale of the independence condition does not warrant Williams's claim that if knowledge is to be of what is there anyway it must be independent of what is there in virtue of people's or the agent's own thoughts and experiences. The objectivity of no domain of thought depends on this condition.

But is not that conclusion premature? It may be thought that while in general views and thoughts about matters whose existence depends on psychological or social facts are objective, there is a special case against the objectivity of evaluative thought arising out of its possible dependence on social facts. If it turns out — it may be argued — that if value propositions are capable of being true or false then their truth-value depends on social facts, then normative or evaluative thought cannot be objective.

This particular objection to the objectivity of practical thought concentrates on what I called the relevance condition. Practical thought appears to meet the other conditions we canvassed. The real doubt about its objectivity is: does it meet the relevance condition? Are there grounds that are not merely persuasive but logically relevant to the confirmation or disconfirmation of any practical thought? The most promising attempt to provide an affirmative answer relies on the use of thick concepts. But thick concepts seem to depend on a shared culture with its shared acceptance of various values. Hence it seems that the thick concept solution to the problem of the relevance condition makes the truth of evaluative propositions depend on the social facts of shared views.

This is where the objection is directed: if it turns out that if practical propositions are true or false they are so in virtue of social facts, then they are not capable of being either true or false.

The objection is a serious one. Thick concepts are indeed crucial to any attempt to establish the objectivity of practical thought and its conformity with the relevance condition. Consider the sort of reasons people give in support of such propositions: Simon should be respected because he acted with great dignity. Sarah deserves promotion for she solved a complicated problem with subtlety and ingenuity. Robin acted well; he kept his head under pressure and showed cool judgment and discrimination in handling his boss. This is a great film: it is easy to understand without being trivial, and it combines humor and wisdom. Typically just about all our evaluative reasoning is saturated with thick concepts of a variety of kinds. Both conclusions and reasons for them are typically expressed by the use of thick evaluative concepts. An account of the relevant reasons that support or undermine evaluative or normative propositions will largely consist in an explanation of the relations between thick concepts. But, and that is where the objection starts, mastery of thick concepts depends on shared understandings and shared judgments. These shared judgments both enable us to understand the meaning of thick evaluative terms, *and incline us to accept the legitimacy of their use.* There is no independent way of validating the legitimacy of the use of thick concepts. Hence, the validity of evaluative propositions, if it depends on thick concepts, depends on shared understandings and judgments, that is, on social facts. The truth or correctness of value propositions cannot, however, depend on social facts. Such dependence will make value judgments contingent, for the facts they depend on are contingent, and arbitrary, for whether or not one has cogent reasons to accept them will depend on the evaluatively arbitrary fact of one's membership in one culture or another. Worst of all, if the truth conditions of evaluative propositions are contingent social facts, then they cannot be normative; they are merely statements of those facts whose existence renders them true.

Since the normative cannot depend on social facts it cannot depend on thick concepts, and given the absence of any other plausible account of the way practical thought meets the relevance condition, we must conclude that it lacks objectivity.

B. *Types of Social Dependence*

To evaluate the objection we need to investigate the ways, if any, in which value judgments depend on shared understandings and judgments. This requires relying on assumptions that cannot be explored here. The observations that follow will, therefore, be tentative and subject to much further clarification and further supporting arguments.[45] I will be relying on one crucial distinction, the distinction between practices that create or sustain the existence of goods and values and practices that are conditions for access to such good or values. On the one hand, it is possible that values and goods are created or maintained in existence by social practices and the shared beliefs and understandings that are part of them. I will call practices that bring into existence goods or values, or sustain them in existence, sustaining practices. On the other hand, it is possible that shared understandings affect not the existence of values and goods, but our ability to learn of them and perhaps to benefit from them. Such practices control access to the values and goods concerned. Quite likely the social dependence of values and goods takes many and varied forms. I will briefly delineate four fairly typical types of case, starting with the closest to dependence of value on practice.

"Socially Created" Goods: Local Goods

The existence of some goods seems to be clearly socially dependent. It used to be important for young women, of a certain class, to walk only with short and measured steps, or for men to wear wigs when out of their homes. There were social advantages to behaving in accordance with conventions of manners and disadvantages attached to flouting them. Conventions of manner, fashion, and deportment vary over time and space. A particular form of manner or dress can lose the meaning it has and acquire a different, even contradictory meaning. It can have different, even mutually exclusive meanings in different places at the same time. Moreover, within a single country it can have one meaning in one subculture and another, even incompatible meaning in another subculture. In the same place and at the same time what earns kudos in one class may earn the disrespect of another, et cetera.

In matters of fashion and manners what is valuable depends on what people do, that is, on conventional conduct, but also on shared attitudes and reactions, on a shared meaning associated with different modes of conduct, deportment, or dress. The dependence is multifaceted. There is more than one value to be realized. In matters of fashion, for example, there are the values, say, of being at the cutting edge of advanced fashion, the value of keeping up with new fashions, the value of merging in the crowd, of being thoroughly conventional and nondistinctive, the value of being charmingly old-fashioned, the value of emphatically asserting one's indifference to fashion, the value of being assertively nonconventional, and many more. When we come to manner the number of different meanings different modes of conduct and address can display is much greater.

The practices and shared meanings of a society determine not only the benchmark of the normal, relative to which the conventional, defiant, cutting edge, et cetera are defined. They also determine which meanings or values (e.g., that of conventionality, defiance, cutting edge) exist relative to the benchmark. Some cultures multiply meanings that turn on subtle distinctions.

In others only a few distinctions determine different meanings. In some societies meanings are fixed and rigid, attached to easily identifiable external cues; in others they are more flexible, more complex in manifestation, allowing for more individual variations and for easier mutation over time.

"Socially Created Goods": The Temporally Unbound Variety

The type of good or social meaning I have in mind here may differ from local goods in degree only, but a difference there is: Take a game, for example, chess, with the goods that playing it makes possible (being good at chess, being a good chess tactician, ingenious at the end game, etc.). Chess was created at a particular time. It makes no sense to think of it as having existed from the creation of the world and only discovered at a certain time. It was invented, created, and developed, not discovered. So it too is socially created or socially constituted, and like all socially created goods and meanings it has an origin in time, and its existence is contingent rather than necessary. It could not have been invented. But in one respect chess is unlike manners. Once invented it is with us forever. Of course it can be forgotten. Times may come when no one will know what chess is, no one will know how to play it. Some games that used to be played by people during the flowering of Maya civilization in the Yucatan, for example, are lost to us. But that is mere loss of knowledge, loss of access to a good. We can rediscover how to play these games. There is a sense in which once the game is invented it remains in existence for ever, or at least for as long as it is logically possible for it to be (if lost) rediscovered.[46]

Many other goods belong to this kind. Think of New York Jewish humor. Enjoying it, being good at telling good New York Jewish jokes and witticisms, or being able to display that sense of humor in one's conversation is valuable and admirable. Like chess, New York Jewish humor and other goods of this kind are generated by a particular culture and did not exist beforehand. This sense of humor developed and emerged during a particular period in the history of New York. It did not exist as a timeless form of humor to be discovered by New York Jews in the nineteenth or twentieth century. Like all socially constituted goods, New York Jewish humor enjoys a contingent existence. It might not have come into existence. But, unlike fashion and like chess, once it has been developed it remains in existence forever (or for as long as it can be – should it be lost – rediscovered). It is quite likely that times will come when people will not understand this form of humor. It also likely that a time will come when there will be no one around capable of understanding it. But these are contingent facts, which do not limit the possibility that it will be rediscovered. What goes for New York Jewish humor goes for classical ballet, the novel, opera, and a large number of other goods that are culturally constituted in similar ways.

Wherein lies the difference between the two categories of socially created goods? In the possibility of enjoying them outside the cultures that bred and sustained them. Suppose you discover a game that has long been forgotten or a form of music no longer practiced in your culture. It is in principle possible to discover what they were, to come to understand them and the cultures that sustained them. That would involve understanding what was good in them. Once one understands those goods one can enjoy them, one can engage in them in the right way, bringing one the intrinsic benefits that they brought people in the cultures where they were practiced. Naturally this requires further conditions, one needs to be good at games, have willing partners to play with, be musical, et cetera. But in principle those goods though created and practiced in one culture can be enjoyed by people in other cultures, even by individuals who live in cultures where the game or form of music did not take root. Not so with regard to local goods. While we can learn and appreciate the fashions or manners of previous times or faraway places, we cannot enjoy their benefits unless they become the fashions and manners of our society.[47]

Goods That Are Not Socially Created – with Limited, Culturally Conditioned Accessibility

Sunsets are not constituted by social practices and shared meanings, nor are beautiful sunsets, nor the beauty of beautiful sunsets.[48] There were beautiful sunsets on earth at least since its atmosphere acquired its present constitution. There probably were beautiful sunsets before the emergence of animal life on the earth. It is possible, however, that there were periods when people did not enjoy beautiful sunsets and did not find them attractive in any aesthetic way at all. It is also likely that after people developed an aesthetic response to natural phenomena, they differed in what they found valuable in nature and in the values they found in what was valuable. Possibly there are psychological universals that determine a degree of similarity in sensitivity across cultures. But perusal of works of art suggests that whatever the similarities the differences in aesthetic responses to, and appreciation of, nature among cultures are considerable. Moreover, the responses to, and appreciation of, the same natural phenomenon (e.g., sunsets) may be incompatible, in that no person can appreciate all aspects of the beauty of a sunset at the same time, without being ambivalent about the phenomena he is reacting to. For example, the beauty of the sea, the same sea in the same conditions, can be perceived as due to its tranquil and harmonious character by a holiday maker on an afternoon walk, and due to its hidden awesome power by a fisherman who knows its fickleness.

It is possible that the sea has all these qualities. This is easy to explain if these are relational qualities, for example. If anything is beautiful if and only if it looks beautiful, beauty is a property of appearance, a matter of how things appear. The appearance of things is an objective matter about which mistakes can be made.[49] One may, for example, mistakenly think that a good-looking person is rather plain. Yet some properties of the appearance of things are relational: some may relate to how they appear in daytime and others to their nocturnal appearance, et cetera.

Objective though they are, not everyone can perceive the way things appear. To be capable of perceiving the appearance of things one may need to be acculturated in suitable ways. Let us think of the values that became prevalent with the Romantic Movement in the eighteenth century. We can understand them and relate to them, as we are the children of the Romantic Movement. They are easier to appreciate for some than for others, and perhaps no one can appreciate all of them any more. But since Romanticism, they have become in principle available to people. Romanticism made forms of appreciation of nature possible that were not possible before. But Romanticism no more changed nature, or the appearance of nature, by creating new valuable features in it than the development of humans or other animals with color vision added color to objects in the world. Red is not made red by the existence of people who can perceive it as red, and beautiful sunsets are not made beautiful by the existence of people who can appreciate their beauty. Culture does not create the beauty of nature. It merely enables us to become aware of it, to come to understand and enjoy it.

Goods with Universal, Culturally Conditioned Access

Some goods may be even more independent of social practices: not only are they not created by social practices, access to them is not restricted by social practices either. Even though sunsets are not man-made, nor is their beauty, the appreciation of their beauty is made possible by culture. One may feel that they are as local and time-bound as all the socially created goods briefly discussed above. Whether culture determines access rather than existence can be felt to be of little significance. What matters is accessibility. Consider the relation of value to personhood. Persons are rational beings, that is, they possess the ability to perceive that some things are good or bad in various ways and to respond appropriately. They should find out enough about value to enable them to conduct themselves sensibly. They bear responsibility to find out enough about value, but that responsibility is limited by accessibility. They cannot come to appreciate normative aspects of the world that are not accessible to them. Three points seem to bear this out:

1. People cannot be blamed for not being guided by values they could not know about.

2. People's conduct cannot be morally wrong for disregarding or violating values or rules they could not in principle know.
3. It is, of course, possible that lack of access to values will impoverish a person's life and will render it less rich and admirable, and so forth, than it could have been had that person the ability in principle to understand and engage in more valuable activities. Similarly, lack of access to values may coarsen a person's character.

Access to a value, rather than its existence, is decisive in evaluations that presuppose responsibility, be they evaluations of people's actions, life, or character. Furthermore, for evaluations of life and character that do not presuppose responsibility, evaluation of them as limited, or coarse, or rich and refined, it does not matter whether the absence of a good from a person's life was due to its nonexistence or to its inaccessibility. Either way, the absence of the good from a person's life may be coarsening or impoverishing. These observations would justify the view that so far as the kinds of values and goods considered so far go there is no significant normative difference between socially created values and those that are not so created, but whose accessibility is socially dependent. If this is all there is to say on the subject, then a fairly strong form of social relativism might be vindicated. Are there any normative considerations which are universally accessible, that is, which are within the reach of all people, of whatever time or place, at least in principle?

A full answer to the question is beyond the scope of the present discussion.[50] For our purposes suffice it to say that one objection to the possibility of universally accessible normative considerations is mistaken. Consider the sort of normative considerations often advanced as universal and timeless. For example: It is always wrong to murder an innocent person.[51] If we can judge people to have acted wrongly in having committed murder we must assume that it was possible for them to know that they should not perform the actions that are the murder of innocent people. But we need not assume that they must have been able to understand the concept "murder," "person," "innocent," "intention," and "killing," which we use to articulate and explain this rule. Arguably, even before these concepts were available to people they had other ways of categorizing mental states, other ways of marking transgressions, other ways of marking animals that, as we now know, belong to the species *Homo sapiens*. Their concepts and generalizations may have been based on false beliefs, and we may find them inadequate in many ways. But they may have enabled them to know that the acts that in fact constitute murder of innocent people are wrong. That is enough to establish that they had the access to the norm that is a precondition of being able to blame them for its violation. If people at all times had access to the norms, in one form or another, then we have here an example of a consideration, to which there is universal access, though that access is culturally determined.

C. Social Dependence and Objectivity

What conclusions regarding the objectivity of value can be drawn from this fourfold classification, assuming that it is basically sound? First, we need to distinguish the social dependence of values from the social dependence of access to them. Second, while all but the most abstract values, goods, and other normative considerations are referred to by the use of thick terms, only some of them are socially created.

My observations at the beginning of this part[52] showed that social dependence does not necessarily pose a threat to objectivity. I believe that most people worry less about the objectivity of local goods, as I called them, than about the objectivity of socially created goods that are not local or those that are not socially created at all. The doubt about the objectivity of value does not arise from the contingency of the social on which all value allegedly depends, but from the suspicion that since knowledge of what is valuable depends on mastery of "thick" concepts, it is suspect.

One additional source of suspicion that values that are socially constructed cannot be objective should be mentioned. It is sometimes assumed that if some good or value is socially created and sustained, then the reason for its being good is that it is accepted as good, that people think it is good, or variants on these. This is not at all so. Consider chess: neither the reasons for making one move rather than another in the course of the game nor the reasons for playing the game involve any appeal to the social practice that created the game. Similarly, we can give reasons for thinking one joke better than another, or one piano sonata better than another, but they will not and should not include an appeal to the fact that these goods are socially created. A joke is good because it is funny, because it has more than one sting, because it takes the mickey out of the pompous, who deserve the treatment, because it points out human foibles, and so forth. A piano sonata is good because it is full of musical ideas, ingenious variations, suspense and surprise, tension and its resolution, because it mixes moods, speaks to the emotions, and so on. The fact that a good is socially constituted is no more reason for its value than the fact that a chair is a product of human design is a reason for thinking it a good chair. The same goes for all artifacts and for all socially constituted goods (see the qualification in the next paragraph). It must be so, for otherwise it would not be possible to distinguish good social creations, or artifacts, from bad ones.

It is true that practices and shared beliefs are (part of the) means by which we identify goods that are socially created or maintained. But identifying what is the good is not the same as explaining what it is that makes it good or why it is good rather than bad.

Local goods may be thought to be a special case since they tend to be conventional goods. That is why some feel less suspicious of them. They feel that we understand the nature of conventions. After all they have received the seal of approval of game theory. Moreover, it may be thought that with conventional goods the explanation for what is good about this mode of conduct, or dress, et cetera, is clear: it is good because that is how people generally behave, how they dress, and so on. This is, however, at best only part of the explanation.[53] The rest has to account for the reason for conforming to the conventional norm. We understand conventions only when we understand the good they are thought to achieve and whether they in fact lead to good or ill.

The values served by conventional goods explain what, if anything, is good in the conventions and enable us to distinguish between good and bad conventions. I emphasize this point for it shows that the explanation of the goodness of any good or valuable thing or option has to be relatively independent of the social practices that create that good. Only thus can we acknowledge that social conditions can also lead to bad practices, which will be mistakenly taken by their participants as good ones. In "Moral Change and Social Relativism"[54] I suggested a different argument to the same effect, namely, that the inherent intelligibility of values means that they have to be somewhat independent of social practices. The two arguments are two aspects of the same thought.

These arguments do not show that normative properties are not socially created. They show that they are not all conventional, and that their normative nature must be explained normatively and cannot be explained in nonnormative terms. But there can be social practices or other social phenomena that can only be identified in normative terms, and such social practices can be said to give rise to new normative properties consistently with the arguments above. We learn that not all goods are socially created not from the argument above but by examining the nature of the various goods (as was sketched in the previous section). The preceding argument is meant to show that even if all goods are socially created (and they are not) it does not follow that the reasons that explain why they are good, what makes them good, consist in an appeal to the fact that the relevant social practices exist. They must consist in pointing to good-making properties of the social practices concerned.

These remarks may lead to the opposite objection, namely, that socially created goods are not socially created at all. The goods involved in them are timeless, only the ways they are realized are local. But while that may be true of some instances, it is not generally true. For example, observing rules of polite behavior tends to make one feel comfortable in social situations and facilitates interaction with others. That good is neither conventional nor socially created. It is timeless. But to say this is to abstract from the differences between different societies and different codes of good behavior. The abstract value of facilitating interactions may be the correct value to apply to the situation, yet it leaves out information that only a concrete and localized description of the good of polite behavior in one or another social setting can convey. Concrete socially created values must be subsumed under abstract universal values, or they will be unintelligible. But they are no "mere" instantiations of universal values. They are distinctive specific goods, which can be enjoyed only if created by social practices.[55]

D. Objectivity and Thick Concepts

Can the objectivity of "thick" concepts be defended? Suspicion of their use can now be seen to be independent of any doubts arising from the alleged social dependence of all value. But suspect they remain. I have already dismissed some of these suspicions. It is true that what we believe may well depend on which evaluative concepts we became familiar with first and which evaluative beliefs we acquired first. That is a result of the path-dependence of epistemic justification, a feature of epistemic justification in all fields of knowledge. Furthermore, it is true that there is no hope of a Peircean convergence regarding evaluative beliefs. There is no reason to think that there is a meaningful ideal situation in which the views of all competent believers will converge. Yet again, we saw reason to doubt the cogency of the requirement of such convergence as a precondition of the possibility of knowledge. Both these observations mean that there is an inevitable contingency not only about our evaluative beliefs, but also in the account of their epistemic justification. What we know and what we do not know is partly a matter of the accident of our circumstances, and even the best epistemic justification possible cannot rid our beliefs of an element of luck. But epistemic luck is a feature of the conditions of knowledge in general. It is not a circumstance special to evaluative beliefs, and it does not negate the possibility of knowledge.

There remains, however, another, though related, source of doubt in the objectivity of evaluative beliefs, if that objectivity depends on deploying "thick" concepts. There is the familiar charge that the thick concepts of different cultures, or of different moral or religious outlooks, are incommensurate. Concepts that belong to one of these systems of thought cannot be explained in terms of concepts belonging to another. These thick concepts, the argument proceeds, are essential for the expression of the systems of thought to which they belong. The views of each system cannot, therefore, be expressed or explained using the concepts of another system. This leads the objector to the conclusion that even when one can be confident that one's evaluative beliefs are justified from within one's own system of thought, one has to acknowledge that that is only a relative justification. Incompatible beliefs enjoy equally cogent justification within other systems of thought. Furthermore, the arguments refuting the other system of thought as a whole to one's own satisfaction are themselves relative to one's own system of thought. The rival system is not only impregnable in its own terms, but it quite likely contains within itself cogent arguments refuting one's own system of thought.

According to the objector it follows that there is no rational way to adjudicate between different systems of thought.[56] This would seem inconsistent with the objectivity of evaluative thought. For, the objector points out, many conflicting evaluative thoughts have equal credentials. Therefore, none of them can be correct or true. The argument is not merely that they cannot be known to be correct or true. That would have been the case had there been nonrelational grounds establishing one rather than the other which people cannot, not even in principle, come to know.[57] But, according to the objector's argument, the failure is not of ability to know. There are no such grounds, therefore there is nothing to know.

Much has been written about the coherence of the incommensurability claim that underlies the objection. I will put such doubts to one side. The objection is also vulnerable on other grounds. It relies heavily on the inability to explain the concepts of one culture, or system of thought, using those of another. But how important is this limitation? The argument is often discussed as revolving not on the relations between concepts belonging to two different systems of thought, but on the relation between the meanings of terms in two languages. In the development of languages, however, new terms are often added whose meaning cannot be precisely explained using the other terms of the language. We learn their meaning in part through use, and by ostension, and only in part by locating their meaning relative to that of other words.[58] We do the same when we encounter concepts in a foreign culture. Words are added to the language often borrowed from the other language, whose meaning is learned not exclusively through explanation, but by ostension, and through habituation to aspects of the alien culture that they signify.

There is little doubt that often we fail to understand concepts embedded in a culture or system of thought that is alien to us. But is there any reason to think that even given favorable conditions we could not master them? That they cannot be exhaustively or satisfactorily explained using our concepts does not establish that conclusion, for we can learn them directly, by being exposed to their use, rather than through translation. Sometimes we could do so by actually living in the alien society; at other times it is possible to learn their meaning by learning about that society and reconstructing in imagination, or simulation, its ways and beliefs.

To claim that members of one culture cannot in any way come to understand the concepts of another amounts to the implausible claim that people have the capacity to acquire the concepts of one culture only. Once they have done so their conceptual capacity is exhausted or perhaps blocked. This seems an implausible supposition.

I can think of only one possible reason for it. Complete understanding of a concept – and it is important to remember that understanding is a matter of degree – involves knowing its relations with all the concepts one understands. Take, for example, the relation "being incompatible with." One does not understand what it is to be blue if one does not know that it excludes being red, nor what it is to be just if one does not know that it excludes being unfair. It follows that in a way the more concepts one has already acquired the more difficult it is for one to acquire new ones, for one would have to understand whether they are or are not compatible with those one has already mastered. Could it not therefore be the case that for this reason those who mastered the concepts of our culture cannot understand those of ancient alien civilizations? Our inability to understand their concepts is no sign of reduced mental ability. Rather, to understand their concepts we have to know the degree to which they are compatible with ours. Members of those ancient civilizations themselves did not have that knowledge. Since they did not know our concepts they did not have to know how our concepts relate to theirs in order to understand theirs. We do, and this is why we cannot understand their concepts.

At this point the argument that systems of thought are incommensurate because their concepts are not mutually translatable has been abandoned in favor of the assertion that systems of thought are incommensurate because no one can master the concepts of more than one of them. The new contention is, however, implausible. It flies in the face of the evidence. There were and are people who inhabited more than one culture and understood both. It also overlooks the fact that our own culture contains concepts derived from different systems of thought, which have not merged together. While some of us do not have use for concepts such as grace, sacred, blessed, prayer, and others, for the most part we manage to understand them, when we try. Finally, the conclusion exaggerates the conceptual insularity of different cultures. To be sure there are many culture-specific concepts, that is, concepts that evolved in one culture and have no parallels in others. But they are embedded in a conceptual framework that includes many concepts bridging the cultural gap or having at least near relatives in other cultures. It seems safe to dismiss the thesis that no person can master concepts of more than one culture and, with it, the thesis that there are past or present cultures whose concepts cannot in principle be understood by us.[59]

It may be worth pointing out that the considerations I advanced here are consistent with the view expressed in Part II about the essentially local character of evaluative concepts, or of many of them, and of the nonexistence of a Peirceian ideal condition from which everything can be known. There I was arguing that it is impossible, even if only because of the impossibility of knowing the future, for anyone to master all the evaluative concepts. Here, I argued that there is no general reason to think that no one can come to know and understand more than one of the existing systems of thought. This conclusion can be reinforced to the effect that no past or present human culture and its concepts are beyond the comprehension of people for whom it is an alien culture. There are no human cultural islands that cannot be understood by anyone other than their members.

At this point one may be tempted to resuscitate the challenge to the objectivity of evaluative thought, while abandoning the conceptual incommensurability thesis. One may argue that (1) all justification is internal to a system of thought, and that (2) there is no way of adjudicating between beliefs belonging to different systems of thought, and since (3) some beliefs belonging to different systems of thought are incompatible and cannot both be true, on pain of contradiction, it follows that no beliefs are true. As before, this argument presupposes (1) that evaluative beliefs are true only if there are reasons that explain how it is that they are true, and (2) that evaluative reasons are in principle available to people, though not necessarily to everyone. For reasons we cannot explore here these seem reasonable assumptions.

This challenge to the objectivity of evaluative thought is ill-founded. It is true that all justifications are relative: they are all addressed to an actual or potential audience, addressing the doubts of *that* audience and relying on what *that* audience accepts. The relativity of justifications is itself a result both of the parochial character of (many) evaluative concepts and of the path dependence of epistemic justifications. So long as all the different justifications are consistent, that relativity does not undermine the objectivity of evaluative thought. Nor does it follow from the relativity of justification that there is no way of adjudicating between incompatible thoughts or beliefs.

More generally I suspect that not infrequently the sense that incompatible evaluative propositions have equal credentials and therefore neither can be true results from a failure to distinguish two types of incompatibility. Two evaluative propositions can be (1) inconsistent with each other, or they can (2) express values, virtues, or ideals that cannot both be realized in the life of a single person. The second kind of incompatibility does not undermine the objectivity of evaluative thought. It merely leads to value pluralism.

The first kind of incompatibility is relevant to the debate on objectivity. Given the two presuppositions I accepted it must be the case that only one of two inconsistent propositions can be adequately supported by reasons. But we have to distinguish epistemic from constitutive reasons (though they may overlap). Two people can have adequate epistemic reasons for accepting each of two inconsistent propositions. These could be as banal as that different people, whose judgment they have good reason to trust but whose beliefs are inconsistent with each other, have advised them. Even constitutive reasons can conflict as there may be something to be said for both sides of an evaluative dispute (constitutive reasons are often prima facie). But evaluative propositions and their negations cannot both enjoy adequate or completely vindicatory support by reason. None of the considerations I canvassed in this article suggest that inconsistent evaluative propositions do enjoy adequate or vindicatory support by reasons.

This has been a long and mostly negative discussion. There may be reasons for rejecting the objectivity of evaluative thought. I offered various considerations to show that many arguments offered as justifying such rejection do not succeed in doing so. The constructive contribution of my arguments is in showing how doubts about objectivity can arise out of a misunderstanding of objectivity and of justification. If you set us an unachievable target you will be able to show that we fail to achieve it. It is instructive to see how we were victims of an overdemanding and overrigid conception of justification and objectivity. But the misguided allure of these "high ideals" is not confined to evaluative thought. Those who succumb to them are entrapped by confusions in other areas of thought as well.

Notes

1. Unless otherwise indicated, when referring to what people think, I have in mind the thought (or thought-content) rather than the act or activity of thinking.

2. Bear in mind that it would be odd actually to talk of people's impartiality unless someone challenged it or unless the circumstances of the action invite doubts about it.

   At the hands of some contractarian or constructivist philosophers impartiality extends in another direction as well: in matters of ethics what impartial judges accept is thereby made true. But I will not explore the contractarian uses of the notion.

3. Though nothing much depends on the way domains are demarcated. The criteria of objectivity determine whether a domain is objective or not, whichever way it is carved.

4. For example, Marmor, "Three Concepts of Objectivity" in A. Marmor (ed.), *Law and Interpretation* (Oxford: Clarendon, 1995).

5. D. Wiggins, "Objective and Subjective in Ethics, with Two Postscripts About Truth" in B. Hooker (ed.), *Truth in Ethics* (Oxford: Blackwell, 1996), p. 36.

6. Wiggins's own view is explained in "What Would Be a Substantive Theory of Truth?" in Z. van Straaten (ed.), *Philosophical Subjects: Essays Presented to P. F. Strawson* (Oxford: Oxford University Press, 1980).

7. Responsibility, rather than more narrowly moral responsibility.

8. Whether this applies to epistemic objectivity in all its variants is open to doubt. Perhaps the capacity to be epistemically objective (one version of epistemic objectivity noted above) is an exception. The question whether or not one is responsible for not being objective in that sense involves considerations of aspects of responsibility that cannot be pursued here.

9. And this may account for the tendency to classify them as subjective.

10. Some would make this the first and most important condition of objectivity. One way of formulating it is: A domain is objective if thoughts belonging to it deal with matters about which there are propositions that are true or false (or correct or incorrect, or more or less correct or incorrect). I state the condition in this way, rather than by saying that those thoughts express propositions that are true or false, in order to allow for the possibility of thoughts that are objective, and belong to an objective domain, but express propositions that are neither true nor false.

11. B. Williams, *Descartes* (London: Harvester, 1978), p. 64.

12. I am using a realist mode of expression ("about a reality") in a weak sense, in which we could say of arithmetical propositions that they are about numbers and their relations, without being committed to Platonism about numbers. This weak sense is explained in the second half of the independence condition.

13. In "What Would Be a Substantive Theory of Truth?" (*Philosphical Subjects*), Wiggins suggests as a mark of truth that a statement's being true or not is independent of any

particular subject's means of appraising its truth-value. This goes beyond the independence condition. Practical or evaluative thought does not conform with this condition
under some natural interpretations of it, but is objective. Some of the discussion in the
sequel bears on the reasons for rejecting Wiggins's condition.

14. Many would claim – Williams observes – that we are now familiar with the situation of
doing with less than an absolute conception, and can, as modern persons and unlike the
ambitious or complacent thinkers of earlier centuries, operate with a picture of the world
that at the reflexive level we can recognize to be thoroughly relative to our language, our
conceptual scheme – most generally, to our situation. But it is doubtful to what extent we
really can operate with such a picture, and doubtful whether such views do not implicitly
rely, in their self-understanding, on some presumed absolute conception, a framework
within which our situation can be comprehensively related to other possible situations.
(*Descartes,* p. 68.) We should agree that the notion of "relative reality" does not make
much sense. There is no interesting sense in which something can be the case relative to
us, but not be the case relative to others, unless, as Williams observes, such claims
presuppose a common frame of reference.

15. Such an isolationist position seems to be endorsed by Dworkin in "Objectivity and Truth:
You'd Better Believe It," *Philosophy & Public Affairs* 25 (1996), p. 87.

16. It is not clear whether as formulated by Williams the condition would rule out perspec-
tivalist accounts of truth or of reality that are not self-contradictory. For a claim that there
can be coherent perspectivalism see S. D. Hales, "A Consistent Relativism," *Mind* 106
(1997):33.

17. This also explains why there is safety in numbers. The more criteria we have the firmer
our grasp of the concept, for cumulatively they eliminate the possibility of misunderstandings relative to known questions. On the other hand they open up more possibilities
of hitherto unthought of questions regarding which they are vague and need refinement.

18. Cf. B. Williams, "Truth in Ethics" in Hooker (ed.), *Truth in Ethics,* p. 25. (Note that this
example merely illustrates the possibility of additional, logically independent, conditions. It does not illustrate any puzzles they may be called for to dispel). My espousal of
the long route is in line with Dworkin's position in "Objectivity and Truth." There he
warns against taking it for granted that conditions for the objectivity of one domain (say
relating to material objects) apply also to all other domains (say that which relates to
mathematics or to values).

19. This objection is based on claims endorsed by several philosophers, including Dummett,
Wiggins, Williams, and Crispin Wright in *Truth and Objectivity* (Cambridge, Mass.:
Harvard University Press, 1992).

20. *Truth and Objectivity,* chaps. 1 and 2.

21. Cf., for example, B. Williams, "Truth in Ethics," pp. 19–20 and elsewhere.

22. In the sense with which the phrase was introduced by J. Mackie in Chapter 1 of *Ethics:
Inventing Right and Wrong* (London: Penguin, 1977).

23. For example, Marmor, "Three Concepts of Objectivity," and Pettit and Leiter in the
present volume.

24. "Truth in Ethics," in *Truth in Ethics,* p. 3. It may be that Wright's argument here is the
argument Dworkin tries to make in his "Objectivity and Truth: You'd Better Believe It."

25. Given that mastery of concepts is a matter of degree, everything I say in the text has to be
modulated to allow, e.g., for a more imperfect mastery of a greater number of concepts.

26. *The View From Nowhere* (New York: Oxford University Press, 1986), p. 5. He also says

that, "To acquire a more objective understanding of some aspect of life or the world, we step back from our initial view of it and form a new conception which has that view and its relation to the world as its object. In other words we place ourselves in the world that is to be understood" (ibid., p.4). Here Nagel seems to be saying that a belief about the world is more subjective than a belief about my having a belief about the world. But my beliefs about the content of the theory of quantum mechanics are not more subjective than my belief that I have certain beliefs about quantum mechanics. They are simply different. I will assume that the quotation above is simply an unhappy formulation of the idea I quoted in the main text.

27. Ibid., p. 4.
28. This issue is relevant to the standing of perceptually dependent properties, e.g., color properties, and I will not pursue it here.
29. From "A Critical Review of Berkeley's Idealism," in Charles S. Peirce, *Selected Writings (Values in a World of Chance)*, ed. Philip P. Wiener (New York: Dover, 1966), p. 82; *Descartes*, p. 244.
30. Ibid., p. 245.
31. Ibid., p. 248.
32. See H. Putnam, "Bernard Williams and the Absolute Conception of the World" in *Renewing Philosophy* (Cambridge, Mass.: Harvard University Press, 1992), p. 80, and J. McDowell, "Aesthetic Value, Objectivity, and the Fabric of the World" in E. Schaper (ed.), *Pleasure, Preference, and Value* (Cambridge: Cambridge University Press, 1983), p. 1.
33. *Ethics and the Limits of Philosophy* (London: Fontana Press/Collins 1985), p. 140.
34. Ibid.
35. It is illuminatingly discussed by Wright in *Truth and Objectivity*, e.g., pp. 88–94.
36. C. Wright's condition of cognitive command (*Truth and Objectivity*, pp. 92–93) disregards the existence of rational underdetermination in its assertion that a discourse exhibits cognitive command only if all disagreements can be explained by "divergent input." On pp. 95ff, Wright has an interesting discussion of the related topic of the degree to which reason can be permissive only, but he does not fully adjust his conclusions to allow for its insights.
37. "Objectivity and the Science-Ethics Distinction," in Putnam, *Realism with a Human Face* (Cambridge, Mass.: Harvard University Press, 1990).
38. For a critique of the absolute conception that argues that science too needs perspectival concepts, see Putnam, "Objectivity and the Science-Ethics Distinction." Note that to establish his case Putnam has to show not only that different systems of representations can be used in science, but also that they employ what I call parochial concepts.
39. There may or may not be reasons to think that some perceptual concepts, those designating the so-called secondary qualities, designate relational properties of things. For example, there may or may not be reason to think that they designate how things when observed strike the observer, rather than how they are when not observed. Williams advances some arguments to that effect, and their examination is irrelevant to my argument here. The only relevant point is that the fact that perceptual concepts are local is not such an argument.
40. This is one of the points made by McDowell, "Aesthetic Value, Objectivity, and the Fabric of the World."
41. It may be worth noting that the rejection of this option is not just an endorsement of the

"Neurath's boat" understanding of the pursuit of knowledge. Those who accept that we must start from here, i.e., from the beliefs we happen to have, can be wedded to an ideal convergence test or some other test of the kind here rejected.

42. Perhaps it is helpful to warn here that this reference to a holistic approach is not an endorsement of an epistemic approach based on coherence in any shape or form. I have explained some of the reasons for this in *Ethics in the Public Domain* (Oxford: Clarendon Press, 1994), essay 13: "The Relevance of Coherence."

43. Williams, *Descartes,* p. 64

44. I am assuming a club which is not legally incorporated.

45. They will also be crude in not drawing some elementary distinctions. I will refer to goods, values, valuables, norms, considerations which determine that an action is right or wrong, etc., without trying to distinguish between them. For present purposes such distinctions are immaterial. Furthermore, I will use examples, implying that they are examples of genuine goods, or values. Their purpose is to illustrate abstract general points. It is not my suggestion that everything that is endorsed by a local culture is good for that reason, and the examples can be substituted with others by those who doubt their credentials. Finally, I will consider only beliefs about intrinsic goods and will avoid any reference to instrumental goods.

46. It is true that chess may be forgotten and then be reinvented rather than rediscovered. That would be the case if its reemergence is independent of knowledge of its previous existence. But this seems to be consistent with my claim: So long as it can be re-discovered there is something to rediscover.

47. Two qualifications do not erode the contrast I draw in the text. First, there are "deviant" ways of enjoying local goods in alien cultures: it could, e.g., mark one as an eccentric. Similarly, there is usually a whole network of meaning associated with all goods – socially constituted or not – which is lost when they are moved from one context to another. Playing chess in seventeenth-century Paris invokes different meanings than playing in Washington Square in New York City today.

48. I will call any good, norm, or value that is not socially constituted "universal," even though it may not be strictly universal, as its existence may be conditioned by other factors.

49. See generally, P. M. S. Hacker, *Appearance and Reality* (Oxford: Blackwell, 1988).

50. See my discussion of the universality of value in "Moral Change and Social Relativism," in E. F. Paul et al. (eds), *Cultural Pluralism and Moral Knowledge* (Cambridge: Cambridge University Press, 1994). Among other things I discuss there the possibility of applying judgements that presuppose responsibility, to people, their life, character or actions, by values that were not created until a later time. In the present discussion I ignore that possibility.

51. I present a simplified and inaccurate norm, to avoid complicated substantive moral issues.

52. See "Thick Concepts and the Social Connections."

53. At best for, as was noted in discussing local goods, typically a single conventional standard provides an opportunity for a variety of goods, some of which depend not on conformity but on deviation from it (e.g., the good of being an unconventional person, or one with a strong individual taste).

54. In *Cultural Pluralism and Moral Knowledge.*

55. I have argued this and some other points made in the current section and the next one in "Moral Change and Social Relativism."

56. My formulation of the objection is not meant to capture the precise argument of any writer, though it borrows from points advanced by a number of philosophers. For example, some aspects of such a view were elaborated by A. MacIntyre in his Gifford lectures. Davidson's "On the Very Idea of a Conceptual Scheme" is the best-known attempt to refute such views. But see Hacker, *Appearance and Reality.*

57. The argument presupposes, correctly, that evaluative beliefs are not about brute facts. What value things have is an intelligible matter. Necessarily if something has a value in one way or another then there are reasons which explain this fact.

58. The *Oxford English Dictionary* defines "nerd" as "An insignificant or contemptible person, one who is conventional, affected, or studious; a 'square', a 'swot.'" Surely this misses out a lot that is essential to the understanding of the term in contemporary, especially American culture. The *OED* instances the following (from an ad in the *New York Times,* 1978): "The nerdiest nerds on TV are really smart cookies," a quote made mysterious rather than explained by their definition.

59. This remark is confined to cultures of creatures who share our perceptual capacities and emotional make-up.

6

Embracing Objectivity in Ethics

PHILIP PETTIT

This chapter is written in support of an objectivist position in ethics. The first part of the chapter attempts to characterize the objectivism defended. And the second presents some arguments that should help to make the objectivism in question appealing.

I characterize ethical objectivism by three claims. First, semantic objectivism: the claim that ethical evaluations posit values – including, of course, disvalues – and do not serve just to express feelings or anything of that kind. Second, ontological objectivism: the claim that there really are ethical values available for evaluations to posit, so that evaluations are not undercut by massive error.[1] And third, justificatory objectivism: the claim that, though ethical justification may not dictate a unique verdict in every case, the verdicts it delivers are equally relevant for every person; they are based on neutral values that have the same significance for all.

Having characterized ethical objectivism in this way, I go on to present some arguments in its defense. With each of the first two claims, I argue that the claim is inherently plausible and bolster this by showing that the main reason why opponents reject it is not compelling. In the case of the third claim, justificatory objectivism, I take a more direct approach. I present considerations that tend to undermine the opposing position, spending only a little time in defending the objectivistic alternative against attack.

Before coming to the main parts of my discussion, however, I should say something on what I have in mind when I speak of ethical values. Ethical values provide grounds for the assessment of the things that people individually and collectively do. What distinguishes them from other grounds of assessment is that they underpin a sort of assessment that has a characteristically authoritative standing. The criticism of an option on grounds of manners or prudence or law may be endorsed by an agent, even someone who is perfectly sincere, without having an effect on their choice; the agent may justify indifference to that criticism by arguing that in the case on hand it would be wrong of them – ethically wrong of them – to honor the demands of etiquette or prudence or law. But the criticism of an option by reference to ethical values does not leave the same leeway. Under a more or less shared sense of priorities, agents cannot expect to be able to justify indifference to such a criticism by arguing that it would be wrong of them in terms of etiquette or prudence or law, or indeed in any other terms, to honor the demands of ethics. Ethical values are grounds of assessment that are distinguished from other practical criteria of evaluation by the enjoyment of a certain priority.

Systems of justification connect in any society with distinct sets of more or less conventionally recognized norms: norms of etiquette and prudence and law, of course, but also norms of an ethical kind. But doesn't that mean that there is no need to accord any system of justification a priority over others? Doesn't it mean that we should be open as theorists to the discovery that even if our society gives priority to ethical norms and ethical justification, it is perfectly possible that different norms and different forms of justification have priority in other societies? Doesn't it mean that we cannot use the priority claim as a general way of distinguishing ethical values from other criteria of practical evaluation?

Not from my point of view. The challenge just presented supposes that as etiquette and prudence and law are descriptively demarcated realms of norm and assessment, so too with ethics; as there is a descriptively identifiable point of view, and in the nature of the case a limited point of view, associated with the other realms, so there is a similarly limited ethical point of view. But those of us who believe in the priority of ethical justification will reject this supposition. We will say that what distinguishes ethical justification is not the particular norms it invokes but rather the role it plays in relation to justification of the other sorts. We will say that the criterion of ethical as distinct from other kinds of assessment is precisely the fact that it enjoys a certain sort of priority in people's justificatory practices.[2]

People may sometimes speak of what is ethically required or permitted, of course, with implicit scare quotes around the word "ethical" or "moral." In this case they refer to what accords with the ethical norms recognized in their culture, not necessarily with the norms that they themselves would uphold; the point of the scare quotes is to mark that distance. But in its primary, committed form, talk of ethical justifiability refers to justifiability in the ultimate currency of justification: justifiability by criteria that cannot be suspended in the manner of the criteria associated with etiquette and other systems.

You want to know, then, whether those in another society are arguing in ethical terms about the justifiability of an action? Ask whether or not they regard the assessment at issue as the sort that can be set aside in the way that most of us are occasionally willing to set aside assessments by reference to etiquette or prudence or legality. If the assessment sought is not susceptible to that sort of suspension, then what is sought is precisely an ethical evaluation of the act. Or so at any rate I shall assume. Ethical values are those values that people invoke in the sort of assessment that they do not treat as suspendable in the relevant sense. Ethical values provide the ultimate or reserve currency in which people seek to gauge the justifiability of what they and others do.

One final comment. A number of contemporary philosophers are antimoralists and reject the view that moral considerations override all competing reasons.[3] Is my characterization of ethical values inconsistent with their point of view? Not necessarily. I say that within our justificatory practices ethical values are distinguished by the priority they enjoy. Antimoralists can be cast, perhaps with a little regimentation, as rejecting the universal relevance of such justificatory practices; they can be taken to say that people should not always be required to justify themselves in the manner that would introduce ethical considerations. I return to their point of view at the end of this essay.

I. A Characterization of Ethical Objectivism

To say that ethical values are objective is, by my lights, to defend three distinct, objectivistic claims: semantic, ontological, and justificatory. I shall approach the characterization of objectivism by discussing these doctrines and explaining why each, in its particular realm, looks to be a natural part of an overall objectivist position.

A. Semantic Objectivism

To be a semantic objectivist about any area of discourse is to hold that the sentences in that area are regularly used with the intention of expressing or communicating states of belief and knowledge – cognitive attitudes – as to how things are in the relevant domain. It is to defend a cognitivist picture of the purpose – the purpose as revealed in common practice – for which participants in the discourse resort to those sentences. They resort to those sentences in order to report on how things are, according to their own view of things. But though the primary account of semantic objectivism refers us to the belief-expressing intention of speakers, that account also connects with other, perhaps more familiar characterizations. These generally associate cognitivism about any discourse with the claim that relevant utterances are assertoric and truth-conditional in character.

It is common since Frege to distinguish between the different forces with which a sentence may be uttered or used. Take a sentence like "James is going to town." This sentence, despite the indicative mood, may be uttered with interrogative or imperative or optative or exclamatory force, not just with assertoric. It may be uttered in a tone of voice that indicates that the speaker is asking a question or giving an order or making a wish or expressing amazement as distinct from simply reporting a matter of fact. It may be used so that it is equivalent in usage to "Is James going to town?" or "Let James go to town" or "Would that James would go to town" or "James, in town!"

Semantic objectivists about any area of discourse, under our initial account, are bound to hold that sentences in the discourse can be used with assertoric force. This is because only sentences with assertoric force can be used with the intention of expressing cognitive attitudes. Sentences that lack all assertoric force can register the intentions or wishes or feelings of speakers but not – not, at least, in a direct fashion – their beliefs. Thus semantic objectivism entails the claim that the utterances in the discourse under consideration include assertions.

When a sentence is used assertorically to report a matter of fact, not just to formulate a question or a command, and not just to express a wish or a feeling or anything of that kind, then the utterance – the sentence in use – is presumptively truth-conditional. It directs us to a condition, presumptively well defined, such that it is true if that condition obtains, false if it does not obtain. The condition may turn out to be not well defined; it may be like the condition answering to "That is a dagger," where there is nothing for the demonstrative to pick out. In that case the sentence is presumptively truth-conditonal but not actually so. It is presumptively apt to be true or false but, because of not managing to pick out a condition by which its truth-value can be determined, it is not actually so.

We began with a characterization under which semantic objectivism about any discourse holds that the sentences are regularly used with the intention of expressing cognitive attitudes. We saw that that entails the claim that in such employment the sentences are used with assertoric force. And we now see that it therefore entails the claim that in such employment the sentences are presumptively truth-conditional or truth-apt. Do those entailments exhaust the content of semantic objectivism? Does semantic objectivism amount to a doctrine that we might describe as truth-conditionalism or, more pedantically, presumptive truth-conditionalism?

I think that this is indeed what semantic objectivism amounts to, at least in the ethical case. There may be a concept of truth or truth-aptness that allows us to say that a discourse is assertoric and truth-conditional, yet not fit to express belief.[4] But that is not the concept with which we ordinarily work, since any sentences that are allowed to be true or false raise a question for us as to whether we should believe them.[5] Semantic objectivism in ethics amounts to nothing more or less than truth-conditionalism. Or so at any rate I shall assume.[6]

Expressivism

But if that is what semantic objectivism amounts to in ethics, then what do opponents say? They must deny that the sentences in the area are used with the intention of expressing beliefs or, equivalently, that they are presumptively truth-conditional. Perhaps some sentences wear the surface appearance of assertions, and perhaps there is even an honorific sense in which they can pass as true or false, but semantic nonobjectivists must hold that proper analysis will reveal them to be nonassertoric expressions of noncognitive attitudes. The view taken of the would-be assertions will be that they are expressions of such attitudes, not attempts to say anything about the world: not even attempts to say that the speaker has the attitudes expressed.

The attitude allegedly expressed in ethical assessments may be an emotion or sentiment, for example, so that saying that something is good or right or whatever amounts, at least in significant part, to a positive exclamation on a par with "Wow!" or "Bravo!"[7] Or it may be a prescriptive attitude, most plausibly an attitude of prescribing something universally, so that saying that something is right amounts to enjoining or commanding that anyone in the relevant situation should perform that act.[8] Expressivism, as it is often called, represents a broad family of alternatives to semantic objectivism.

My own belief is that expressivism, characterized in this more or less standard manner, is much more problematic than is generally believed. The sentences that allegedly express emotive or prescriptive attitudes are intentionally produced in ordinary, sincere usage – they are not like reflexes of approval or disapproval – and so they must be the product of a belief on the agent's part that he or she does indeed have those attitudes. Why don't they serve to express that belief, then, at the same time that they serve to express the attitude in question? Why don't they serve in the double role – the role of simultaneously expressing an attitude and the belief that one has that attitude – exemplified by a sentence like "I approve"? If these questions cannot be satisfactorily answered, then expressivism collapses into something like the subjectivist doctrine described by G. E. Moore.[9] According to this doctrine, ethical evaluations have truth-conditions but all that it takes to make them true is that the subject has the attitudes they allegedly report. This is not the place to develop that criticism, however, and I shall proceed on the assumption that expressivism is not an inherently problematic alternative to semantic objectivism.[10]

Semantic objectivists about ethics deny that ethical sentences are used only with the intention of expressing emotional or prescriptive attitudes or anything of that kind; they reject all forms of the expressivism just characterized. They say that when people speak of things being fair or just, when they condemn certain actions as being cruel or intemperate, or when they settle on a choice as the desirable or right one to take, then they mean to be identifying and ascribing properties that answer to the names of fairness and justice, cruelty and intemperance, desirability and rightness. Semantic objectivists hold that when people provide ethical assessments in such terms, then they mean to posit the reality of the values and disvalues in question and to pronounce on the distribution of those properties across different arrangements and actions and choices. The ethical assessments are used with the intention of expressing beliefs in those distributions, so the view goes; they are used in a way that supposes that they are truth-conditional and truth-apt and so fitted to the expression of such beliefs.

One caveat, however. While semantic objectivists deny that ethical utterances are used only with the intention of expressing emotional or prescriptive attitudes and the like, they can still recognize a place for such noncognitive attitudes. Suppose that the property that is ascribed in an ethical assertion, according to their view, is identified as the property in virtue of which an option evokes a certain response under certain conditions: this, in the way that the property of being admirable is identified by reference to the response of admiration. In that case someone who uses an ethical assertion to express a belief in the presence of the property will often express also the presence of the noncognitive attitude. Someone who says that some choice was admirable will not only express a belief that it was admirable but also a feeling of admiration for the act. Semantic objectivists about ethics do not have to say that ethical utterances express beliefs and nothing but beliefs; they need only say that beliefs figure crucially among the attitudes that the utterances express.

Ethical Objectivity and Semantic Objectivity

How reasonable is it to tie a belief in ethical objectivity to a semantic objectivism – a cognitivism – about ethical assessments? When we consider traditional emotivist positions as exemplars of expressivism, it may seem entirely compelling, for those positions give ethical evaluations a decidedly particularistic, even capricious, cast: they make evaluations look like affective hiccups that have no objective significance. But I should stress that not all expressivist views of ethics are of this kind and that tying ethical objectivism to a semantic objectivism about evaluation is not quite as uncontroversial as might be thought.

Take the expressivist view that ethical evaluations express universal prescriptions. Someone who defends such a view, like R. M. Hare,[11] may think that human beings are similar enough for it to be the case that what is universally prescribable for one will be universally prescribable for others. Thus they may think that there is room for debate about what is right – what is right by anyone's lights – and that sustained debate should identify the right choice in any decision. That sort of prescriptivism is objectivist in the perfectly ordinary sense that it sees ethical evaluation as an enterprise in which people can expect to be rationally brought to a common mind. While it does not posit objective values – that is, objective properties that can be a matter of cognition – it does represent ethical assessment as bearing on rationally and commonly resoluble questions. While not semantically objectivist it is, as we might say, intersubjectivist; it does not allow ethics to sink in a quagmire of individually variable and more or less capricious responses.

Prescriptivism is not the only expressivist position that is intersubjectivist, even rationalist, in this sense. Simon Blackburn and Allan Gibbard have argued, for example, that even if ethical evaluations express sentiments, it does not follow that just about anything goes in the realm of those emotions.[12] Someone can find themselves in trouble with others – perhaps also in trouble with their more reflective self – for the sentiments they express in ethical evaluation. And taking their stand on the side of their present sentiments, someone can say here and now that even were their present sentiments different – even if their sentiments about cruelly teasing a child were different – it would be wrong to act in a manner allowed by those changed feelings: it would be wrong to tease a child cruelly.[13] Under this sort of view, as under prescriptivism, we may expect the task of ethical assessment to present itself as a more or less rationally resoluble challenge.

Notwithstanding the capacity of various expressivist positions to vindicate intersubjectivism, however, I am going to assume here that ethical objectivism is committed to a nonexpressivist view: that is, in effect, to semantic objectivism. In fairness to the opposition it is important to recognize that expressivism does not necessarily give us a deflationary or debunking view of ethical debate: that it can sustain an intersubjectivist attitude. But still the expressivist position, even in its intersubjectivist forms, falls well short of what I shall take here to represent an objectivist approach.[14]

B. Ontological Objectivism

Consistently with being a semantic objectivist about any area of discourse, however, it is possible to take a fairly dim view of that discourse. In particular, it is possible to hold that while participants do indeed use sentences with the intention of expressing beliefs, and while the sentences are presumptively truth-conditional, actually the entities characteristically posited by those sentences and beliefs – the entities distinctive of the domain of discourse in question – are a chimera. Thus the idea would be that notwithstanding the cognitivist aspirations of participants, the discourse in question is undercut by massive error.

What would be the effect of such massive error on the status of a discourse? What in particular would be the effect of such error about values? Suppose we were to conclude that people are mistaken in thinking that there are values and disvalues answering to terms like "just" and "inequitable," "right" and "wrong" and that their beliefs in the distribution of such properties fail for the reason that there are no properties available to be distributed. What in that case should we say about the status of ethical discourse?

We might say either of two things. We might maintain that while ethical assessments are presumptively truth-conditional, the truth-conditions that they aspire to pick out are not well defined; they are like the truth-condition of a sentence such as "That is a dagger," where there is nothing for the demonstrative to refer to. In that case we would say that though presumptively truth-conditional, the assessments are not actually so; they are neither true nor false, because they do not successfully pick out conditions by which their truth or falsehood is determined.

Alternatively, however, we might have a view of the truth-conditions that the assessments aspire to pick out such that though there are no values or disvalues, still the truth-conditions are well-defined. We might deny that in saying an action is fair, for example, people are ascribing that property, presumptively available for demonstration, which goes by the name of "fairness"; if that is how things were, then the nonreality of the property would leave the truth-condition of the sentence ill-defined. We might hold instead that in saying such a thing people are asserting, first, that there is a property that deserves to go by the name of "fairness" and, second, that the action has the property in question. If we held that view, then the nonreality of the property would not mean that the truth-condition was ill-defined; it would just mean that the condition was unfulfilled and that the sentence was false.

On this second view, then, error about the reality of values would impact, not on the truth-conditionality or truth-aptness of ethical assessments, but on their truth-value. It would entail that any sentence of the form "X is fair," "X is right," "X is cruel," "X is unjust" – assuming these are ethical assessments – is false. It is false, not for the contingent reason that X lacks the property ascribed, but for the deeper reason that there is no property for X to have or lack. More generally, this second view would mean that ethical assessments that are not subject to external negation – as in "It is not the case that X is fair," "It is not the case that X is wrong" – all come out as false.

We need not judge on which of these views would be the more compelling one to take in the case of there being no values and disvalues of the kind that ethical discourse, according to semantic objectivism, posits. Under either view the participants in the discourse would suffer from massive error: in the first case, from error about the availability of truth-conditions for their assessments; in the second case, from error about the fulfillment of the truth-conditions available. Someone who defends either view maintains that ordinary people are deceived about values and disvalues; each amounts to a form of eliminativism about such entities.

It is a striking feature of moral philosophy that the possibility of being ontologically (as distinct from semantically) nonobjectivist about ethical discourse – the possibility of ethical eliminativism – has only recently been identified.[15] But once the possibility is identified, it is clear that anyone who aspires to defend ethical objectivism must reject it. That is my second claim in characterization of an objectivist position in ethics. Ethical objectivism, so I say, is bound to uphold not just semantic objectivism about ethical discourse but also ontological. It is bound to maintain that not only do ethical assessments posit values and disvalues, those properties are rightly posited: they are, as we say, objective realities.

There is unlikely to be any challenge to the claim that if semantic objectivists about ethics are to count as full-blown ethical objectivists, then they must embrace ontological objectivism too. We saw that expressivism can make some claim to be consistent with objectivism; if it does not cast ethical evaluations as purporting to say how things objectively are, it can at least give support to an intersubjectivist view of ethical debate. But eliminativism can make no claims of this kind. On the ontological issue of the reality of values and disvalues it epitomizes the attitude of someone who wants to reject ethical objectivism.

Objective but Not Transcendent Values

But if ontological objectivism is a necessary part of an overall objectivist position, there may be a question as to whether it needs strengthening. The suggestion would be that ethical objectivists may have to claim more on the ontological front than just that values are objective realities. They may have to claim that values are objective realities that enjoy a certain independence of human beings, even a certain lack of connection with them. They may have to claim that values, as I shall say, are transcendent realities.

Before considering this suggestion, it will be useful to make a minor concession. It is possible to imagine someone who is a semantic and ontological objectivist about ethical discourse, but only because they maintain a very debunking construal of that discourse. They interpret ethical assessments in such a manner that their truth-conditions fall well short of what they intuitively seem to be. Consider the subjectivism described by G. E. Moore,[16] for example; I suggested earlier that expressivism may collapse into such a doctrine. According to subjectivism all that is said in the claim that something is good or right is that the speaker approves of it – or, in a more plausible version, that it satisfies (the speaker's) presupposed standards[17] – and all that is required for there to be ethical values, then, is that the speaker does indeed have such attitudes of approval or such standards. The subjectivist construal of ethical assessments is counterintuitively debunking, running against our sense that ethical evaluations have the same truth-conditions as they are uttered now by one person, now another, and running against our assumption that we approve of things because they have certain values, not the other way around.[18] It would be misleading to say that someone who held by such a position – someone who defended semantic and ontological objectivism relative to such an interpretation of ethical assessments – was an ethical objectivist. Or so at any rate I am happy to concede.[19]

But let us assume, reasonably, that semantic and ontological objectivism are upheld relative to an interpretation of ethical assessments that is not debunking in this way. The question then is whether something more than the objectivist commitment is required at the ontological level for a full-blown ethical objectivism. Do values and disvalues have to be, not just objective realities, but realities of transcendent significance?

What would it be for ethical values to be transcendent? There are two salient possibilities. The first is that there are many different conceptions of what it is to be truth-apt or truth-conditional and that the values posited in ethical discourse are transcendent so far as ethical sentences are truth-conditional in a heavyweight rather than a lightweight sense.[20] The other possibility is that there is only one conception of truth-aptness or truth-conditionality for sentences and that the values posited in ethical discourse are transcendent so far as the truth-conditions of ethical sentences, like the truth-conditions of sentences in physics and theology, bear on how things are in the world at large – the natural and perhaps nonnatural world – and not on how things are related to us human beings.[21]

I prefer to think of the transcendence issue in the second manner. There is only one way for sentences to be truth-conditional, I believe: by being used in ordinary circumstances with the intention of expressing beliefs, as I suggested earlier. But there are many varieties in which truth-conditions may come. Some conditions may bear on how things are with us human beings, for example, or with our responses to things, and others may bear on how things are in realms and in respects that have little or no special connection to our species. The transcendence issue is whether the truth-conditions of ethical sentences bear primarily on us and the relations that things have to us or whether they bear primarily on the nature of the nonhuman world. When we speak of what is amusing or disgusting or colored, we speak of things as they relate to us. When we speak of what has positive electrical charge, or what weighs heavier than what, or of the creation of the universe by a benevolent god, then we speak of things as they are independently of us. The transcendence issue is whether ethical sentences belong with sentences in the former or with sentences in the latter category.[22]

My reason for preferring this way of formulating the question is that it provides a perfectly good account of it, without running into the sorts of problems that are bound to go with letting the conception of truth-aptness – and therefore truth – go plural and ambiguous.[23] The conception of what it is to be wealthy may be the same for different societies consistently with wealth requiring many more possessions and capabilities in an advanced society than it would require in a traditional community.[24] And similarly the conception of what it is to be truth-apt and the conception of what it is to be true may be the same for different discourses consistently with truth-aptness and truth making very different requirements in different domains; in some domains truth may require the nonhuman world to assume a distinctive configuration, in others it may require little more than the availability of a certain pattern in human responses to things.[25]

We can return finally to the question raised earlier. Do ethical objectivists have to think about values and disvalues in a transcendent way? Do they have to think that the truth-conditions of ethical sentences bear primarily on how the nonhuman world is and that the things that make such sentences true may have no special connection to the human species? Do they have to think of ethical values and disvalues as comets that streak into the atmosphere of human thought, imposing on us demands that come truly from without? Or can ethical objectivists cast values and disvalues in a more anthropocentric light? Can they see them, for example, as features of the world that assume shape and salience, and that attract our attention, only in virtue of producing certain responses in us? Can they see them in the way most of us see colors: as properties of things, and perhaps independently describable properties of things, that are unified and important only in virtue of their association with our color sensations?

I propose that we should not associate ethical objectivism with a belief in transcendent values, for two reasons. One is that it is hard to see how there could be transcendent values consistently with a naturalistic picture of the universe: consistently with a picture, roughly, under which all that there is in the empirical world is composed of microphysical elements and is governed by microphysical laws.[26] Only the presence of Platonic properties breaking in upon our attention from a nonnatural sphere – only the reality of things like Plato's form of the good – would seem to be capable of vindicating ethical transcendence. Many of us will want to reject such properties and it would seem to be a good idea to construe ethical objectivism so that it stands some chance of being true in the purely naturalistic world that we countenance.

The other reason for not associating ethical objectivism with transcendence is nicely complementary to the first consideration. By traditional lights it would be an important win for those who believe in the objectivity of ethics to be able to argue that values and disvalues are on a par, for example, with colors.[27] After all, color appearances are remarkably constant as between different lights and different observers and where there are divergences, we readily account for them by reference to factors that are reasonably cast as perturbances.[28] Moreover this convergence on the colors of things is produced in the context of a semantically and ontologically objectivist framework; it is not just the intersubjectivist sort of convergence for which certain expressivists might look. If values and disvalues could be made out to have a status like that which colors enjoy, then intuitively that would be a big win for those who believe in the objectivity of ethics.

I think that these considerations ought to persuade us to dissociate objectivism from a belief in transcendent values. If the two seem to be connected, that may only be because objectivity is often contrasted, not with nonobjectivity, but with subjectivity.[29] The construal of objectivity as the opposite of subjectivity may suggest that someone who espouses ethical objectivism in any full sense of the term must be opposed to a broadly subjective or anthropocentric view of the values and disvalues countenanced. But this consideration ought to have no hold on us. For the sense of objectivity that is at issue in our discussion, of course, is the sense in which the antonym is nonobjectivity, not subjectivity. Ontological objectivism will be vindicated by the reality of any ethical values, even values that are decidedly immanent to human life: even values that do not have a quasi-religious transcendence.[30]

In suggesting that subjectivism was a counterintuitive account of the content of ethical evaluation, I argued that it offended against the common assumption that we approve of things because they have certain values, not the other way around.[31] It should be noticed in this connection that taking values to be immanent to human life does not mean rejecting that assumption. Colors are immanent to human life in the intended sense and yet we have no hesitation in thinking that when we see something as red, and conditions are normal, then we do so because it is red. Perhaps there is a sense in which red things are red because we see them as red: it is because we see them that way that they and not some other class of things are called by the word "red." But in the primary causal sense, it is clear that we see things as red because they are red, and not the other way around.[32]

C. Justificatory Objectivism

We have argued so far that on the issues surveyed ethical objectivism requires no less and no more than semantic and ontological objectivism. No less, because it must reject both expressivism and eliminativism. No more, because it need not embrace such further doctrines as a belief in transcendent values and disvalues. But the issues surveyed are not all the issues there are in this realm. For besides the question of whether ethical evaluations are presumptively truth-conditional, and besides the question of whether the values and disvalues postulated are objective realities, there is a question as to how ethical values and disvalues serve in people's attempts to assess what they do: ultimately, in people's attempts to justify their choices to one another.

The question here is whether there is a single set of values and disvalues such that each person is required to invoke those properties in any bedrock justification of choice or action. Consistently with semantic and ontological objectivism, there may be no such single pool of justificatory values and disvalues. There may be no single currency of justification, and no exchange system that might enable us to construct one. Each individual, or each among a certain set of groups or cultures or societies, may have to draw on a different set of values as the ultimate justifiers by which to assess choice. Values and disvalues may vary from individual to individual or from group to group, so that assessment and justification are always relative to the position of the valuer and a certain relativism is vindicated.

As ethical objectivism is opposed to expressivism and eliminativism, so it is naturally opposed to any such form of relativism. Consider the theist who says that there is a god. We do not ask such a person whether they think that there is one god or many, for the presupposition of avowing that there is a god is that there is at most one; the existence claim is normally tied to a uniqueness assumption. What goes for the theist goes, in parallel, for the ethical objectivist. When the objectivist says that there are objective values and disvalues, we naturally presume that they are expressing a belief in a single set of such entities. It would be downright Pickwickian of someone to say that there are objective values and disvalues and then to add that not only are there objective values and disvalues, there are as many sets of values and disvalues as there are valuational positions.

There is another way of bringing out the natural opposition between anything that deserves the name of ethical objectivism and the belief that values and disvalues vary between individuals or groups, so that justification is relativized to the valuer's position. This is to draw attention to the fact that the word "objective" has a dual connotation in ordinary usage. Under the first connotation, anything that is described as objective belongs with the world that we human beings confront; it is not part of our imagining or invention. Under the second, anything that is described as objective belongs equally to all of us human beings; it is common, intersubjective property. To argue that ethical objectivism is consistent with some form of relativization would be to work against the grain of this second connotation.

Justification, Substantive and Isomorphic

There may be a difficulty in seeing, not that objectivism must reject any form of relativism, but that there is any serious position there for objectivism to reject. By the account given earlier, ethics has to do essentially with assessment and justification. And if two people belong to different valuational positions, acknowledging different values and disvalues, doesn't that mean that neither will be able to justify to the other those choices that are supported by unshared values?

Ethical relativism would certainly mean that neither will be able to justify such choices to the other in the straightforward or substantive sense of pointing to commonly recognized values that support it. Neither will be able to display the choice as one that is compelling from both perspectives. But there is a weaker sense of justification available even in everyday life and the relativist can argue that such justification is consistent with a relativity of values and disvalues.

Even if my values and disvalues are different from yours and justify different things from yours, it may be a matter of common belief between us that were you in my valuational position then you would value the things that I currently value and justify the things that I currently justify. With some of my current choices, then, I won't be able to present them as substantively justifiable from your point of view. But I will be able to present them as isomorphically justifiable, so to speak. I will be able to argue that these are choices that you would condone were you in my position, even if they are choices you currently criticize. And what I am able to do in relation to you, you may be able to do in relation to me. We can each justify ourselves to the other, if not in terms of substantive justifiability, at least in terms of isomorphic.

The isomorphic sort of justification that relativism could continue to permit is already familiar from everyday life. Often we are unable to persuade one another of the truth of our respective beliefs – say, beliefs of a religious character – and of the choices that they lead us to make. But in such cases we still have resort, quite naturally, to a second-grade way of justifying those choices. I argue with you that were you in my position – did you have my upbringing, or whatever – then you would accept what I believe and condone what I choose. This practice shows that isomorphic justifiability has a place in everyday life and that the relativist need not be cast as revising our notions of justification.

Relativism, Idiolectical and Indexical

We have argued that relativism is a possible position and that ethical objectivists are required to reject it. A last question, however, bears on what might be involved in embracing a relativist view and, by implication, what is involved in upholding the objectivist position.

The classical form of relativism would say that while people in different positions employ the same evaluative terms or concepts, and employ them to express the same beliefs, an evaluation can be true at one valuational position and false at another; there is truth-for-this-position and truth-for-that but no such thing as truth, period. This relativism about truth is hard to square with the fact that in asserting the doctrine in question, we must assume that it is true: and presumably assume that it is true, period. And besides, relativism about truth does not fit with what we have been assuming up to this point about truth-aptness and truth. Thus I propose not to consider such a form of relativism here. In any case neglecting it should not make for much of a loss, since there are two other forms of relativism that may capture much of what relativists about truth have wanted to maintain about ethics.

Where the relativist about truth assumes that people in different positions employ the same ethical terms or concepts, and employ them to express the same beliefs, the other two sorts of relativists deny those respective assumptions. The first sort argues that in different positions people employ different terms or concepts; the second argues that in different positions people employ the same terms or concepts but to express different beliefs. The first relativist says that each position offers an idiolectical language that those in other positions may not understand. The second says that while there are not different evaluative idiolects – while our languages of evaluation are identical or intertranslatable – the common terms used in fundamental assessment include terms that are indexical in the manner of "I," "you," "here" and "now" and serve to formulate different beliefs, different bedrock evaluations. The beliefs will be different in the way in which my belief that I am hungry is different from your belief that you are hungry: they will have different truth-conditons.

Idiolectical relativism may take the radical but practically not very relevant form of arguing that some cultures are so distant from one another that there is no translating the evaluative terms of either into the terms of the other; they are, as it is often said, incommensurable. Alternatively it may take the more domestic, and more threatening form of saying that while we use lexemes like "kind" and "fair" and "right" in common, these do not always function in the same way within our different perspectives; what we mean by them may vary between speakers. Whether in exotic or domestic form, however, idiolectical relativism will be objectionable to anyone who believes in the objectivity of ethical values. The objectivist will say that there are values and disvalues available such that they offer the right referents for the terms in question and that while there may be differences in how people use the terms, there ought to be a permanent possibility of resolving those differences, or of explaining the failure of resolution in a way that keeps meaning and reference common.[33]

Indexical relativism comes in two main varieties, one analytical, the other normative. Analytical indexicalism argues, in a debunking account of evaluative content, that what "That is V" means in my mouth, where "V" is "desirable" or "right" or whatever, is that I approve in some way – or for a group to which I belong, that we approve in some way – of the option or proposal in question. When I say that something is desirable, or right, I mean that it satisfies my or our standards.[34] I may think that everyone ought to satisfy my standards but if the indexicalism is truly relativist in spirit, I will think that everyone ought to satisfy their own standards: they ought to do what is desirable-by-their-lights or right-by-their-lights. I agreed in the last section to assume that ethical assessments were not to be interpreted in such a counterintutive, debunking way and I shall concentrate here on the normative version of indexical relativism.

What the normative indexicalist holds is that the expressions that identify the ultimate justifiers of choice are indexical expressions that refer us explicitly to concerns like, in my own case: preserving my integrity, keeping my promises, and furthering my long-term interests, the welfare of my children, the happiness of my friends, or the good of my country. The claim will be, in relativist spirit, that everyone's choices have to be justified by reference to some ultimate set of values, and while we may use the same evaluative language to express those values, there need be no one ultimate set of values by reference to which the choices have to be justified. This is because indexicalized values like the welfare of my children or my friends may figure among my ultimate justifiers, the welfare of your children and your friends among yours. All justifications end somewhere but there will be nowhere that all justifications end.

Normative indexicalism is a common creed, because it is implicit in every form of nonconsequentialism. Consequentialists say, roughly, that the right option in any choice is that which maximizes expected, neutral value: that which best promotes the realization of nonindexical goods. Opponents of consequentialism say that, no, the right option is not that which best promotes such neutral goods.[35] They say that the right option may often be a function of an agent-relative value such as the preservation of the agent's integrity, the keeping of their promises, or the nurture of their children. In effect they defend normative indexicalism.[36] The varieties of nonconsequentialism are endless. The right option may be that which manifests virtue, for example, as virtue ethicists say, where manifesting virtue does not require promoting virtue more generally.[37] Or that which conforms to what would be supported in a moral contract, as contractualists hold, where conformity does not enjoin promoting conformity more generally.[38] Or that which is universally prescribable, where performing the prescribable does not mean promoting its general performance.[39] Or anything of the kind.

To sum up, then, the rejection of relativism has deep implications. It involves not just the belief that truth is not relative to position, and not just the belief that our terms of evaluation and justification can in principle be rendered commensurable; it also involves a belief in the soundness of a broadly consequentialist position. While ethical objectivism is quite intuitively linked with justificatory as well as with semantic and ontological objectivism, it may be surprising that the justifications linkage involves a consequentialist commitment.

II. A Defense of Ethical Objectivism

My characterization of ethical objectivism may or may not be found intuitive. It may be regarded as a fair analysis of the sort of doctrine that deserves to be called by that name. Or it may be taken as an entirely stipulative account of what the name shall be used to mean in these discussions. But however it is understood, it gives us the questions with which we shall be concerned in the remainder of the paper. I want to reveal the strength of the argument for ethical objectivism. And so I need to look in turn at the case for semantic objectivism, the case for ontological objectivism, and the case for justificatory objectivism.

A. *Semantic Objectivism*

Semantic objectivists hold that ethical sentences are often used with the intention of expressing beliefs and that they are therefore presumptively truth-conditional. Thus the first issue is whether semantic objectivists are right in making this claim.

There are three distinctive ways in which we treat ordinary assertions. First, of course, we stand over them or, precisely, assert them. Second, we treat them as capable of being denied, as when someone asserts the counterpart sentence that begins with words like "It is not the case that . . ." And third, we regard them as capable of being, not denied, but supposed: in particular, capable of being used within the antecedent of a conditional that tells us what would follow in some sense from the truth of the assertion.

The most distinctive form of treatment among these three is the embedding of the asserted sentence in the antecedent place of a conditional. For whatever may be said about standing over and denying other utterances, it seems fairly clear that we embed only assertions in the antecedents of conditionals. Take any assertion of the form "It is the case that p." We can always imagine usages – sensible, straightforward, and indeed assertoric usages – for words of the form "If it is the case that p, then q." And we can easily make sense of the point of such usages, even if we disagree on details. Given that the sentence "It is the case that p" can serve to express a belief, the conditional "If it is the case that p, then q" may serve to reveal what follows according to my beliefs when those beliefs are minimally revised to include the belief that p. Or it may serve to describe what would follow in the objective world in the event of that world retaining its current history and/or laws and yet – perhaps impossibly, according to my current beliefs – being a p-world. It may serve to reveal the implications, in any such sense, of the world's being of a p-character.

But while this is so with assertions, it does not appear to be the case with sentences that have nonassertoric force. Take any straightforward question or prescription or wish or exclamation: "Is it the case that p?," "Make it the case that p," "Would that p," "Wow: p!" It appears that we cannot retain the marker of nonassertoric force and embed the sentence in the antecedent of a conditional. We cannot say "If is it the case that p, then q"; or "If make it the case that p, then q"; or "If would that p, then q"; or "If wow: p, then q." But more important even than this consideration is the fact that we cannot readily identify a point for such nonassertoric conditionals. The conditionals cannot elucidate the implications of the world being of a p-character, since the antecedent clauses do not correspond to assertions that express a belief that it is of that character. So what on earth could they be used to do?

In view of the sorts of considerations just rehearsed, Peter Geach[40] proposed that we use the antecedent-place test to determine whether or not evaluations are assertoric, presumptively truth-conditional, and intended to express belief contents. And, as he himself argued, the antecedent-place test strongly suggests that evaluations are of an assertoric kind. Take any evaluation such as "it is cruel to torture cats," or "an equal distribution of benefits would be fair," or "it is always right to insist on honesty among public officials." Any of those sentences can be fitted readily into the antecedent of a conditional and in each case it is easy to give a straightforward gloss on why the conditional makes sense. We can readily say, for example, that if it is always right to insist on honesty among public officials, then it must always be feasible for such officials to behave honestly. And we can easily explain what is going on in such a conditional, or so at least it seems. Plausibly, the conditional displays what follows according to our beliefs from the world being such that insistence on honesty is always right; revise that belief set so that it includes the belief about the rightness of insisting on honesty and, at least under a minimal revision, it is going to include the belief in the feasibility of honesty.

I had said that the first issue in defending semantic objectivists is whether their claim that we treat evaluations as ordinary truth-apt assertions is borne out in everyday practice. We certainly assert and deny evaluations in the ordinary manner and, so it now appears, we embed them in the antecedent places of conditionals in the manner that is particularly characteristic of asserted sentences. The evidence, on the face of it, is that semantic objectivism is correct. Evaluations are presumptively truth-conditional assertions that are intended to express the contents of beliefs. They are of a kind with all of the other sorts of sentences in which we aspire to say how the world is and not just to raise questions, give orders, make wishes, or express feelings.

But of course that is not the end of the matter. For, unsurprisingly, there have been a number of theoretical attempts to explain how evaluations can pass the antecent-place test while not counting as assertions proper: while only counting, in Michael Dummett's phrase, as quasi-assertions.[41] The idea, roughly, is that even if I only mean to prescribe or exclaim in saying that something is right, the conditional that begins "If it is right that such and such" can serve to express what would have to be the case, under certain constraints, were the choice to wring prescription or exclamation from me. This may look like an ad hoc response to the argument for semantic objectivism: an epicycle designed for the preservation of a less and less compelling position.[42] But we cannot dismiss it out of hand and we cannot say that the evidence of our evaluative performance is straightforwardly inconsistent with an expressivist, nonobjectivist position.

What we can say, however, is that since semantic objectivism makes more straightforward sense of our evaluative performance – of the way we treat ethical evaluations – then the onus of proof lies with expressivists. It is up to them to tell us why semantic objectivism is so repellent and why we should be driven to a position that requires a nonstraightforward account of our evaluative performance: in particular, a nonstraightforward account of the point in embedding evaluations in the antecedent places of conditionals.

The main reason why many expressivists shy away from semantic objectivism is that in their view semantic objectivism leads to an eliminativism about values. They think that ontological objectivism cannot be defended, on the grounds that values and disvalues would be mysterious entities to countenance. And so they reason that if they take evaluations to be intended as expressions of belief – if they go along with semantic objectivism – they will have to say that ordinary evaluators are subject to massive error: that the world does not provide the sorts of values and disvalues that people posit.[43] This reason for rejecting semantic objectivism may or may not be an appropriate one. But we need not consider it in any case at this point in our discussion. It will come up when we look at what there is to be said against ontological objectivism and when we consider, in effect, whether semantic objectivism has to lead to ethical eliminativism.

The Argument from No-Fault Disagreement

Is there any other, more independent reason why expressivists might think that semantic objectivism is untenable? There is one argument that appears, more or less tangentially, in many discussions and I will devote the remainder of this defense of semantic objectivism to examining it. Let us suppose that we ordinary speakers do take ethical evaluations as truth-conditional expressions of beliefs; let us suppose that semantic objectivism is true. The argument I have in mind holds that that supposition has implications – in particular, implications to do with the quantity and quality of agreement available on ethical questions – that are not borne out in practice. The hypothesis of semantic objectivism may be reduced, if not to absurdity, at least to implausibility; it supports expectations that are not fulfilled.

Fully fleshed out, the argument needs not just the supposition that we ordinary speakers treat evaluations as the expressions of beliefs but also some ancillary assumptions. It supposes that we ordinary speakers are conversationalists who speak to one another, not just to ourselves. It supposes that in speaking to one another, we often differ in what we assert and deny: we address sentences with the same truth-conditions and we express belief and disbelief, respectively, in their fulfillment. And it supposes that when we differ in this way, we each manage to sustain the belief that, marginal indeterminacies or vaguenesses aside, the difference can in principle be resolved on the basis of evidence: on the basis, ultimately, of how the world appears to be. We may actually resolve the difference, so that resolubility in principle is established by resolution in practice. Or we may find reason to explain the lack of resolution in practice, consistently with resolubility in principle. We may explain the nonresolution by orthogonal differences of belief, for example, or by differences in the credible evidence at one another's disposal, or by the intrusion of some inappropriate influences – some incompetence or inattention or partiality – on the belief-forming practice of the other.[44]

I am happy to go along with all of these suppositions, for I believe that we ordinary speakers do indeed conform to the conversational or dialogical image described.[45] So what now is the argument I mentioned against semantic objectivism? The argument holds that under these extra suppositions semantic objectivism would lead us to expect, if not more actual agreement on ethical matters than we actually get, at least a higher level of discontent with disagreement.

It is certainly accurate to say that under the suppositions given, there ought to be a certain discontent among ordinary speakers about disagreement in matters ethical. There ought to be a pervasive assumption that, marginal indeterminacies apart, someone is wrong in the case of disagreement and that the disagreement must be explicable in a way that does not dismiss some parties to the debate in an ad hoc way. It must be explicable by differences in the evidence available, or in the vividness with which evidence is available, on the different sides; or by differences in matters of orthogonal belief, for example, differences of a religious or ideological character; or by more or less restricted differences in susceptibility or exposure to influences that warp our belief-forming capacities: for example, by the presence of a certain bias or illogic.

The claim of those who rely on this argument, then, will be that actually we everyday evaluators take a much more laissez-faire attitude to ethical disagreement than semantic objectivism would predict. Ethical disagreement is a common-or-garden-variety phenomenon – this part of the claim can be readily admitted – and, so it is alleged, we are in the habit of treating many instances of disagreement, in Huw Price's[46] phrase, as no-fault disagreements. We may fight about what is actually to be done in this or that situation but we will not bother debating about the disagreement, as if the sharing of evidence, or the sharing of inferential intuition, would establish consensus. And we do not suppose that the disagreement is in need of some special explanation. We treat ethical disagreement, so it is maintained, as not having any particular significance for what there is; we do not see it as a disagreement about a matter of fact.

If this argument is sound in alleging that we regularly treat ethical disagreement as fault-free, then that will provide some support for an expressivist reading of ethical evaluation. We ordinary folk may admit certain limited indeterminacies in ethical matters, consistently with treating ethical utterances as intentionally expressing beliefs; after all, we standardly treat vague utterances as expressive of belief: more on this in the last section. But we can hardly admit wholesale indeterminacy – we can hardly treat all disagreements as fault-free – consistently with regarding evaluations as truth-conditional expressions of belief. Or at least we cannot do so, short of embracing something like the counterintuitive doctrine that G. E. Moore[47] described as subjectivism; according to this doctrine, as we saw earlier, each of us self-ascribes an attitude of approval or disapproval in making an evaluation and so we do not contradict one another in making what look like conflicting evaluations.

Does this argument give a good reason for rejecting semantic objectivism and, subjectivism aside, for embracing some form of expressivism? I do not think so. For the fact is that we do not generally treat ethical disagreement in the laid-back, tolerant manner alleged. Suppose you say that a particular way of dealing with the examination of students is fair and I say that it is not; suppose you say, for example, that teachers should have the right to determine, without appeal, ten percent of the overall mark allocated. Assume that neither of us has power to determine what actually happens in any examinations, so that there is no practical matter at issue. Are we likely to treat one another's claims in the way that we might treat expressions of taste about such a question? Are we each likely to regard the claim of the other as a confession of feeling or inclination or whatever, not as something that challenges our own view of the world? Surely not.

We are much more likely to open up an argument about the two claims, looking at what each would imply in practice, looking at the parallel claims to which it would give countenance, invoking the values and disvalues that we see in play, and so on. You will argue that teachers have special knowledge of their students' abilities, I will argue that giving teachers the power claimed would enable them to exercise favoritism and would induce an ingratiating mentality in students. We may then go on to debate the importance of special knowledge among assessors and the danger of giving discretion to those with power over others. And, pushing further, we may well find ouselves in deeper and deeper waters, as we examine the merits and the demerits of the larger schemes that would seem to sink or swim with the rival proposals for teacher involvement. There is no point, however, at which it is plausible to forecast that we will call it a day and recognize that there is fault on neither side of our disagreement. We may call it a day for reasons of exhaustion or despair, but those are reasons that may weigh with us in debates on the most objective and tractable of issues.

But can this be right? One of the most common themes in contemporary circles is precisely that ethical value, like beauty, is in the eye of the beholder – or at least of the beholder's reference group – and that we ought to rejoice in this diversity, not deny it. I say in response that while that metacomment certainly offers supporting testimony in favor of expressivism, it does not constitute supporting evidence. For what we need to look at is not what people say about ethical evaluation but what they show in their practices of negotiating the ethical differences that matter to them. And what they show, so I have been arguing, is that they regard ethical divergence as significant and troubling; they do not take it lightly, and certainly they do not celebrate it.

My line against the argument from no-fault disagreement will be supported, not just by those inclined toward semantic objectivism, but also by all of those who are attracted toward what I described as intersubjectivist forms of expressivism. Such thinkers suggest that resolution on ethical matters ought to be attainable in principle and that disagreements ought never to be taken lightly.

They see ethical debate as a continuing conversation and they give little coun-tenance to the no-fault disagreements that are allegedly acknowledged among people who differ in their ethical evaluations.

The belief that ethical disagreements have a no-fault character and argue for a lack of semantic objectivity in evaluations may derive a spurious plausibility from the high level of disagreements that actually obtain in the ethical realm: that is, from what is described by John Mackie as "the well-known variation in moral codes from one society to another and from one period to another, and also the differences in moral beliefs between different groups and classes within a complex community."[48] But the disagreements that actually obtain are probably no more marked than the differences we find on undoubtedly factual issues such as the origin of our species, the existence of god, and the perfor-mance of various political systems. We may disagree across cultural and other boundaries about the justifiability of treating women in a certain fashion and about the desirability of capital punishment. But such disagreements are quite consistent with agreement on deeper matters like the justice of treating similar cases similarly or of allowing no one arbitrary, unchallengeable discretion over the destiny of another.

Even if ethical disagreements were decidedly more marked than disagree-ments in nonethical matters, however, this ought not to persuade us that people treat evaluations as nonassertoric. For in most cases the disagreements can be explained in a manner that is consistent with their status as assertions and people regularly resort to such explanations. Thus they quote differences in religious belief, or differences in beliefs about relevant empirical matters, in accounting for why they take varying views of the morality of abortion or artificial contraception. And where no such differences are in evidence, people have resort, however reluctantly, to seeing those with whom they differ as being unduly influenced by irrelevant pressures: by a wish to remain faithful to a certain tradition, for example, or by the desire to be able to rationalize an independently appealing course of action, or by a commitment to a certain posture in politics. The point is that conversation on ethical matters goes on and on, and that people show no sign of declaring the exercise void or pointless; they display a sustained belief in the assertoric and truth-conditional character of their contributions.[49]

B. Ontological Objectivism

So much by way of arguing that semantic objectivism about ethical discourse is plausible and that the main, independent argument against it – the argument from no-fault disagreement – is not persuasive; we ordinary folk do not often countenance no-fault disagreements and we do not display a willingness to treat ethical evaluations as less than properly assertoric. But it is one thing to hold that participants in ethical discourse regard their claims and counterclaims as truth-conditional assertions about how things are. It is another to maintain that there really are values and disvalues of the sort invoked and that there is a fact of the matter as to whether their distribution conforms to this or that alleged pattern. To maintain this is to espouse ontological as well as semantic objectivism – it is to reject not just ethical expressivism but also ethical eliminativism – and I turn now to argue for the plausibility of such a thesis.

The fact that people practice ethical conversation suggests, if semantic objectivism is correct, that they succeed in finding something to talk about. If there were no such thing as ethical values and disvalues, then we would expect ordinary people to have tumbled to their unreality: the fact that they continue in discussion as if such values remained steadfastly available would certainly require special explanation. This means, then, that just as the onus on the issue of semantic objectivism lies squarely with those of an expressivist outlook, so the onus on the issue of ontological objectivism lies on the side of eliminativists. Expressivists and eliminativists are alike in denying the ethical appearances: in holding that things in the ethical domain are not what they seem to be. It is up to them rather than their opponents, therefore, to say why they maintain their particular position.

The Arguments from the Queerness of Values

So what is the main argument that moves eliminativists to claim that ordinary people are massively mistaken in the values and disvalues they countenance? It has been, and I think that it still is, what John Mackie described as the argument from queerness.[50] Values and disvalues are properties such that to recognize their presence is, *eo ipso,* to have at least a reason of some sort for choosing or not choosing the bearer; they display what Mackie describes as intrinsic prescriptivity. But what in the world – what in the ordinary, empirical world – could such intrinsically prescriptive properties be? They seem entirely out of keeping with the features to which science and common sense otherwise direct us; they are one of a kind and to that extent they are dubious or suspect posits.

The problem that Mackie finds with values – and, by extension, disvalues – comes out in the conception that he entertains of what values would have to be. "Plato's Forms give a dramatic picture of what objective values would have to be. The Form of the Good is such that knowledge of it provides the knower with both a direction and an overriding motive; something's being good both tells the person who knows this to pursue it and makes him pursue it."[51] Something's being good wreaks this magic, indeed, independently of contingent dispositions and desires; "the end has to-be-pursuedness somehow built into it."

In presenting this conception of objective values, Mackie shows that he thinks such values would have to be like comets, in our earlier metaphor, that streak into the atmosphere of the moral world and that command attention and attraction in a wholly mysterious fashion. I agree that if the intrinsic prescriptivity of values meant that they had to have this unfamiliar character, then it would be hard to countenance values. But I believe that we can make sense of that prescriptivity, and combat the argument from queerness, under a very different account of what values are. Under this account values turn out to be, not realities of purely transcendent significance, but realities that have a markedly immanent, anthropocentric character.

There are two distinct aspects to the intrinsic prescriptivity that bothers Mackie and others. The first problem that such eliminativists find with values is that the identification of a value in an option provides a justifying reason, other things being equal, for concluding that the option is right or, if rightness is the value in question, for choosing the option. There is an inferential, albeit defeasible, linkage between the ascription of other values to an option and the ascription of rightness and between the ascription of rightness and the choice of that option. Or so it is, at any rate, according to people's ordinary practices. As my reason for judging that q may be that p and that if p then q, so my reason for choosing an option may be that it is right and my reason for judging that it is right may be that it is the only fair choice, or the only loyal choice, or whatever. Values are inherently reason-giving; they are, to stick with Mackie's terminology, intrinsic justifiers.

If the first problem that eliminativists associate with the intrinsic prescriptivity of value is its capacity to provide justificatory reason for choice, the second problem is its capacity to provide motivational reason. Not only do we generally assume that values can provide grounds of justification, we also conduct ethical conversation on the assumption that if someone sees a certain value in one or another option, then they will generally tend to choose that option. We assume that there is an intimate, not merely inductive, association between evaluation and desire. Holding by a positive evaluative belief goes naturally with attraction, holding by a negative one with aversion. The linkage holds most saliently at the level of *pro tanto* evaluation, for we expect that anything that is thought in a certain regard desirable will tend to be desired under that aspect. But we also generally expect a linkage between the option that is finally judged to be right and the option that is effectively desired or preferred. If either linkage fails, then we think that there must be a special explanation: say, an explanation by reference to weakness of will or some such form of practical unreason.[52]

It may seem that the motivational problem is not really distinct from the justificatory one. There is no parallel problem, after all, about how the beliefs in certain premises are noninductively associated with a belief in the conclusion. But the parallel between the theoretical and practical cases is only partial. For by many lights the beliefs in certain premises are not really distinct from the belief in any conclusion that they more or less immediately support. The existence conditions for the beliefs in the premises require the presence of the belief in the conclusion; or if the existence conditions do not require the presence of that belief, the conditions under which someone counts as properly and rationally believing in the premises do. But by most lights any beliefs, even beliefs that are evaluative in nature, are separated by a gulf from desire. Beliefs are ways of registering what is the case and, being of a receptive or passive character, are bound to be distinct from something as action-centered as a desire or disposition to choose.[53]

The distinction between the two problems of queerness comes out in the fact that they each have a distinct Humean origin. The first problem is that if there were objective values, then there would be no is-ought gap: facts about values would entail oughts. The second problem is that if there were objective values, then beliefs and desires would not be distinct existences: the belief that an option is valuable in some way would be associated in more than an inductive fashion with a desire for that option; reason would sometimes be the master, not the slave, of the passions.

Moral Functionalism

In order to combat these arguments, I first need to set out a positive view of the content and character of ethical judgments. The only way of establishing that ontological objectivity is proof against the arguments is to show that there is a plausible, semantically objectivist construal of ethical assertions such that no one can complain on either count of queerness about the values and disvalues countenanced: no one can say that the entities in question are too queer to be taken seriously. My own favored position on the character and content of ethical judgments is moral or ethical functionalism.[54] I will describe and defend this view in outline before coming back to Mackie's two arguments.

The first thing to say in introduction to moral functionalism is that it is a generalization of a better-known position that is sometimes described as moral dispositionalism.[55] Think of the way we learn to use a color term like "red" of things that are disposed to look red to normal observers in normal conditions. Moral dispositionalism argues, in parallel, that we learn to use a value term like "desirable" of things that are disposed to look attractive under specifications that also require a normal and even ideal perspective: in this case, one characterized by the absence of bias and partisanship, a unified and coherent set of desires, full and vivid information about alternatives and consequences, and the like. The term picks out the property that plays or realizes the dispositional role of making things look attractive under relevant conditions, as "red" picks out the property that plays or realizes the dispositional role of making things look red in normal circumstances. (Or so at least I shall assume: I put aside, as orthogonal to my discussion, the possibility of taking the term to pick out the higher-order property of having a property that makes things look suitably attractive: that is, of taking the term to refer to the role-property, not the realizer-property.)

Moral functionalism holds that a value term like "desirable" refers, not to the realizer of a simple dispositional role – not to the property that makes things look attractive under certain conditions – but to the realizer of a more encompassing role. That is the sense in which it generalizes dispositionalism. It holds that a term like "desirable" refers to the property that not only makes things look attractive under certain conditions but that also satisfies a number of other connections.[56] What sorts of other connections? Briefly, those that prove to be taken for granted – and it may not be immediately clear what these are – among people who understand the word.

Consider the range of ethical terms that stretch from thick terms like "fair" and "generous" and "sympathetic" to terms like "ought" and "should" and "right" and that include also terms like "praise" and "blame" and "justify." When we come to master any such term, when we come to understand its meaning and its reference – assuming that we agree in the meaning and reference assigned – we do so in virtue of coming to accept certain shared working assumptions. We come to share assumptions about the sorts of things that are fair or right or praiseworthy, for example; about the sorts of connections that hold between the properties that these terms pick out; and about the sorts of responses we expect in people who come to assign such properties to the options they contemplate.

According to moral functionalism, these shared assumptions will guide us in our usage of the terms, will enable us to use the terms to a communicative purpose, and will provide us with a common basis on which to debate differences in particular assessments. In judging that an option is fair I will be influenced by the fact that it is importantly similar to certain paradigm cases of fairness, that it appeals to me as soon as I adopt an impartial, detached stance on the alternatives, that it thereby presents itself as a candidate for being the right thing to choose, and so on. In saying that it is fair I will communicate to others who understand the word that the option has the presumptively unique property that makes it look similar to certain paradigms, that makes it impartially appealing, that gives grounds for regarding it as the right option to choose, and the like. And in going on to argue with you the case for its being fair I will draw on such shared assumptions about the marks of fairness – or I may work my way toward a shared revision of those assumptions – trying to show that it does indeed have those marks.

The moral functionalist picture is that each of the terms in our shared moral vocabulary – and I am continuing to assume that this is shared – picks out a presumptively unique property by the fact of that property's satisfying the sorts of working assumptions mentioned. The term picks out that property that realizes the role described in those assumptions. The role may be causal, as in the expectation that something that is fair will arouse the desire of the impartial. Or the role may be inferential, as in the expectation that something that is fair will be a candidate for being the right choice.

The terms in our moral vocabulary will not pick out corresponding role-playing properties one by one, of course, in an atomistic fashion. If the functionalist picture is to be plausible, then it must involve the assumption that moral terms are networked with one another.[57] I learn the meaning of "fair" by seeing the connections of the property, not just with paradigms, but also with the properties picked out by other moral terms: with rightness, as in learning that fairness is a reason why something may be right; with politeness, as in learning that fairness is a more important rightness-maker than politeness; with impartiality, as in learning that impartial people tend to desire fair outcomes; with justification, as in learning that the fairness of an option chosen may enable me to justify myself to others in making that choice; and so on. And if I learn the meaning of "fair" by seeing the connections between fairness and the properties picked out by other moral terms, then I at the same time learn the meanings of those other terms by seeing the connections of the properties they pick out with one another. Mastering the vocabulary of morality has to be a holistic matter; it has to involve easing oneself simultaneously into the meanings of a whole range of terms, not building up an understanding of those terms one by one. In learning the terms, to invoke a Wittgensteinian phrase, light dawns slowly over the whole.

We can sum up these comments by saying that according to moral functionalism mastering a shared moral vocabulary amounts to endorsing a shared moral theory: a shared view of how moral properties connect with one another and with certain nonmoral properties. Moral functionalism amounts to a theory-theory of moral vocabulary: a theory according to which competence in moral reasoning itself involves commitment to a theory. Moral reasoners are, inevitably, moral theorists.

But it would be quite misleading to complete the exposition of moral functionalism at this point. For there are three distinctive claims that it will maintain in regard to the shared moral theory that it imputes to ordinary folk. And it is important that we understand these before we return to Mackie's arguments against ethical objectivism. The claims are, respectively, that the theory ascribed to participants in moral discourse is an evolving theory, that it is a modest theory, and, perhaps most important of all, that it is a practice-based or practical theory.

An Evolving Theory

The theory ascribed to ordinary people by moral functionalism is evolving or developmental or dynamic in character. While ethical debate starts from the assumption that participants share enough of a background theory to be able to talk to one another – they do not pass one another in the night, each pursuing quite different questions – still there is always a possibility, in the course of the debate, that one or more of them will come to amend the theory from which they began: the theory that debate forces them to articulate. That theory is never fixed in finished form; it is never proof against revision. On the contrary, ethical debate is inherently and systematically open to the possibility of theoretical reform.

The reason that the background theory espoused in moral debate is evolving in this way is that ethical reasoning proceeds via what John Rawls[58] has described as the method of reflective equilibrium. According to Rawls, ethical reasoning always involves moving to and fro between background moral theory and foreground moral judgments in the search for an equilibrium: in particular, an equilibrium that can be shared among the different people who are party to the debate.[59] The idea is that any commitment or consensus in moral theory is always subject to destabilization as new issues for moral adjudication come on the agenda or indeed as old issues return to that agenda. Maybe it was taken for granted that such and such a general connection characterizes a certain moral property but if the assumption leads to moral judgments that prove difficult to endorse then it is liable to be amended in the search for a better equilibrium of theory and judgment.

It should not be surprising that the moral theory that permeates ethical reasoning and discussion has this provisional and evolving character. The purpose of ethical debate is to resolve live and open issues and it would be amazing if the theory that it presupposes – the theory that it has to presuppose if the terms of the debate are to enjoy an established meaning and reference – was immune to reconsideration. In this respect folk moral theory contrasts sharply with the folk psychological theory that is often said to shape our usage of terms that bear on perceptions and sensations, memories and expectations, judgments and beliefs, intentions and desires, and so on. While that folk psychology may have to be revised in order to be squared with new discoveries in cognitive and neural science, and even perhaps with novel and challenging cultures, it is not systematically exposed to reasons for reconsideration in the same fashion as our folk moral views.

A Modest Theory

The second thing to note about the moral theory that functionalism ascribes to ordinary folk is that it is modest in character. It does not commit the folk to the reality of values and disvalues that are radically discontinuous with the sorts of realities countenanced in common sense and in natural science. The posits of folk moral theory, so it turns out, can be seen as familiar, even humdrum in nature.

For all that we have said up to this point, admittedly, the properties picked out by moral terms – the properties that play the requisite moral roles – might be of just about any character. But as a matter of fact the moral theory counte-nanced by the folk includes a principle that severely constrains the character they can have. In particular, the principle constrains the character of those properties in a manner that ensures the modesty of folk moral theory.

According to this principle, if two items differ in regard to a moral or more generally an evaluative property, then they also differ in a purely descriptive way. We ordinary folk endorse that presumption in countenancing the chal-lenge to back up any evaluative discrimination – any discrimination to the effect that this is right and that is wrong, for example, this is just and that is unjust, he is virtuous and she unvirtuous – with a discrimination of a purely descriptive kind. Our legitimating that sort of challenge means that by our lights no evaluative difference is possible without a descriptive difference. No evaluative difference is possible even between whole possible worlds without some descriptive difference in those worlds.[60] Evaluative specifications, as it is now often put, supervene on descriptive specifications.

This supervenience of the evaluative on the descriptive has dramatic im-plications for the nature of those properties that play moral-theoretical roles. Any property that we identify as the realizer of such a role – the property that we identify as rightness, or fairness, or impartiality, for example – must be descriptively specifiable. There must be a descriptive way of marking every difference that the presence of such a property makes. And so, in principle, there must be a descriptive mode of picking out all and only the bearers of the property; the property must have a descriptive character.

What makes a specification evaluative, it may be asked, what descriptive? I assume that an evaluative specification, but not a descriptive specification, will connect with presumptions about justification and the like. Thus it will be true according to those presumptions that any evaluatively specified property, taken as such, can play a justificatory sort of role whereas nothing of the kind will be true according to the presumptions in relation to descriptively specified properties.[61]

Folk moral theory is modest, then, in the sense that the properties to which it is committed are all taken to be capable of descriptive specification. They are capable of specification in terms that are of a kind with the terms from common sense and natural science in which we describe the world around us. There is nothing mysterious, say, nothing intrinsically evaluative, about such proper-ties; they are ontologically run-of-the-mill. What is the property of rightness, for example? It is that descriptive property – though we have no prospect of giving its descriptive specification – that plays the corresponding role in our folk moral theory. It is that descriptively specifiable property that makes an option imperative for the agent, that makes any similar option imperative for any similar agent, that is instantiated in virtue of such and such values, and that serves to make an option unobjectionable, to attract agents who are not weak of will, to connect reliably with virtue, and so on.

In discussing the requirements for ontological objectivism I said that while objectivists do not have to think that values are transcendent entities, they must think that values are such as to vindicate the common assumption that we approve of things because they have certain values, not the other way around.[62] Not only must values be capable of descriptive specification, as is easily granted under the moral-functionalist picture, it is also necessary that the descriptive character of the values enable us to uphold this assumption.

What it is in descriptive terms that makes an option kind or cruel, then, must be independent of our approving or disapproving of such an option; it must not consist in the fact of eliciting approval or disapproval, as under a subjectivist view. And what it is that makes the option kind or cruel must be something that can register with us and lead us to approve or disapprove of the option. It must be a descriptive property, like the property that leads us to describe something as red or yellow, that is sufficiently unified and salient to make an impact upon us.

To require that this is so, however, is not to compromise in any serious way the modesty of the theory that functionalism ascribes to participants in moral discourse. For on the most intuitive reading of ethical discourse, as already noted, we participants do not intend just to record the fact that we approve or disapprove when we make ethical evaluations; we intend to ascribe independent properties to the things evaluated. And it is hard to see how we could target those properties semantically – how we could pick them out by the use of terms like "kind" and "cruel," or "right" and "wrong"[63] – if they were not sufficiently unified or salient to make an impact upon us.[64]

A Practical Theory

The third and last feature to notice about the participant theory ascribed by moral functionalism is that it is practice-based or practical in character; or, more exactly, that the mode in which ordinary folk believe it is practice-based or practical.[65] Two examples will make clear the sort of thing that I have in mind.

Consider the way that we reason in accordance with *modus ponens* or *modus tollens* in being disposed, whenever we think that all As are Bs, to argue our way from A to B; from not B to not A; from not A to possibly B, possibly not B; and from B to possibly A, possibly not A. We may instantiate those dispositions without having the logician's ability to formulate the principle in question, and without even being aware that there is a principle. We certainly believe the principle but we do not believe it in intellectual or judgmental mode. And yet neither do we believe it just in the sense of behaving as if it were true, for we believe all necessary truths, and so all necessary principles of reasoning in this way, even ones that have no such presence in our ratiocinative dispositions.[66] We believe the principle, so I shall say, in a practice-based or practical manner.

Consider again the way that we reason when we allow appearances of a color like red to dictate a judgment that things are red, at least when we have no evidence of perceptual abnormality; and when we allow the judgment that things are red to generate an expectation that, at least in the absence of abnormalities, they will look red. We may not be able to formulate the principle of reasoning according to which something is red if and only if it looks red to normal observers in normal conditions. We may not even have the word "normal" at our disposal. As used by theorists, "normal" observers and conditions may refer to such observers and conditions as are of a kind with those that pass muster in our practice of resolving discrepancies across time and people by discounting some of the discrepant responses. Thus we do not believe the principle in a judgmental way. As in the other case, however, neither do we believe it just in a behavioral manner: just in the sense of behaving as if it were true. We believe it in a practice-based or practical way.

These forms of practical belief in a principle of reasoning display the following characteristics. We focus on instances of the reasoning as items of attention. We are disposed, at least when we are relatively clear-minded, to treat just such instances as valid: that is, we are disposed to judge that the premises support the conclusion. And we can be said to believe in a case-by-case way of those instances that they are valid; we can be said to believe the principle that unifies the instances *in sensu diviso,* though not *in sensu composito.*[67] The practical belief makes itself felt in the fact that once we come to understand a sentence that formulates the principle, then we are in a position to see that our reasoning habits already committed us to that principle; we can see that we held by it even prior to having words in which to express it.

The theory that functionalism ascribes to participants in moral disourse is naturally represented as a matter of practical, not of judgmental, belief. How do people come to believe that there are paradigms of fairness: say, depending on context, a principle of equal allocation or a principle like "I cut, you choose"? Not necessarily by explicitly registering that such examples are paradigms but simply by treating them as more or less nonnegotiable instances. How do they come to hold that fairness is a *pro tanto* reason for thinking an option is the right one to choose? Not necessarily by spelling out that principle of inference but simply by being disposed to treat fairness, other things being equal, as a reason for ascribing rightness. How do they come to hold that fairness is descriptively supervenient? Not necessarily by giving their assent to a principle of supervenience but simply by being disposed to reason from the claim that two or more options differ in fairness to the conclusion that there is some descriptive difference between them. How do they subscribe to the claim that fairness makes an option attractive, at least for those who see things clearly and fully and are not subject to bias or ennui or any such malaise:[68] at least for those who are ideally situated? Not necessarily by adverting to that connection in so many words: they may not even have words available to describe what is required. Simply by treating attractiveness in the apparent absence of nonideal factors as a reason for predicating fairness and by expecting that of which fairness is predicated to prove attractive in the absence of those factors.

The functionalist idea, then, is that competence in moral vocabulary amounts to sharing in a lived theory – a *Lebenstheorie* – that shows up only occasionally in explicit, judgmental remarks. The theory permeates the patterns of perceptual and judgmental reasoning, even the patterns of motivation and attraction, that go with being able to tell fair from biased, kind from cruel, right from wrong and with being able to debate with others, and indeed with oneself, about how this or that option should be ethically characterized. The mode of existence of the theory is decidedly nonintellectual. It lives in the habits of reason, in the habits of perception and even in the habits of the heart.

In describing the moral theory postulated by functionalism I have had to speak of the nonideal factors that may affect the judgment of fairness or rightness or, more generally, of desirability in any regard. But how should we define nonideal factors? They cannot be defined, on pain of vacuity, just as those factors that block the inference from attractive to desirable. But neither can nonideal factors be defined just by a list of items, as when we are told that bias and passion and ennui and lack of this or that sort of information are all nonideal. For the list of nonideal factors in the case of moral perception, like the list of nonideal factors in the case of color perception, is open in principle to further addition. Nonideal factors may be identified as factors of a kind that the list illustrates but they cannot be exhausted by any available list. Thus the question remains as to how that kind is to be specified.

The best account of the kind in question drives us back to people's natural habits and practices in negotiating questions of desirability. I call it an "ethocentric" account, because the Greek word "ethos" can mean either habit or practice. The account becomes available, even salient, once we recognize that ordinary people believe the moral theory that functionalism ascribes to them, only in a practice-based or practical mode.

Suppose that in comparing judgments on what is desirable in this or that way, people are guided in part by their own desiderative inclinations or lack of them: this, in the way that they are guided by their color sensations, or the lack of such sensations, in debating about matters of color. Suppose that they back away from the judgmental inclinations associated with their desire or lack of desire – they suspend the tendency to describe the apparently attractive as genuinely attractive, the apparently nonattractive as genuinely nonattractive – when their desires come apart, whether as between persons or times: this, in the way that they question their color sensations when their sensations come apart. And suppose, finally, that they seek the resolution of such discrepancy and the determination of what is genuinely attractive – of what is desirable – by looking on one or the other side for factors that would suggest that the desire or lack of desire in that quarter signifies nothing: it is the product of irrelevant factors akin to the perturbations that may affect color sensation and is not a reliable index of something's being desirable or nondesirable.

These suppositions fit naturally with the sort of moral dispositionalism that functionalism generalizes, and they correspond with how ordinary people actually behave in discussing matters of desirability, whether with themselves or others. I shall assume, then, that they are fulfilled. People think of any variety of desirability, so the suppositions suggest, as a property that will generally show up in the way in which it makes things reliably attractive at different times and to different individuals. Where attractions come apart, then, people will look for a compelling basis on which to dismiss one or more of the desiderative responses. They will look for a noncollusive, objectively motivated basis for resolving the question as to whether a certain desirable property is or is not present.

Assuming the fulfillment of the suppositions described, we can offer a ready and plausible account of nonideal factors.[69] We can identify them as factors such that, at least among people who are not otherwise divided, their identification as grounds for dismissing discrepant responses would maximize noncollusive agreement on what is desirable, and what not. This definition assumes that the practices ascribed to people – the practices that involve taking certain desires as an index of a presumptive desirability – are sound. Nonideal factors, according to the definition, are those influences that a maximally satisfactory implementation of the practices would identify as grounds for dismissing the presence or the absence of a particular desire as an index of the presence or the absence of a corresponding desirable property.

This simple account avoids the problems with the approaches that resort to a whatever-it-takes line or to a finite list of examples. It is not definitionally vacuous, in the manner of the first approach, yet unlike the second approach, it manages to be open-ended. We are put in a position where it can be a matter of discovery that nonideal factors come into play with an interested as distinct from a disinterested perspective, an uninformed as distinct from a better-informed standpoint, a reflective as distinct from a passionate point of view. As we discover that color does not show up reliably in sodium lighting, so we discover that no one is a reliable judge in their own case. And so on.

Apart from enabling us theorists to identify and itemize nonideal factors, the ethocentric account also gives us a plausible account of how such factors will present themselves to people in the practice of moral judgment. Resolving this or that discrepancy, and thereby coming to a mind on how things really are in respect of desirability, people will see some such factors as obstacles or limitations that undermine the significance of their desires or nondesires as indices of desirability; they will see them, in a normative light, as things that get in the way of perceiving what is desirable. And generalizing from some such examples, they can see nonideal factors in general – if they ever give them a name – as those that are of a kind with the examples. The same sort of story that must apply in the color case will apply equally well here.

Against the Arguments from Queerness

We may return at last to Mackie's argument against ontological objectivism about ethics. The argument divides into an argument from the justificatory queerness of values and an argument from their motivational queerness. The justificatory argument goes as follows.

1. Objective values would have to be intrinsic justifiers.
2. No natural properties could serve in this role.
3. Therefore there are no values in the natural world.

I accept the first premise of this argument, believing that values are primarily distinguished by the ways in which they provide justificatory reason, other things being equal, for this or that judgment of rightness, or this or that actual choice. But I reject the second premise and so find the overall argument unsound. Our discussion of moral functionalism shows that certain natural properties can serve in the required role, where properties are understood as properties of the sort that are countenanced in common sense and in science.

What our discussion of functionalism shows, more precisely, is that there is a sense of "intrinsic justifier" such that natural properties can serve in an intrinsically justificatory role. If a natural property is identified as the bearer of a moral-theoretical role such as that which is ascribed to fairness, then it is a priori that any option that is distinguished by having that property, taken as such – taken under its role-playing aspect – will, other things equal, be the right option to choose and will represent the justified choice. We do not know which descriptive or natural property plays the fairness role, not knowing enough about the actual world. But no matter how the actual world is, and no matter which property plays the fairness role, fairness is guaranteed to connect with rightness. The way in which the term "fair" is mastered – the network of presumptions that govern its usage – ensures that an option that is distinguished by its fairness will, when other things are equal, be the right option to take. In that sense there will be an a priori connection between fairness – fairness, when other things are equal – and rightness.[70]

The fact that there is an a priori connection of this kind between one or another moral property and justifiability shows that such properties can serve as intrinsic justifiers. If Mackie overlooked that possibility, I suspect that the reason is that he focused on moral properties in themselves, not under their aspect as deservers of the names given them in moral discourse. He did not see that no matter how morally inert a natural property is in itself, it can serve, qua realizer of a moral role, in a justificatory part.

Mackie's argument from motivational queerness runs on roughly parallel lines to the argument from justificatory queerness.

1. Objective values would have to be such that ascribing them is noninductively associated with the presence of a corresponding desire.
2. Natural properties are such that ascribing them cannot be noninductively associated with the presence of a corresponding desire.
3. Therefore there are no objective values in the natural world.

My complaint about this argument, like my complaint about the argument from justificatory queerness, is that the second premise is false. As I assume that values are intrinsic justifiers of choice, so I am happy to assume that there is a noninductive association between the ascription of *pro tanto* or final value to an option and the presence of a corresponding qualified or unqualified desire. But as I think that certain natural properties, taken as fulfilling a suitable role, can be intrinsic justifiers, so I believe that the ascription of such natural properties can be noninductively associated with the presence of desire.

As a generalized version of moral dispositionalism, functionalism assumes that folk theory posits a connection between something's being desirable and its looking attractive, at least under conditions where nonideal factors are absent; we discussed this above. According to folk theory, what it is to be desirable is, in part, to be ideally attractive in this way. When someone judges that an option is desirable, then, they imply that it is such that they would desire it — they would desire it, taking it as an option for their actual self and situation[71] — were they free of such obstacles and limitations; they imply that it is the genuinely or ideally attractive option.

Suppose now that I come to judge that an option is desirable — or indeed not desirable — by partial reliance on the principle that links what is attractive in situations where nothing is amiss to what is desirable. Assuming that I believe that principle in practical mode, then, I will ordinarily form the judgment that an option is desirable through finding it attractive — through coming to desire it — in circumstances where nothing seems, rightly or wrongly, to be amiss: in circumstances where I do not believe that any nonideal factor is at work.[72] And that means in turn that my evaluative judgments will generally have a desiderative character. The way in which the judgments are maintained will involve the presence of desires. And so the acts or states of judgment will not leave me cold. They will be noninductively associated with the presence of corresponding desires.[73]

The argument from the motivational queerness of values assumes that as natural properties cannot be intrinsic justifiers, so the ascription of a natural property cannot be noninductively associated with the presence of a corresponding desire. But that premise in the argument is false, as this discussion of the ascription of desirability reveals. Thus the argument from motivational queerness offers no more persuasive a case for ethical eliminativism than did the argument from justificatory queerness. Ontological objectivism about ethical values is not as vulnerable to criticism as Mackie and other eliminativists have assumed.

One concluding remark to this defense of ontological objectivism. Even if it is not vulnerable to eliminativist objections, ontological objectivism may still be false. The reality of objective values – and indeed disvalues – will be established to the extent that the practices of ordinary moral reasoners and discussants are vindicated. But it could prove that those practices break down. People might fail to identify agreed sources of perturbation and limitation, for example, and might fail to discriminate any single set of conditions that are favorable for the identification of value. Or an individual person might fail in that way over time. The only possible conclusion, then, would be that there are no values, or at least no complete set of values, of the kind adumbrated in ethical discourse. Indeed we might expect that conclusion to surface in ordinary practice, with a developing recognition of no-fault disagreements and with a drift away from seeing evaluations as assertoric and truth-conditional.[74]

The upshot is that if we are to be ontological objectivists, if we are to hold that there are properties available to play the roles distinguished in folk moral theory, then our objectivism has to have a provisional character. We do not know what will emerge in the course of ethical discourse, any more than we know what will emerge in the course of scientific. We do not know whether that discourse will prove to be a fruitful conversational program or even whether it will sustain a fruitful one-person conversation across time. We may judge that so far the discourse is doing well and that its success bears witness to the reality of values, conceived in a functionalist way. But we should recognize that the issue of whether there really are values remains *sub judice:* it remains to be determined by the future career of ethical argument.[75]

C. Justificatory Objectivism

I have tried to show why semantic and ontological objectivism about ethical values represents a plausible and coherent position: one that is not vulnerable to arguments from no-fault disagreement or from the justificatory or motivational queeress of values. I have done this, in particular, from within a functionalist account of what positing and ascribing values involves. This semantic-cum-ontological objectivism represents a form of moral realism, as that term is now generally used.[76]

The objectivism that I sketched earlier, however, and the objectivism that I want to maintain here, amounts to more than just a realist position about ethical values. It also involves the claim that there is one and only one set of values on the basis of which ethical justification can be secured. It involves the rejection of relativism as well as the rejection of expressivism and eliminativism.

I distinguished two coherent forms of ethical relativism, one of which I described as idiolectical, the other as indexical. Idiolectical relativism holds that despite appearances – despite appearances of synonymy or trans-latability – different individuals or groups do not use moral terms with the same meanings in order to frame their ethical judgments; each has a more or less distinctive idiolect. Indexical relativism holds that they do use such terms with the same meanings but that they do not use them to express the same contents; the expressions that articulate their fundamental values include in-dexical terms like "I" or "we" and have different interpretations in different mouths.

In discussing expressivism and eliminativism I argued, first, that each doctrine ran against common presumptions and, second, that the main sort of argument used in its defense was not persuasive. In discussing relativism I will take a more direct approach. With relativism, or at least with indexical relativ-ism, there is less profit in discussing where the onus of proof lies; and equally, in the space available, there is less prospect of providing an adequate response to the many arguments invoked in its defense.[77]

Against Idiolectical Relativism

Why would anyone be an idiolectical relativist, arguing that even within the same linguistic community what people mean by the word "right," to take the most central moral term, may differ from individual to individual, or group to group? The obvious answer is that such a difference of meaning would account for the extensive divergence in the use of the word "right." It would cease to give that divergence the aspect of a disagreement, of course – and indeed it would give the lie to people's sense of disagreeing with one another – but it would have the benefit of restoring conversational peace. It would reconcile people to one another, presenting what looked like substantial disagreements as merely terminological differences.

Assume that a number of people – at the limit this may be the same person at different times – use a term like "right" with the same meaning and reference. What are the factors that serve to determine that meaning and reference? According to the moral functionalism by which I hold, the things that those who use the term believe in common about its actual and possible instances are the things that they take for granted, though perhaps without thinking much about them and perhaps without being able to spell them out linguistically. The candidates for fixing meaning are, in a word, their shared working assumptions about right options, where many of those assumptions may have the status of practical, not judgmental, beliefs. They are things to which people commit themselves so far as they treat certain examples as paradigms of rightness, for example, so far as they recognize certain constraints on how to argue for the rightness of an option, so far as they give certain grounds in support of claims of rightness, and so far as they countenance certain sorts of challenges to those claims.

Idiolectical relativists hold that the working presumptions surrounding a term like "right" vary from person to person, or group to group; the term is answerable in those different contexts of usage to different background principles. They need not say that as a matter of fact this difference in meaning is transparent to participants in moral discourse. They may hold that while everyone takes certain principles for granted in learning to apply the term "right," and while most of those principles are common property, that is not a stable dispensation.

According to this instability claim, what people will find when they reflect on those principles and their implications for particular cases – what they will find when they look for a reflective equilibrium between their principles and the particular judgments that attract them – is that they differ in which principles they are disposed to treat as nonnegotiable: they differ in which principles they authorize as a priori. There may be a loose set of presumptions from which people all start in learning the use of "right" and other moral terms, then, but the theory adumbrated in the ways in which they come to apply those terms is liable to vary between individuals or groups. And as the theory varies, so too will the meaning. It will transpire that the individuals or groups use the term "right," and perhaps other terms too, with different senses. It will transpire that much moral discourse is vitiated by ambiguity.

While it is certainly coherent, I do not think that this form of relativism is very plausible. There are two grounds of objection, one a general consideration against idiolectical relativism, the other a specific objection to relativism about rightness and other value properties.

As a general position, idiolectical relativism supposes that we are each guided in our usage of relevant terms by presumptions that we individually own: by presumptions that represent a sort of private property. It is this supposition that leaves room for the discovery – and the distinctively relativist claim – that, as it turns out, those guiding presumptions differ between individuals or groups. The lesson of ethical debate, so the relativist claim goes, is that the things that we treat as nonnegotiable and a priori in the domain of the relevant terms vary from person to person or at least from subculture to subculture. We each use the same terms, or we each use what are regarded as translational counterparts, but we do not use them with the same meanings and we do not use them to express the same belief contents.

The general problem that I find with this sort of idiolectical relativism is that it fails to allow for the extent to which we treat one another as more or less equal authorities, at least outside realms of scientific expertise, in debating about any area of discourse.[78] If we treated our guiding presumptions in the use of any term as private property, then there is no obvious reason why we should balk at discrepancy with how others apply the word and why we should work at seeking to explain away the difference; there is no reason why we should authorize one another, holding open the possibility that it is us and not others who are mistaken. If our words are answerable only to our own, private presumptions, then why not treat discrepancies of application across individuals as signs of a difference in the guiding presumptions: signs of a difference in meaning?

I believe that the fact of conversational authorization argues for quite a different model from the one assumed by idiolectical relativists. This does not suppose that we each use our words under the guidance of private presumptions and then look to see if, as an empirical, contingent matter, others use the words in the same way. The model is that we each use our words on the assumption that there are guiding presumptions available in common to different people – they are common, not private, property – and that if the terms have the meaning and reference on which we presume then disagreements with others must be resoluble in principle. The condition on which the terms will prove to have their apparent meaning and their presumed reference – the condition on which ordinary users will treat the terms as possessed of such regular semantic credentials – is that disagreements between people in how the terms are applied never come to seem inherently irresoluble. Whatever disagreements remain in practice, after the best efforts at discussion, look from each side to be explicable by reference to different bodies of information or insight, or different perturbing factors, or something of that kind. People may have recourse, eventually, to a hypothesis of different, idiolectical meanings; but that will be a last recourse that they access only with reluctance.

My general problem with idiolectical relativism is that it fails to take account of the extent to which people authorize one another in conversation and give sustenance to this model of communication. Even in translation, when we seek to get in contact with those from a different linguistic community, the model of achieving understanding is that we can each make it a matter of shared belief that the translational counterparts identified are answerable to common presumptions. If a disagreement in usage appears between us, that is not treated as evidence in the first place of a translational mistake, but as something that should lend itself to resolution, or to the explanation of non-resolution, in the ordinary manner.

Where this first objection to idiolectical relativism is general in character, my second objection bears on idiolectical relativism about ethics in particular. Consistently with the line just argued, people in different subcultures or linguistic communities may agree that with a certain term or a certain set of translational counterparts there really is a difference – ideally, an independently intelligible difference – in the background presumptions to which they hold it answerable and that, at least in a limited range of cases, this makes for no-fault disagreements about application. One group uses "red" to cover a range that overlaps into a range for which the other group uses "orange." Or whatever. But there is a special difficulty about imagining that this happens in any large measure with the term "right" or with other moral terms; and that is my second objection to idiolectical relativism.

The special difficulty is that whereas a term like "red" is used only for purposes of discrimination and categorization, "right" and other moral terms are used for the purpose of assessment and justification. Were people to agree across different subcultures – or, by extension, across different linguistic communities – that "right" meant something different in each context then that would make for a major difficulty. It would mean that they could not begin to argue with one another about matters of justification. It would mean that they could not hope to use the term for the purpose for which it is primarily designed.

With a term like "right" perhaps the most important working presumption, upheld on all sides, is that if the parties in a particular debate appear to be using the term in accordance with different presumptions, then something has to change. Let the term be guided by different presumptions, let the term be declared systematically ambiguous, and it will cease to serve its primary role. Thus the condition on which the term should survive in our conversations – the condition on which we should remain committed to ethical discussions – is that we can succeed in avoiding a declaration of ambiguity.

It may be this point that influenced W. B. Gallie in his introduction of the notion of an essentially contested concept.[79] Gallie noticed that with a wide range of terms – evaluative terms, in particular – people appear unwilling to reconcile their differences by each agreeing that they use the terms in different, more or less idiolectical senses. They each go on claiming that in the one and only proper sense of the term, what they hold is true and what their opponents say is false; they are each unwilling to let the term go, allowing it to subdivide into different disambiguations. In maintaining that the purpose served by a term like "right" rules out reconciliation by disambiguation, I am saying in effect that it is an essentially contested concept.

The two objections mentioned should serve, I think, to undermine the attractions of the idiolectical form of ethical relativism. Perhaps such relativism holds out the prospect of peace, allowing the parties in ethical debate to think that they are each right and that only terminological differences are getting in the way. But the peace that is adumbrated is the peace of the sepulchre: the peace that comes with the expiry, not the consummation, of ethical debate.

Finally, however, a concession. Consistently with idiolectical relativism being unsound, what may indeed happen in ethical discourse is that certain limited indeterminacies are identified and insulated. While people may use moral terms with the same meaning and reference, they may use them in such a way that for certain limited cases there is no fact of the matter as to what is right and what is wrong; that may be essentially indeterminate. Being committed to the objectivity of moral theory in all of the senses explained so far is consistent with acknowledging this limited indeterminacy. It is consistent with thinking that commitment to a version of the folk moral theory does not necessarily provide one with a complete ordering of the options that come up for decision.

Suppose that people all agree on the rightness-making power of fairness and kindness, for example, and on the other connections that we generally expect fairness and kindness and indeed rightness to satisfy. It may be, for all that agreement, that they are inclined to assign different degrees of right-making power to fairness and kindness. Some weight fairness very heavily in relation to kindness, others weight it less heavily – perhaps individuals differ between times – and the difference shows up in the different judgments of rightness that they are individually disposed to make of certain hypothetical, maybe even of certain actual, choices.

This sort of possibility can be internalized in people's ordinary practices, with the recognition that there is no fact of the matter as to what is right in the cases where their weighting inclinations lead them to differ. People may make a working presumption of the fact that their weighting inclinations with properties like fairness and kindness come apart at the margins and they may let that impact on the intended reference of "right" and indeed also of "fair" and "kind." The term "right" will not refer to the property that goes with any one individual's judgmental dispositions, even in the absence of nonideal factors; it will not go idiolectical. The term will be used to refer to what the different properties targeted in people's dispositions have in common; it will be used to refer, not to any unique property, but to the set of properties that coincide in those cases, and only those cases, where agreement is accessible.

On this account, then, "right" will have a marginal indeterminacy akin to the more systematic indeterminacy of vague terms like "bald" or "thin" or "handsome." Different subjects will have marginally different tendencies to precisify the term and make judgments of rightness in particular cases. And in those marginal cases where precisifications come apart, it will be indeterminate whether any of the relevant options is right or wrong: this, in the way in which it may be indeterminate whether someone is bald. There will be a fact of the matter as to whether an option is right or not right only in cases where precisifications converge.

This concession is important, because it shows how the rejection of idiolectical relativism can be squared with intuitions of indeterminacy that many will find compelling in the ethical realm.[80] But this is not the place to develop the implications of that concession, nor indeed to deal with the difficult issues to which it gives rise.[81] My ambition is to show how objectivism can be reasonably sustained, not to paint in the details of a plausible objectivistic outlook.

Against Indexical Relativism

Idiolectical relativism says that different individuals or groups use moral terms with different meanings and that evaluations, therefore, express different contents across those differences. Indexical relativism allows that all individuals and groups use relevant terms with the same meanings or with roughly the same meanings. But it argues nonetheless that in virtue of the indexicality of some of the terms used, people's fundamental evaluations can express different contents in the mouths of different speakers.

I shall not say much about indexical relativism in the analytical form in which it claims that certain evaluative terms are covertly indexical. According to analytical indexicalism what I often mean by "right" or any such term is "right-for-me," and what you mean is "right-for-you," so that we may be speaking at cross-purposes in debating whether something is right or not. I have been assuming throughout this chapter that any such approach is counterintuitively debunking of our ordinary usage. And the considerations raised against idiolectical relativism show why. The considerations about our mutually authorizing one another in evaluative conversation argue against any such indexical variation in the reference of "right" and the like, as they argue against any idiolectical variation in meaning. I return to the point later.

We are mainly concerned with indexical relativism in the normative form in which it claims, in nonconsequentialist vein, that the basic justifiers of people's choices may involve a self-reflexive reference. They may involve a reference to the preservation of the agent's own virtue, or the doing of their own contractual part in some arrangement, or the advancement of the interests of their own children or friends, or whatever.

I am committed to the rejection of such nonconsequentialism and what I will do here in defense of the commitment is to present a serious problem that faces any nonconsequentialist view.[82] As a consequentialist, I argue that when we try to identify the final, a priori presumptions about rightness – when we try to revise and regiment our received moral theory in this regard – we must recognize that the right option in any choice is the option that maximizes the expected realization of neutral values, where neutral values may include not just properties like fairness and kindness but also reflexive properties like that of parents looking after their children.[83] My argument will be that if we do not do this – if we espouse nonconsequentialism – then we shall find ourselves unable to give due weight to one of the most deeply seated presumptions that we make in moral reasoning: the principle that justifications should always be universalizable.[84] I shall assume that the universalizability constraint on justification is irresistible and I shall argue that nonconsequentialism cannot easily satisfy it.

The universalizability presumption holds that if two choice scenarios differ in regard only to particulars, then whatever option is right in one scenario, the counterpart option must be right in the other. If I face a choice between helping my friends or my country, and you face a choice between helping your friends and your country, and if the general features of our situations are indiscernible, then whatever is right for me, the corresponding option must be right for you. I cannot be so relatively important, nor you so unimportant, that the sort of thing that is right for me is not right for you. Nor can our friends or countries differ in importance in a way that would make for a difference in rightness. If the situations contrast only in matters of individual identity, not in any nonindividual or universal respects, then there can be no difference in matters of rightness. Any claim that it is right for individual A to help A's friends or to keep A's promises or whatever must be universalizable into a claim that applies to any individual of the relevant kind: any individual who is similar to A in relevant respects.

The tension between admitting universalizability and being a nonconsequentialist can be best brought out by means of an example. Suppose that nonconsequentialism is sound, so that the basic justifiers of choice include values that are relativized to different positions; they include agent-relative and group-relative values like the success of my country, the welfare of my children, the keeping of my promises, or the cultivation of my integrity. And suppose, to take a target case, that France's decision to test nuclear weapons in 1995 is to be justified in nonconsequentialist fashion by reference to such a group-relative value; that decision was defended by President Chirac, after all, on the grounds that it was in the higher interest of his country. What then might a nonconsequentialist President Chirac say, in response to the demand that he should be able to universalize the justification and show that it does not presuppose that his country is special?

One thing that he might say is that any nuclear power is permitted or obliged to test its weapons, subject to provisos that are allegedly met in the French case. But while this response would have the merit of being straightforward and nonchauvinistic – it does not treat France as special – it is not consistent with the assumption that the decision is justified in a nonconsequentialist way by a group-relative value. The response says that whatever consideration makes it right for France to test its nuclear weapons, that same consideration makes it right for any nuclear power – or at least any nuclear power that satisfies the provisos – to do so. It is a consideration that requires or permits all nuclear powers, and not just France, to test their weapons. But the sort of thing that would justify all nuclear powers in testing their weapons has to be neutral as between those who identify with France and those who identify with other countries. It has to be a consideration that by President Chirac's lights would not only justify France in testing its weapons but also justify any other country in doing so.

This response to the universalizability challenge, then, gives the game away to the opposition. In making the response, President Chirac would represent himself as committed to justifying choice by reference to neutral reasons or values and as believing that those considerations require or at least permit the testing of nuclear weapons. And he would suggest that if those reasons lead him to test France's nuclear weapons, and not anyone else's, that is just because he has the power of controlling nuclear tests only in relation to France. Suppose that he thinks there is a requirement involved, not just a permission. In this response to the universalizability challenge, then, he will imply that if he could best promote the testing of nuclear weapons by stopping France from testing its weapons – the scenario is unlikely but not impossible – then that is what he should do. He implies that he is the servant of the impersonal good.

Is there any other response that President Chirac might offer to the demand to show that his decision is universalizable? The question is a pressing one for nonconsequentialists, because if no such response can be identified, then the universalizability constraint is going to make their position hard to maintain. In the absence of an alternative response, it will seem that the universalizability constraint is inconsistent with the nonconsequentialist claim that the basic justifiers of choice may include nonneutral values.

But, as it turns out, there is another response that President Chirac might make to the universalizability challenge. He might say, not that it is right in his terms for any power to test its weapons, but rather that as it is right in his terms for France to test its weapons, so he is prepared to admit that it is right in the terms of other nuclear leaders to test the weapons that their individual countries possess. He might not endorse the universal claim that it is right for every nuclear power, or at least every power in France's position, to test its weapons. Rather he might defend the claim that for every nuclear power in France's position, it is going to be right in the terms of that power's leaders and citizens that it should test its weapons.

The sort of response envisaged here is the only alternative that I see to the response that plays into the hands of consequentialists. And the response can be readily generalized.

Take any particular claim that it is right for individual A to do something like helping their children, respecting the rights of those they deal with, or maintaining their integrity, where in each case the action advances a cause that falls particularly to them. Suppose that we challenge A, or A's champion, as to how far they are prepared to universalize this claim of rightness. One response will certainly be the familiar one that it is right for any agent, or any agent in similar circumstances, to try to advance their cause; this suggests that the rightness of A's $\emptyset$-ing is determined by something that equally determines the rightness of anyone's acting in the corresponding way and that it is determined therefore in the neutral, consequentialist manner. But there is also another response that will be available, in principle, in any such case.

This will be to say that for any X, where "X" varies over A and B and other possible agents, it is right-in-X's-terms for X to try to advance their cause. It may not be right, period, for A to advance their cause but, so it is suggested, that sense of rightness is irrelevant or nonexistent. The point is that it is right-in-A's-terms for A to try to advance their cause – it is A-right, as we may say – and the answer to the universalizability challenge is that for any X it is X-right

for them to try to advance their cause. As it is A-right for A to help their
children, to keep their promises, to maintain their integrity, or whatever, so it is
B-right for B, and C-right for C to take corresponding courses of action.

The first response to the universalizability challenge assumes that universalizability is to be understood in a neutral way, so far as it takes rightness to be
a property that is common to all perspectives. The second response rejects this
line, taking rightness itself, at least in certain contexts, to be a relativized
property. If universalizability is taken in the neutral way, so it will be argued, it
should be no surprise that taking up the challenge to universalize any judgment
of rightness will mean endorsing neutral reasons and going over to a consequentialist point of view. But if universalizability is itself taken in a relativized
way, so that X-rightness replaces rightness period, then it should equally be
no surprise that the challenge can be handled without recourse to consequentialism.

The drift of my argument against nonconsequentialism should now be clear.
In order to defend the normative indexicalist claim that basic justifiers may
include relativized values such as the welfare of the agent's children, the
fortune of the agent's country, the agent's own integrity, or something of the
kind, it appears that nonconsequentialists must have resort to the analytical
thesis that the term "right," at least in some uses, is covertly indexical. If they
are to make sense of the universalizability constraint, and stop it from driving
them into the consequentialist camp, then they must embrace a counterintuitive
and debunking analysis of the most central of all ethical terms.

The claim that "right" is covertly indexical is implausible in itself, as we
have already mentioned, because it postulates a widespread and implausible
failure of mutual comprehension among those involved in ethical debate. One
person says that an action is right, another that it is wrong, but in many cases
there is no issue at all between them; there is only the practical clash that goes
with one saying "I approve" and the other "I disapprove." What the first
person, A, means is that it is right-in-A's-terms; what the second person, B,
means is that it is right-in-B's-terms. What were they arguing about, then?
Nothing, it seems; or at least nothing distinctively ethical. They were confused
by the nonindexical feel of a term like "right" into treating it as having a
common meaning and reference for them both. This is an implausible view and
a view that is deeply condescending in its attitude toward ordinary participants
in ethical debate.

But apart from the inherent implausibility of taking "right" to be covertly
indexical, the use of such a step in order to neutralize the effect of the universalizability challenge leaves nonconsequentialists in an unhappy position. One
way of underlining that fact is to say that from their point of view morality is
not going to look very different from prudence.

"Prudent" is covertly indexical so far as it always means "prudent-for-X."
Moreover, "prudent-for-X" is typically used to justify actions that are in X's

interest; it is not as if the predicate is ever used to discern what is prudent-for-X among Y's actions. Something parallel holds for "right" in the position to which our argument drives the nonconsequentialist. 'Right' in suitable contexts has got to mean 'right-for-X' and if it is to be of use to nonconsequentialists in answering the universalizability challenge it has got to be fitted in particular for justifying actions that serve X in a way that they may not serve others. While serving X, indeed, the actions to be justified by reference to what is right-for-X may positively frustrate others: while preserving X's integrity they may make it very difficult for others to do so; or while promoting the interests of X's children, they may jeopardize the interests of other people's children.

But in ordinary moral thinking, we contrast the demands of rightness with the promptings of prudence, and in general with any self-interested promptings, and treat them as having a greater authority. And if we think that our acting in prudence's name is really the right thing to do – the right thing, and not just a sign of our moral failure – then we are willing to give this a neutral justification; we are prepared to think that what justifies us in doing so is the neutral sort of consideration that would justify anyone in our position taking that line. Those who relativize rightness and use relativized rightness to justify a person's preserving their integrity, helping their children, or whatever, lose this contrast between rightness and prudence. They make rightness out to be a sort of prudence that lies beyond the need or possibility of neutral justification.

When you are called upon to justify a choice to me, it will not be intuitively sufficient for you to show me how prudent the choice was from your point of view. So it was prudent. Fine. But was it right? Was it something that you can represent, to those of us who do not necessarily share your prudential interests, as a justifiable action? You may explain your action to us by citing its prudential character. You may even give us a perspective from which we can excuse your doing what you did, recognising that it is justifiable in an isomorphic way; we can recognize that in your situation perhaps we too would have been moved by the corresponding prudential consideration. But you cannot justify the action in the sense in which we asked for justification, simply by showing that you were prudent. What we are looking for, intuitively, is substantive justification, not justification of the isomorphic sort, and the problem on the relativized picture of rightness, as that is used by nonconsequentialists, is that there will often be no such justification available; the appeal to rightness will do no better in justificatory terms than the appeal to prudence.

These considerations show that in being driven to indexicalize and relativize rightness nonconsequentialism would require a deep revision in our ordinary ways of thinking and that we should not contemplate that revision without considerable reluctance. The relativization of rightness in question would make moral discourse and moral exchange radically incapable of unifying the different points of view of different people. It would give a philosophical basis to despair about the prospect that people might reconcile their different interests and commitments by appealing to moral argument. Such despair may yet be borne out in the development of our species but it is surely inconsistent with the hope around which moral argument continues to be built. This is the hope that by weaning ourselves away from more partial perspectives, and by submitting ourselves to the demands of fairness and equality and rationality and the like, we may yet manage to see things from a common, moral point of view. It is the hope, in a word, that ethical objectivism is sound.

The Possibility of Justificatory Objectivism

A full defense of consequentialism would need, not just to establish the case for believing that the ultimate justifiers of choice must be neutral in character, but also to silence the general misgivings and the specific objections that prevent many thinkers from giving that case a proper hearing. The general misgivings stem from the belief that consequentialism has to recommend a mode of decision making in which our ordinary moral psychology is upturned and agents adopt a casuistical, detached profile: a profile in which they can countenance the claims of friends and family, for example, only to the extent that looking after them happens to be the best way of furthering the impersonal good. The specific objections are that consequentialism would support the intuitively wrong choices; or would support the right choices for the wrong reasons; or would represent supererogatory, often heroic, choices as the only right one to take; and so on.

I cannot address all such complaints here.[85] But it may be useful if I say something, in conclusion, on the reservation about consequentialism that is espoused by those I described in my introduction as antimoralists. They suggest that going over to the sort of justificatory objectivism defended here would make life exceedingly impoverished. It would undermine our particularistic attachment to family and friends, for example, as well as our single-minded commitment to the hobbies and projects that mark out our individuality. This thought leads them to counsel, in my formulation, that such attachments and commitments should be placed beyond the bounds of ethical assessment; people should not be exposed to the corrosive effects of having to justify those attachments and commitments in ethical terms.

What I want to say is that this reaction to impartial morality – in particular, to the brand of justificatory objectivism that I have defended here – is mistaken and unnecessary. It overlooks the fact that the objectivism in question is, precisely, justificatory. The position I adopt does not recommend that people conduct their lives under the explicit control of neutral values, only that they conduct their lives in a way that is neutrally justifiable. Thus there is no ground for the stipulation, itself inherently counterintuitive, that in certain areas of life moral assessment should be kept at bay.

The facts that antimoralists emphasize are, first, that we all care for certain other people in their own right, not for what they represent; second, that we are creatures of particularistic inclinations and enthusiasms whose very identity and sense of self is tied up with taking those promptings seriously; and, third, that in many contexts and connections acknowledging a requirement to check one's responses by reference to neutral values defies deeply laid instincts and intuitions.[86] But I am happy to admit these facts, consistently with embracing justificatory objectivism. For it is entirely likely that if the facts are indeed sound – as I take them to be – then people will be justified in giving themselves over, no doubt within certain limits, to the personal attachments and the particularistic projects in question. The demands of neutral value can scarcely call for a pattern of decision, or a mode of decision making, that would undermine love and affection and our individuating sense of self; after all, such a life would do very badly by way of furthering any plausible set of values.

Yet even this observation may not be sufficient to silence the complaints of antimoralists. For they may say that if I admit the requirement to do only that which is objectively justifiable, then I must admit the further requirement to check that that which I do is objectively justifiable. And if I admit that checking requirement, then I betray the personal ideal of a life in which certain personal attachments and particularistic commitments are more or less sacrosanct. I give myself over instead to a moralistic ideal in which I only help my friends, for example, when I have the extra thought – one thought too many, in Bernard Williams's[87] phrase – that this is the right thing to do. I deny myself the possibility of expressing the way I am and feel and think, without first doing an ethical quality-check.

I agree with antimoralists, not only that we should not undermine personal attachments and particularistic commitments, but also that doing such ethical quality-checks would have an undermining effect. But there is no difficulty for justificatory objectivism in this admission. For if quality-checks would undermine such attachments and commitments, then it will be objectively justifiable, indeed objectively obligatory, to avoid such checking. People should take enough thought, in occasional moments of reflection, to make sure that certain patterns of unchecked spontaneity do indeed promise to be objectively justifiable by the values they espouse. But they should not drive unchecked spontaneity out of their lives by constant recourse to quality-checks.

The agents I envisage, then, can be decidedly spontaneous consistently with embracing a justificatory form of objectivism. Their consequentialism will mean that they occasionally reflect on the justifiability of their lives – hardly an objectionable feature – and that otherwise they satisfy a purely counterfactual requirement, not a requirement that imposes a pattern of actual self-monitoring.[88] What counterfactual requirement, in particular? I suggest this: that for any pattern of behavior that the agents manifest, it will be the case that did they think it was objectively unjustified then they would not manifest it.

Satisfying this requirement does not require any extra thought of the kind that Williams criticizes. What it requires is rather the absence of a thought: the absence of a thought that the pattern of action in question is objectively un-justified. Hardly an excessive requirement, that. And certainly not a require-ment to embarrass us about embracing objectivity in ethics.[89]

Notes

1. In terminology used by Ronald Dworkin ("Objectivity and Truth," *Philosophy & Public Affairs* 25 (1996): 87–139), opponents of semantic objectivism claim to reject ethical objectivity in a way that is neutral as between different ethical claims – the status of those claims is reinterpreted but their validity is not necessarily challenged – while opponents of ontological objectivism acknowledge that their rejection of ethical objectivity means that ordinary ethical evaluators are subject to massive error. Dworkin denies that seman-tic nonobjectivists can be as neutral as they claim.
2. J. L. Mackie, *Ethics* (Harmondsworth: Penguin, 1977), pp. 27–30.
3. See Susan Wolf, "Moral Saints," *Journal of Philosophy* 79 (1982): 419–439; Michael Stocker, "The Schizophrenia of Modern Ethical Theory," *Journal of Philosophy* 73 (1976): 453–466; Bernard Williams, *Ethics and the Limits of Philosophy* (Cambridge, Mass.: Harvard University Press, 1985); and, for an overview, Brian Leiter, "Nietzsche and the Morality Critics," *Ethics* 107 (1997): 250–285.
4. Crispin Wright, *Truth and Objectivity* (Cambridge, Mass.: Harvard University Press, 1992), p. 35.
5. Frank Jackson, Graham Oppy, and Michael Smith, "Minimalism and Truth-Aptness," *Mind* 103 (1994): 287–302, at p. 295.
6. Others may say that truth-conditionalism is weaker than semantic objectivism without committing themselves to a novel concept of truth-aptness. They may hold that while truth-aptness in general connects with belief, the only issue for participants in certain discourses may be, not whether to believe the relevant truth-apt sentences, but whether to treat them for certain purposes as if they were true: whether to treat them as expressing useful fictions. Such a fictionalist view has been defended with regard to theoretical, scientific discourse, e.g., and discourse on possibilities and necessities (Bas Van Fraassen, *The Scientific Image* [Oxford: Oxford University Press, 1980]; G. Rosen, "Modal Fictionalism," *Mind* 99 (1990): 327–354]). It might in principle be explored in the case of ethics too.
7. A. J. Ayer, *Language, Truth, and Logic* (London: Gollancz, 1946); C. Stevenson, *Ethics and Language* (New Haven: Yale University Press, 1941).
8. R. M. Hare, *Moral Thinking* (Oxford: Oxford University Press, 1981).
9. See G. E. Moore, *Ethics* (Oxford: Oxford University Press, 1912).
10. See Frank Jackson and Philip Pettit, "A Problem for Expressivists," *Analysis* 58 (1998): 39–51.
11. Hare, *Moral Thinking*.
12. Simon Blackburn, *Spreading the Word* (Oxford: Oxford University Press, 1984) and *Essays in Quasi-Realism* (Oxford: Oxford University Press, 1993); Allan Gibbard, *Wise Choices, Apt Feelings: A Theory of Normative Judgement* (Cambridge, Mass.: Harvard University Press, 1990).

13. Martin Davies and Lloyd Humbertstone, "Two Notions of Necessity," *Philosophical Studies* 48 (1981): 1–30, at pp. 22–25.

14. I should mention that I am ignoring one possible but very implausible position. This would hold that while expressivism in some form is true, so that people do not mean to posit values in making ethical assessments, actually there are such values in the world. This is implausible because it supposes that the entities in question can be identified as ethical values independently of any connection with the terms in which people make ethical assessments. My thanks to Christine Tappolet for drawing my attention to this possibility.

15. Mackie, *Ethics*.

16. Moore, *Ethics*.

17. James Dreier, "Internalism and Speaker Relativism," *Ethics* 101 (1990): 6–26.

18. Gilbert Harman, *The Nature of Morality* (New York: Oxford University Press, 1977).

19. Philip Pettit, "Evaluative 'Realism' and Interpretation," in S. Holtzman and C. Leich (eds.), *Wittgenstein: To Follow a Rule* (London: Routledge & Kegan Paul, 1981), p. 225; Peter Railton, "Moral Realism: Prospects and Problems," in W. Sinnott-Armstrong and M. Timmons (eds.), *Moral Knowledge?: New Readings in Moral Epistemology* (New York: Oxford University Press, 1996), p. 55.

20. Paul Horwich (*Truth* [Oxford: Blackwell, 1990]) and Crispin Wright (*Truth and Objectivity*) would prefer to cast this view as bearing on the appropriate conception of truth: truth for sentences, taken as already interpreted, already possessed of truth-conditions. Jackson et al., "Minimalism and Truth-Aptness," p. 300. I follow Jackson, Oppy, and Smith in thinking that the more perspicuous way of casting it is as an issue about the conception of truth-conditionality or truth-aptness that is appropriate for sentences.

21. Philip Pettit, "Realism and Truth: A Comment on Crispin Wright's *Truth and Objectivity*," *Philosophy & Phenomenological Research* 56 (1996): 883–890; see also Geoffrey Sayre-McCord, "Introduction" to *Essays on Moral Realism* (Ithaca: Cornell University Press, 1988).

22. This issue arises whether or not you think, as indeed I do, that the meaning and reference of basic, undefined terms is partly fixed on the basis of the primitive responses elicited by the referents: whether or not you believe in a global form of response-dependence. See Philip Pettit, "Realism and Response-Dependence," *Mind* 100 (1991): 587–626.

23. See Frank Jackson, "Realism, Truth, and Truth-Aptness," *Philosophical Books* 35 (1994): 162–169; Christine Tappolet, "Mixed Inferences: A Problem for Pluralism about Truth Predicates," *Analysis* 57 (1997).

24. Amartya Sen, "Poor, Relatively Speaking," *Oxford Economic Papers* 35 (1983): 153–168.

25. Pettit, "Realism and Truth."

26. Philip Pettit, "A Definition of Physicalism," *Analysis* 53 (1993): 213–223; Frank Jackson, *From Metaphysics to Ethics: A Defence of Conceptual Analysis* (Oxford: Oxford University Press, 1998).

27. David Wiggins, *Needs, Values, Truth* (Oxford: Basil Blackwell, 1987).

28. David R. Hilbert, *Color and Color Perception* (Stanford: Center for the Study of Language and Information, 1987).

29. David Wiggins, "Objective and Subjective Ethics, with Two Postscripts About Truth," *Ratio* 8 (1995): 243–258.

30. Particularists, as they are called, sometimes seem to imply that though evaluative predicates collect things into descriptive or natural classes, there need be no descriptive pattern common to members of such a class: there may be nothing about the class such that exposure to a subset would enable a person to extrapolate reliably to other members. See, e.g., Jonathan Dancy, *Moral Reasons* (Oxford: Blackwell, 1993); David McNaughton, *Moral Vision* (Oxford: Blackwell, 1988); and Mark Timmons, "Outline of a Contextualist Moral Epistemology," in W. Sinnott-Armstrong and M. Timmons (eds.), *MoralKnowledge?*. I reject such a suggestion, believing that evaluative properties must have a descriptive salience sufficient to enable us – finite minds responsive to natural features of the world – to cotton on to those properties. See Frank Jackson, Philip Pettit, and Michael Smith, "Ethical Particularism and Patterns," in B. Hooker & M. Little (eds.), *Particularism* (Cambridge University Press, forthcoming). I do not go into the matter here, because it would take us too far afield.

31. Harman, *The Nature of Morality.*

32. Pettit, "Realism and Response-Dependence."

33. See Wiggins, *Needs, Values, Truth;* Susan Hurley, *Natural Reasons* (New York: Oxford University Press, 1989).

34. Dreier, "Internalism and Speaker Relativism."

35. Philip Pettit, "The Consequentialist Perspective," in Marcia Baron, Philip Pettit, and Michael Slote, *Three Methods of Ethics* (Oxford: Blackwell, 1997).

36. Philip Pettit, "Consequentialism," in Peter Singer (ed.), *A Companion to Ethics* (Oxford: Blackwell, 1991); "The Consequentialist Perspective."

37. Justin Oakley, "Varieties of Virtue Ethics," *Ratio* 9 (1996): 128–152.

38. T. M. Scanlon, "Contractualism and Utilitarianism," in A. Sen and B. Williams (eds.), *Utilitarianism and Beyond* (Cambridge: Cambridge University Press, 1982).

39. Hare, *Moral Thinking.* For ease of presentation I am neglecting the fact that there is a second way of being a consequentialist apart from maintaining that the right option is identified in the first place as that which maximizes expected value. This would involve holding that while the right option is identified in the first place by reference to the manifestation of virtue, or the satisfaction of an ideal contract, or the performance of what is universally prescribable, it turns out that satisfying any such condition involves maximizing expected value. Hare defends such a downstream consequentialism in deriving utilitarianism from his universal prescriptivism (but see Philip Pettit, "Universalizability without Utilitarianism," *Mind* 96 [1987]: 74–82); he does so, incidentally, from within an expressivist approach. I defend consequentialism in its upstream variety in Pettit, "The Consequentialist Perspective."

40. Peter Geach, *Logic Matters* (Oxford: Blackwell, 1972), chap. 8.

41. Michael Dummett, *Frege: Philosophy of Language* (London: Duckworth, 1973), chap. 10; Simon Blackburn, *Spreading the Word* and *Essays in Quasi-Realism;* see too Jackson, *From Metaphysics to Ethics.*

42. For a critique see M. Van Roojen, "Expressivism and Irrationality," *Philosophical Review* 105 (1996): 311–335.

43. Gibbard, *Wise Choices, Apt Feelings,* p. 154.

44. Why only, of the other? Because there is a pragmatic inconsistency in thinking that while I actually believe that p, I would believe that not p in the event of escaping this or that inappropriate limitation of evidence or competence or whatever. There is a contrast here, of course, with the case of desire since I may have to acknowledge that my actual desires

do not correspond, for reasons of weakness, to what I know I would desire if I were not subject to this or that bad influence.

45. Philip Pettit, *The Common Mind: An Essay on Psychology, Society, and Politics* (1993; reprint, with a new postscript, New York: Oxford University Press, 1996); Gerald Postema, "Public Practical Reasoning: An Archaeology," *Social Philosophy and Policy* 12 (1995): 43–86; Philip Pettit and Michael Smith, "Freedom in Belief and Desire," *Journal of Philosophy* 93 (1996): 429–449.

46. Huw Price, *Facts and the Function of Truth* (Oxford: Blackwell, 1988).

47. Moore, *Ethics.*

48. Mackie, *Ethics,* p. 36.

49. See Michelle M. Moody-Adams, *Fieldwork in Familiar Places: Morality, Culture, and Philosophy* (Cambridge, Mass: Harvard University Press, 1997), on related themes.

50. Mackie, *Ethics,* pp. 38–42.

51. Ibid., p. 40.

52. Philip Pettit and Michael Smith, "Practical Unreason," *Mind* 102 (1993): 53–80.

53. Michael Smith, "The Humean Theory of Motivation," *Mind* 96 (1987): 36–61.

54. Frank Jackson, "Critical Notice of Susan Hurley's 'Natural Reasons,'" *Australasian Journal of Philosophy* 70 (1992): 475–487; Frank Jackson and Philip Pettit, "Moral Functionalism," *Philosophical Quarterly* 45 (1995): 20–40, and "Moral Functionalism, Supervenience, and Reductionism," *Philosophical Quarterly* 46 (1996): 82–86; Pettit, "The Consequentialist Perspective"; Jackson, *From Metaphysics to Ethics.*

55. See Mark Johnston, "Dispositional Theories of Value," *Proceedings of the Aristotelian Society,* supp. vol. 63 (1989): 139–174; David Lewis, "Dispositional Theories of Value," *Proceedings of the Aristotelian Society,* supp. vol. 63 (1989): 113–137; John McDowell, "Values and Secondary Properties," in T. Honderich (ed.), *Morality and Objectivity* (London: Routledge, 1985); Michael Smith, "Dispositional Theories of Value," *Proceedings of the Aristotelian Society,* supp. vol. 63 (1989): 89–111, and *The Moral Problem* (Oxford: Blackwell, 1994).

56. See Hurley, *Natural Reasons;* cf. W. V. O. Quine, *From a Logical Point of View* (Cambridge, Mass: Harvard University Press, 1953), and *The Roots of Reference* (La Salle: Open Court Publishers, 1974).

57. David Lewis, *Philosophical Papers* (Oxford: Blackwell, 1983), essay 6; Jackson, *From Metaphysics to Ethics,* chap. 6.

58. John Rawls, *A Theory of Justice* (Oxford: Oxford University Press, 1971).

59. Rawls, *Political Liberalism* (New York: Columbia University Press, 1993), p. 121.

60. Jackson and Pettit, "Moral Functionalism."

61. The claim that every evaluative property – every evaluatively specifiable property – is also descriptively specifiable is a very substantive thesis. An evaluative property will not be descriptively specifiable just because it can be indirectly identified, say as the property that so and so is thinking about, in descriptive terms. Such an indirect identification picks out the property only by means of its having the distinct descriptive property that so and so is thinking about it. A descriptive specification proper will pick out the property without relying on such further connections (see M. Van Roojen, "Moral Functionalism and Moral Reduction," *Philosophical Quarterly* 46 [1996]: 77–81; and Jackson and Pettit, "Moral Functionalism, Supervenience, and Reductionism").

62. Harman, *The Nature of Morality.*

63. Pettit, "The Consequentialist Perspective," p. 117.

64. Jackson et al., "Ethical Particularism and Patterns."

65. Philip Pettit, "Practical Belief and Philosophical Theory," *Australasian Journal of Philosophy* 76 (1998): 15–33.

66. Robert Stalnaker, *Inquiry* (Cambridge, Mass.: MIT Press, 1984).

67. David Lewis, *Convention* (Cambridge, Mass.: Harvard University Press, 1969), p. 67.

68. Stocker, "The Schizophrenia of Modern Ethical Theory."

69. Philip Pettit, "A Theory of Normal and Ideal Conditions," *Philosophical Studies* 66 (1999): 21–44.

70. Robert Stalnaker, "Assertion," in P. Cole (ed.), *Syntax and Semantics* (New York: Academic Press, 1978).

71. Pettit and Smith, "Practical Unreason."

72. Notice, for the record, that all that is required is an absence of belief in the presence of nonideal factors, not the presence of a belief in the absence of nonideal factors; this makes the account less demanding and more plausible.

73. Pettit, "Realism and Response-Dependence"; Jackson and Pettit, "Moral Functionalism."

74. See Price, *Facts and the Function of Truth.*

75. This slant may make my approach congenial to someone like Ronald Dworkin ("Objectivity and Truth") who wants to hold that the only grounds for debating skeptical issues about ethics are grounds internal to ethical debate.

76. Sayre-McCord, introduction to *Essays on Moral Realism.*

77. Pettit, "The Consequentialist Perspective."

78. Pettit, *The Common Mind,* chap. 4; Pettit and Smith, "Freedom in Belief and Desire."

79. W. B. Gallie, "Essentially Contested Concepts," *Proceedings of the Aristotelian Society* 56 (1955–56): 167–198; see also William Connolly, *The Terms of Political Discourse* (Princeton: Princeton University Press, 1983).

80. Pettit, "Evaluative 'Realism' and Interpretation."

81. See John Broome, "Incommensurable Values," in R. Crisp and B. Hooker (eds.), *Essays in Honour of James Griffin* (Oxford: Oxford University Press, 1998).

82. Pettit, "The Consequentialist Perspective," and, for a detailed presentation, "Nonconsequentialism and Universalizability," *Philosphical Quarterly* 50(2000): 175–190.

83. The upstream consequentialist, to use an earlier description, will hold that this is an a priori and axiomatic assumption; the downstream consequentialist will maintain that it derives, perhaps a priori, perhaps not, from such an assumption: say, as in the case of Hare (*Moral Thinking*), from the assumption that the right option in any choice is that which is universally prescribable. The argument here supports consequentialism as such, whereas in "The Consequentialist Perspective" I argue in favor of upstream consequentialism in particular.

84. See Wlodzimierz Rabinowitz, *Universalizability* (Dordrecht: D. Reidel, 1979).

85. See Pettit, "The Consequentialist Perspective."

86. Leiter, "Nietzsche and the Morality Critics;" Pettit, "The Consequentialist Perspective."

87. Bernard Williams, *Moral Luck* (Cambridge: Cambridge University Press, 1981), p. 18.

88. Peter Railton, "Alienation, Consequentialism, and the Demands of Morality," *Philosophy and Public Affairs* 13 (1984): 134–171.

89. In completing this essay I was greatly helped by detailed comments from Brian Leiter and his colleagues, Cory Juhl and Robert C. Koons, and by suggestions from Frank Jackson, Ellie Mason, Don Regan, and Michael Smith.

7

Pathetic Ethics

DAVID SOSA

The battle for territory between subjectivist and objectivist ideologies is ultimately global war: truth itself is under siege.[1] One theater in which the fighting has been elegantly fierce is ethics. But it is not always clear for whom or what the troops are fighting. If your flag is just realism, for example, you could be Swiss about the engagement. But realists are reasonably suspicious of the antirealist *tendencies* of subjectivism (however this is ultimately defined) – it introduces a significant discontinuity between ethics and, for example, physics (which can be taken as paradigmatically *real*). A different realist may worry rather that objectivity in ethics will commit us to "queer" properties and lead ultimately to an error theory or to eliminativism. So realists enter the fray, on either side.

So-called sensibility theories[2] seek to negotiate a cease-fire. They grow with the thought that ethics must have *something* important to do with agents and their sensibilities. And they develop on analogy with views of secondary qualities, proposing a variety of analytic connections between moral properties and subjective states. What the proposals have in common is that in them the instantiation of ethical properties is viewed as not entirely independent of human psychological reactions. Still, such instantiation, when it occurs, is there to be cognized. There is nothing queer about ethical properties: they are intelligibly rooted in ethical thought or feeling. An ethical reaction, however, is not itself merely the expression of preference or the issuance of an imperative. It is an essentially cognitive response to ethical properties.

I think there is something importantly wrong with sensibility theories. Ultimately, their flaw is that they are, in a word, pathetic.[3] One way to bring this out is to review how these theories arise in response to John Mackie's error theory. Part of the problem, it seems to me, is that Mackie has been rejected for the wrong reasons. Though I too find his view problematic, sensibility theorists have been misled by an underappreciation of Mackie. Reviewing his contribution, we better understand and more effectively resist the appeal of the proffered alternative.

Explaining the persistence of our allegedly erroneous commitment to objectivity in ethics, Mackie appeals to Hume's remark about the mind's "propensity to spread itself on external objects."[4] Compare the "pathetic fallacy": "If a fungus, say, fills us with disgust, we may be inclined to ascribe to the fungus itself a non-natural quality of foulness" (*Ethics,* 42).[5] This inclination can lead us into error. The features of the object that produce our disgust in no way *resemble* that experience. They are simply natural qualities. The relevant features (or even their conjunction) do not, it seems, have "to-be-disgusted-by" built in intrinsically. And moreover, our actually being disgusted is a product of our own sensibility as much as it is a result of the natural qualities of the fungus that lead to our disgust. Here the idea of an illegitimate spreading of our own feelings onto the external object is clear. The question is whether ethical properties are another case in point.

To preview, our dialectic will proceed as follows. First, we review Mackie's seminal metaethical statement. Some of McDowell's early development of sensibility theory, to which we proceed, was explicitly in response to Mackie. Where Mackie saw ordinary morality committed to an error, in virtue of its commitment to objectivity, McDowell finds ordinary morality innocent, in spite of recognizing that commitment. The question is whether the commitment to objectivity stands a chance of being satisfied. Mackie does not think so; and given *Mackie's* interpretation of the commitment, McDowell would agree that it is unsatisfiable. But according to McDowell, that interpretation is optional. Properly understood, the commitment to objectivity implicit in commonsense moral discourse and practice *can* be satisfied. This requires a reconceptualization of the variety of objectivity in play. As we'll see, David Wiggins too develops, apparently simultaneously, a position similar to McDowell's.

But their position suffers at least two important disadvantages. First, the sensibility theories offered are circular. They appeal to the very moral notions under analysis. Does the circularity vitiate the account? I will argue that it does. Second, Mackie's interpretation of commonsense morality's commitment to objectivity is the more plausible. Accordingly, unless moral value is after all objective in Mackie's sense, we appear to be forced to an error theory.

Since the late 1980s there has been a second wave of the *kind* of theory McDowell and Wiggins proposed. Crispin Wright and Mark Johnston,[6] sensitive to criticisms of McDowell made by Simon Blackburn,[7] have developed versions of sensibility theory that take seriously the analogy with secondary qualities but qualify it in order to avoid difficulties of the McDowell/Wiggins view. We will see, however, that these new versions also come with their own new problems.

I propose, then, to challenge the rejection of the variety of objectivity (commitment to which) Mackie feared would lead inevitably to an error theory. Because sensibility theories cannot effect the desired truce, a view of moral value according to which it is in relevant respects more like a *primary* quality merits further development. Admittedly I do not develop a positive proposal as an alternative.[8] But if such a view is ultimately incoherent, an error theory, or skepticism, and some post hoc revisionism, are our lot. The point of the present chapter is to reintroduce the possibility of a more robust objectivity in ethics by challenging an increasingly popular class of views that reject it. Sensibility theories proceed from an implausible interpretation of moral phenomenology and appear unpromising if not empty. In their understanding of morality, they give the wrong role to human subjective response.

I. Problems from Mackie

A. A Fertile Idea

Although the locus classicus may be Hume,[9] contemporary sensibility theories develop in response to Mackie. Mackie begins *Ethics: Inventing Right and Wrong* with a "bald statement of the thesis" of his Chapter 1: "There are no objective values" (*Ethics,* 15). And he articulates his basic anti-objectivist metaethical claim in relation to moral reasoning: made fully explicit, moral reasoning must contain as input something that cannot be objectively validated, something whose truth, validity, or authority "is constituted by our choosing or deciding to think in a certain way" (*Ethics,* 30).

Pay close attention to Mackie's drawing (*Ethics,* 19) of a close "analogy with colours." He draws the analogy with a specific purpose in mind: to clarify the distinction between conceptual and factual analysis in ethics. But he found the productive vein tapped earlier by Hume.

Boyle and Locke claimed that "colours as they occur in material things consist simply in patterns of arrangement and movement of minute particles on the surfaces of objects, which . . . enable these objects to produce colour sensations in us; but that colours *as we see them* do not literally belong to the surfaces of material things" (cited in *Ethics,* 18–19; emphasis added). Mackie makes the point that whether Locke and Boyle were right cannot be settled merely by linguistic inquiry. Whatever the nature of our color claims, there is a residual question about the nature of the colors themselves. The development of color science and more detailed knowledge about the mechanism of color vision has had a significant impact on the question. Beside the specific use to which he puts it, Mackie's analogy also provides a useful model by which to understand him. His position with respect to moral value is akin to Locke's on color. Ethical value, *as we understand it* (viz. objectively), does not literally belong to anything. What ethical value things have is not as we ordinarily understand it.

B. Queerness

Mackie deploys two arguments for the view that there are no objective values. The first is a familiar argument from relativity. But there is also a second, the argument from queerness. The substance of this objection was already, I would argue, a part of his rejection of any "naturalist descriptivist" position. Mackie's idea is that a naturalist can hold that moral claims are committed to *something* objective, some natural descriptive facts, but not that they are committed to objective value. Such a view misses, Mackie claims, the categorical imperative force of moral assertion: if moral claims assert only that some natural state of affairs obtains, then no prescription is forthcoming except relative to subjective desires, preferences, and so forth. This presupposes, what he now makes explicit in the argument from queerness, that no natural entity or feature can be intrinsically prescriptive. Objective values, if there were any, would be "utterly different from anything else in the universe" (*Ethics,* 38).

Mackie cannot understand the idea of an end having "to-be-pursuedness" built in, independently of any subjective desire or preference. Hume famously argued that reason (we can generalize to all of what we might call the "cognitive attitudes") cannot motivate the will. Only desires (generalize to the "conative attitudes") have that force. To suppose that some objects of cognition can, after all, influence the will independently of any conation is to postulate something "of a quite different order from anything else with which we are acquainted" (*Ethics,* 40). It is hard to see how such a thing, a categorically prescriptive characteristic, could be related to the natural. According to Mackie, and before him Moore, there must be *some* supervenience of the ethical on the natural. But if value is objective, what could that relation be?

So far I have emphasized only the metaphysical edge of the argument from queerness. But the argument has an epistemological edge too. In accord with their being metaphysically extraordinary, objective values would apparently require an extraordinary epistemology. If we are aware of moral value, then, it seems, it is not in the mundane way by which we become aware of anything else. According to Mackie, our ordinary forms of perception cannot make us aware of the "authoritative prescriptivity" (*Ethics,* 39) of value, so they cannot make us aware of value. We need some special sort of intuition; this need is a disadvantage of the view that espouses objective moral value.

Worse, "[i]t is not even sufficient to postulate a faculty which 'sees' the wrongness: something must be postulated which can see at once the natural features that constitute the cruelty, and the wrongness, and the mysterious consequential link between the two" (*Ethics,* 41). I must confess, however, that I don't know why Mackie says this. Why must we postulate such a super-faculty? Why wouldn't a faculty that can appreciate categorical prescriptivity when it sees it suffice? The faculty that sees the natural features that constitute the cruelty could just be our standard sensory capacity. Moral sense could be sensitivity to the imperatives that might arise. And it may be philosophical reflection that's needed to understand the categorical link between the natural features and the wrongness. Perhaps most moral agents would never "see" the "mysterious link." Why should they?

C. A Slide to Avoid

There is the threat of a slide in the above reasoning concerning queerness. I'm not sure that Mackie makes it. But I want to raise the issue if only to be able to refer back to it later. No one denies that moral claims involve an element of *intensionality.* From claims like "it is (would be) wrong for S to do A" or "S should not do A," it follows neither that S does A, nor that S fails to do A. Similarly from the fact, if it were one, that feature F has "to-be-pursuedness" built in, it does not follow that F is in fact pursued. All that follows is that F is *to be* pursued. The slide to avoid (at least without further argument) is *from* a kind of intensionality, *out of* it. Consider the following quotation from Mackie. "An objective good would be sought by anyone who was acquainted with it, not because of any contingent fact that this person, or every person, is so constituted that he desires this end, but just because the end has to-be-pursuedness somehow built into it" (*Ethics,* 40). This seems to make the slide. Whether an objective good *would* be sought by anyone who was acquainted with it need *not* be independent of that person's desires, preferences, and so forth. What is independent of that person's subjectivity is its "to be" pursuedness. The imperative, the categorical demand (the satisfaction of which cannot be inferred), that the subject pursue the good obtains whatever the agent's attitudes toward it. But whether the agent actually seeks the good or would seek the good depends on what she wants or prefers or would want or prefer.

If objective value is queer, it is not because its existence would entail the existence of motivations that are independent of conative attitudes. The existence of objective value would, given the considerations that have been adduced so far, entail the existence only of *demands for* motivation (indeed, perhaps for something else: for action) – demands that obtain independently of the conative attitudes. Watch the scopes: (i) demand for (motivation that is independent of conative attitudes), (ii) (demand for motivation) that is independent of conative attitudes. It's the demand that's independent, not the motivation.

Now it may be that Mackie finds unintelligible even the existence of a *demand* for action that is independent of conative attitudes. But insofar as his view inherits the plausibility of Hume's observation that beliefs cannot, by themselves, motivate, the view is not entitled to reject the existence of objective moral value. Perhaps motivation is always, even in some sense is necessarily, a product of affective attitudes. But that doesn't entail that nothing could *call* for a motivation or for a course of action independently of any conative attitude. The Humean observation simply does not apply directly. And the notion of a *demand* here is not extravagant: it is just a reflex of the categorical imperative force of moral assertion – a point Mackie himself stresses. That the imperative force is categorical is tantamount to its desire independence; that the categorical is an imperative is tantamount to its making a demand. Once we are clear about what would *not* follow from the postulation of objective moral values, however (no spooky desire-independent motivations), is it still so clear that they are queer? The issue will rearise significantly below toward the end of this chapter.

II. McDowell's Secondary Qualities

A. Problematic

McDowell begins his "Values and Secondary Qualities"[10] by trying to re-introduce us to a problematic: Mackie insisted, and McDowell agrees, that ordinary evaluative thought "presents itself as a matter of" sensitivity to aspects of the world. Noncognitivists, for whom moral judgments are not truth evaluable, cannot thereby capture the nature of moral *experience*. The experience of making a moral judgment is as of making a truth-evaluable judgment – it is as of attributing a real (moral) property. Noncognitivists do not, admittedly, base their view on any phenomenology; their idea is that the truth evaluable cannot, by itself, be motivational. McDowell now claims that this noncognitivist view (the truth-evaluable can't be motivational), combined with Mackie's view about how value "presents itself," makes the phenomenology of evaluation involve a "mere incoherence." Why?

Evaluative thought would be "presenting itself" as what it cannot possibly be. It would be presenting itself as *evaluative* and hence necessarily motivational; but it would also be presenting itself as truth evaluable. And the noncognitivist view is that nothing could be both. Mackie sees that some kinds of truth-evaluable claims *can,* after all, be motivational. Only claims of "objective" fact cannot be. According to McDowell, this insight (that some instances of the truth evaluable *can* be motivational) "clears away the only obstacle to accepting [Mackie's] phenomenological claim" (VSQ, 110) by removing the implication that the phenomenology of evaluation [necessarily] involves an incoherence. Noncognitivism must now be seen, says McDowell, as offering a *correction* to the phenomenology: it is misleading of evaluative thought to present itself as sensitivity to aspects of the world. In fact, evaluative thought is a matter of *expression.* And so it should present itself that way. We should attempt to alter the phenomenology accordingly. Finally, according to McDowell, "In Mackie's view, the correction is called for" (VSQ, 110).

A problem with McDowell's analysis is that Mackie need not call for a *noncognitivist* correction. It is a different correction to the phenomenology of evaluation, one that has not yet been so much as implicated by McDowell's discussion, that Mackie's view requires. What needs fixing is just our *objectifying* tendency. Moreover, McDowell's putting the point by referring to Mackie's *removal* of an incoherence in the phenomenology of evaluation may be obfuscatory. Mackie's own view of unreconstructed moral phenomenology incorporates the incoherence. According to Mackie too, ordinary evaluative thought presents itself as what it cannot possibly be. It presents itself as a matter of sensitivity to objective aspects of the world. And Mackie admits that claims of objective fact cannot be motivational. The correction called for by Mackie is simply the removal of the objectifying tendency: a recognition that moral value is ultimately *invented* and is not built in to the fabric of the world.

McDowell will suggest that Mackie attributes an unmerited plausibility to the thesis that the phenomenology of value needs correcting. The reason for Mackie's mistake, according to McDowell, is a "false picture of what one is committed to if one resists" (VSQ, 110) the thesis. According to McDowell, we can in a way agree with Mackie about the phenomenology while rejecting the error theory: the phenomenology, in representing the evaluative as objective, need not be committing an error.

B. A False Picture

It is thus agreed that evaluative judgment appears to be an exercise of sensitivity to aspects of the world. Assuming we accept that appearance, what is the nature of this sensitivity? According to McDowell, a perceptual "model" is "virtually irresistible" (VSQ, 110). But to what does that model commit us? Mackie implicitly held that the model is perceptual awareness of *primary* qualities. This, according to McDowell, stacks the deck in favor of Mackie's error theory – this is the crux of the allegedly "false picture of what one is committed to if one resists" Mackie's view.

Following Locke, Mackie takes secondary-quality perception, untutored, to involve a projective error. According to McDowell, Locke and Mackie hold that "we are prone to conceive secondary-quality experience in a way that would be appropriate for experience of primary qualities" (VSQ, 111). But McDowell is at least misleading here. The error that Locke and now Mackie point to is not in our "conception of secondary-quality experience." Until Locke, we probably had nothing so robust as a *conception* of secondary-quality experience. Even now most secondary-quality perceivers probably have no distinct conception of secondary-quality experience. What we do have is the phenomenology of secondary-quality experiences. We have the experiences; and they involve a phenomenology. And according to Locke, that phenomenology is misleadingly indistinct from the phenomenology of primary-quality experience.

When we see the color of an object, the experience is relevantly akin to seeing the object's shape. In each case there is the sense that the experience is a response to a feature of the object that the object has independently of that or any other similar experience – a feature the experience *resembles* but in no way *constitutes*. In the case of primary-quality experience, that sense is correct. Not so for secondary-quality experience. In any case, it seems, McDowell finds this conception of secondary-quality experience "seriously mistaken." That is, apparently, McDowell thinks it is wrong to suppose that, untutored, the phenomenology of primary- and secondary-quality experience is similar in the way Locke and Mackie do.

C. Self-Consciously-Secondary-Quality Experience

"A secondary quality is a property the ascription of which to an object is not adequately understood except as true, if it is true, in virtue of the object's disposition to present a certain sort of perceptual appearance" (VSQ, 111). This incorporates an ambiguity: what variety of *understanding* is in question? If McDowell meant only that the (philosophical) fact of the matter is that secondary qualities are dispositions to produce certain sorts of perceptual experience, then there need be no disagreement with Locke and Mackie. Mackie, you recall, favors a correction to our phenomenology. Untutored, it involves a projective error; but when we discover that objects have no quality that resembles our untutored experience thereof, then we can correct our experience. McDowell: "a predication *understood* only in [terms of some microscopic textural property of the object's surface] – not in terms of how the object would look – would not be an ascription of a secondary quality" (VSQ, 112; emphasis added). Again, what is the nature of the understanding in question?

McDowell has an answer. The understanding is phenomenological. According to McDowell, the ascription or predication of a secondary quality presents itself as the predication of a property that is essentially a matter of being disposed to look a certain way. "What would one expect it to be like to experience something's being such as to look red, if not to experience the thing in question (in the right circumstances) as looking, precisely, red?" (VSQ, 112). In other words, our experiences of things' looking red *are* experiences of things' being such as to look red. This is a troubling feature of McDowell's view.

For my part, I would expect the experience of something's being such as to look red (if I could possibly have such an experience, about which I remain unsure) to be quite different from the experience of something's looking red. For example, couldn't a color-blind person, who in one good sense cannot experience anything as looking red, still experience some things as being such as to look red? Maybe he has some reliable way of distinguishing red objects. And (switching to different sense modalities) experiencing the *smell* of a fresh lime might serve better than any tasting as the experience of something's being *such as* to *taste* tart. So McDowell may illegitimately eliminate an important phenomenological distinction in his attempt to introduce another.

The phenomenological distinction he is trying to introduce is between secondary-quality experience and primary-quality experience. In Mackie's Lockean view, naive perceptual consciousness stands accused of (mis)taking secondary qualities for primary qualities. We have secondary-quality ideas that are phenomenologically indistinguishable, in respect of primacy, from primary-quality ideas: but while primary-quality ideas resemble their objects, secondary-quality ideas do not. McDowell finds this view not only wrong but incoherent. According to him the view requires two things:

First, that colours figure in perceptual experience neutrally, so to speak, rather than as essentially phenomenal qualities of objects, qualities that could not be adequately *conceived* except in terms of how their possessors would look; and second, that we command a concept of resemblance that would enable us to construct notions of possible primary qualities out of the idea of resemblance to such neutral elements of experience. (VSQ, 113; emphasis added)

As we've seen, he denies that the first condition is satisfied. (Notice the switch to the terminology of "conception" from that of "understanding.") But at this point he focuses on the second condition. He finds it "quite unclear" (VSQ, 113) what sense we could make of a notion of resemblance to redness-as-it-figures-in-our-experience other than in phenomenological respects. If the notion of resemblance is analyzed in phenomenological respects, then we have no conception of the possible primary qualities other than in terms of how they would look; redness as it figures in our experience would prove to be "stubbornly phenomenal." For McDowell, the property that an object is represented as having, already in secondary-quality *experience,* is "distinctively phenomenal."

Claiming to find something unclear, even quite unclear, is insufficient argument. The concept of resemblance that would enable us to construct a notion of (what is in fact a secondary quality but is) a possible primary quality from "neutral" elements of experience is just that notion of resemblance involved in the claim that primary-quality ideas resemble their objects. Perhaps this notion needs further elucidation; but it has not been shown incoherent. Secondary qualities are supposed to resemble our ideas in just the way primary qualities actually do resemble our ideas. In both cases the property figures in experience neutrally, in the sense that it does *not* (contra McDowell) present itself as essentially subjective. In both cases the phenomenology is as of a property that *resembles* the experience. And, so far as I can tell, there is no incoherence in this prephilosophical conception of secondary-quality experience. According to Locke and Mackie, our phenomenology, does, however, turn out to have been misleading: as a matter of fact (but not simply as a matter of logic), there are no properties of objects that resemble our ideas of secondary qualities (in the sense in which there *are* properties of objects that resemble our ideas of primary qualities).

McDowell thinks that "no notion of resemblance could get us from an *essentially* experiential state of affairs to the concept of a feature of objects intelligible otherwise than in terms of how its possessors would strike us"

(VSQ, 115; emphasis added). I'm not sure what (other than possibly begging a question) the "essentially" is doing in this claim. If it is just redundant, if all experiential states are essentially experiential, then it may be innocent. But if it is supposed to somehow make the resemblance impossible, then it begs the question. Redness-as-it-figures-in-experience is an experiential property; perhaps it is even essentially experiential. And the nature of the resemblance claimed is a matter for investigation. But why *can't* something that is essentially experiential resemble something that is not (other than in respect of subjectivity)? This is not addressed.

It is instructive that McDowell notes, in passing, that a version of this point "tells . . . against the Lockean conception of *shapes*" (VSQ, 115; emphasis added). So McDowell would apparently reject the use of resemblance altogether. He says that "[e]xplaining 'ideas' as 'intentional objects' should direct our attention to the relation between how things are and how an experience represents them as being – in fact identity, not resemblance" (VSQ, 114). He wants properties of objects to be the very elements of experience. It is not that we have subjective phenomena that *resemble* (except in the limiting sense of identity) the properties that are their objects; no, our experiences are simply constituted by properties that ordinary objects can instantiate. At least this seems to be the view McDowell is bruiting.

This contrasts with an alternative "picture": "a confronted external reality, conceived as having only an objective nature, is processed through a structured 'subjectivity,' conceived in [an] objectivistic manner" (VSQ, 117). The objectivistic conception in question is supposed to consist in taking phenomenological representation to be a matter of experience being constituted by intrinsically representational elements. Redness-in-experience, in virtue of its intrinsic nature, represents redness itself.

It thus becomes clearer that it's nothing particular about its account of *secondary*-quality experience that inclines McDowell to reject this picture. What he means to suggest (unsuccessfully, I think, to this point), is that this picture threatens to "cut us off" from even the *primary* qualities of the objects we perceive (VSQ, 117). Primary-quality experience too is essentially subjective; its elements can no more *resemble* their objects, if these are to be fully *objective,* than can the elements of secondary-quality experience.

It is not easy, however, to view McDowell's recommendation as a real alternative. Although the elements of experience, because they are essentially subjective, allegedly cannot *resemble* what is objective, they can nevertheless be *identical* to what is not essentially subjective. Primary-quality experience is partly constituted by not-exclusively-phenomenal properties. The constitution of secondary-quality experience, by contrast, is by phenomenal properties. But this seems to undermine the earlier argument: if there is no problem with not-essentially-phenomenal properties *constituting* subjective experience, there should be still less of a problem about the elements of subjective experience *resembling* not-essentially-phenomenal properties.

McDowell's opponent may believe that experience is constituted by intrinsically representational elements. It is another step, though one we may well want to take, to hold that experience is constituted by *essentially* representational elements. Not everything intrinsic is essential. The target view is, perhaps, that the elements of experience are "individuated" by their representational character. What it is to be one of these elements is just to represent as it does; and again, they represent as they do in virtue of what they are intrinsically like. Experience is thus supposed, by McDowell's opponents, to be intrinsically representational, essentially representational, and essentially phenomenological – *what it is* amounts to *what it is like to have it.* If experience is both essentially representational and essentially phenomenological, then it must be that its representational character just *is* what it is like to have it.

McDowell rejects this view because he finds it "hard to see how a difference in respect of objectivity [between primary and secondary qualities] could show up in their representational significance" (VSQ, 115). But why should it show up *there?* What's the argument for the idea that perceptual experience must disclose the *nature* of its objects? Why can't reasoning, philosophical analysis, and even scientific theorizing all be necessary – perception providing only some input to the question and even sometimes providing misleading input, input that must be corrected by the other epistemic faculties? That the situation is otherwise appears simply to be asserted.

This is a general problem with the position McDowell is trying to develop. It is as if everything we might come to know about some objective matters is already present in a corresponding experience. We can *perceive* natures. Phenomenology discloses essences. This is deeply problematic. Though McDowell calls it a "gratuitous slur on perceptual 'common sense' to accuse it of [what he considers] a wildly problematic understanding of itself" (VSQ, 113), the fact is that perception, at least, has no *understanding* of itself at all. Common sense does have a (rather superficial and subject to correction) understanding of perception: in some cases experience is misleading. Sometimes the properties of objects are not exactly as they seemed; and sometimes, perhaps, there really aren't any such properties at all (and the line between these two cases is notoriously difficult to draw). Although the discovery that perception has misled us can result from additional experience, the contents of the original experience may have been simply erroneous.

When we look at a color picture in the newspaper, we have the experience as of a fully "dissectably" colored area. That experience is misleading. Look closer, with a magnifying glass for example, and you discover that the color of the area is not fully dissectable. Not every part of the area has the color that the area as a whole appears from a distance to have. The ordinary phenomenology represents the area as having a uniformly dissectable color, as being such that each sub-area has the same color as the whole. Does this indicate some wildly problematic understanding of itself by perceptual common sense? No. It indicates a kind of illusion we are subject to in experience. Secondary-quality experience is supposed to be a similar phenomenon (the analogy is quite apt). We are under the illusion that the object has a property that resembles our experience (in the way primary qualities actually often do resemble our experiences). As a matter of fact, the property of the object which our experience is *of* (and this needs to be explicated – though McDowell does not explicitly raise a problem here) does not resemble it.

D. Reality

In section 4 of "Values and Secondary Qualities," McDowell challenges Mackie's reason for rejecting the objectivity of secondary qualities. Of course, given McDowell's recommended revision of our conception of secondary qualities, Mackie's skeptical reasoning would have to apply in a different way, to take account of the "less extravagant construal [McDowell has] suggested for the thought that secondary qualities genuinely characterize objects" (VSQ, 117) – less extravagant because it is no longer required, for objectivity, to be independent of human sensibility in general. Objectivity is now understood simply as a matter of being there to be experienced, an aspect of the world rather than a figment of the experience supposed to be *of* it, a property genuinely possessed by objects that confront us. But all this is compatible with some of these properties having an essentially phenomenal character in the sense that experiencing them is necessarily an experience as of something's being disposed to present a certain sort of perceptual appearance.

The skeptical argument McDowell attributes to Mackie appeals to explanatory idleness. We don't need to affirm that an object actually has any property resembling what it is taken in experience to have in order to explain that experience. I'm not sure this really is Mackie's argument, at least not in *Ethics*. It does not seem to me to be near the surface in the argument from queerness, as McDowell suggests (VSQ, 118). In any case, McDowell points out a weakness in the argument: "the right explanatory test is not whether something pulls its own weight in the favoured explanation . . . but whether the explainer can consistently deny its reality" (VSQ, 118). The fact that a property does not appear in the best explanation of a phenomenon does not suffice to impugn its reality; it must be the case, at least, that accepting the best explanation is consistent with denying its existence. The existence of many properties that do not *appear in* the best explanation may still be *implied by* the properties that do appear. So even if a property is explanatorily idle, it may still be objectively real, so long as it is implied by the best explanation of corresponding phenomena.

Still, McDowell does think there is after all an important disanalogy between the case of secondary qualities and the case of values. Although these features (secondary qualities and values) are said to be alike in that experiences of them are unintelligible except as experiences as of essentially subjective properties – except as experiences as of properties "that can be understood adequately only in terms of the appropriate modification of human (or similar) sensibility" (VSQ, 118) – they are also distinct in that value experiences are also experiences as of properties that *merit* the appropriate sensible reaction. This introduces a significant new element into the issue.

McDowell attempts to "elaborate" this point in connection with "danger or the fearful." Setting aside the obvious difference between danger and the fearful, let's focus on the fearful. Sometimes, when we are experiencing fear, we also have the sense that the situation merits it: The situation *is* fearful, and as a justifiable result, we are afraid. (There are also cases, which we can ignore, of diffuse but recalcitrant anxiety accompanied by the depressing sense that the situation does not merit it.) So the fearful is like the good in this sense. And though it may be coherent to suppose that the fearful is best understood as a property of situations that is not independent of human sensibility – that what is fearful is so in virtue of being such as to produce fear in subjects like us – there is the question of how to make appropriate room for the possibility of *criticism*. Our experiencing a situation as *to be feared* appears to be subject to rational revision. We might, while continuing to be afraid, come to think that in fact there is nothing to fear. We may come to feel that our fear is misplaced. How to make room for rational disagreement about what is in fact fearful?

Recall the pathetic fallacy. Is the disgusting like the fearful? Do we make sense of disgust by "seeing it as a response to objects that *merit* such a response, or as the intelligibly defective product of a propensity towards responses that would be intelligible in that way" (VSQ, 119)? Presumably not. Unlike the fearful, and unlike the good, the disgusting lacks what McDowell wants to call "objectivity." McDowell is suggesting that for the disgusting the image of projection is appropriate, but that not so for ethics. The problem, however, is that we still have not been told what this *meriting* of a response amounts to.[11] So we do not know how to capture the difference in a way that will rule *in* the fearful and the good and rule *out* the disgusting. The most natural way to accommodate this consideration is by means of the rejected primary-quality model.

By the end of "Values and Secondary Qualities," McDowell sees himself as having begun to sketch an intermediate position. He rejects both intuitionistic Platonism and projectivist sentimentalism (and of course the idea that there is an exhaustive opposition between them). He has no patience for what he appears to consider the burlesque of an epistemology offered by the Platonist, and anyway cannot take seriously the idea of primary-quality-like properties *demanding* human affective responses. What is right about intuitionist Platonism, however, is its view of evaluative experience as a matter of *sensitivity* to aspects of the world rather than of *projection* of sentiment (by means of an erroneous attribution of a property to which the sentiment is anyway supposed to be a response). Projectivist sentimentalism, on the other hand, gets this wrong. Mackie, and since him Blackburn, are said to have a *thin* conception of reality, a conception on which there is nothing in the world that *answers* to our experience of value. Evaluative experience involves an erroneous projection onto a value-free reality. According to McDowell, reality does have values built in; those built-in values are, essentially, subjective-response producers.

In section 3 of "Values and Secondary Qualities," McDowell had distinguished two conceptions of objectivity (VSQ, 113–114): (i) "what it is for something to have [the quality] can be adequately understood otherwise than in terms of dispositions to give rise to subjective states," and (ii) "[the quality] is there to be experienced, as opposed to being a mere figment of the subjective state that purports to be an experience of it." An important thrust of McDowell's paper is that a quality can be objective in sense (ii) without needing to be objective in sense (i). McDowell alleges that it is confusion on this score that leads Mackie to skepticism about objective moral value and to the error theory.

Later, however, McDowell draws the distinction slightly differently. (i) is redrawn (VSQ, 115–116) so that whether a quality is objective depends on whether *experience* represents it as being essentially phenomenal. Mackie would *insist* that value is objective according to the redrawn sense (i) – evaluative experience does not represent value properties as essentially phenomenal. Mackie, recall, claims to be engaging in a kind of ontological analysis; and because value is subjective in the *original* sense (i), its being objective in this *redrawn* sense (i) leads precisely to his error-theory. Only now do we locate the heart of the disagreement between Mackie and McDowell. If we accept McDowell's redrawing of the first kind of objectivity, so that whether a quality is objective depends on whether experience represents it as being essentially phenomenal, then Mackie finds qualities to be objective and McDowell holds them to be subjective.

This is ironic because it is Mackie whose overall position is the *denial* of objective moral value and McDowell whose position is to affirm a kind of objectivity. But that's because although Mackie believes value is objective in the redrawn sense of (i), he finds nothing in the world that actually answers to the objective conception implicit in our experience. We might say he finds value to be *objective* in experience and in implicit conception, but *subjective,* using the original sense (i), in independent reality. McDowell by contrast emphasizes the objectivity of value in sense (ii). But he claims that our evaluative experience is already constituted by the essential phenomenality of value. So McDowell would hold that value is subjective in experience – subjective in the redrawn sense (i). That experience is not mistaken, however: value *is* subjective in the original sense (i). Our evaluative experience is thus objective in representing value as (as subjective as) it is.

E. A Projection of Error into Metaethics

Simon Blackburn claims that his own "quasi-realism"[12] coherently combines projectivism with an earned right to a standard deployment of the notion of truth. Projectivism does *threaten* to lead to noncognitivism: if "ethical remarks . . . express attitudes or sentiments"[13] it is hard to see how they are even *apt* for truth evaluability. Blackburn tries to find room for truth evaluability, in something other than an error-theoretic way, in the projectivist paradigm. Because the attitudes expressed in ethical remarks are the "upshot" of sensibilities that are themselves "subject to attitudes of approbation or disapprobation" and "a matter for argument and criticism," truth "can now be explained in terms of the fact that the sensibility from which the attitude issues stands up to the appropriate kind of criticism" (PTE, 217). Although McDowell finds it "hard to imagine that anyone would explicitly deny that if truth in ethics is available, it needs to be earned," he will argue that "a crucial issue opens up when one sets out to be less schematic" about "an account of the nature of the criticism to which ethical sensibilities are subject" (PTE, 216).

The point of the image of projection is to explain certain seeming features of reality as reflections of our subjective responses to a world that really contains no such features. Now this explanatory direction seems to require a corresponding priority, in the order of understanding, between the projected response and the apparent feature: we ought to be able to focus our thought on the response without needing to exploit the concept of the apparent feature that is supposed to result from projecting the response. . . . The question, now, is this: if in connection with some range of concepts whose application engages distinctive aspects of our subjective make-up in the sort of way that seems characteristic of evaluative concepts, we reject the kind of realism that construes subjective responses as perceptions of associated features of reality . . . , are we entitled to assume that the responses enjoy this kind of explanatory priority, as projectivism seems to require? (PTE, 218)

McDowell thinks the answer is no. And since projectivism does reject that kind of realism, it cannot satisfy the requirement about explanatory priority. McDowell recommends his own alternative. Remain realist (i.e. do not accept projectivism), thereby avoiding the requirement of an explanatorily *prior* understanding of our subjective responses, and nourish the realist aspiration by observing that ethical sensibility is susceptible to *reason* (all this while admitting the essentially response-dependent character of ethical value itself).

McDowell's alternative is developed on analogy to the comic and its associated response, amusement. We can be realists about comedy: amusement can be understood as a response to the comic qualities of a joke, for example. Jokes that are funny really do have comic qualities that are there for us to respond to. But those qualities are not wholly prior to the sentiment of amusement: what it is to be funny is, precisely, to be disposed to produce amusement. Neither, however, is the sentiment in question prior to the quality: there is no understanding the relevant response, amusement, independently of its being a matter of finding something *funny*. *Laughter,* for example, would not suffice because, as we know, we laugh at things that are not funny and fail to laugh at what is funny.

This is the essence of the "no-priority view" that McDowell seeks to defend: "a position which says that the extra features are neither parents nor children of our sentiments, but – if we must find an apt metaphor from the field of kinship relations – siblings" (PTE, 219). This view, rejecting the idea that value is *projected onto* a fundamentally value-free world, dodges the demand, otherwise implicit in earning a right to truth, for a corresponding explanatory priority. We need not seek "a conception of what it is to be funny on the basis of principles for ranking senses of humor which would have to be established from outside the propensity to find things funny" (PTE, 220). Instead we focus on the funny itself in discriminating between more or less refined senses of humor; and we do this while admitting that the funny is a matter of producing amusement in refined senses of humor. Our conception of greater and less refinement and discrimination in senses of humor will be "derivative from an understanding of what it is for things to be really funny" (PTE, 220). At the same time, what it is for things to be funny will be conceived in terms of their producing amusement in people with a good sense of humor.

McDowell's position is threatened by vicious circularity. It is impossible to explain a feature F in terms of a feature G and at the same time explain (in the same sense of explanation) feature G in terms of feature F. Nothing can *derive* from itself; and no two things can both be derivative from each other. If G-ness derives from F-ness, then F-ness does not derive from G-ness. McDowell is not unaware of the threat. But he is not impressed: "understanding the genesis of the 'new creation' [ethics] may be understanding an interlocking complex of subjective and objective or response and feature responded to" (PTE, 223). Some kinds of "interlocking," however, are incompatible with understanding.

Blackburn raises a similar issue. He says that McDowell's suggestion shirks a plainly necessary explanatory task. We want to fit the commitments implicit in our "activity of moralizing, or reaction of finding things funny . . . into a metaphysical view which can properly be hostile to an unanalysed and *sui generis* area of moral or humorous . . . facts" (PTE, 221, citing Blackburn). Blackburn worries that McDowell's position provides no connection between such truths and devices whereby we might know about them.

McDowell responds, a bit gnomically, that his aim is to "locate" the activity and reactions in the "appropriate space of reasons" (PTE, 221). He admits that no particular judgment is a sacrosanct starting point, immune to critical scrutiny; but he denies that we must earn the right to truth from an initial position "in which *all* such verdicts or judgments are suspended at once" (PTE, 222). The issue, however, is whether, if we allow *any* such judgments or verdicts, and discriminate better or worse senses of humor on that basis, we can then use the resulting conception of comic sensibility in an *explanation of* or in *understanding* (McDowell's terms) something's humor.

The same issue rearises in connection with McDowell's view that we can protect our right to conditionals of the form "if it had not been the case that the act was wrong, I would not have become committed to the belief that the act was wrong" (our having a right to such conditionals serving as a mark of objectivity) by establishing that one would not have arrived at (become committed to?) the belief that the act was wrong

had it not been for good reasons for it, *with the excellence of the reasons vindicated from within the relevant way of thinking. . . .* We have no point of vantage on the question what can be the case, that is, what can be a fact, external to the modes of thought and speech we know our way around in, with whatever understanding of what counts as better and worse execution of them our mastery of them can give us. (PTE, 222; emphasis added)

McDowell's position thus aims at "an epistemology that centres on the notion of susceptibility to reasons" (PTE, 221) where the reasons in question can themselves be partly constituted by ethical concepts. Critical scrutiny need not involve stepping outside the point of view constituted by an ethical sensibility.

Another, perhaps sharper, way of putting the point about the threat of circularity is in terms of the resulting *weakness* of the condition for objectivity. According to McDowell's view, it seems, truth and objectivity can be earned through susceptibility to reasons. But what is *that?* What kind of susceptibility? What kinds of reason? What distinguishes a "reason-susceptible" ethical stance from one that is deeply arbitrary? The difference should have something to do with the relevance of (good) reasons to take the ethical stance. But now what makes something a good ethical reason? What makes a reason relevant? If these questions will be answered from within the ethical sensibility at issue, it is unclear how to avoid the arbitrary.

Imagine: my ethical stance is the result of overwhelming oppression. My ethical beliefs, as well as my belief that an act is right just in case my oppressors approve, have been forcefully *required* of me. My ethical sensibility is affected only by alterations in what my oppressors sanction; no other considerations touch me. Is my stance susceptible to *ethical* reasons? Certainly it is subject to the will of my oppressors. This does not look much like susceptibility to ethical reasons; but then *that* appears to be a judgment from outside the moral system in question. The idea that "susceptibility to reasons" might suffice to objectify a domain builds a lot into the variety of susceptibility in question. In particular, it may need to build in (surreptitiously) what it is trying to leave out: an *external* grounding for ethics.

McDowell mentions Alasdair MacIntyre's claim that, as things stand, we cannot distinguish, "among methods of inducing people to change their minds on ethical matters, between making reasons available to them on the one hand and manipulating them in ways that have nothing in particular to do with rationality on the other" (PTE, 217). He holds that "if there is enough substance to [our understanding of better and worse execution of ethical thought and speech] to enable us to rule out a position like MacIntyre's with a clear conscience, that is what it is for truth to be attainable in such thought and speech" (PTE, 222). Unfortunately, unless whether a manipulation has anything "in particular to do with rationality" is determined from *outside* an ethical sensibility, and it certainly seems that McDowell would be opposed to any such view, we cannot rule out a position like MacIntyre's with a clear conscience. We might rule it out; but our conscience should be shadowed by the realization of the parochialism of that ruling. And we should be dissatisfied by an objectivity that we recognize to be so deeply self-centered.

III. A Prehensile Subjectivism

Attention to the threat of circularity in McDowell is preparatory: Wiggins is faced with the same threat. We'll proceed by focusing, intermittently, on key passages.

What traditional subjectivists [those that preceded "Moore's celebrated and influential critique of subjectivism"[14]] have really wanted to convey is not so much definition as commentary. Chiefly they have wanted to persuade us that, when we consider whether or not *x* is good or right or beautiful, there is no appeal to anything that is more fundamental than actually possible human sentiments. (SS, 188)

This is, in the first instance, a comment about what there is *appeal to* when we *consider* whether *x* is good or right or beautiful. But the notion of what might be appealed to in a consideration is somewhat obscure. An opponent of subjectivism need not deny that, in some sense, actually possible human sentiments are appealed to in considerations of value. The objectivist might still insist that these sentiments have no role in the *constitution* of ethical properties themselves. Compare what are agreed to be primary qualities: shape, for example. When we consider whether or not *x* is round, is there appeal to anything more fundamental than sensory experience? One needn't be a radical empiricist to accept that we have no a priori access to the shapes of objects. But that our consideration of an object's shape can ("appeal to" or) be based on, ultimately, only our sensory experience does not amount to, or force, the conclusion that shape is a subjective quality.[15]

Wiggins, like McDowell and Mackie, finds the analogy with color suggestive. According to him, "it is simply obvious that colour is something subjective" (SS, 189). Although this may be premature, the issue for Wiggins is "to develop and amplify the subjectivist claim that *x* is good if and only if *x* is such as to arouse/such as to make appropriate the sentiment of approbation" without "traducing" that claim or "treating it unfairly as a definition or an analysis" (SS, 190).

He urges that there are "two main ways." The first is Hume's projectivism. Wiggins himself aims to provide the second way to develop the subjectivist claim (SS, §§ 8–9). The crucial difference, between Hume's way and Wiggins' alternative, is that Hume, holding that "values are merely phantasms of the feelings, or gildings or stainings with colours borrowed from internal sentiment[,] . . . must never look to objects and properties themselves in characterizing the difference between good and bad judgments in taste and morals" (SS, 192–193). Ultimately, unacceptably, this leads Hume to a "*non*-subjective foundation" for his subjectivism as well as to a "substantial conception of a nearly homogeneous human nature" (SS, 193).

This "paradox" leads Wiggins away from Hume's "official theory." Wiggins seizes upon a different sort of Humean suggestion concerning "qualities in objects that are fitted by nature to produce particular . . . feelings."

> Suppose that objects that regularly please or help or amuse us . . . or harm or annoy or vex us . . . in various ways come to be grouped together by us under various categories or classifications to which we give various avowedly anthropocentric names; and suppose they come to be grouped together as they are precisely *because* they are such as to please, help, amuse us, . . . or harm, annoy, vex us . . . in their various ways. There will be then no saying, very often, what properties these names stand for independently of the reactions they provoke. (The point of calling this position subjectivism is that the properties in question are explained by reference to the reactions of human subjects.) But equally – at least when the system of properties and reactions diversifies, complicates, and enriches itself – there will often be no saying exactly *what* reaction a thing with the associated property will provoke without direct or indirect allusion to the property itself. (SS, 195)

This passage clearly exhibits a deep problem with early sensibility theories: if the objects come to be grouped together as they are *because* they are such as to please, help, amuse, harm, annoy, or vex us, then there is some *priority* of the sentiments in question with respect to the groupings. It is because of their production of certain sentiments that the objects *come to be* grouped together under categories to which we give anthropocentric names. And again the "point of calling this position subjectivism is that the properties in question are *explained by* reference to the reactions of human subjects" [emphasis added]. Explanation, recall, is necessarily asymmetric. But then we cannot accept that there is "no saying exactly *what* reaction a thing with the associated property will provoke without direct or indirect allusion to the property itself."

If there is no identifying the reaction in question without at least implicit reference to the property, then objects cannot be understood to be grouped together as instances of the properties as a result of their tendency to produce reactions in us. What I mean to suggest is that Wiggins's account of the properties' *derivation* gives a kind of priority to human reactions that he cannot then eliminate by insisting that the reactions cannot be identified except by alluding to those same properties.

Wiggins's "sensible" subjectivism, like McDowell's self-styled objectivism, is developed on analogy with the comic.

[W]hen we dispute whether *x* is really funny, there is a whole wealth of considerations and explanations we can adduce, and by no means all of them have to be given in terms simply synonymous or interdefinable with "funny." . . . [Even if "funny" is an irreducibly subjective predicate,] [t]hese diverse and supporting considerations will . . . serve a[ ] purpose. By means of them, one person can improve another's grasp of the concept of the funny; and one person can improve another's focus or discrimination of what *is* funny. (SS, 195–96)

Of course, this is all supposed to provide a model for the moral case. How satisfactory a model is it? Wiggins suggests that considerations – not all of which need be given in terms interdefinable with "funny" – can be adduced in order to *improve* one another's discrimination of what is funny. So improvement with respect to comic sensibility is supposed to be possible. But what, on the model Wiggins is developing, can such improvement amount to? Is the improvement in question anything other than more-faithful adherence to a more-widely-popular way of responding? Wiggins helps himself to a language of "improvement," "refinement," and "keenness"; so far, however, this is to assert, not to explicate, the compatibility of his subjectivism with concepts that cohere more naturally with objectivist positions.

One question concerns the standard of refinement. Improvement is improvement along a dimension; what defines the relevant dimension? The objectivist has a view; the dimension is defined by the properties themselves. Our reactions, because they are not metaphysically *prior to* the properties, can be more or less *sensitive to* them. Wiggins wants the same idea to apply to his subjectivism. But if the properties are *derivative* from our reactions, if things have the properties only *because* we have the reactions we do, if the properties are *explained* by our reactions, then the metaphor of our reactions' being better or worse approximations of what is anyway there is ruled out. A given reaction may still be more or less faithful to the reactions, taken generally, that determine the properties; so there is room for criticism of any individual reaction in terms of others. But refinement is then, presumably, a matter of blending in perfectly, having the average reactions, lack of individuality or uniqueness: accuracy becomes, essentially, *compliance.*

Wiggins argues that

we must keep faith in another way with Hume's desire to maintain the sovereignty of subjects simultaneously with the distinction between sound and mistaken judgment. We shall do this by insisting that *genuinely* [funny/appalling/shocking/consoling/ reassuring/ disgusting/pleasant/delightful/ . . .] things are things that not only [amuse/ appall/shock/console/reassure/disgust/please/delight/ . . .] but have these effects precisely because they *are* [funny/appalling/shocking/consoling/reassuring/disgusting/ pleasant/delightful/ . . .] – at the same time insisting that this "because" introduces an explanation that both explains and justifies. (SS, 199–200)

Again, subjects are sovereign (!). Nonetheless, we can distinguish between sound and mistaken judgment. And we can do this, Wiggins urges, by insisting that the genuinely funny is that which not only amuses, but does so *because* it is funny. The comic properties of genuinely funny things justify and explain our amusement; when we are amused by what is not funny, our amusement cannot be so explained. So, explanatorily idle "comic properties" do not, when instantiated, yield genuine instances of the funny.

But the problem of circularity that besets McDowell is, ironically, highlighted by Wiggins's bracketing of funny/appalling/shocking/consoling/ reassuring/disgusting/ pleasant/delightful. What, indeed, is the difference between the appalling and the consoling? Appalling things appall; and consoling things console. But to be appalled is to find something appalling and to be consoled is to find something consoling. The genuinely appalling appalls because it is appalling; the genuinely consoling consoles because it is consoling. Similarly for the other property/response pairs that Wiggins lists. If there is no "object-independent and property-independent, 'purely phenomenological' or 'purely introspective' account of amusement" (SS, 195) or of these other responses, then Wiggins has not yet said enough for us to distinguish the matched pairs in his list from one another.[16]

It is striking that immediately after the passage quoted above, Wiggins uses an especially inapt analogy for how the various effects can be explained and justified: "in *something* like the way in which 'there is a marked tendency for us all to think that $7 + 5 = 12$, and this tendency exists because there is really nothing to think about what $7 + 5$ is' explains a tendency *by* justifying it" (SS, 200). What's striking is that arithmetic facts appear to be an extreme example of the *non*-subjective. There being nothing else to think about what $7 + 5$ equals is independent of what any of us, or all of us, might be, or have been, disposed to think. Ultimately, the tendency is explained by the arithmetic facts; and, of course, the arithmetic facts are not in turn explained or justified by the tendency.

Wiggins does worry that an opponent of his view might protest that he is (in a phrase, for a different purpose, of Bernard Williams's) confusing resonance with reference. Wiggins is trying to formulate a variant upon "classical" (presumably Humean) subjectivism. The opponent objects that he is "trying to ground . . . a distinction between what is really ∅ and not really ∅ upon what are by [his] own account mere responses – upon a convergence in the inclinations various people feel or do not feel to say that *x* is ∅ or that *x* is not ∅" (SS, 204). Wiggins answers that the reactions he has been "speaking of are not 'mere' responses. They are responses that are correct when and only when they are occasioned by what has the corresponding property ø and are occasioned by it because it *is* ø" (SS, 204–05). But this makes matters worse.

If Wiggins is trying to ground a distinction between what is really ø and not really ø upon *correct* responses, where responses are correct when and only when they are occasioned by what [really] has the corresponding property ø and are occasioned by it because it *is* ø, then his task is clearly hopeless. There can be no grounding, no explanation, in terms that presuppose what is to be grounded or explained. What is to be explained is the difference between really being ø and not really being ø. This is explained in terms of a kind of response. What kind of response? Those that are occasioned by things that are really ø and because those things are really ø. But the difference between things that are really ø and those that aren't was what was to be explained. We have made no progress.

In a revealing statement, Wiggins insists that subjectivism does not "insulate from criticism the attitudes and responses that sustain glib, lazy, or otherwise suspect predications" (SS, 207). But to what *variety* of criticism does it leave those predications open? If the standards for refinement are to be found from within the moral system in question, perhaps only glib, lazy, or otherwise suspect criticisms will be applicable. The predicative practice will survive (take on a "life of its own" – see SS, 196) and evolve. Intuitively "mistaken" reactions – for example, glib and lazy indifference in the face of gross injustice – may "catch on and survive, and then . . . evolve further, and generate further [mistaken?] property, response pairs." It is not clear that a pathologically glib and lazy ethical system is differentially less *fit,* evolutionarily. Indeed, it would seem to be at least as self-supporting and self-perpetuating as preferred alternatives. A superficial look at the history of civilization may support this view (though I would not draw any definite conclusions). Given conceivable relations among antecedent distributions of resources and a disposition to such systems, there is reason to suppose such systems will show greater adaptive advantage. In short, for all we know, Wiggins's position may be a meta*un*ethics rather than a metaethics.

IV. The Wright Stuff

A. Basics

Sensibility theories themselves have evolved since their early development. Crispin Wright has sketched[17] a position that, while opposed to sensibility theories like those of McDowell and Wiggins, retains some of their basic features. His opposition to their view is based on the idea that moral judgment has no distinctive phenomenology. Moral judgment, according to Wright, does not encompass any distinctive kinds of psychological effect. It's true that valuing is necessarily linked to the state of *caring;* but Wright thinks valuing is dispassionate and has the caring as a consequence, not as a constitutive aspect. In any case, the caring in question is not a particular kind of caring.

This is a striking point on the part of Wright because, as we know, McDowell and Wiggins themselves deny that there is a distinctive moral phenomenology. That's why they define the responses that are to ground evaluative properties in terms of those same properties. There is no independent way of identifying the response of *amusement,* for example, according to McDowell, except that it is a matter of finding something *funny.* But Wright may think, plausibly, that this nevertheless points up a disanalogy between secondary qualities and evaluative properties. For the experience of red *does* have a distinctive phenomenology, qualitatively identifiable independently of the secondary quality itself.

Wright deepens this by connecting it to what he considers a more basic point. "If our experience of secondary qualities provides a model of anything, then it is of a notion of experience which is, up to a point at least, *raw*" (MVP, 12). Not every aspect of a color experience is a deployment of conceptual resources. Even when it is affected and conditioned by concepts, phenomenology maintains a degree of independence. Wright doubts that there is anything of sufficient rawness in the phenomenology of moral judgment to give the notion of "moral experience" any work to do. We cannot make sense of someone's finding something phenomenologically to be immoral while possessing no moral concepts.

This is where the dialectic becomes especially complex. Wright now thinks he has shown a certain view to be bankrupt. The unacceptable view exploits the secondary-quality analogy in a specific way. We cannot view our appreciation of moral value as modeled by our perception of secondary qualities. That perceptual model demands a kind of phenomenology that has a "raw" element – the model demands the availability of a kind of phenomenology that is potentially preconceptual. And this is what the evaluative will not provide. There is no distinctive evaluative phenomenology, or so Wright urges. Therefore the "perceptualist" application of the secondary-quality analogy fails. But the insight embedded in drawing the analogy, Wright believes, can still be preserved. The insight consists in the idea that the subjectivity of moral *judgment* can be "harmonised" with moral realism in the way that a proper understanding of secondary qualities and secondary-quality experience can yield a harmonious mix of realism and subjectivism.

Importantly, Wright's development of the analogy will jettison the notion of a distinctively moral *experience* and replace it with the notion of distinctively moral *beliefs* – beliefs whose formation is analytically tied to a disposition to certain sorts of practical concern (MVP, 13). How does Wright's development proceed? He starts with what he calls, using a term of Mark Johnston's, the "*basic equation*" for "red":

x is red ↔ for any *S:* if *S* were perceptually normal and were to encounter *x* in perceptually normal conditions, *S* would experience *x* as red. (MVP, 14)

Wright imagines modifying this by replacing the condition involving a distinctive experience ("*S* would experience *x* as red") with a condition demanding a distinctive belief.

Red

x is red ↔ for any *S:* if *S* knows which object *x* is, and knowingly observes it in plain view in normal perceptual conditions; and is fully attentive to this observation; and is perceptually normal and is prey to no other cognitive disfunction; and is free of doubt about the satisfaction of any of these conditions – *then* if *S* forms a belief about *x*'s colour, that belief will be that *x* is red. (MVP, 15)

The strategy is promising; but raises a question. This new equation (like the basic equation before it) involves the notion of *normality*. How is that to be understood?

Wright distinguishes (MVP, 15–16) a *conduciveness* interpretation of normality from a statistical interpretation. On the conduciveness interpretation, the amended basic equation appears to hold true a priori. On the statistical interpretation, things are a bit more complicated.

It would, I think, subserve the correctness of *Red* if we glossed the notion of normal perceptual function as: perceptual function of a kind which is actually typical of human beings. But it will not do so to gloss "normal perceptual circumstances." The conditions which actually usually prevail during winter in Spitzbergen, for instance, or in a normal photographic dark-room, are not suited for colour appraisal. A good description of conditions which are, optimally, so suited would be: conditions of illumination like those which actually typically obtain at noon on a cloudy summer's day out of doors and out of shadow. Even here "typically" is required because such conditions are sometimes disturbed by solar eclipses, nuclear explosions, dust storms and volcanic discharges. So there is still an element of statisticality. But notice: when both uses of the notion of normality are so interpreted, in broadly statistical terms, *Red* continues not merely to hold true but to hold true *a priori*. For our knowledge that typical visual functioning and conditions of illumination like those I just broadly statistically characterised are conducive for the appraisal of colour is not *a posteriori* knowledge. (MVP, 16)

I think Wright is too quick in making these claims about color. He thinks our knowledge that certain conditions are conducive to color appraisal might be a priori. It might be an a priori truth that, for example, illumination like that *typically* obtaining at noon on a cloudy summer's day is conducive to color appraisal. But I'm skeptical. For all we might have known a priori, couldn't it have been the case that color appraisal is best carried out in photographic darkrooms? Conditions conducive to color appraisal come to be known to us only through experience, it seems; our knowledge that certain conditions are so conducive can be justified only empirically. Wright's opposing opinion is, according even to him, "crucial in what follows" (MVP, 16).

At this point, Wright marks an alleged disanalogy between secondary and primary qualities. The contrast, ultimately, involves the possibility of producing a priori true basic equations for primary qualities on the model of those we have seen for secondary qualities. His contention is that the analogous basic equations would not be true a priori – not even after judicious refinement (or if they were, there would still be another crucial disanalogy concerning the independence of the concepts used in specifying the relevant conditions and the concepts under analysis).

He considers a "canonical biconditional" for "approximately square."

x is approximately square $\leftrightarrow$ if the four sides and four interior angles of x were to be correctly measured, and no change were to take place in the shape or size of x during the process, then the sides would be determined to be approximately equal in length, and the angles would be determined to approximate right angles. (MVP, 19)

He considers this in order to bring out the fact that

[I]t is not *a priori* true, but merely a deep fact of experience, that our (best) judgements of approximate shape, made on the basis of predominantly visual observations, usually "pan out" when appraised in accordance with more refined operational techniques. . . . It is not *a priori* true that the world in which we actually live allows reliable perceptual appraisal of approximate shape – is not, for example, a world in which the paths travelled by photons are subject to grossly distorting forces. (MVP, 20)

The problem is that this is supposed to be by way of contrast with the case of secondary qualities. As I noted above, however, it's not clear that the contrast holds. Isn't it also knowable only a posteriori that the world in which we actually live allows reliable perceptual appraisal of color? that it is not, for example, a world in which the paths traveled by photons are subject to grossly distorting forces? Actually, I don't feel certain whether these are a priori or a posteriori; but I do not in any case see the alleged variation between the case of primary qualities and that of secondary qualities.

The upshot for Wright is that we have "a satisfying account of what is subjective and what is objective in secondary quality ascription, and how the element of subjectivity is compatible with objectivity" (MVP, 21). And "[t]he question is, do ascriptions of moral quality provide another illustration?" His answer, ultimately, is that the ascription of moral qualities is fundamentally different from secondary-quality ascription, but that the latter may point us in the direction of a related way of harmonizing a subjective element with objectivity in ethics.

Moral experience, unlike secondary-quality experience, has no distinctive phenomenology. But by substituting moral beliefs for moral experience in a nonreductive account of evaluative properties, we can produce a priori true basic equations that characterize evaluative properties. Even so, the satisfaction of the relevant conditions in *Moral* cannot be independent of the extension of moral concepts themselves.

Moral

P ↔ for any *S*: if *S* scrutinises the motives, consequences, and for Jones, foreseeable consequences in the context of the remark; and does this in a fashion which involves no error concerning nonmoral fact or logic, and embraces all *morally-relevant* considerations; and if *S* gives all this the fullest attention, and so is victim to no error or oversight concerning any relevant aspect of his/her deliberations; and if *S* is a *morally-suitable* subject – accepts *the right moral principles,* or has *the right moral intuitions or sentiments,* or whatever; and if *S* has no doubt about the satisfaction of any of these conditions, *then* if *S* forms a moral evaluation of Jones' remark, that evaluation will be that *P.* (MVP, 22–23, emphasis added)

Here we find a fundamental breakdown in the analogy between moral and secondary qualities:

[P]roper pedigree for visual appraisals of colour is a matter of meeting conditions whose satisfaction in a particular case does not directly depend on what the extension of colour predicates is; proper pedigree for moral judgments, by contrast, is a matter of meeting conditions the satisfaction of some of which is, irreducibly, a moral question. (MVP, 23–24)

This is now a familiar problem for sensibility theories. Wright draws two important consequences. First, "the extension of the truth predicate among ascriptions of moral quality may not be thought of as determined by our best beliefs" and second, "judgments of moral quality cannot *inherit* objectivity in the way in which . . . judgments of secondary quality can" (MVP, 24) These consequences *appear* to favor a projectivist view (or even an error theory) over a view like that of McDowell and Wiggins's, Wright admits. But he thinks it would be premature to recoil from the analogy with secondary qualities directly into a projectivist or an error theory. Another possibility is to see moral epistemology as *"self-contained"* – an idea that Wright thinks, controversially, has a prima facie analog in mathematical judgment. Wright appears optimistic that we will accordingly find harmony at last. I worry about emptiness.

B. Struth!

Later, in "Truth in Ethics,"[18] Wright attempts to substantiate his optimism. Like McDowell, he too I think subtly misunderstands the import of Mackie's error theory.[19] He finds that theory "unlikely . . . [to] serve [as] a satisfactory moral theory" because it "relegates moral discourse to bad faith." If there is something to this, so far I think Wright's case for it (TE, 2–3) is insufficient.

The critical point for Wright, to begin with, is that the error theory forgoes any conception of a *"proper basis"* for moral sentiment – "the world is unsuited to confer truth on any of our claims about what is right." (TE, 2). But we see that Wright bases this criticism on the idea that according to the error theory, "it is of the essence of moral judgment to aim at the truth" even when "there is no moral truth to hit" (TE, 2). This understanding of the error theory's predicament, however, may conflate two ideas from Mackie.

Mackie is almost certainly a cognitivist. He does think that moral judgments aim at the truth. And he might well think that it is of the essence of moral judgments that they aim at the truth. But it is not clear that Mackie would support the idea that there are no truths of the sort that it is of the essence of moral judgments to aim at. He denies that there are any *objective* moral truths; and he thinks that moral judgments do, *in fact,* aim at objectivity. But it is not clear, to me at least, that he thinks *it is of the essence of* moral judgments to aim at objective truth. It is not clear that he would think anything that did not aim at objectivity was ipso facto not a moral judgment. His claim about the objectivity to which moral judgment aims appears to be more of an observation, a generalization from introspection. Indeed, refraining from attributing to him the stronger claim would make sense of his readiness, in later chapters, to make moral judgments. Mackie might view cognitivism as a nonnegotiable feature of morality, while consistently maintaining that the implicit commitment to objectivity of our actual moral practice is in principle separable.

In any case, Wright canvasses a possible response to his criticism, a response in support of Mackie's position: perhaps there is some subsidiary norm relative to which moral judgments, all of which are equally false, can be assessed. The making of moral judgments can be rendered reasonable by appeal to this subsidiary norm and the charge of bad faith could be dissolved. But this strategy invites what Wright considers a good question.

[I]f, among the welter of falsehoods which we enunciate in moral discourse, there is a good distinction to be drawn between those which are acceptable in the light of some such subsidiary norm and those which are not . . . then why insist on construing *truth* for moral discourse in terms which motivate a charge of global error, rather than explicate it in terms of the satisfaction of the putative subsidiary norm, whatever it is? (TE, 3)

Indeed. Simply substitute "objectively true" for "true" (and analogously for the cognates) and let some form of subjective truth constitute the subsidiary norm and you get a question to which Mackie could answer as follows: "only because doing so would be revisionary of what is implicit in our actual moral phenomenology; nevertheless, the revision may be called for." In other words, what there is a welter of, according to Mackie, is claims to *objective* moral truth. No claim to objective moral truth can be made good; and all such claims are thus false. But such claims may satisfy certain, admittedly ultimately subjective, standards. It may then be appropriate to *redefine* moral truth in terms of the satisfaction of those standards. But such an account would be revisionary: ordinary moral practice is, as a matter of contingent fact, implicitly committed to the objectivity of moral judgments. The charge of global error is appropriate – but the error has not been alleged as *pathological*.

Summarizing broadly, Wright is attempting to show that antirealists need not give up the notion of truth in ethics. Some but not all moral judgments will still be *superassertible* (TE, 9): "superassertible" will effectively function as a truth predicate, a predicate that validates the basic platitudes about truth that Wright elsewhere argues[20] are constitutive of the notion of truth.

Superassertibility is "an absolute notion: a statement is superassertible if it is assertible in some state of information and then remains so no matter how that state of information is enlarged upon or improved" (TE, 10). And assertibility is a matter of meeting the standards (the "discipline" in Wright's terminology) that govern the discourse in question. These standards are "*language-game internal*," internal to the discourse. We thus dispense with the notion of *correspondence* (though we could innocently retain the locution, if we chose). Truth is ultimately defined from *within* the discourse. Wright's discussion here hearkens back to his earlier ideas about the "self-containment" of moral epistemology.

But Wright misses at least *my* inclinations when he claims: "What those whose intuitive inclination is to moral realism really want, I suggest, is not truth as representation – realism as properly understood – but a certain kind of objectivity in moral appraisal: ideally, precisely that a tendency towards convergence in the conception of what is morally important and how much importance it has, be indeed intrinsic to moral thinking itself" (TE, 18).

Intersubjectivity (or even "that a tendency towards convergence be intrinsic") will not satisfy the intuitive demand for realism and objectivity. If I am concerned that a particular agent might, even in ideal conditions of "information," make errors in moral judgment, why should I think it metaphysically impossible that we *all* make moral errors, even that we all *tend* to make moral errors, even under conditions of increasing (nonmoral) information? One needn't be so pessimistic as to think that what is true in morality is "altogether beyond our ken" (TE, 13) in order to hold that what is true in morality is always, even in conditions of full nonmoral information (even if a judgment is superassertible), independent of what we judge – though we may often judge correctly. What is *potentially* beyond our ken might fail actually to be beyond our ken. Of course, Wright's tendentious characterization of the realist alternative ("the idea that . . . the connection between prosecution of best method and getting at the truth is, at bottom, 'serendipitous'" [TE, 9]) makes that an easier target. But to hold that two things are metaphysically independent is far from holding that they might not overlap in *systematic*, rather than merely serendipitous, ways. So we set Wright's sensibility theory aside too, as we proceed.

V. Hyperthalamic Ethics?

A.

Mark Johnston begins his discussion[21] with Hume. In a pair of quotations, Hume first compares "vice and virtue" to colors and other secondary qualities, which "according to the modern philosophy [e.g., Locke's] are not qualities in the object but perceptions in the mind." But in the second quotation Hume expresses some hesitation in connection with the error-theoretic aspect of "modern philosophy," comparing the claim that "snow is neither cold nor white" to a "paradox." If we admit the analogy with secondary qualities and deny the view that such qualities are not "in the object," we get what might be the "motto" for "analogists" such as McDowell and Wiggins.

With what conception of secondary qualities might the analogists be operating? Johnston begins with a simple "dispositional conception":

x is red iff *x* is disposed to look such and so (ostended) way to standard perceivers as they actually are under standard conditions as they actually are. (DTV, 140)

Such an account would have three virtues. First, predications involving '*x* is red' would be truth-evaluable in a straightforward way. Second, "predicating '*x* is red' could be part of straightforward causal/dispositional explanations of why those things look red to perceivers" (DTV, 140). And third, the dispositional account does not devolve into a "simple subjectivism or idealism": the phrase "as they actually are" enables the biconditional to count *x* as red even if, standard perceivers or standard conditions being different, it were not disposed to look such and so (ostended) way to standard perceivers under standard conditions (just so long as it *were* disposed to look that way to standard perceivers *as they actually are . . .*).

These three virtues allow the dispositional conception to "confound" three kinds of theories: noncognitivism about color, error theories about color, and "delayed-reaction" color realism that sees "a problem about how remarks of the form '*x* is red' could be truth evaluable given their causal origin in our responses, a problem which requires a substantial explanation of how we come to 'earn the right' to express our experiences in terms of judgments about external things" (DTV, 141).

The analogy between the evaluative and the colored thus holds out the promise of a corresponding effect on noncognitivism, error theory, or quasi-realism in ethics. But Johnston insists that this promise is conditioned by just which analogy is deployed. There are important disanalogies.

First, in the evaluative domain (at least once we go beyond the sensuous aesthetic values) there is no very good analog of our ordinary perception of secondary qualities. "[V]alues are not in general the object of any perceptual or quasi-perceptual faculty or sense" (DTV, 142).[22] Second, according to Johnston, "talk about red, colour or secondary qualities, while talk of determinables, is still relatively detailed talk. However, talk about value is talk at a level of almost fantastic abstraction" (DTV, 143). I worry that the disanalogy claimed by Johnston may be the product of an unfair comparison: redness is in some sense a more specific property than simply being valuable. But can we say the same for *having a secondary quality?* Is talk about value really talk at a level of more fantastic abstraction than talk of being a secondary quality? I'm not yet convinced.

In any case, Johnston claims other disanalogies. According to him, the prospects for an analysis or definitional reduction are brighter in the case of colors than they are with respect to the evaluative.

[W]e can rely upon the neophyte's quality space and a cannily chosen collection of foils and paradigms to make salient a way things look . . . we could [accordingly] give a substantive specification of standard perceivers and standard conditions without even covertly using the notions of being red . . . [and] we would here have defined a colour concept ostensively and without relying upon any colour concept as opposed to colour sample.

However, nothing like this will be plausible in the case of the concept of being a valuable state of affairs. . . . There is a colour (appearance) solid but no value (appearance) solid. (DTV, 143–144).

Finally fourth, and this further supports the differential prospects for definitional reduction in the two domains, the concept of finding good reason to value a state of affairs appears to depend on the concept of value itself: x is a good reason for valuing y only if valuing y because of x is itself *valuable. Good reason* is itself an evaluative concept: noticing this forces us to give up the "analytically reductive game with respect to the universal predicate of favourable assessment of states of affair" (DTV, 144).

But, Johnston goes on to claim, that is not the only game suggested by the analogy. "The most plausible, if highly generalizing, way of taking the analogy is this: evaluational concepts, like secondary quality concepts as understood by the analogists, are 'response-dependent' concepts" (DTV, 144). What is response-dependence? Johnston defines this as a matter of a concept's being "interdependent with or dependent upon the concept of certain subjects' responses under certain conditions" (DTV, 145).[23] With respect to any such concept something of the following form will hold a priori:

x is C iff In K, S's are disposed to produce x-directed response R (or [iff] x is such as to produce R in S's under conditions K). (DTV, 145)

Some obvious examples of response-dependent concepts would be the *nauseating,* the *embarrassing,* the *irritating,* and the *credible* (DTV, 146). And the best examples of response-*in*dependent concepts are from theoretical science, logic, and mathematics. Johnston cautions us not to confuse the concept of a subject's employing a concept with the concept so employed (DTV, 146).

Now, Johnston thinks that "[m]any pivotal issues in philosophy . . . can be cast in terms of whether and in what way the central concepts in those areas are response-dependent" (DTV, 146). This is because philosophers often seek a "qualified realism" about the relevant areas of discourse. A qualified realism would assert that "the discourse in question serves up genuine candidates for truth and falsity, and that, nonetheless, the subject matter which makes statements of the discourse true or false is *not wholly independent of* the cognitive or affective responses of the speakers of the discourse" (DTV, 144; emphasis added). The "basic problem" is to explain the variety of *dependence* contemplated by such a qualified realism without reducing the view to some kind of idealism. Opposing Dummett's semantic antirealism and Putnam's internal realism,[24] Johnston prefers *local* and *topic-specific* qualified realisms and rejects a response-dependent conception of truth.

Johnston stresses that the characterization of response-dependent concepts does not imply that they admit of a *reductive* definition in terms of subjects' responses, and he reminds us of the "explicit allowance for conceptual interdependence." He notes, moreover, the possibility that the biconditional that shows a concept to be response-dependent might be, strictly speaking, circular. If our aim is only the exhibition of conceptual connections, however, this circularity is no vice (DTV, 147).

We thus see how a response-dependent account of the central concepts of a given area of discourse can amount to a qualified realism about that area. It can be a realist (as opposed to *irrealist*) conception of the area because it can allow genuine instances of the relevant concepts to exist, realist (as opposed to *idealist*) conception because it can allow that instances of the concept could exist even if the relevant conditions and responders had been different, and a realist (as opposed to *antirealist, internal realist,* or *pragmatist*) conception because it can deny those views' commitment to a response-dependent conception of truth. But the realism is nevertheless qualified precisely in its denial that the concepts in question are independent of the concept of subjects' responses under specified conditions.

This much smartly sets the stage for Johnston's central concern: whether "the notion of value, the all purpose notion of favourable assessment of states of affair, is a response-dependent notion" (DTV, 148). He is not prepared to endorse just any response-dependent account of value (indeed in his next section he subtly critiques David Lewis's elegant proposal); but he will ultimately propose an alternative of his own.

B.

Johnston's proposal proceeds in stages. First, we must broaden our conception of reasonableness to encompass that more substantive variety "which we look for in both practical and theoretical matters" (DTV, 162). Accordingly, Johnston offers the following:

(1) x is a value iff substantive reason is on the side of valuing x. (DTV, 162)

This is supposed to be uncontroversial. The right-hand side may be a kind of paraphrase of the left. But we can articulate the claim, and make it more controversial, by adding the following:

(2) y is a substantive reason for/against valuing x iff we are disposed stably to take it to be so under conditions of increasing information and critical reflection. (DTV, 162)

If under some conditions we take y to be a substantive reason for valuing x, and if critical reflection on more inclusive states of information yields the same result (with respect to y's being a substantive reason for valuing x), then we are disposed stably to take y to be a substantive reason for valuing x. (2) raises a question about which methods for weighing substantive reasons are acceptable. Surely not just any method for weighing substantive reason, such that relative to it, we are stably disposed to take y to be a substantive reason for valuing x, suffices to make y in fact a substantive reason for valuing x. Johnston suggests the following:

(3) A method for weighing substantive reasons is an acceptable method for determining whether the weight of substantive reason is on the side of valuing x iff we are stably disposed to take it to be so under conditions of increasing information and critical reflection (DTV, 163).

I worry about the adequacy of (3) as a response to the possible difficulty with (2). After all, surely not just any method for considering the acceptability of methods for weighing substantive reasons will do. There may be methods for judging the acceptability of a method for weighing substantive reasons such that, relative to them, we are stably disposed to judge the method acceptable when in fact it is not. At least, this seems no less likely than the analogous claim with respect to (2), to which Johnston himself appears to be sensitive in offering us (3). In any case, we are led immediately to (4):

(4) Substantive reason is on the side of valuing x iff this is so according to one and all [acceptable] methods of weighing the reasons for and against valuing x. (DTV, 163–64)

Together, (1) through (4) constitute Johnston's (dispositional and) response-dependent account of value. The notion of substantive reason used in the account of value given by (1) is response-dependent as made explicit by (2) and (3). "There are no substantive reasons which we cannot get to in principle from here, although getting to them may involve a gradual but thorough re-working of what we take to be substantive reasons, the appropriate methods of weighing them and perhaps also the correct styles of critical reflection" (DTV, 164).

A worry I expressed above rearises here: couldn't arriving at substantive reasons sometimes involve a reworking of our methods of reworking? If so, might not such reasons be in principle inaccessible to us? Couldn't we be wrong *all the way down?* Johnston says (DTV, 164), "[i]f we think of our present system of substantive reasonableness on the model of Neurath's ship, not only may the ship require considerable overhaul but so also may our methods of overhauling it." But so also might our way of changing our method of overhauling the ship, and so also might our process for changing the way we change the method by which we overhaul the ship, and so on and on without end. If there is no level of our system of practical reason that is not in need of overhaul, then it may be that some substantive reasons are, after all, *hyper-external.*[25]

After a discussion of the variety of relativism entrained by the response-dependent account he favors (DTV, § VI, 166–170), Johnston returns (DTV, § VII, 170–174) to the residual appeal of response-independent accounts of value. He admits that a response-dependent account should be offered as a "partly revisionary account." But I question his sympathetic use of the quotation from Wittgenstein:

The right road is the road which leads to an *arbitrarily* predetermined end and it is quite clear to us all that there is no sense in talking about the right road apart from such a predetermined goal. . . . I think it would have to be the road which *everybody* on seeing it would, *with logical necessity* have to go or feel ashamed for not going.[26] (cited by Johnston, DTV, 170–171)

While Johnston finds something in this sort of robust objectivity, he holds that Mackie successfully stigmatized it as an error at the heart of our thought about value. And Johnston's account is meant to "eliminate precisely this error of supposing that the demands of value or substantive practical reason are thoroughly independent of our tendency to respond to such demands" (DTV, 171). I am troubled because Wittgenstein is stressing the kind of *internalism* that Johnston himself has earlier (DTV, 160–161) in effect rejected. Why should a defender of a response-independent account, of all positions, be viewed as committed to such a strong variety of internalism?

According to a response-independent conception of value, there are evaluative demands built into the world in such a way that any responsible agent *should,* on pain of evaluative error, respect. The evaluative, to be response independent, need not be thought of as a product of rationality.[27] Did Mackie successfully stigmatize *this* view of "the objectively prescriptive"? Not if, as I suggest, he commits the slide to avoid. The fact that we can make no sense of a demand for a motive-independent-motivation (these would be queer) does not entail that we can make no sense of a motive-independent-demand for a motivation. The response-independent theorist is committed only to the latter.

We might consider other possible manifestations of the projective error Mackie finds embedded in our ordinary moral discourse and practice. Take Plato's *Euthyphro*. The Socratic argument exhibited there (at 10B–11B) is, Johnston admits, "the characteristic bugbear of response-dependent accounts" (DTV, 172). Johnston points out that his account will "allow many instances of this form of argument as showing that *certain* dependencies are not relevant to the correct account of value. . . . Something is valued by the ideal observer because it is valuable, i.e., in accord with substantive practical reason. It is not valuable because it is valued by the ideal observer" (DTV, 172).

But at the next level, when we consider the nature of substantive reasons, Johnston must "take care" and "dig in." He can admit an "explanatory element in the remark that we take something to be a reason because it is a reason" (DTV, 172); but he will insist that whatever is a reason is so precisely because we would take it to be so as we approach ideal conditions. Otherwise we illegitimately require *hyper-external* reasons.

It is not easy to see how to argue about this. But Johnston offers (DTV, 172–173) one argument in support of his view. If there were hyper-external reasons, by what consideration could we be led to believe that we have ever been in contact with one? Given a response-independent conception of substantive reason, the following claim

(H) The substantive reasons are to be discovered by taking into account relevant information and critically reflecting on it.

appears to be a merely contingent empirical hypothesis. And, according to Johnston there is something "essentially bogus" (DTV, 173) about the idea of finding empirical support for the claim that we discover the substantive reasons through reflection on information.

If a response-independent conception of substantive reason must regard (H) as contingent, then perhaps Johnston has a powerful argument. But I'm not convinced the position is committed to that. Notice that (H) is a thesis about how substantive reasons are to be *discovered,* not about what they *are.* It may be a priori that a set of facts are to be discovered in some way, even though perfect exercise of the recommended method is no *guarantee* of success. Johnston himself wants to allow some response-independent concepts – he rejects (DTV, 145) one kind of response-dependent account of *truth.* Is he now prevented from maintaining a priori theses about how the instantiation of those concepts is to be discovered? I don't see why. Facts about how discoveries occur *when they do* may be knowable a priori even while the possibility of error is persistent. Our metaethics had better not manifest a *hypo*-objectifying, hyperthalamic error.[28]

VI. Forward to the Past

To recapitulate briefly, sensibility theories are troubled. There needs to be some constraint on the subjective reactions that properly count as constituting ethical value. But no noncircular account appears plausible – for two reasons. First, there seems to be no way to characterize the *kind* of reaction that is relevant – unlike color experience, moral experience is not phenomenologically distinctive. But if moral experience is constituted by cognitive states, and the relevant individuation of cognitive states is in terms of their *contents,* then specification of the relevant kind of reaction will presuppose the concept whose nature is under investigation. Second, even assuming there were no circularity in defining the notion of a moral judgment and then using it to understand moral properties, not just any exercise of moral judgment should be relevant to the determination of moral properties. Presumably only *good* (or appropriate, or morally or ethically sensitive) uses of moral judgment should qualify. But this is a small circle of concepts. Can we be confident that it will distinguish ethics from etiquette?

More recently, Wright and Johnston have tried to rehabilitate sensibility theory, reducing its reductive ambition and jettisoning the perceptualist metaphor implicit in McDowell and Wiggins's development of the secondary-quality analogy. Wright's discussion relies ultimately on the possibility of a substantive "self-contained" moral epistemology. His talk of standards that are "language-game internal," however, is reminiscent of the McDowell/Wiggins view, if now shorn of its perceptualist trappings. And though such a view need not be *false,* I have tried to raise a doubt about its explanatory adequacy.

Johnston's introduction of the general notion of a "response-dependent concept" is promising. Like Wright's idea of concepts for which a characteristic sort of biconditional – one making essential reference to human subjective responses – is a priori, response-dependence bids fair to give us an understanding of how the normative might both *demand* certain attitudes from us while, in another sense, being *constituted* by those very attitudes. Of course Johnston faces an analog of the issue that threatens other sensibility theories. According to him, the relevant concepts are response-dependent *all the way down:* value is defined in terms of the balance of substantive reason, substantive reason is defined in terms of our disposition to find a reason substantive (according to an acceptable method for weighing reasons), and the acceptability of methods for weighing reasons is defined in terms of our disposition to find such methods acceptable.

The opposing attitude is suspicious of making the metaphysical depend on the epistemic in this way. A healthy modesty about our epistemic capacity nourishes the worry that we just *might* be wrong all the way down. This modesty finds expression in an echo of *Euthyphro*. Isn't the practice of finding something a good reason itself "answerable" to an independent reality in the following sense: in the best cases we find something a good reason for something else *because it is?*

If sensibility theory's heroic effort to reconceptualize objectivity fails, we are thrown back on Mackie's interpretation. According to Mackie, and according to his conception of objectivity, ethics is not objective. Our commonsense conception of it is in error. We go wrong in seeing ethical properties as objective, *that is* — for this is now what objectivity will be — as built into the fabric of the world independently of any subjective responses to those properties. To correct the error, we must slough off these objectivist tendencies and face the subjectivist reality squarely. This need not force us to noncognitivism — just to a better appreciation of the nature of what is cognized. We are not noncognitivist about the disgusting, or about the funny, appalling, and so on. Neither should we be noncognitivist about the ethical. But we cannot be objectivist without error.

On the other hand, any sort of projectivism will have its own disadvantages. Indeed, it is partly recoil from Hume's "gilding and staining" metaphor that leads to sensibility theory in the first place. Again, Mackie himself points out that ordinary moral phenomenology is committed to the objectivity of morality. Our sense of moral outrage upon witnessing some act of wanton cruelty is experienced as a response to features of the situation that are anyway there. McDowell finds an important difference between evaluative properties and their secondary-quality cousins (not siblings) in the fact that evaluative properties can be said to *merit* the very responses in terms of which they are conceived. And Wiggins doubts that life can be meaningful if value is not seen as, in some sense, *transcending* our valuations: "no attempt to make sense of the human condition can make sense of it if it treats the objects of psychological states as unequal partners or derivative elements in the conceptual structure of values and states and their objects."[29] We are referred to Aristotle (though unsympathetically, by Wiggins, who finds it an overreaction): "We desire the object because it seems good to us, rather than the object's seeming good to us because we desire it."[30]

Perhaps it is time to reconsider the rejection of a full-blooded, *hardcore* objectivity, this notwithstanding various derogatory claims about whether the position can be "taken seriously," "is intelligible," or "incoherent."

Of all the possible objectivist positions available in the logical space left by the denial of subjectivism, Platonism is one of the least tempting. Hardly anyone holds it, there is little point in arguing against it, and there is not very much to say about it. Any subjectivists who take it to be their most serious opposition are wasting their time on a straw man, and underestimating the strength of their objectivist opposition. . . . [I] assume that in ethics, at least, Platonism is not a live option.[31]

Exactly *why,* however, can't evaluative properties be more like primary qualities than they are like either projections or secondary qualities?

It should be admitted right away that there is a bit (or perhaps a *variety*) of subjectivism that is right. Never mind ethical properties – the very *bearers* of ethical properties depend on the existence of subjective agents. Whatever we take as the primary bearers of ethical property, whether these be intentional actions, complexes involving subjects, or just subjects individually, subjectivity is an essential element in the very constitution of the bearers of ethical properties. So the field of ethics is bound up with subjectivity in an intimate way. Notice that this seems different from, say, physics generally. There is a kind of discontinuity brought on simply in virtue of the metaphysics of the subject matter. Ethical properties are significantly different from physical properties because, whatever their nature, the former, though not the latter, could in no way obtain without the existence of agents – what could have them? Of course, if we are ultimately physicalist about the mind, this distinction dissolves.

Ethics is intimately bound up with subjectivity in a further way: part of what makes an action right has *something* to do with how that action relates to subjective agents. Such notions as intent, happiness, pleasure and pain, duty, and rights appear to be inseparable from subjectivity (as do the virtues of courage, loyalty, generosity, justice, benevolence, etc.). To the extent that those notions are relevant to the ethical status of an act, that status is not independent of subjectivity. Whatever the final form of our normative theory, it seems antecedently clear that what makes an action ethically right or good will have *something* to do with how things stand (or stood or will stand) with subjective agents. It will be some properties of subjects – either the agent herself or the agent together with various affected parties – that will make the agent's action have the ethical status it does. Exactly which properties of which subjects is a matter for normative theory. But no plausible normative theory leaves subjectivity out of the picture entirely.

These two roles for subjectivity mark an interesting division, incidentally, between ethics and aesthetics, it seems to me. The subject matter of aesthetics *need not* involve subjectivity. Beautiful things need not have any mentality as a constituent part. Consider the following passage from Putnam's *Reason, Truth, and History.*

An ant is crawling along a patch of sand. As it crawls, it traces a line in the sand. By pure chance the line that it traces curves and recrosses itself in such a way that it ends up looking like a recognizable caricature of Winston Churchill. Has the ant traced a picture of Winston Churchill, a picture that *depicts* Churchill?[32]

Putnam doubts the pattern produced would be *meaningful.* Whatever we think of Putnam's point, there should be little doubt that the ant might produce a *beautiful* pattern. That we might value more a duplicate pattern produced by intentional agency shows only that we have more values than the purely aesthetic, it seems to me. The natural majesty of the Grand Canyon does not depend on a divine provenance; and we delight, when Voyager sends back pictures of Jupiter's surface, at the discovery of so much beauty, so far from home. We may say then, perhaps surprisingly, that aesthetics is in this way *more* objective than ethics.

The existence of subjects is thus a precondition on the obtaining of ethical properties; and how things stand with subjects will be in some way relevant to the determination of the ethical status of actions. So much forces us toward a particular sort of subjectivism in ethics. But sensibility theories press for something else. They see the nature of ethical properties as significantly inter-related with ethical *attitudes* – a specifically *cognitive* response is singled out as distinctively relevant. We have an incipient *epistemicism*[33] associated with sensibility theories. Subjective evaluations are held to be interdependent with ethical value. It is this element for which I do not see sufficient justification.

Sensibility theories appear to represent an unholy matrimony between two quite different ideas. First, the idea implicit in the analogy with secondary qualities is that the features in question are *constituted* by subjective reactions, objects have the properties *in virtue of* subjects' having those reactions, the features have no reality *beyond* that given them by the existence of the relevant subjective reactions. This idea alone is insufficient to sustain a "sensible" subjectivism, objectivity of the sort McDowell pursues, mainly because there is no independently specifiable variety of subjective reaction in terms of which to analyze the evaluative properties.

A second, very different idea is borrowed from an antirealist current (whose roots are in verificationism). That current is opposed to the idea that there might be truths that will outrun all of our best theories, no matter how much those theories are improved. This is the central idea of, for example, Putnam's "internal" or "pragmatic" realism, and whatever we may think of that so-called realism, there is an important difference between it and the central idea of the analogy with secondary qualities. Sensibility theories in ethics in this way go beyond subjectivism to a form of epistemicism. In admitting that evaluative properties are subjective in the two ways discussed above – the existence of subjects is a precondition of the obtaining of ethical properties and the ethical status of an act is not independent of the subjective states of the agents involved – we in no way commit ourselves to the epistemicism implicit in latter-day subjectivism.

The alternative floated here, then, is that ethics is subjective insofar as its subject matter essentially involves subjects and insofar as the applicability of its characteristic properties and predicates is not independent of the distribu-tion of subjective states among the subjects involved in the ethically evaluable situation. What I allege to be irrelevant, however, is how things stand with subjects who are not involved in the ethically evaluable state: how things stand (or would stand, under specified conditions, or are disposed to stand) with actual or potential *evaluators* (that do not themselves figure in the situation) is independent of the ethical status of actions. Given that certain agents act from a vicious character, or a bad will, or produce a balance of pain over pleasure or unhappiness over happiness, the ethical status of their act is settled, and any potential evaluator's disposition to *judge* the act bad, or to have a con- or pro-attitude toward it, simply reflects their ethical acumen. Ethics is accordingly objective while still reflecting a kind of subjectivity. What could be wrong with such a view?

Recall an important passage in McDowell. "[I]t seems impossible – at least on reflection – to take seriously the idea of something that is like a primary quality in being simply *there,* independently of human sensibility, but is nevertheless intrinsically (not conditionally on contingencies about human sensibility) *such as to* elicit some 'attitude' or state of will from someone who becomes aware of it" (VSQ, 111; emphasis added). McDowell will have to do much better, in rejecting this view, than to report his inability to take it seriously. In the meanwhile, be aware of the threat of what I earlier called the "slide to avoid." Can a quality be "such as to" elicit a state of will even if many who are, in some sense, aware of it, do not acquire the state? The wording is, I think, critically indeterminate. Certainly I can elicit a response (to a party invitation, for example, I can add 'RSVP') and not get one. It is not at all impossible, or even difficult, to take seriously (indeed, to *accept*) the idea that something that is like a primary quality in being simply there, independently of human sensibility, is nevertheless intrinsically such as to elicit a state of will from someone who becomes aware of it (perhaps the state of will is in some sense demanded even of those who are *not* aware of it). Why couldn't a primary quality in the relevant sense *demand* an affective attitude?

The issue of internalism is confusing because it encompasses not only the question (i) of whether the obtaining of a property could possibly demand, independently of any subjective reactions, an affective state, but also the question (ii) of whether a subject could *judge* that a property obtains without being in the relevant affective state.[34] The case of color is again instructive. Even if it were the case that an object's being red were analytically tied to the obtaining of certain independently specifiable subjective states, it would not follow that someone could not judge that something is red without being in or even having a tendency to be in that subjective state. Color-blind people, exploiting testimony, can judge and even know that things have certain colors, colors they cannot see.

For evaluative properties too, there is the possibility that ethical value be analytically tied to the obtaining of certain independently specifiable subjective states, but that someone judges that a circumstance has positive value without being positively motivated toward it. "There is a name for not being motivated by what one judges valuable. It is of course 'weakness of will' . . .

[w]eakness of will . . . can disrupt the expected connection between judging something valuable and desiring it in the extended sense" (DTV, 161).

Avoiding the slide, and appreciating the weakness of any plausible internalism, we see that Platonism[35] has less against it than might be supposed. The demand that ethical properties be partly constituted by subjective responses may be guided by an exaggerated internalism. Objective properties can demand responses, responses that for one reason or another they may not get. And disaffection, alienation, weakness, self-deception, and other psychological phenomena can disjoin an agent's psyche so that her cognitive and conative states do not march in lockstep. Some may be inclined to call this, when it occurs, a form of irrationality. But I for one find that too simple – for one thing, finding oneself with a recalcitrant will can rationally lead one to alter one's judgments.[36]

My purpose in this chapter has been to reflect critically on a kind of meta-ethical view that has been growing in popularity since at least the early 1980s. Sensibility theories emphasize, in one way or another, an analogy with secondary qualities. Ethical judgments can be objective in a manner not unlike color judgments. While the differences may be as important as the similarities (and what these differences might be is, as we've seen, a matter of some controversy), a common thread is that the ethical facts are not independent of our best judgments about what those facts are. This enables a "qualified realism" according to which we can make sense of *error* in ethical judgment while still capturing the sense that the ethical facts are in some important sense *up to us*.

I think the sense in which the ethical facts are up to us is far weaker than sensibility theory claims. The ethical facts are fixed by features of the ethical situation. Some of these will include, of course, whether agents are in pain, whether agents intend to do harm, whether agents are acting in expression of a virtuous character, and so on. But given those facts, the ethical status of the act is fixed and whatever anyone might think, no matter what their state of non-moral information, is beside the point. Of course, if they are morally sensitive, they will likely judge correctly. But to the extent there is a real issue between sensibility theory and the kind of opponent I have been trying to give content, it is better understood in connection with the following quotation from Wright.

One basic form of opposition between realist and anti-realist views of a discourse will be between those who think of the truth of a statement as constituted in some substantial relation of fit or representation – the traditional imagery of the mirror – and those who conceive, or might as well conceive, of truth as superassertibility, as durable satisfaction of the discourse's internal disciplinary constraints. (TE, 11)

There is an important difference between supposing that moral reality is independent of human subjectivity (of course it is not – whether an act is wrong is not utterly independent of who gets hurt) and supposing that moral reality owes something to "the standards that inform our conception of responsible discourse about it" (TE, 17). Standards, and conceptions of responsible discourse, are ultimately epistemic notions. We commit the pathetic fallacy when we mistake features of our own responses to a situation for features of the situation itself. There is *some* property defined by sensibility theory. It is a relational property that a situation has (very roughly) just in case we would be disposed, under conditions understood as ideal (in nonmoral respects), to have a certain kind of pro-attitude toward it. My worry is that a theory that takes that to be an *ethical* property commits the pathetic fallacy. We are mistaking features (defined in terms) of our own responses to the situation for features of the situation itself. And in ethics, as in so many other areas, though it's not certain we'll always get it wrong, there's also no metaphysical guarantee that we must eventually get it right.[37]

Notes

1. See, for example, Hilary Putnam's *The Many Faces of Realism* (1987).
2. Apparently originally by Stephen Darwall, Allan Gibbard, and Peter Railton, "Toward *Fin de Siècle* Ethics: Some Trends," *Philosophical Review* 101 (1992): 115–189. Page references to its reprinting as chap. 1 of Darwall et al. (eds.), *Moral Discourse and Practice: Some Philosophical Approaches* (New York: Oxford University Press, 1997).
3. In the sense of definition 4 in the *OED*, 2nd ed., Oxford University Press (1989): "4. Pertaining or relating to the passions or emotions of the mind." Cf. definition 3 of "pathos": "In reference to art, especially ancient Greek art: The quality of the transient or emotional, as opposed to the permanent or ideal: see *ethos* 2." The referenced entry 2 for "ethos" is remarkable: "In reference to ancient æsthetic criticism and rhetoric; Aristotle's statement that Polygnotus excelled all other painters in the representation of 'ethos' apparently meant simply that his pictures expressed 'character'; but as Aristotle elsewhere says that this painter portrayed men as nobler than they really are, some modern writers have taken *ethos* to mean 'ideal excellence.' The opposition of *ethos* and *pathos* ('character' and 'emotion'), often wrongly ascribed to Aristotle's theory of art as expounded in the *Poetics,* really belongs only to Greek rhetoric." And consider the accompanying quotation: "1881 *Q. Rev.* Oct. 542 The real is preferred to the ideal, transient emotion to permanent lineaments, pathos to ethos."
4. Cited in John L. Mackie, *Ethics: Inventing Right and Wrong* (Harmondsworth, Middlesex: Penguin, 1977) [hereafter cited as *Ethics*], p. 42.
5. The phrase "pathetic fallacy" was first used by John Ruskin to label a different sort of peccadillo: 1856 Ruskin *Mod. Paint.* III. iv. xii. Sect. 5. 160 "All violent feelings . . . produce . . . a falseness in . . . impressions of external things, which I would generally characterize as the 'Pathetic fallacy'." But Eliot gave Ruskin's point a twist: 1856 Geo. Eliot in *Westm. Rev.* Apr. 631 "Mr. Ruskin . . . enters on his special subject, namely landscape painting. With that intense interest in landscape, which is a peculiar characteristic of modern times, is associated the 'Pathetic Fallacy' – the transference to external objects of the spectator's own emotions." In any case, Mackie's use is slightly different again: we do not suspect the fungus itself has feelings of disgust; rather that it has some property to which our disgust is a direct and appropriate response.

6. Also David Lewis ("Dispositional Theories of Value," *Proceedings of the Aristotelian Society,* supp. vol. 63 [1989]: 113–137) and Michael Smith ("Dispositional Theories of Value," *Proceedings of the Aristotelian Society,* supp. vol. 63 [1989]: 89–111), whose views, however, have specific features that take them outside the scope of the present essay.

7. Simon Blackburn, "Errors and the Phenomenology of Value," in T. Hondereich (ed.), *Morality and Objectivity* (London: Routledge & Kegan Paul, 1985).

8. Moreover, I attend to projectivist and eliminativist alternatives only obliquely.

9. See, for example, Appendix I to Hume's *Enquiry Concerning the Principles of Morals.*

10. John McDowell, "Values and Secondary Qualities," in T. Hondereich (ed.), *Morality and Objectivity* (London: Routledge & Kegan Paul, 1985) [cited hereafter as VSQ].

11. McDowell's attempt to address this concern is clearest in his later "Projection and Truth in Ethics" in S. Darwall et al. (eds.), *Moral Discourse and Practice: Some Philosophical Approaches* (Oxford: Oxford University Press, 1997), which we will discuss below.

12. See his *Essays in Quasi-Realism* (New York: Oxford University Press, 1993).

13. Cited in John McDowell, "Projection and Truth in Ethics," p. 216 [cited hereafter as PTE].

14. David Wiggins, "A Sensible Subjectivism?" [cited hereafter as SS] in *Needs, Values, and Truth: Essays in the Philosophy of Value* (Oxford: Blackwell, 1987), p. 186.

15. Compare Mark Johnston's point about verificationism. Mark Johnston, "Dispositional Theories of Value," *Proceedings of the Aristotelian Society,* supp. vol. 63 (1989): 139–174, p. 146.

16. In a similar vein, Darwall et al. note, "A peg that fits a round hole has a particular shape; so does a hole that fits a square peg; but what shape in particular do an otherwise unspecified peg and hole have thanks to the fact that they fit each other?" *"Fin de Siècle* Ethics," p. 21.

17. Crispin Wright, "Moral Values, Projection, and Secondary Qualities" [cited hereafter as MVP], *Proceedings of the Aristotelian Society,* supp. vol. 62 (1988): 1–26; Wright, *Truth and Objectivity* (Cambridge, Mass.: Harvard University Press, 1992) [cited hereafter as TO].

18. Crispin Wright, "Truth in Ethics" [cited hereafter as TE], in B. Hooker (ed.), *Truth in Ethics* (Oxford: Blackwell, 1996).

19. Together with Blackburn's discussion ("Errors," pp. 1–4), which I do not address here, this may constitute a third such failure.

20. In, inter alia, *Truth and Objectivity* (1992).

21. Johnston, "Dispositional Theories of Value," [cited hereafter as DTV], p. 139.

22. This sort of criticism is made by others too. See Blackburn, "Errors," p. 14.

23. Actually at first he gives this only as a necessary condition; but in the following paragraph he affirms its sufficiency.

24. His arguments against those overambitious responses to the basic problem are spelled out in detail in his "Objectivity Refigured: Pragmatism Without Verificationism," in J. Haldane and C. Wright (eds.), *Reality, Representation, and Projection* (New York: Oxford University Press, 1993).

25. "[H]yper-external reasons, reasons which could in principle outrun any tendency of ours to accept them as reasons, even under conditions of increasing information and critical reflection" (DTV, 172).

26. From Ludwig Wittgenstein, "Lecture on Ethics," *Philosophical Review* 74 (1965): 3–11.

27. Though this is one way, indeed Kant's, of securing the result. It is also, differently, Michael Smith's. Michael Smith, *The Moral Problem* (Cambridge, Mass.: Blackwell, 1994). Smith's contribution to the Aristotelian Society symposium on dispositional theories of value appears with Lewis's and Johnston's. Smith, "Dispositional Theories of Value."

28. It's worth noting that Johnston has begun developing an attractive and more qualified conception of the scope of response-dependent accounts. "Are Manifest Qualities Response-Dependent?" *Monist* 81 (1998): 3–43. It is not clear whether this new conception remains susceptible to the critical considerations adduced here: if what substantive reason is on the side of valuing is (in his terms) "manifest," then it would seem Johnston has revised his view in a way that would make it immune to the worries I raise (and more sympathetic to the alternative implicated here).

29. David Wiggins, "Truth, Invention, and the Meaning of Life," *Proceedings of the British Academy* 62 (1976): 331–378. Reprinted in his *Needs, Values, and Truth,* pp. 87–137. See p. 106 (page references to its reprinting in *Needs, Values, and Truth*).

30. Ibid.

31. Susan Hurley, *Natural Reasons* (New York: Oxford University Press, 1989).

32. Hilary Putnam, *Reason, Truth, and History* (New York: Cambridge University Press, 1981), p. 1.

33. Say that "epistemicism" with respect to an area is a matter of holding that the truth of claims in that area depends on our tendency to find them true.

34. Cf. also Darwall's distinction between *existence internalism* and *judgment internalism,* Stephen Darwall, *Impartial Reason* (Ithaca: Cornell University Press, 1983), pp. 54–55; and Brink's distinction between "agent" and "appraiser" internalism, David Brink, *Moral Realism and the Foundations of Ethics* (Cambridge: Cambridge University Press, 1989), p. 40.

35. "Platonism" might be inapt: there need be no commitment to an intuitionistic epistemology, and the view that ethical properties occupy an abstract Platonic realm is optional. The position is constituted by holding ethical properties to be akin to primary qualities in their independence from subjective judgment (though with the qualifications noted). If sensibility theories constitute a "reactionary" realism, perhaps "Anti-Reactionary Realism" is a better term.

36. Such a view put me at odds with Michael Smith's well-developed view (e.g., Smith, "Dispositional Theories of Value"; Smith, *The Moral Problem;* Smith, "Internalism's Wheel," in Hooker (ed.), *Truth in Ethics,* of the consequences for ethical theory of internalism. His work is part of a significant literature on that subject. Considerations of space prohibit a discussion that takes account of it. I hope to pursue the issue elsewhere.

37. My thanks to Mark Johnston, conversations with whom shaped some of my thinking on these issues, to Brian Leiter for useful comments, written and oral, throughout the development of this essay (and for making it possible in the first place), to Dan Bonevac and Cory Juhl for critical discussion, and to the participants in my metaphysics seminar here at Austin in Spring 1998.

Bibliography

This bibliography is long but does not purport to be comprehensive. I have concentrated on the important literature on moral objectivity that *postdates* the 1988 Sayre-McCord collection on moral realism (below), which itself contains a useful bibliography that the reader should consult for earlier literature on the point. (See also, for metaethics literature [broadly construed], the useful bibliography in Darwall, Gibbard, and Railton (1997), as well as the wide-ranging on-line "Bibliography of Metaethics," compiled by Jimmy Lenman, at: http://www.gla.ac.uk/Acad/Philosophy/Lenman/bib.html.) I also, of course, have given special attention to literature – old and recent – on objectivity in law. I am grateful to Michael Durham (J.D., Ph.D. candidate, Yale) and Chad Mc-Cracken (J.D., Ph.D., University of Texas, Austin) for assistance in preparing this bibliography. – BL

Adams, David M. "Objectivity, Moral Truth, and Constitutional Doctrine: A Comment on R. George Wright's 'Is Natural Law Theory of Any Use in Constitutional Interpretation?'" *Southern California Interdisciplinary Law Journal* 4 (1995): 489–500.

Alexander, Larry, and Ken Kress. "Against Legal Principles," in A. Marmor (ed.), *Law and Interpretation: Essays in Legal Philosophy.* Oxford: Clarendon Press, 1995.

Altham, J. E. J. and Ross Harrison (eds.). *World, Mind, and Ethics: Essays on the Ethical Philosophy of Bernard Williams.* Cambridge: Cambridge University Press, 1995.

Amselek, Paul, and Neil MacCormick (eds.), *Controversies About Law's Ontology.* Edinburgh: Edinburgh University Press, 1991.

Anderson, Elizabeth. *Value in Ethics and Economics.* Cambridge, Mass.: Harvard University Press, 1993.

Arneson, Richard. "Metaethics and Corrective Justice," *Arizona Law Review* 37 (1995): 33–43.

Arrington, Robert L. (ed.). *Rationalism, Realism, and Relativism: Perspectives in Contemporary Moral Epistemology.* Ithaca: Cornell University Press, 1989.

Audi, Robert. "Moral Epistemology and the Supervenience of Ethical Concepts," *Southern Journal of Philosophy* 29 Supp. (1990): 1–24.

"Ethical Naturalism and the Explanatory Power of Moral Concepts," in S. Wagner and R.

Warner (eds.), *Naturalism: A Critical Appraisal*. Notre Dame: Notre Dame University Press, 1993.

"Intuitionism, Pluralism, and the Foundations of Ethics," in W. Sinnott-Armstrong and M. Timmons (eds.), *Moral Knowledge?: New Readings in Moral Epistemology*. New York: Oxford University Press, 1996.

Moral Knowledge and Ethical Character. New York: Oxford University Press, 1997.

Bennett, Robert W. "Objectivity in Constitutional Law," *University of Pennsylvania Law Review* 132 (1984): 445–496.

Bix, Brian. "H. L. A. Hart and the 'Open Texture' of Language," *Law and Philosophy* 10 (1991): 51–72.

Law, Language, and Legal Determinacy. Oxford: Clarendon Press, 1993.

Blackburn, Simon. "How to be an Ethical Antirealist," in P. French et al. (eds.), *Realism and Antirealism. Midwest Studies in Philosophy,* vol. 12. Minneapolis: University of Minnesota Press, 1988.

"Manifesting Realism," in P. French et al. (eds.), *Realism and Antirealism. Midwest Studies in Philosophy* 12 (1988). Minneapolis: University of Minnesota Press, 1988.

"Through Thick and Thin," *Proceedings of the Aristotelian Society,* supp. vol. 66 (1992): 285–299.

"Wise Feelings, Apt Reading," *Ethics* 102 (1992): 342–356.

Essays in Quasi-Realism. Oxford: Oxford University Press, 1993.

"The Flight to Reality," in R. Hursthouse et al. (eds.), *Virtues and Reasons: Philippa Foot and Moral Theory*. Oxford: Clarendon Press, 1995.

"Securing the Nots: Moral Epistemology for the Quasi-Realist," in W. Sinnott-Armstrong & M. Timmons (eds.), *Moral Knowledge?: New Readings in Moral Epistemology*. New York: Oxford University Press, 1996.

"Moral Relativism and Moral Objectivity," *Philosophy & Phenomenological Research* 58 (1998): 195–198.

Bloomfield, Paul. "Of *Goodness* and *Healthiness:* A Viable Moral Ontology," *Philosophical Studies* 87 (1997): 309–332.

"Prescriptions Are Assertions: An Essay in Moral Syntax," *American Philosophical Quarterly* 35 (1998): 1–20.

Blumenson, Eric. "Mapping the Limits of Skepticism in Law and Morals," *Texas Law Review* 74 (1996): 523–576.

Boghossian, Paul, and J. David Velleman. "Colour as a Secondary Quality," *Mind* 98 (1989): 81–103.

Boyle, Joseph. "Natural Law and the Ethics of Traditions," in R. George (ed.), *Natural Law Theory: Contemporary Essays*. Oxford: Clarendon Press, 1995.

Brandt, R. B. "Foundationalism for Moral Theory," in J. Couture and K. Nielsen (eds.), *On the Relevance of Metaethics: New Essays on Metaethics. Canadian Journal of Philosophy,* supp. vol. 21. Calgary: Calgary University Press, 1996.

"Science as a Basis for Moral Theory," in W. Sinnott-Armstrong and M. Timmons (eds.), *Moral Knowledge?: New Readings in Moral Epistemology*. New York: Oxford University Press, 1996.

Bransen, Jan, and Marc Slors (eds.). *The Problematic Reality of Values*. Assen: Van Gorcum, 1996.

Brest, Paul. "Indeterminacy and Interest," *Stanford Law Review* 34 (1982): 765–773.

Brink, David. "Legal Theory, Legal Interpretation, and Judicial Review," *Philosophy & Public Affairs* 17 (1988): 105–148.

Moral Realism and the Foundations of Ethics. Cambridge: Cambridge University Press, 1989.

"Semantics and Legal Interpretation (Further Thoughts)," *Canadian Journal of Law and Jurisprudence* 2 (1989): 181–191.

"Moral Realism Defended," in L. Pojman (ed.), *Ethical Theory.* Belmont: Wadsworth, 1997.

Broekman, Jan M. "Beyond Legal Gaps," *Law and Philosophy* 4 (1985): 217–237.

Brower, Bruce. "Dispositional Ethical Realism," *Ethics* 103 (1993): 221–249.

Brown, Mark R., and Andrew C. Greenberg. "On Formally Undecidable Propositions of Law: Legal Indeterminacy and the Implications of Metamathematics," *Hastings Law Journal* 43 (1992): 1439–1488.

Bulygin, Eugenio. "Norms and Logic: Kelsen and Weinberger on the Ontology of Norms," *Law and Philosophy* 4 (1985): 145–163.

Bunge, Mario. "A New Look at Moral Realism," in E. Valdés et al. (eds.), *Normative Systems in Legal and Moral Theory:* Festschrift *for Carlos E. Alchourrón and Eugenio Bulygin.* Berlin: Duncker & Humbolt, 1997.

Burns, Arnold. "Disenchantment," *Ethical Perspectives* 1 (1994): 145–155.

Burton, Mark. "Determinacy, Indeterminacy, and Rhetoric in a Pluralist World," *Melbourne University Law Review* 21 (1997): 544–583.

Burton, Stephan L. "'Thick' Concepts Revised," *Analysis* 52 (1992): 28–32.

"Reply to Garrard and McNaughton," *Analysis* 53 (1993): 59–61.

Butchvarov, Panayot. "Realism in Ethics," in P. French et al. (eds.), *Realism and Antirealism. Midwest Studies in Philosophy,* vol. 12. Minneapolis: University of Minnesota Press, 1988.

Skepticism in Ethics. Bloomington: Indiana University Press, 1989.

Carlson, George R. "Moral Realism and Wanton Cruelty," *Philosophia* 24 (1994): 49–56.

Carlson, Thomas L. "Gibbard's Conceptual Scheme for Moral Philosophy," *Philosophy & Phenomenological Research* 52 (1992): 953–956.

Casati, Roberto, and Christine Tappolet (eds.). *Response-Dependence. European "Review" of Philosophy,* vol. 3. Stanford: CSLI Publications, 1998.

Chappell, T. D. J. "The Incompleat Projectivist: How To Be an Objectivist and an Attitudinist," *Philosophical Quarterly* 48 (1998): 50–66.

Cohen, Joshua. "The Arc of the Moral Universe," *Philosophy & Public Affairs* 26 (1997): 91–134.

Coleman, Jules. "The Practice of Corrective Justice," *Arizona Law Review* 37 (1995): 15–31.

"Truth and Objectivity in Law," *Legal Theory* 1 (1995): 33–68.

Coleman, Jules, and Brian Leiter. "Determinacy, Objectivity, and Authority," *University of Pennsylvania Law Review* 142 (1993): 549–637. Also in A. Marmor (ed.), *Law and Interpretation: Essays in Legal Philosophy.* Oxford: Clarendon Press, 1995.

Collier, John, and Michael Stingl. "Evolutionary Naturalism and the Objectivity of Morality," in P. Thompson (ed.), *Issues in Evolutionary Ethics.* Albany: SUNY Press, 1995.

Copp, David. "Explanation and Justification in Ethics," *Ethics* 100 (1990): 237–258.

"Moral Realism: Facts and Norms," *Ethics* 101 (1991): 610–624.

"Moral Skepticism," *Philosophical Studies* 62 (1991): 203–233.

Morality, Normativity, and Society. New York: Oxford University Press, 1995.

"Moral Knowledge in Society-Centered Moral Theory," in W. Sinnott-Armstrong and M. Timmons (eds.), *Moral Knowledge?: New Readings in Moral Epistemology.* New York: Oxford University Press, 1996.

"Moral Obligation and Moral Motivation," in J. Couture and K. Nielsen (eds.), *On the Relevance of Metaethics: New Essays on Metaethics. Canadian Journal of Philosophy,* supp. vol. 21. Calgary: Calgary University Press, 1996.

"Belief, Reason, and Motivation: Michael Smith's *The Moral Problem." Ethics* 108 (1997): 33–54.

Couture, Jocelyne, and Kai Nielsen (eds.). *On the Relevance of Metaethics: New Essays on Metaethics. Canadian Journal of Philosophy,* supp. vol. 21. Calgary: Calgary University Press, 1996.

Crisp, Roger. "Naturalism and Non-Naturalism in Ethics," in S. Lovibond and S. Williams (eds.), *Essays for David Wiggins: Identity, Truth, and Value.* Oxford: Blackwell, 1996.

Currie, Gregory. "Interpretation and Objectivity," *Mind* 102 (1993): 413–428.

D'Amato, Anthony. "Aspects of Deconstruction: Refuting Indeterminacy with One Bold Thought," *Northwestern University Law Review* 85 (1990): 113–127.

"Aspects of Deconstruction: The Failure of the Word 'Bird,'" *Northwestern University Law Review* 84 (1990): 536–541.

"Pragmatic Indeterminacy," *Northwestern University Law Review* 85 (1990): 148–189.

Dancy, Jonathan. *Moral Reasons.* Oxford: Blackwell, 1993.

"In Defence of Thick Concepts," in P. French et al. (eds.), *Moral Concepts. Midwest Studies in Philosophy* 20 (1996). Notre Dame: Notre Dame University Press, 1996.

"Real Values in a Humean Context," *Ratio* 9 (1996): 171–183.

D'Arms, Justin, and Daniel Jacobson. "Expressivism, Morality, and the Emotions," *Ethics* 104 (1994): 739–763.

Darwall, Stephen. "Moore to Stevenson," in R. Cavalier et al. (eds.), *Ethics in the History of Western Philosophy.* Basingstoke: Macmillan, 1989.

"Expressivist Relativism?" *Philosophy & Phenomenological Research* 58 (1998): 183–188.

Darwall, Stephen, Allan Gibbard, and Peter Railton. "Toward *Fin de Siècle* Ethics: Some Trends," *Philosophical Review* 101 (1992): 115–189.

(eds.). *Moral Discourse and Practice: Some Philosophical Approaches.* New York: Oxford University Press, 1997.

Dascal, Marcelo, and Jerzy Wróblewski. "Transparency and Doubt: Understanding and Interpretation in Pragmatics and in Law," *Law and Philosophy* 7 (1988): 203–224.

DeCew, Judith Wagner. "Moral Conflicts and Ethical Relativism," *Ethics* 101 (1990): 27–41.

Divers, John, and Alexander Miller. "Rethinking Realism," *Mind* 103 (1994): 521–533.

"Why Expressivists About Value Should Not Love Minimalism About Truth," *Analysis* 54 (1994): 12–19.

"Platitudes and Attitudes: A Minimalist Conception of Belief," *Analysis* 55 (1995): 37–44.

Dreier, James. "Internalism and Speaker Relativism," *Ethics* 101 (1990): 6–26.

"The Supervenience Argument Against Moral Realism," *Southern Journal of Philosophy* 30.3 (Fall 1992): 13–38.

"Accepting Agent-Centered Norms: A Problem for Non-Cognitivists and a Suggestion for Solving It," *Australasian Journal of Philosophy* 74 (1996): 409–422.

"Expressivist Embeddings and Minimalist Truth," *Philosophical Studies* 83 (1996): 29–51.

Dworkin, Ronald. "Can Rights Be Controversial?" in *Taking Rights Seriously.* Cambridge, Mass.: Harvard University Press, 1977.

"Law as Interpretation," *Texas Law Review* 60 (1982): 527–550.

"My Reply to Stanley Fish (and Walter Benn Michaels): Please Don't Talk About Objectivity Anymore," in W. Mitchell (ed.), *The Politics of Interpretation.* Chicago: Chicago University Press, 1983.

"Is There Really No Right Answer in Hard Cases?" in *A Matter of Principle.* Cambridge, Mass.: Harvard University Press, 1985.

"On Interpretation and Objectivity," in *A Matter of Principle,* Cambridge, Mass.: Harvard University Press, 1985.

Law's Empire. Cambridge, Mass.: Harvard University Press, 1986.

"Pragmatism, Right Answers, and True Banality," in M. Brint and W. Weaver (eds.), *Pragmatism in Law and Society.* Boulder: Westview, 1991.

"Objectivity and Truth: You'd Better Believe It," *Philosophy & Public Affairs* 25 (1996): 87–139.

Edgington, Dorothy. "Truth, Objectivity, Counterfactuals, and Gibbard," *Mind* 106 (1997): 107–116.

Edmundson, William A. "Transparency and Indeterminacy in the Liberal Critique of Critical Legal Studies," *Seton Hall Law Review* 24 (1993): 557–602.

"The Antinomy of Coherence and Determinacy," *Iowa Law Review* 82 (1996): 1–20.

Edwards, Jim. "Debates About Realism Transposed to a New Key," *Mind* 103 (1994): 59–72.

"Is Tennant Selling Truth Short?" *Analysis* 57 (1997): 152–158.

Ellis, Brian. *Truth and Objectivity.* Cambridge: Blackwell, 1990.

Endicott, Timothy A. O. "Linguistic Indeterminacy," *Oxford Journal of Legal Studies* 16 (1996): 667–697.

"Vagueness and Legal Theory," *Legal Theory* 3 (1997): 37–63.

Vagueness in Law. Oxford: Clarendon Press, forthcoming.

Epstein, Richard A. "Some Doubts on Constitutional Indeterminacy," *Harvard Journal of Law and Public Policy* 19 (1996): 363–373.

Feldman, Heidi Li. "Objectivity in Legal Judgment," *Michigan Law Review* 92 (1994): 1187–1255.

Field, Hartry. "Disquotational Truth and Functionally Defective Discourse," *Philosophical Review* 103 (1994): 405–452.

Fine, Arthur. "The Viewpoint of No One in Particular," *Proceedings & Addresses of the American Philosophical Association* 72 (1998): 9–20.

Fish, Stanley. "Interpretation and the Pluralist Vision," *Texas Law Review* 60 (1982): 495–505.

"Working on the Chain Gang: Interpretation in Law and Literature," *Texas Law Review* 60 (1982): 551–567.

"Wrong Again," *Texas Law Review* 62 (1983): 299–316.

"Fish v. Fiss," *Stanford Law Review* 36 (1984): 1325–1347.

"Still Wrong After All These Years," *Law and Philosophy* 6 (1987): 401–418.

Doing What Comes Naturally. Durham, North Carolina: Duke University Press, 1989.

Fiss, Owen. "Objectivity and Interpretation," *Stanford Law Review* 34 (1982): 739–763.

"Conventionalism," *Southern California Law Review* 58 (1985): 177–197.

Folina, Janet. "Putnam, Realism, and Truth," *Synthèse* 103 (1995): 141–152.

Francis, Leslie Pickering. "Legal Truth and Moral Realism," *Southern Methodist University Law Review* 50 (1997):1721–1754.

French, Peter et al. (eds.). *Realism and Antirealism. Midwest Studies in Philosophy,* vol. 12. Minneapolis: University of Minnesota Press, 1988.

Gampel, Eric H. "A Defense of the Autonomy of Ethics: Why Value Is Not Like Water," *Canadian Journal of Philosophy* 26 (1996): 191–209.

"Ethics, Reference, and Natural Kinds," *Philosophical Papers* 26 (1997): 147–163.

Garner, Richard T. "On the Genuine Queerness of Moral Properties and Facts," *Australasian Journal of Philosophy* 68 (1990): 137–141.

Garrard, Eve, and David McNaughton. "Thick Concepts Revisited: A Reply to Burton," *Analysis* 53 (1993): 57–58.

Geach, Peter (ed.). *Logic and Ethics.* Dordrecht: Kluwer, 1991.

George, Robert P. (ed.). *Natural Law Theory: Contemporary Essays.* Oxford: Clarendon Press, 1995.

"Natural Law and Human Nature," in R. George (ed.), *Natural Law Theory.* Oxford: Clarendon Press, 1995.

"A Defense of the New Natural Law Theory," *American Journal of Jurisprudence* 41 (1996): 47–61.

"Law, Democracy, and Moral Disagreement," *Harvard Law Review* 110 (1997): 1388–1406.

Gewirth, Alan. "Is Cultural Pluralism Relevant to Moral Knowledge," *Social Philosophy and Policy* 11 (1994): 22–43. Also in E. Paul et al. (eds.), *Cultural Pluralism and Moral Knowledge.* Cambridge: Cambridge University Press, 1994.

Gibbard, Allan. *Wise Choices, Apt Feelings: A Theory of Normative Judgment.* Cambridge, Mass.: Harvard University Press, 1990.

"Moral Concepts: Substance and Sentiment," *Philosophical Perspectives* 6 (1992): 199–221.

"Reply to Blackburn, Carson, Hill, and Railton," *Philosophy & Phenomenological Research* 52 (1992): 943–945.

"Thick Concepts and Warrant for Feelings," in *Proceedings of the Aristotelian Society Supplement,* vol. 66. London: Russell, 1992.

"Reply to Sinnott-Armstrong," *Philosophical Studies* 69 (1993): 315–327.

"Projection, Quasi-Realism, and Sophisticated Realism," *Mind* 105 (1996): 331–335.

Gilbert, Alan. *Democratic Individuality.* Cambridge: Cambridge University Press, 1990.

Goldman, Alan. *Moral Knowledge.* London: Routledge, 1988.

"Aesthetic Versus Moral Evaluations," *Philosophy & Phenomenological Research* 50 (1990): 715–744.

"Skepticism About Goodness and Rightness," *Southern Journal of Philosophy* 29 Supp. (1990): 167–183.

"The Expressivist Theory of Normative Judgment," *Inquiry* 34 (1992): 509–523.

Goldstick, D. "The Causal Argument Against Ethical Objectivity," in D. Odegard (ed.), *Ethics and Justification.* Edmonton, Alberta: Academic Printing & Publishing, 1988.

Goldsworthy, Jeffrey. "Some Scepticism About Moral Realism," *Law and Philosophy* 14 (1995): 357–374.

"Fact and Value in the New Natural Law Theory," *American Journal of Jurisprudence* 41 (1996): 21–46.

Gormally, Luke (ed.). *Moral Truth and Moral Tradition: Essays in Honour of Peter Geach and Elizabeth Anscombe.* Portland, Oregon: Four Courts Press, 1994.

Graff, Gerald. "'Keep Off the Grass,' 'Drop Dead,' and Other Indeterminacies: A Response to Sanford Levinson," *Texas Law Review* 50 (1990): 405–413.

Greenawalt, Kent. "How Law Can Be Determinate," *UCLA Law Review* 38 (1990): 1–86.
Law and Objectivity. New York: Oxford University Press, 1992.
"Interpretation and Judgment," *Yale Journal of Law & the Humanities* 9 (1997): 415–435.
"The Nature of Rules and the Meaning of Meaning," *Notre Dame Law Review* 72 (1997): 1449–1477.

Griffin, James. *Value Judgment: Improving Our Ethical Beliefs.* Oxford: Clarendon Press, 1996.

Haldane, John, and Crispin Wright (eds.). *Reality, Representation, and Projection.* Oxford: Oxford University Press, 1993.

Hale, Bob. "Can There Be a Logic of Attitudes?" in J. Haldane and C. Wright (eds.), *Reality, Representation, and Projection.* Oxford: Oxford University Press, 1993.
"Postscript," in *Reality, Representation, and Projection.* Oxford: Oxford University Press, 1993.

Hampton, Jean. "Hobbes and Ethical Naturalism," *Philosophical Perspectives* 6 (1992): 333–353.
The Authority of Reason. Ed. Richard Healey. Cambridge: Cambridge University Press, 1998.

Hanen, Marsha P. "Feminism, Objectivity, and Legal Truth," in L. Code et al. (eds.), *Feminist Perspectives: Philosophical Essays on Method and Morals.* Toronto: University of Toronto Press, 1988.

Harding, Sandra. "'Strong Objectivity': A Response to the New Objectivity Question," *Synthèse* 104 (1995): 331–349.

Hare, R. M. "Objective Prescriptions," *Philosophy* 35 (Supp.) (1993): 1–17.
"Foundationalism and Coherentism in Ethics," in W. Sinnott-Armstrong and M. Timmons (eds.), *Moral Knowledge?: New Readings in Moral Epistemology.* New York: Oxford University Press, 1996.
"Off on the Wrong Foot," in J. Couture and K. Nielsen (eds.), *On the Relevance of Metaethics: New Essays on Metaethics. Canadian Journal of Philosophy,* supp. vol. 21. Calgary: Calgary University Press, 1996.

Harman, Gilbert. "Moral Diversity as an Argument for Moral Relativism," in D. Odegard and C. Stewart (eds.), *Perspectives on Moral Relativism.* Lilliken: Agathon, 1991.
"Explaining Value," *Social Philosophy and Policy* 11 (1994): 229–248. Also in E. Paul et al. (eds.), *Cultural Pluralism and Moral Knowledge.* Cambridge: Cambridge University Press, 1994.
"Reply to Critics," *Philosophy and Phenomenological Research* 58 (1998): 207–213.

Harman, Gilbert, and Judith Jarvis Thomson. *Moral Relativism and Moral Objectivity.* Oxford: Blackwell, 1996.

Hasnas, John. "Back to the Future: From Critical Legal Studies Forward to Legal Realism, or How Not to Miss the Point of the Indeterminacy Argument," *Duke Law Journal* 45 (1995): 84–132.

Hegland, Kenney. "Goodbye to Deconstruction," *Southern California Law Review* 58 (1985): 1203–1221.

"Goodbye to 2525," *Northwestern University Law Review* 85 (1990): 128–133.

"Indeterminacy: I Hardly Knew Thee," *Arizona Law Review* 33 (1991): 509–527.

Heinaman, Robert (ed.). *Aristotle and Moral Realism.* Boulder: Westview Press, 1995.

Herget, James E. "Unearthing the Origins of a Radical Idea: The Case of Legal Indeterminacy," *American Journal of Legal History* 39 (1995): 59–70.

Hetherington, Stephen Cade. "Sceptical Insulation and Sceptical Objectivity," *Australasian Journal of Philosophy* 72 (1994): 411–425.

Hill, Jr., Thomas E. "Gibbard on Morality and Sentiment," *Philosophy & Phenomenological Research* 52 (1992): 957–960.

Hodges, Wilfred. "Logic, Truth, and Moral Judgements," in S. Lovibond and S. Williams (eds.), *Essays for David Wiggins: Identity, Truth, and Value.* Oxford: Blackwell, 1996.

Hooker, Brad (ed.). *Truth in Ethics.* Oxford: Blackwell, 1996.

Horgan, Terence. "Wright's 'Truth and Objectivity,'" *Noûs* 29 (1995): 127–138.

Horgan, Terence, and Mark Timmons. "New Wave Moral Realism Meets Moral Twin Earth," *Journal of Philosophical Research* 16 (1991): 447–465.

"Troubles for New Wave Moral Semantics: The 'Open Question Argument' Revived," *Philosophical Papers* 21 (1992): 153–175.

"Troubles on Moral Twin Earth: Moral Queerness Revived," *Synthèse* 92 (1992): 221–260.

"Troubles for Michael Smith's Metaethical Rationalism," *Philosophical Papers* 25 (1996): 203–231.

Horwich, Paul. *Truth.* Oxford: Blackwell, 1990.

"Gibbard's Theory of Norms," *Philosophy & Public Affairs* 22 (1993): 67–79.

"The Essence of Expressivism," *Analysis* 54 (1994): 19–20.

Hurley, Susan. *Natural Reasons: Personality and Polity.* New York: Oxford University Press, 1989.

Jack, Julie. "Meaning-Norms and Objectivity," in P. Geach (ed.), *Logic and Ethics.* Dordrecht: Kluwer, 1991.

Jackson, Frank. "Realism, Truth, and Truth-Aptness," *Philosophical Books* 35 (1994): 162–169.

Jackson, Frank, Graham Oppy, and Michael Smith. "Minimalism and Truth-Aptness," *Mind* 103 (1994): 287–302.

Jackson, Frank, and Philip Pettit. "Moral Functionalism and Moral Motivation," *Philosophical Quarterly* 45 (1995): 20–40.

"Moral Functionalism, Supervenience, and Reductionism," *Philosophical Quarterly* 46 (1996): 82–86.

Jacobs, Jonathan. "Practical Wisdom, Objectivity, and Relativism," *American Philosophical Quarterly* 26 (1989): 199–209.

"Moral Imagination, Objectivity, and Practical Wisdom," *International Philosophical Quarterly* 31 (1991): 23–37.

Jacobs, Jonathan, and John Zeis. "Theism and Moral Objectivity," *American Catholic Philosophical Quarterly* 66 (1992): 429–445.

Jacobsen, Rockney. "Semantic Character and Expressive Content," *Philosophical Papers* 26 (1997): 129–146.

Jardine, Nicholas. "Science, Ethics, and Objectivity," in J. Altham and R. Harrison (eds.),

World, Mind, and Ethics: Essays on the Ethical Philosophy of Bernard Williams. Cambridge: Cambridge University Press, 1995.

Johnston, Mark. "Dispositional Theories of Value," in *Proceedings of the Aristotelian Society* Supp. vol. 63 (1989): 139–174.

"Objectivity Refigured: Pragmatism Without Verificationism," in J. Haldane and C. Wright (eds.), *Reality, Representation, and Projection.* Oxford: Oxford University Press, 1993.

Kairys, David. Introduction to D. Kairys (ed.), *The Politics of Law: A Progressive Critique.* New York: Pantheon Books, 1982.

Kane, Robert. *Through the Moral Maze: Searching for Absolute Values in a Pluralistic World.* New York: Paragon Books, 1994.

Kennedy, Duncan. "Form and Substance in Private Law Adjudication," *Harvard Law Review* 89 (1976): 1685–1778.

A Critique of Adjudication: fin de siècle. Cambridge, Mass.: Harvard University Press, 1997.

Kitcher, Philip. *The Advancement of Science.* Oxford: Oxford University Press, 1993.

Korsgaard, Christine. *The Sources of Normativity.* Cambridge: Cambridge University Press, 1996.

Kosso, Peter. "Science and Objectivity," *Journal of Philosophy* 86 (1989): 245–257.

Kraemer, Eric Russert. "On the Moral Twin Earth Challenge to New-Wave Moral Realism," *Journal of Philosophical Research* 16 (1991): 467–472.

Kramer, Matthew. "What Good Is Truth?" *Canadian Journal of Law and Jurisprudence* 5 (1992): 309–319.

Krausz, Michael (ed.). *Relativism.* Notre Dame: Notre Dame University Press, 1989.

Kress, Ken. "Legal Indeterminacy," *California Law Review* 77 (1989): 283–337.

"A Preface to Epistemological Indeterminacy," *Northwestern University Law Review* 85 (1990): 134–147.

"Modern Jurisprudence, Postmodern Jurisprudence, and Truth," *Michigan Law Review* 95 (1997): 1871–1926.

Kukathas, Chandran. "Explaining Moral Variety," *Social Philosophy and Policy* 11 (1994): 1–21. Also in E. Paul et al. (eds.), *Cultural Pluralism and Moral Knowledge.* Cambridge: Cambridge University Press, 1994.

Kutz, Christopher J. "Just Disagreement: Indeterminacy and Rationality in the Rule of Law," *Yale Law Journal* 103 (1994): 997–1030.

Landers, Scott. "Wittgenstein, Realism, and CLS: Undermining Rule Skepticism," *Law and Philosophy* 9 (1990): 177–203.

Lawson, Gary. "Legal Indeterminacy: Its Cause and Cure," *Harvard Journal of Law and Public Policy* 19 (1996): 411–428.

Leiter, Brian. "Objectivity and the Problems of Jurisprudence," *Texas Law Review* 72 (1993): 187–209.

"Perspectivism in Nietzsche's *Genealogy of Morals,*" in R. L. Schacht (ed.), *Nietzsche, Genealogy, Morality: Essays on Nietzsche's "Genealogy of Morals."* Berkeley: University of California Press, 1994.

"The Middle Way," *Legal Theory* 1 (1995): 21–31.

"Tort Theory and the Objectivity of Corrective Justice," *Arizona Law Review* 37 (1995): 45–51.

"Legal Indeterminacy," *Legal Theory* 1 (1995): 481–492.

"Explanation and Legal Theory," *Iowa Law Review* 82 (1997): 905–909.

"Moral Facts and Best Explanations," *Social Philosophy & Policy* (forthcoming).

Levinson, Sanford. "Law as Literature," *Texas Law Review* 60 (1982): 373–403.

"What Do Lawyers Know (and What Do They Do with Their Knowledge)?: Comments on Schauer and Moore," *Southern California Law Review* 58 (1985): 441–458.

Lewis, David. "Dispositional Theories of Value," in *Proceedings of the Aristotelian Society* Supp. vol. 63 (1989): 113–137.

Lieberman, Marcel. *Commitment, Value, and Moral Realism.* New York: Cambridge University Press, 1998.

Lipkin, Robert Justin. "Beyond Skepticism, Foundationalism, and the New Fuzziness: The Role of Wide Reflective Equilibrium in Legal Theory," *Cornell Law Review* 75 (1990): 811–877.

"Indeterminacy, Justification, and Truth in Constitutional Theory," *Fordham Law Review* 60 (1992): 595–642.

Little, Margaret Olivia. "Moral Realism I: Naturalism," *Philosophical Books* 35 (1994): 145–153.

"Moral Realism II: Non-Naturalism," *Philosophical Books* 35 (1994): 225–233.

Loeb, Don. "Generality and Moral Justification," *Philosophy & Phenomenological Research* 56 (1996): 79–96.

"Must a Moral Irrealist Be a Pragmatist?" *American Philosophical Quarterly* 33 (1996): 225–233.

Lovibond, Sabina. "Ethical Upbringing: From Connivance to Cognition," in S. Lovibond and S. Williams (eds.), *Essays for David Wiggins: Identity, Truth, and Value.* Oxford: Blackwell, 1996.

MacIntyre, Alasdair. "Moral Relativism: Truth and Justification," in L. Gormally (ed.), *Moral Truth and Moral Tradition: Essays in Honour of Peter Geach and Elizabeth Anscombe.* Portland: Four Courts Press, 1994.

Mackie, John. "The Third Theory of Law," in M. Cohen (ed.), *Ronald Dworkin and Contemporary Jurisprudence.* London: Duckworth, 1983.

Margolis, Joseph. *The Truth About Relativism.* Cambridge: Blackwell, 1991.

"Moral Realism and the Meaning of Life," *Philosophical Forum* 22 (1990): 19–48.

Marmor, Andrei. "Three Concepts of Objectivity," in A. Marmor (ed.), *Law and Interpretation: Essays in Legal Philosophy.* Oxford: Clarendon Press, 1995.

"An Essay on the Objectivity of Law," in B. Bix (ed.), *Analyzing Law: New Essays in Legal Theory.* Oxford: Clarendon Press, 1998.

Mason, H. E. "Realistic Interpretations of Moral Questions," in P. French et al. (eds.), *Realism and Antirealism. Midwest Studies in Philosophy,* vol. 12. Minneapolis: University of Minnesota Press, 1988.

McDowell, John. *Mind and World.* Cambridge, Mass.: Harvard University Press, 1994.

"Two Sorts of Naturalism," in R. Hursthouse et al. (eds.), *Virtues and Reasons: Philippa Foot and Moral Theory.* Oxford: Clarendon Press, 1995.

"Projection and Truth in Ethics," in S. Darwall et al. (eds.), *Moral Discourse and Practice: Some Philosophical Approaches.* Oxford: Oxford University Press, 1997.

McFarland, Duncan, and Alexander Miller. "Response-Dependence Without Reduction?" *Australasian Journal of Philosophy* 76 (1998): 407–425.

McNaughton, David. *Moral Vision: An Introduction to Moral Theory.* Oxford: Blackwell, 1988.

Mendola, Joseph. "Normative Realism, or Bernard Williams and Ethics at the Limit," *Australasian Journal of Philosophy* 67 (1989): 306–318.

"Objective Value and Subjective States," *Philosophy and Phenomenological Research* 50 (1990): 695–713.

Menzies, Peter, and Philip Pettit. "Found: The Missing Explanation," *Analysis* 53 (1993): 100–109.

Miller, Alexander. "Objectivity Disfigured: Mark Johnston's Missing-Explanation Argument," *Philosophy & Phenomenological Research* 55 (1995): 857–868.

"An Objection to Smith's Argument for Internalism," *Analysis* 56 (1996): 169–174.

"More Responses to the Missing-Explanation Argument," *Philosophia* 25 (1997): 331–349.

Millon, David. "Objectivity and Democracy," *New York University Law Review* 67 (1992): 1–66.

Mills, Charles W. "Marxism, 'Ideology,' and Moral Objectivism," *Canadian Journal of Philosophy* 24 (1994): 373–393.

Milo, Ronald D. "Skepticism and Moral Justification," *Monist* 76 (1993): 379–393.

"Contractarian Constructivism," *Journal of Philosophy* 92 (1995): 181–204.

Mizzoni, John. "Moral Realism, Objective Values, and J. L. Mackie," *Auslegung* 20 (1995): 11–24.

Moore, Michael S. "The Semantics of Judging," *Southern California Law Review* 54 (1981): 151–295.

"Moral Reality," *Wisconsin Law Review* (1982): 1061–1156.

"A Natural Law Theory of Interpretation," *Southern California Law Review* 58 (1985): 277–398.

"Metaphysics, Epistemology, and Legal Theory," *Southern California Law Review* 60 (1987): 453–506.

"The Interpretive Turn in Modern Theory: A Turn for the Worse?" *Stanford Law Review* 41 (1989): 871–957.

"Law as a Functional Kind," in R. George (ed.), *Natural Law Theory: Contemporary Essays.* Oxford: Clarendon Press, 1992.

"Moral Reality Revisited," *Michigan Law Review* 90 (1992): 2424–2533.

Moser, Paul K. *Philosophy After Objectivity.* Oxford: Oxford University Press, 1993.

Munzer, Stephen R. "Realistic Limits on Realist Interpretation," *Southern California Law Review* 58 (1985): 459–475.

Nagel, Thomas. *The Last Word.* New York: Oxford University Press, 1997.

Nelson, William E. "Standards of Criticism," *Texas Law Review* 60 (1990): 447–493.

Nickel, James W. "Uneasiness About Easy Cases," *Southern California Law Review* 58 (1985): 477–487.

Nielsen, Kai. "Relativism and Wide Reflective Equilibrium," *Monist* 76 (1993): 316–332.

Nozick, Robert. "Invariance and Objectivity," *Proceedings & Addresses of the American Philosophical Association* 72 (1998): 21–48.

Odegard, Douglas, and Carole Stewart (eds.). *Perspectives on Moral Relativism.* Lilliken: Agathon, 1991.

O'Leary-Hawthorne, John, and Graham Oppy. "Minimalism and Truth," *Noûs* 31 (1997): 170–196.

O'Leary-Hawthorne, John, and Huw Price. "How to Stand Up for Non-Cognitivists," *Australasian Journal of Philosophy* 74 (1996): 275–292.

Patterson, Dennis. "Realist Semantics and Legal Theory," *Canadian Journal of Law and Jurisprudence* 2 (1989): 175–191.

"What Was Realism?: A Reply to David Brink," *Canadian Journal of Law and Jurisprudence* 2 (1989): 193–195.

Law and Truth. New York: Oxford University Press, 1996.

Paul, Ellen Frankel et al. (eds.). *Cultural Pluralism and Moral Knowledge.* Cambridge: Cambridge University Press, 1994.

Peczenik, Aleksander. "Moral and Ontological Justification of Legal Reasoning," *Law and Philosophy* 4 (1985): 289–309.

Perry, Michael J. *Morality, Politics, and Law: A Bicentennial Essay.* New York: Oxford University Press, 1988.

"Normative Indeterminacy and the Problem of Judicial Role," *Harvard Journal of Law and Public Policy* 19 (1996): 375–393.

Pettit, Philip. "Realism and Response-Dependence," *Mind* 100 (1991): 587–626.

The Common Mind: An Essay on Psychology, Society, and Politics. New York: Oxford University Press, 1993; with a new postscript, 1996.

"Realism and Truth: A Comment on Crispin Wright's *Truth and Objectivity,*" *Philosophy & Phenomenological Research* 56 (1996): 883–890.

Philips, Michael. *Between Universalism and Skepticism: Ethics as Social Artifact.* New York: Oxford University Press, 1994.

Phillips, David. "How To Be a Moral Relativist," *Southern Journal of Philosophy* 35 (1997): 393–417.

Pigden, Charles R. "Logic and the Autonomy of Ethics," *Australasian Journal of Philosophy* 67 (1989): 127–151.

"Geach on Good," *Philosophical Quarterly* 40 (1990): 129–154.

Platts, Mark. "Hume and Morality as a Matter of Fact," *Mind* 97 (1988): 189–204.

Moral Realities. London: Routledge, 1991.

Postema, Gerald. "Public Practical Reasoning: An Archaeology," *Social Philosophy and Policy* 12 (1995): 43–86.

"Public Practical Reasoning: Political Practice," in I. Shapiro and J. DeCew (eds.), *Theory and Practice. Nomos,* vol. 37. New York: New York University Press, 1995.

Presby, Shannon S. "Interpretivism Naturalized: Dworkin's Minimalist Metaphysics," *Canadian Journal of Law and Jurisprudence* 7 (1994): 303–330.

Price, Huw. *Facts and the Function of Truth.* Oxford: Blackwell, 1988.

Putnam, Hilary. "Objectivity and the Science-Ethics Distinction," in H. Putnam, *Realism with a Human Face.* Cambridge, Mass.: Harvard University Press, 1990.

Realism with a Human Face. Cambridge, Mass.: Harvard University Press, 1990.

"Reply to Mark Timmons," *Erkenntnis* 34 (1991): 416–419.

"Are Moral and Legal Values Made or Discovered?" *Legal Theory* 1 (1995): 5–19.

"Replies to Brian Leiter and Jules Coleman," *Legal Theory* 1 (1995): 69–80.

"Pragmatism and Moral Objectivity," in *Words and Life.* Cambridge, Mass.: Harvard University Press, 1994.

"Pragmatism and Relativism: Universal Values and Traditional Ways of Life," in *Words and Life.* Cambridge, Mass.: Harvard University Press, 1994.

Quinn, Warren. "Putting Rationality in Its Place," in R. Frey and C. Morris (eds.), *Value, Welfare and Morality.* Cambridge: Cambridge University Press, 1993. Also in R. Hursthouse et al. (eds.), *Virtues and Reasons: Philippa Foot and Moral Theory.* Oxford: Clarendon Press, 1995.

Railton, Peter. "Marx and the Objectivity of Science," in F. Suppe and P. Asquith (eds.), *PSA 1984,* vol. 2. Lansing, Mich.: Philosophy of Science Association, 1985.

"Naturalism and Prescriptivity," *Social Philosophy and Policy* 7 (1989): 151–174. Also in E. F. Paul et al. (eds.), *Foundations of Moral and Political Philosophy.* Oxford: Blackwell, 1990.

"Nonfactualism About Normative Discourse," *Philosophy & Phenomenological Research* 52 (1992): 951–968.

"Some Questions About the Justification of Morality," *Philosophical Perspectives* 6 (1992): 27–53.

"What the Noncognitivist Helps Us To See, the Naturalist Must Help Us To Explain," in J. Haldane and C. Wright (eds.), *Reality, Representation, and Projection.* Oxford: Oxford University Press, 1993.

"Reply to David Wiggins," in J. Haldane and C. Wright (eds.) *Reality, Representation, and Projection.* Oxford: Oxford University Press, 1993.

"Subject-ive and Objective," *Ratio* 8 (1995): 259–276.

"Moral Realism: Prospects and Problems," in W. Sinnott-Armstrong and M. Timmons (eds.), *Moral Knowledge? New Readings in Moral Epistemology.* New York: Oxford University Press, 1996.

"Moral Explanation and Moral Objectivity," *Philosophy & Phenomenological Research* 58 (1998): 175–182.

"Red, Bitter, Good," in R. Casati and C. Tappolet (eds.), *Response-Dependence. European "Review" of Philosophy,* vol. 3. Stanford: CSLI Publications, 1998.

"Aesthetic Value, Moral Value, and the Ambitions of Naturalism," in J. Levinson (ed.), *Aesthetics and Ethics: Essays at the Intersection.* Cambridge: Cambridge University Press, 1998.

Raz, Joseph. "Moral Change and Social Relativism," *Social Philosophy and Policy* 11 (1994): 139–158. Also in E. Paul et al. (eds.), *Cultural Pluralism and Moral Knowledge.* Cambridge: Cambridge University Press, 1994.

"Interpretation Without Retrieval," in A. Marmor (ed.), *Law and Interpretation: Essays in Legal Philosophy.* Oxford: Clarendon Press, 1995.

Rescher, Nicholas. *Objectivity.* Notre Dame: Notre Dame University Press, 1997.

Ripstein, Arthur. "Questionable Objectivity," *Noûs* 27 (1993): 355–372.

Rogers, John M., and Robert E. Molzen. "Some Lessons About the Law from Self-Referential Problems in Mathematics," *Michigan Law Review* 90 (1992): 992–1022.

Rorty, Richard. *Objectivity, Relativism, and Truth.* Cambridge: Cambridge University Press, 1991.

Rosati, Connie S. "Naturalism, Normativity, and the Open Question Argument," *Noûs* 29 (1995): 46–70.

"Persons, Perspectives, and Full Information Accounts of the Good," *Ethics* 105 (1995): 296–325.

"Internalism and the Good for a Person," *Ethics* 106 (1996): 297–326.

Rosen, Gideon. "Objectivity and Modern Idealism: What Is the Question?" in M. Michael and J. O'Leary-Hawthorne (eds.), *Philosophy in Mind.* Dordrecht: Kluwer, 1994.

Rosen, Michael. "Must We Return to Moral Realism?" *Inquiry* 34 (1991): 183–194.

Ross, Steven. "The Nature of Moral Facts," *Philosophical Forum* 22 (1991): 243–269.

"The Nature and Limits of Moral Objectivism," *Philosophical Forum* 29 (1998): 28–49.

Rumfitt, Ian. "Truth Wronged," *Ratio* 8 (1995): 100–107.

Sayre-McCord, Geoffrey (ed.). *Essays on Moral Realism.* Ithaca: Cornell University Press, 1988.

"Moral Theory and Explanatory Impotence," in P. French et al. (eds.), *Realism and Anti-realism. Midwest Studies in Philosophy,* vol. 12. Minneapolis: University of Minnesota Press, 1988.

"Being a Realist About Relativism (in Ethics)," *Philosophical Studies* 61 (1991): 155–176.

"Normative Explanations," *Philosophical Perspectives* 6 (1992): 55–71.

"Coherentist Epistemology and Moral Theory," in W. Sinnott-Armstrong and M. Timmons (eds.), *Moral Knowledge?: New Readings in Moral Epistemology.* New York: Oxford University Press, 1996.

"Hume and the Bauhaus Theory of Ethics," in P. French et al. (eds.), *Moral Concepts. Midwest Studies in Philosophy,* vol. 20. Notre Dame: Notre Dame University Press, 1996.

"'Good' on Twin Earth," *Philosophical Issues* 8 (1997): 267–292.

"The Metaethical Problem," *Ethics* 108 (1997): 55–83.

Scanlon, T. M. "Fear of Relativism," in R. Hursthouse et al. (eds.), *Virtues and Reasons: Philippa Foot and Moral Theory.* Oxford: Clarendon Press, 1995.

Schauer, Frederick. "Easy Cases," *Southern California Law Review* 58 (1985): 399–440.

"Formalism," *Yale Law Journal* 97 (1988): 509–548.

Schiffer, Stephen. "Meaning and Value," *Journal of Philosophy* 87 (1990): 602–614.

Schueler, G. F. "Pro-Attitudes and Direction of Fit," *Mind* 100 (1991): 277–281.

"Why Oughts Are Not Facts (or What the Tortoise and Achilles Taught Mrs. Ganderhoot and Me About Practical Reasoning)," *Mind* 104 (1995): 713–723.

Schurz, Gerhard. "How Far Can Hume's Is-Ought Thesis Be Generalized?" *Journal of Philosophical Logic* 20 (1991): 37–95.

Seabright, Paul. "Objectivity, Disagreement, and Projectibility," *Inquiry* 31 (1988): 25–51.

Seanor, Douglas, and N. Fotion (eds.). *Hare and Critics.* Oxford: Clarendon Press, 1988.

Sen, Amartya. *Objectivity and Position.* Lawrence: University of Kansas Press, 1992.

"Positional Objectivity," *Philosophy & Public Affairs* 22 (1993): 126–145.

Seung, T. K. *Intuition and Construction: The Foundation of Normative Theory.* New Haven: Yale University Press, 1993.

Shafer-Landau, Russ. "Ethical Disagreement, Ethical Objectivism, and Moral Indeterminacy," *Philosophy & Phenomenological Research* 54 (1994): 313–344.

"Supervenience and Moral Realism," *Ratio* 7 (1994): 145–152.

"Vagueness, Borderline Cases, and Moral Realism," *American Philosophical Quarterly* 32 (1995): 83–96.

"Moral Judgement and Moral Motivation," *Philosophical Quarterly* 48 (1998) 353–358.

Sherline, Edward. "Moral Realism and Objective Theories of the Right," *Southern Journal of Philosophy* 30.4 (Winter 1992): 127–140.

Simpson, Gerry J., and Hilary Charlesworth. "Objecting to Objectivity: The Radical Challenge to Legal Liberalism," in R. Hunter et al., *Thinking About Law: Perspectives on the History, Philosophy, and Sociology of Law.* St. Leonards, Australia: Allen & Unwin, 1995.

Singer, Joseph. "The Player and the Cards: Nihilism and Legal Theory," *Yale Law Journal* 94 (1984): 1–70.

Sinnott-Armstrong, Walter. "Some Problems for Gibbard's Norm-Expressivism," *Philosophical Studies* 69 (1993): 297–313.

"Moral Skepticism and Justification," in W. Sinnott-Armstrong and M. Timmons (eds.), *Moral Knowledge?: New Readings in Moral Epistemology.* New York: Oxford University Press, 1996.

Sinnott-Armstrong, Walter, and Mark Timmons (eds.). *Moral Knowledge?: New Readings in Moral Epistemology.* New York: Oxford University Press, 1996.

Slote, Michael. "Ethics Naturalized," *Philosophical Perspectives* 6 (1992): 355–376.

Smith, Michael. "Dispositional Theories of Value," in *Proceedings of the Aristotelian Society,* Supp. vol. 63 (1989): 89–111.

"Realism," in P. Singer (ed.), *A Companion to Ethics.* Oxford: Blackwell, 1991.

"Objectivity and Moral Realism: On the Significance of the Phenomenology of Moral Experience," in J. Haldane & C. Wright (eds.), *Reality, Representation, and Projection.* Oxford: Oxford University Press, 1993.

"Minimalism, Truth-Aptitude, and Belief," *Analysis* 54 (1994): 21–26.

The Moral Problem. Oxford: Blackwell, 1994.

"Why Expressivists About Value Should Love Minimalism About Truth," *Analysis* 54 (1994): 1–12.

"Internal Reasons," *Philosophy & Phenomenological Research* 55 (1995): 109–131.

"Internalism's Wheel," *Ratio* 8 (1995): 277–302.

"The Argument for Internal Reason: Reply to Miller," *Analysis* 56 (1996): 175–184.

"Normative Reasons and Full Rationality: Reply to Swanton," *Analysis* 56 (1996): 160–168.

"In Defense of *The Moral Problem:* A Reply to Brink, Copp and Sayre-McCord," *Ethics* 108 (1997): 84–119.

"Response Dependence Without Reduction," in R. Casati & C. Tappolet (eds.), *Response-Dependence. European "Review" of Philosophy,* vol. 3. Stanford: CSLI Publications, 1998.

Solomon, Wm. David. "Moral Realism and the Amoralist," in P. French et al. (eds.), *Realism and Antirealism. Midwest Studies in Philosophy,* vol. 12. Minneapolis: University of Minnesota Press, 1988.

Solum, Lawrence B. "On the Indeterminacy Crisis: Critiquing Critical Dogma," *University of Chicago Law Review* 54 (1987): 462–503.

Sosa, Ernest. "Moral Relativism, Cognitivism, and Defeasible Rules," *Social Philosophy and Policy* 11 (1994): 116–138. Also in E. Paul et al. (eds.), *Cultural Pluralism and Moral Knowledge.* Cambridge: Cambridge University Press, 1994.

"Normative Objectivity," in E. Valdés et al. (eds.), *Normative Systems in Legal and Moral Theory:* Festschrift *for Carlos E. Alchourrón and Eugenio Bulygin.* Berlin: Duncker & Humbolt, 1997.

Stavropoulos, Nicos. *Objectivity in Law.* Oxford: Clarendon Press, 1996.

Stewart, Robert, and Lynn Thomas. "Recent Work on Ethical Relativism," *American Philosophical Quarterly* 28 (1991): 85–100.

Stocker, Michael. "Emotions and Ethical Knowledge: Some Naturalistic Connections," in P. French et al. (eds.), *Philosophical Naturalism. Midwest Studies in Philosophy,* vol. 19. Notre Dame: Notre Dame University Press, 1994.

Stoljar, Daniel. "Emotivism and Truth Conditions," *Philosophical Studies* 70 (1993): 81–101.

Stout, Jeffrey. "Truth, Natural Law, and Ethical Theory," in R. George (ed.), *Natural Law Theory: Contemporary Essays.* Oxford: Clarendon Press, 1992.

Stroud, Sarah. "Moral Relativism and Quasi-Absolutism," *Philosophy & Phenomenological Research* 58 (1998): 189–194.

Sturgeon, Nicholas. "Schiffer on Meaning and Value," *Journal of Philosophy* 87 (1990): 615–616.

"Nonmoral Explanations," *Philosophical Perspectives* 6 (1992): 97–117.

"Moral Disagreement and Moral Relativism," *Social Philosophy and Policy* 11 (1994): 80–115. Also in E. Paul et al. (eds.), *Cultural Pluralism and Moral Knowledge.* Cambridge: Cambridge University Press, 1994.

"Critical Study: Allan Gibbard, *Wise Choices, Apt Feelings,*" *Noûs* 29 (1995): 402–424.

"Evil and Explanation," in J. Couture and K. Nielsen (eds.), *On the Relevance of Metaethics: New Essays on Metaethics. Canadian Journal of Philosophy,* supp. vol. 21 (1995). Calgary: Calgary University Press, 1996.

"Thomson Against Moral Explanations," *Philosophy & Phenomenological Research* 58 (1998): 199–206.

Sturgeon, Scott. "The Epistemic View of Subjectivity," *Journal of Philosophy* 91 (1994): 221–235.

Suttle, Bruce B. "Truth, Morality, and What Differences Make a Difference," *Journal of Value Inquiry* 28 (1994): 437–442.

Svavarsdóttir, Sigrún. "Moral Cognitivism and Motivation," *Philosophical Review* 108 (1999): 161–219.

Swain, Corliss. "Passionate Objectivity," *Noûs* 26 (1992): 465–490.

Talmage, C. Emerson. "Do Survival Values Form a Sufficient Basis for an Objective Morality?: A Realist's Appraisal of the Rules of Human Conduct," *Notre Dame Law Review* 69 (1994): 893–986.

Tännsjö, Torbjörn. *Moral Realism.* Savage, Maryland: Rowman & Littlefield, 1990.

Tappolet, Christine. "Le programme quasi-realiste et le realisme moral," *Studies in Philosophy* 51 (1992): 241–254.

Tasioulas, John. "Consequences of Ethical Relativism," *European Journal of Philosophy* 6 (1998): 172–202.

Teichmann, Roger. "Truth, Assertion, and Warrant," *Philosophical Quarterly* 45 (1995): 78–83.

Tennant, Neil. "On Negation, Truth, and Warranted Assertability," *Analysis* 55 (1995): 98–104.

The Taming of the True. Oxford: Clarendon Press, 1997.

Tersman, Folke. "Non-Cognitivism and Inconsistency," *Southern Journal of Philosophy* 33 (1995): 361–371.

"Crispin Wright on Moral Disagreement," *Philosophical Quarterly* 48 (1998): 359–365.

Thomas, Laurence. "Morality and Human Diversity," *Ethics* 103 (1992): 117–134.

Tilley, J. "Two Kinds of Moral Relativism," *Journal of Value Inquiry* 29 (1995): 187–192.

Timmons, Mark. "On the Epistemic Status of Considered Moral Judgements," *Southern Journal of Philosophy* 29 Supp. (1990): 97–129.

"Putnam's Moral Objectivism," *Erkenntnis* 34 (1991): 371–399.

"Irrealism and Error in Ethics," *Philosophia* 22 (1993): 373–406.

"Moral Justification in Context," *Monist* 76 (1993): 360–378.

"Outline of a Contextualist Moral Epistemology," in W. Sinnott-Armstrong and M. Timmons (eds.), *Moral Knowledge?* New York: Oxford University Press, 1996.

Morality Without Foundations. New York: Oxford University Press, 1998.

Tolhurst, William E. "On the Epistemic Value of Moral Experience," *Southern Journal of Philosophy* 29 Supp. (1990): 67–87.

"Moral Experience and the Internalist Argument Against Moral Realism," *American Philosophical Quarterly* 32 (1995): 187–194.

Tushnet, Mark V. "Following the Rules Laid Down: A Critique of Interpretivism and Neutral Principles," *Harvard Law Review* 96 (1983): 781–827.

"Defending the Indeterminacy Thesis," in B. Bix (ed.), *Analyzing Law: New Essays in Legal Theory.* Oxford: Clarendon Press, 1998.

Unger, Roberto Mangabiera. *The Critical Legal Studies Movement.* Cambridge, Mass.: Harvard University Press, 1986.

Van Der Dussen, W. J. (ed.). *Objectivity, Method, and Point of View.* Leiden: Brill, 1991.

Van Roojen, Mark. "Expressivism and Irrationality," *Philosophical Review* 105 (1996): 311–335.

"Moral Functionalism and Moral Reductionism," *Philosophical Quarterly* 46 (1996): 77–81.

Virvidakis, Stelios. "On Constructing and Discovering Moral Facts (Kantian Autonomy and Moral Truth)," in *Akten des siebenten internationalen Kant-Kongresses.* Bonn: Bouvier, 1990.

Vokey, Daniel. "Objectivity and Moral Judgment: Towards Agreement on Moral Education," *Journal of Moral Education* 19 (1990): 14–23.

Waldron, Jeremy. "The Irrelevance of Moral Objectivity," in R. George (ed.), *Natural Law Theory: Contemporary Essays.* Oxford: Clarendon Press, 1992.

"On the Objectivity of Morals," *California Law Review* 80 (1992): 1361–1411.

"Assurances of Objectivity," *Yale Journal of Law and the Humanities* 5 (1993): 553–568.

"Vagueness in Law and Language: Some Philosophical Issues," *California Law Review* 82 (1994): 509–540

Waller, Bruce. "Moral Conversion Without Moral Realism," *Southern Journal of Philosophy* 30 (1992): 129–137.

"Noncognitivist Moral Realism," *Philosophia* 24 (1994): 57–75.

Walt, Steven. "Practical Reason and the Ontology of Statutes," *Law and Philosophy* 15 (1996): 227–255.

Walzer, Michael. "Objectivity and Social Meaning," in A. Sen and M. Nussbaum (eds.), *Quality of Life.* Oxford: Oxford University Press, 1992.

Warnke, Georgia. "Law, Hermeneutics, and Public Debate," *Yale Journal of Law and Humanities* 9 (1997): 395–413.

"Reply to Greenawalt," *Yale Journal of Law and Humanities* 9 (1997): 437–441.

Wechsler, Herbert. "Toward Neutral Principles in Constitutional Law," *Harvard Law Review* 73 (1959): 1–35.

Wedgewood, Ralph. "Non-Cognitivism, Truth, and Logic," *Philosophical Studies* 86 (1997): 73–91.

"The Essence of Response-Dependence," in R. Casati and C. Tappolet, *Response-Dependence. European "Review" of Philosophy,* vol. 3. Stanford: CSLI Publications, 1998.

Weinberger, Ota. "The Expressive Conception of Norms – An Impasse for the Logic of Norms," *Law and Philosophy* 4 (1985): 165–198.

Weinrib, Ernest. "Legal Formalism: On the Immanent Rationality of Law," *Yale Law Journal* 97 (1988): 949–1016.

Werhane, Patricia H. "Wittgenstein and Moral Realism," *Journal of Value Inquiry* 26 (1992): 381–394.

West, Robin. "Relativism, Objectivity, and Law," *Yale Law Journal* 99 (1990): 1473–1502.

Wiggins, David. "Moral Cognitivism, Moral Relativism, and Motivating Beliefs," *Proceedings of the Aristotelian Society* 91 (1991): 61–85.

"Cognitivism, Naturalism and Normativity: A Reply to Peter Railton," in J. Haldane and C. Wright, *Reality, Representation, and Projection.* Oxford: Oxford University Press, 1993.

"Replies," in S. Lovibond and S. Williams (eds.), *Essays for David Wiggins: Identity, Truth and Value.* Oxford: Blackwell, 1996.

"Objective and Subjective in Ethics, with Two Postscripts About Truth," *Ratio* 8 (1995): 243–258.

Williams, Bernard. "Truth in Ethics," *Ratio* 8 (1995): 227–242.

"Who Needs Ethical Knowledge?" in B. Williams, *Making Sense of Humanity.* Cambridge: Cambridge University Press, 1995.

"History, Morality, and the Test of Reflection," in C. Korsgaard, *The Sources of Normativity.* Ed. Onora O'Neill. Cambridge: Cambridge University Press, 1996.

Wong, David. "A Relativist Alternative to Antirealism," *Journal of Philosophy* 87 (1990): 617–618.

Worley, Sara. "Feminism, Objectivity, and Analytic Philosophy," *Hypatia* 10 (1995): 138–156.

Wright, Crispin. "Moral Values, Projection, and Secondary Qualities," *Proceedings of the Aristotelian Society,* Supp. Vol. 62 (1988): 1–26.

"Realism, Antirealism, Irrealism, Quasi-Realism," in P. French et al. (eds.), *Realism and Antirealism. Midwest Studies in Philosophy,* vol. 12. Minneapolis: University of Minnesota Press, 1988.

Truth and Objectivity. Cambridge, Mass.: Harvard University Press, 1992.

"Truth in Ethics," *Ratio* 8 (1995): 209–226.

Wright, R. George. "The Consequences of Contemporary Legal Relativism," *University of Toledo Law Review* 22 (1990): 73–105.

Reason and Obligation. Lanham, Maryland: University Press of America, 1994.

"Is Natural Law Theory of Any Use in Constitutional Interpretation?" *Southern California Interdisciplinary Law Journal* 4 (1995): 463–487.

"What's Gone Wrong with Legal Theory?: The Three Faces of Our Split Personality," in *Wake Forest Law Review* 33 (1998): 371–411.

Wróblewski, Jerzy. "Legal Language and Legal Interpretation," *Law and Philosophy* 4 (1985): 239–255.

Yablon, Charles M. "The Indeterminacy of the Law: Critical Legal Studies and the Problem of Legal Explanation," *Cardozo Law Review* 6 (1985): 917–945.

"Law and Metaphysics," *Yale Law Journal* 96 (1987): 613–636.

Yasenchuk, Ken. "Assimilative Moral Realism and Supervenience," *Dialogue* 34 (1995): 75–97.

"Moral Realism and the Burden of Argument," *Southern Journal of Philosophy* 35 (1997): 247–264.

Zangwill, Nick. "Quasi-quasi-realism," *Philosophy & Phenomenological Research* 50 (1990): 583–594.

"Moral Modus Ponens," *Ratio* 5 (1992): 177–193.

"Moral Mind-independence," *Australasian Journal of Philosophy* 72 (1994): 205–291.

"Moral Supervenience," in P. French et al. (eds.), *Moral Concepts. Midwest Studies in Philosophy,* vol. 20. Notre Dame: Notre Dame University Press, 1996.

"Explaining Supervenience: Moral and Mental," *Journal of Philosophical Research* 22 (1997): 509–518.

"Direction of Fit and Normative Functionalism," *Philosophical Studies* 91 (1998): 173–203.

Zapf, Christian, and Eben Moglen. "Linguistic Indeterminacy and the Rule of Law: On the Perils of Misunderstanding Wittgenstein," *Georgetown Law Journal* 84 (1996): 485–520.

Zipursky, Benjamin C. "Legal Coherentism," *Southern Methodist University Law Review* 50 (1997): 1679–1720.

Index

The index was prepared by Barry Sharpe and Brian Berry.